History Made, History Imagined

History Made, History Imagined

Contemporary Literature, Poiesis, and the Past

David W. Price

University of Illinois Press

Urbana and Chicago

Library of Congress Cataloging-in-Publication Data
Price, David W. (David Walter), 1957–
History made, history imagined : contemporary literature,
poiesis, and the past / David W. Price.
p.   cm.
Includes bibliographical references (p.   ) and index.
ISBN 0-252-02468-0 (alk. paper)
ISBN 0-252-06776-2 (paperback : alk. paper)
1. History—Philosophy. 2. History—Methodology. I. Title.
D16.8.P737   1999
901—dc21   98-58031
CIP

Contents

Acknowledgments   vii

Abbreviations and Translations   ix

Introduction: Contending with History   1

1. Making the Truth: History, Fiction, and Philosophy   19

2. Imagining the Past: Carlos Fuentes's *Terra Nostra*   48

3. Experiencing the Past: Susan Daitch's *L.C.*   79

4. Critiquing the Past: Salman Rushdie's *Midnight's Children*   121

5. Redeeming the Past: Michel Tournier's *Le Roi des Aulnes*   152

6. Improvising the Past: Ishmael Reed's *Mumbo Jumbo*   180

7. Narrating the Past: Graham Swift's *Waterland*   216

8. Inventing the Past: Mario Vargas Llosa's *El hablador*   259

Postscript: Annihilating the Past   297

Works Cited   315

Index   331

Acknowledgments

Every book owes its existence to the immeasurable help that an author receives over the years. This book is no exception. Early drafts of this manuscript were read and critiqued by Robert Detweiler, Walter L. Reed, and Ricardo Guttiérez-Mouat. Their comments and guidance made it possible for me to reconceive the project as a whole and cast it in its present form.

Rarely can an author survive the vicissitudes of writing without the close support of family and friends. I would never have been able to complete this project had I not received the unwavering support of my parents. The love of Mary Goldschmidt sustained me for many years, and her scholarly expertise improved the quality of my writing. My best friend and colleague, Andy Wilson, helped me in so many ways, from teaching me about the complex issues surrounding the philosophy of history, to listening to early drafts of my chapters, to letting me use his office and computer as I typed the manuscript. Finally, David Cowart was instrumental in bringing this manuscript to light. He read a second draft of the manuscript, and his advice and guidance over the years helped to motivate me as I continued to write and revise.

I would be remiss if I did not convey a debt of gratitude to Keith Reagan and Lois Merry, whose skills at interlibrary loan acquisitions were indispensable for my work over a four-year period. Many thanks go to Donald P. Verene, who taught superb seminars on Hegel and Vico. I must also express my appreciation to Dick Martin, who accepted my manuscript for publication and shepherded it through the review process, and Terry Sears, who was a joy to work with during the final stages of production.

Combined with this wealth of personal support is the support of other publications and publishers. An early version of a portion of chapter 5 appeared as "Salman Rushdie's 'Use and Abuse of History' in *Midnight's Children,*" *Ariel: A Review of International English Literature* 25.2 (1994): 91–107. Many thanks to Victor Ramraj, on behalf of the University of Calgary and the Board of Governors, for granting me permission to include that material here.

A final word is in order here. Intellectual work is a labor of love and passion. Both can be found inscribed in this text.

Abbreviations and Translations

Because the works listed below are cited with such frequency, the following abbreviations will be used throughout this book.

Works by Friedrich Nietzsche

AC   *The Anti-Christ*. In *Twilight of the Idols and The Anti-Christ*. Trans. R. J. Hollingdale. New York: Penguin, 1968.

BGE   *Beyond Good and Evil*. Trans. Walter Kaufmann. New York: Vintage, 1966.

BT   *The Birth of Tragedy*. In *The Birth of Tragedy and The Case of Wagner*. Trans. Walter Kaufmann. New York: Vintage, 1967.

CW   *The Case of Wagner*. In *The Birth of Tragedy and The Case of Wagner*. Trans. Walter Kaufmann. New York: Vintage, 1967.

D   *Daybreak*. Trans. R. J. Hollingdale. Cambridge: Cambridge University Press, 1982.

EH   *Ecce Homo*. Trans. Walter Kaufmann. New York: Vintage, 1969.

GM   *On the Genealogy of Morals*. Trans. Walter Kaufmann. New York: Vintage, 1969.

GS   *The Gay Science*. Trans. Walter Kaufmann. New York: Vintage, 1974.

HTH   *Human, All Too Human: A Book for Free Spirits*. Trans. R. J. Hollingdale. Cambridge: Cambridge University Press, 1986.

NCW   *Nietzsche contra Wagner*. In *The Portable Nietzsche*. Ed. and trans. Walter Kaufmann. New York: Penguin, 1968.

PT   *Philosophy and Truth: Selections from Nietzsche's Notebooks of the Early 1870's*. Ed. and trans. Daniel Breazeale. Atlantic Highlands, N.J.: Humanities Press, 1990.

PTA   *Philosophy in the Tragic Age of the Greeks*. Trans. Marianne Cowan. Chicago: Gateway Editions, 1962.

TI   *Twilight of the Idols*. In *Twilight of the Idols and The Anti-Christ*. Trans. R. J. Hollingdale. New York: Penguin, 1968.

UM   *Untimely Meditations*. Trans. R. J. Hollingdale. Cambridge: Cambridge University Press, 1983.

WP   *The Will to Power.* Trans. Walter Kaufmann and R. J. Hollingdale. Ed. Walter Kaufmann. New York: Vintage, 1968.

Z   *Thus Spoke Zarathustra.* Trans. Walter Kaufmann. New York: Penguin, 1954.

Works by Giambattista Vico

A   *The Autobiography of Giambattista Vico.* Trans. Max Harold Fisch and Thomas Goddard Bergin. Ithaca, N.Y.: Cornell University Press, 1944.

MAW *On the Most Ancient Wisdom of the Italians.* Trans. L. M. Palmer. Ithaca, N.Y.: Cornell University Press, 1988.

NS   *The New Science of Giambattista Vico.* Trans. Thomas Goddard Bergin and Max Harold Fisch. Ithaca, N.Y.: Cornell University Press, 1988.

SM   *On the Study Methods of Our Time.* Trans. Elio Gianturco. Ithaca, N.Y.: Cornell University Press, 1990.

Citations will indicate the work and page number—for example, (BGE 67) refers to page 67 in *Beyond Good and Evil.* The only exception will be citations from *The Will to Power* and *The New Science of Giambattista Vico*, which will indicate the work and paragraph number—for example, (NS ¶ 510) refers to paragraph 510 in the *The New Science of Giambattista Vico.* All translations of foreign-language quotations, unless otherwise noted, are my own.

History Made, History Imagined

Introduction:
Contending with History

History: Ford's "bunk," Stephen's "nightmare," our "problem." Over the last fifty years, the notion of history, its purpose, and even its verifiability have been under intense scrutiny. While observing the *Historikerstreit* in Germany, the controversy surrounding the Enola Gay exhibit at the Smithsonian, the explanations offered about the origins of the Gulf War, and the reasons for the ethnic conflicts in Bosnia and Rwanda, we witness participants in these public debates making appeals to history, a purported-to-be-true story about what happened in the past. And yet, that does not seem to resolve the matter at all. If anything, such controversies express symptoms of much deeper questions that have been gnawing at us for many years—perhaps since Herodotus and Plutarch began to write. Namely, what is history? What purpose does it serve? Does it express the truth? If so, how? If not, what good is it?

As the previously mentioned examples indicate, there is much at stake in this debate. What we say and hold to be true about the past affects enormously what we are capable of doing in the future. The urgency surrounding this line of inquiry takes on added significance as we approach the end of the millennium. Although Walter Benjamin's observation that history is a document of barbarism has become something of a cliché to rival Santayana's concern about repeating past mistakes, it is nonetheless a haunting refrain that profoundly disturbs. And as the twentieth century goes gently into that good night, and the witnesses and survivors of our violent century pass away, we will be left with the fragments of writing, the artifacts, the secondhand memories, the stories and anecdotes, the photos and film footage, videos and cablegrams, in short, the detritus of time—all open to interpretation.

It is my contention, and the purpose of this book to show, that certain novels can provide us with the best means of engaging in historical interpretations. The novels I choose to analyze here are exemplary in that they combine factual and experiential truths and thereby demonstrate that historical narrative cannot solely concern itself with presenting factual information. Concern for the facts is necessary but not sufficient because, as these novels illustrate, each so-called historical act emerges as a response to systems of values, many of which are often opposed to one another. Yet we seldom fail to overlook the one fact that what is true for every historical act is also true for historical narratives; namely, historical narratives create values. In other words, if conventional historical narratives generally concern themselves with epistemological or even ontological questions, they place greater emphasis on causal relationships so as to produce an *explanation* of what occurred in the past. Rarely do such conventional histories draw attention to the notions of value formation as it affected the actualities of the past and as it affects the very construction of the historical narrative itself. The novels I examine here, however, concern themselves with axiological questions. By posing questions of value, these novels attempt to establish an *understanding* of what occurred in the past. These novels accomplish this goal through acts of figuration in the forms of characters and situations that embody values associated with historical (f)acts. At the same time, these novels highlight the manner in which the very structures of the narratives produce and promote certain values; and, in doing so, they indicate that history as a form of writing necessarily produces values (i.e., there is no neutral, value-free history).

As readers of novels in general, we experience the emotional, psychological, and intellectual states of mind that particular characters possess, and this helps us to understand why they act the way they do. To read about Emma Bovary's education, her aspirations, and her dreams, for example, gives us a better understanding of why she seeks out lovers such as Rodolphe and Léon. Similarly, the novels that I write about here, novels that I claim offer us what I will call *poietic* histories, present us with the emotional, psychological, and intellectual dimensions that we experience from the inside of a fictional character or imagined situation. Rather than have an outside observer, the proverbial objective historian, describe events and explain why they occurred, novels of poietic history allow us as readers to experience the struggle to create values in one of several ways. Novels of poietic history can, among other things, place us in the mind of a character, present the fictionalized description of a historical situation, or pose a series of questions about values and choices of action either directly, through narrators or characters, or implicitly, through narrative structure. These strategies of poietic history serve to underscore the fundamental role value formation plays in determining what informed a course of action in the past *and* what informs the historian's selection of evidence gathered together in a narrative that represents what took place in the past. To choose but one example: when, in *Terra Nostra*, Carlos Fuentes creates the character El Señor, a composite figure of several Spanish monarchs, he allows us to see the cultural conflict of values embodied in a character who will expel the Jews and Muslims from Spain, crush the revolt of the *communeros*, and turn all of Spain into a huge mausoleum. Concomitantly, the very structure of *Terra Nostra* reveals to us a system of values that Fuentes chooses to underscore, values that he implies were obscured, lost, or effaced not only through the actions taken by dominant figures in Spanish culture in the fifteenth and sixteenth centuries but also in many narrative accounts about that period. To read of these events from the inside, so to speak, gives us a greater understanding of what occurred and what we have gained or lost in subsequent historical accounts of these events.

Rather than being held captive by the conventions of epistemology, the novel of poietic history provides the perfect discursive space for examining the past by presenting a series of representations of concrete particulars to universal conditions facing every generation. If we live through the imagination, as I believe we do, then these novels provide us with the means to reimagine the reality of the past. The key to the imagination is figuration; every act we commit is a projection of a figured future. A recreation of the past, therefore, would be the projection of the future in the past. In other words, to comprehend fully the reality of the past, we must participate in the processes whereby individuals, peoples, and entire cultures and societies *figured* their futures through imaginative projections of their wills. The novel as poietic history allows us to experience the projections of these wills, be they individual or collective, and thereby better understand why events in the past occurred as they did.

The novelists examined here also often employ the poetic imagination as a means of questioning history, which, in turn, produces a countermemory or counternarrative to the popular and uncritically accepted referent that we take to be the historical past. They produce speculative novels of poietic history in that they expand the referential field of the past so as to provide the grounds upon which to construct a critique of that same past and, at the same time, imagine new possibilities for the future. In addition, their individual poietic histories produce a philosophy of history that combines the perceived-to-be separate forms of literary and philosophical discourse. Through their speculative, poietic histories, these novelists indicate that the imagination remains the source of all "histories."

The salient feature of novels of poietic history discussed thus far has been the focus on the formation of values, both in the actualities of the past and in the construction of the narrative about that past. But as the discussion above indicates, poietic histories also concern themselves with the future. Just as the focus on value formation relates to past actualities and narrative construction, so too the constitutive feature of what might be termed the orientation toward the future relates to past actualities and to narratives about the past. As I have noted, poietic histories allow us to experience how imagined actors in the past projected their futures by engaging in certain acts. By the same token, poietic histories are written so as to affect *our* future, the future of the reading audience. Writers such as Fuentes, Tournier, Daitch, Rushdie, and Vargas Llosa intend for their poietic histories to cause us to rethink the past and reconsider what we might plan for our future. In this regard, poietic history, unlike much conventional history, does not concern itself exclusively with the past. On the contrary, a major goal of any poietic history is to reconfigure the past in ways that will help us to configure our future. History, therefore, becomes something that we can, in Nietzsche's words, use to "further life."

A focus on figurative language, with a special emphasis on the mythic underpinnings of all history, constitutes the third feature of poietic history. Poietic histories never fail to remind us that all histories grow out of mythic structures that make it possible for us to narrate our experiences. Without these structures, we would be incapable of making sense of, or "figuring out," what happened. Just as poietic history directs our attention to questions of value, it also calls attention to the indispensable role narrative must play in constructing the past. Every narrative depends on the figurative capacity of language, the origins of which we can trace back to myth. Thus, many of these writers of poietic history have discovered that tropologics associated with myth provide us with the best means to shift the historical focus away from epistemology and toward axiology while at the same time permitting us to imagine a past that will build a future.

Rather than focus exclusively on questions of verifiability, novelists of poietic history concern themselves with choosing the narrative elements that put into play an array of values that then are offered up for scrutiny. This is not to imply that these novelists ignore evidence or merely fabricate the past. Several of the novels I examine here are filled with information that any trained historian would identify as being factual. Nevertheless, the intent of these novelists is to reconfigure the past through narrative structures that cast light and shadows in new directions and bring before our eyes new ways of conceiving of the past. Common to all of these novelists is the implicit understanding that historical narratives focusing exclusively on questions of verifiability lose sight of why we write history at all. Meaningful histories, histories that can be of use to us, must allow us to sense the past through figurative language. In other words, we must sense the past to make sense of it. The mythic structures, tropes, and varying narrative strategies that one finds in novels of poietic history become the means by which these novelists allow us to experience the past in the present with an eye toward the future.

Once again, the shift of focus away from epistemology and toward axiology serves as a key constitutive feature of poietic history. We can realize this through novels better than any other form of discourse. Neither historiography nor philosophy, as they are commonly defined, can achieve what novels can. We need only look at one of the most celebrated novels about history—Leo Tolstoy's *War and Peace*—to see what inherent powers obtain in the novel, particularly when it comes to examining the concept of history.

At the end of his magnum opus, Tolstoy declares that history remains an "insoluble mystery presented by the incompatibility of free will and inevitability" because "the union of these two contradictions has already taken place" (1340). Whereas theology, ethics, and philosophy explore possible relationships between freedom and inevitability, history, according to Tolstoy, engages in no similar speculative endeavors because the relation of free will to inevitability achieves a certain finality *in the past.* Tolstoy's attempt to solve the mystery in *War and Peace,* a novel that questions the relation of freedom and inevitability in history, ends in failure; but it is a glorious failure because he does succeed in inaugurating a genuine, speculative questioning of what it means to write history. As part of his initial strategy, Tolstoy develops an elaborate narrative structure based on metonymy (i.e., the lives of Andrew, Pierre, and Natasha are related to and indeed contiguous with the much broader fabric of Russian society), but, after well over a thousand pages consisting of fifteen books and an epilogue, Tolstoy, exasperated and exhausted, turns to the primary trope of metaphor.

In the second epilogue, Tolstoy produces a series of metaphors designed to explain why there can be no adequate explanations of history. History is a locomotive, money, a log being hauled, a moving ship, and electricity, among other things. In each instance, the metaphor expresses the inadequacy of differing historical perspectives. As the narrator tells us, "various historians take forces of different kinds, all of which are incommensurate with the movement observed" (1321). In other words, when historians attempt to explain an event, the whole of history is greater than the sum of its causal parts; no single identifiable force or combination of forces can account for a historical occurrence. Each of Tolstoy's metaphors expresses this general idea *except* the metaphor of money. When the narrator constructs the history-as-money metaphor, he broaches the subject of history as text; and, in so doing, he opens up a rich and allusive intertextual field.

By declaring that "the science of history up to now is like money in circulation—paper and coin" (1321), Tolstoy attempts to discredit traditional historical accounts. Historical biographies are like paper money with no real "security behind them" (1321), he argues. Universal and cultural histories, on the other hand, are money made of metal, but this money lacks "the specific gravity of gold" (1321). In both instances, the narrator appeals to a system of valuation based on gold, a substance that, for Tolstoy, has both exchange *and* use value. Ignoring for a moment the fact that Marx and Tolstoy hold diametrically opposed views of gold, one could say that in *War and Peace*, Tolstoy suggests that in the textual economy of the production of "history," historical texts constitute a type of surplus value; they are a form of value removed from the content of genuine historicity. Although, as Hayden White has argued, Marx's analysis of value grows out of his recognition of the metaphoric relationship between commodities (*Metahistory* 281–330), and Tolstoy's historical insights develop from metaphors he crafted in the course of writing a novel, it is metaphor that, for both writers, builds a way toward understanding.

Tolstoy's *War and Peace* underscores the importance of viewing history as a form of textual production; I have stressed the metaphor of money so as to establish a virtual intertextual bridge between Tolstoy and Marx and thereby reach two other philosophers in whose writings the image of the coin also circulates quite freely. Friedrich Nietzsche uses the coin image to tell us that truth is metaphorical. This means, of course, that truth is a lie. Nietzsche's pronouncement that truths are illusions has become, by now, all too familiar. Truths, he declares, "are metaphors that have become worn out and have been drained of sensuous force, coins that have lost their embossing and are now considered as metal and no longer as coins" (PT 84). Giambattista Vico, by way of contrast, uses money and the image of coins to discuss the origin of language. The earliest Gentile nations, argues Vico, "expressed themselves by gestures," "used signs to fix the boundaries of their estates," and "made use of money" (NS ¶ 434). These three "incontrovertible truths" allow Vico to explore the linguistic underpinnings of social institutions in Western culture. When Vico claims that naming, money, and the law all stem from the same root (e.g., Vico points out that the Greek *nomos* signifies law and from it we get *nomisma*, money; similarly, the French *loi* is related to *aloi*, or money) he engages in speculation— a theoretical enterprise rooted in the imagination. The key to Vico's *New Science*, therefore, is metaphorical speech, which he calls Poetic Wisdom.

Tolstoy, Nietzsche, Vico, and Marx conduct a questioning of history based on a notion of metaphorics, and for each writer the coin serves as the metaphor of their respective methods. Tolstoy rejects the metonymic structure of narrative histories that are responsible for the notions of agency, subjectivity, and causality, and he does so through argument based on metaphor. Nietzsche, conversely, employs a genealogical method of linguistic analysis to repudiate Christian morality by showing that the opposition of good and evil is socially constructed at a particular moment in time. To replace rational metaphysics with a poetic metaphysics based on metaphoric structuration characterizes Vico's entire philosophic project. And Marx, by way of contrast, revolts against the capitalist economic system and uncovers the metaphorics of exchange valuation. Common to each of these writers is a commitment to the reexamination of history as idea and a refusal to accept history as given.

The seven authors whose works I analyze in the chapters that follow share a similar commitment to the reexamination of history. Like Tolstoy, Vico, Marx, and Nietzsche, these seven contemporary novelists stress the textuality of history. They call into question the historicity of popular notions of the past, accounts that have been inscribed in the collective memory of the tribe, accounts that deny their significatory status by repeatedly appealing to a referent of "what really happened."

By conducting a questioning of history, these authors write poietic histories. In their novels, they oppose what many believe to be the essential difference between history and literature. I will argue that the novelists examined here articulate a new relation between these two discursive forms. By positioning themselves between literature and history, these seven novelists ostensibly associate themselves with a long tradition of the novel, one that roughly began with the works of Sir Walter Scott, and, at the same time, engage in a form of contemporary political practice, one that indicates that history is really a form of *poiesis*, the act of making in language. The novelists of poietic history remind us that the actualities of the past were shaped by competing systems of values, some of which were eclipsed over time. The novels they produce underscore the conflict of opposing values through characterization, setting, and narration. Of equal importance to these novelists, however, remains the question of how those actualities of the past come to be recorded in language. The fundamental act of narration itself expresses a system of values, and each of these novelists exploits this very fact to explore the axiological dimensions of making history through acts of imagination *in language*.

These novelists return to Tolstoy's laws of necessity and belief in free will to explore, if not solve, what Tolstoy characterizes as an "insoluble mystery." "Reason gives expression to the laws of inevitability," writes Tolstoy. "Consciousness gives expression to the essence of freedom" (1347). For Tolstoy, this means that "Freedom is the content. Inevitability is the form"; and "only by uniting them do we get a clear conception of man's life" (1347). The writers I examine here choose to write novels because the novel can unify content and form, reason and consciousness, inevitability and freedom *in writing*. Through their respective narrative constructions, they engage in the questioning of history, a questioning that must itself produce a history (*histoire, historia, storia, Geschichte*); but this questioning only obtains in the form of the novel, which constitutes the discursive space in which such a questioning can occur. Just as Vico attempts to recover the concrete experience of human history through the poetic imagination, these contemporary novelists avoid a reflective mode of writing and prefer, instead, writing as imagistic forming, an activity that serves as the principal part of a mediating process Paul Ricoeur refers to as "configuration." Like Nietzsche, these writers elicit a countermemory, one that seeks to rupture the condensation of memory, myth, and worn metaphor that has become our historical "truth." The production of a countermemory allows us to see, as through the eyes of Walter Benjamin's angel, the "single catastrophe" as opposed to the "chain of events" that comprise the "storm . . . we call progress" (257–58). In addition, these writers heed Marx's call not merely to interpret the world but to change it. Through their novels, these writers explode the univocal expression of history as a description of "what really happened" and replace it with a polyvocality of competing discourses, languages, and points of view. This emphasis on the many voices of the past makes it possible for us to conceive of a past that is more than a dead letter; it will help us to understand and experience the past as a dynamic flow of values in a force field that can be reconfigured in ways to help transform our future.

At this point, I feel it necessary to warn prospective readers that this study is not an examination of the "historical novel." I do not suggest that the novelists I study here continue the tradition of novel writing often associated with the names Walter Scott, Alessandro Manzoni, and Heinrich Mann. According to Georg Lukács, the historical novel first appeared after the French Revolution, and it was through such a mass experience that people began "to comprehend their own existence as something historically conditioned, . . . to see in history something which deeply affects their daily lives" (*Historical Novel* 24). For Lukács, the "increasing historical awareness of the decisive role played in human progress by the struggle of classes in history" becomes the key to this new self-consciousness (27). Consequently, true historical novels, as Lukács defines them, must record the struggles among classes; and, in the works of Walter Scott, he perceived not only "the direct continuation of the great realistic social novel of the eighteenth century" (31) but also a depiction of the development of English society as a series of "ceaseless class struggles and their bloody resolution in great or small, successful or abortive uprisings" (32). Typically, a Scott novel possesses a mediocre figure as a central character who witnesses the clash of classes or cultures (e.g., the Scottish Highlanders and the English in *Waverley*), and whose function, claims Lukács, is to "bring the extremes whose struggle fills the novel" together (36). Scott does not try to concentrate his efforts on representing major, real-life historical figures, such as Bonnie Prince Charlie; such characters play only a peripheral role, if they appear at all. Rather, as Lukács sees it, Scott's genius lies in his ability to create "historical-social types" (35) that themselves reflect the "quality of the inner life, the morality, heroism, capacity for sacrifice, steadfastness etc., peculiar to a given age" (50).

From this paradigm, we would surmise that a contemporary version of the classical historical novel would retain three main characteristics: a lack of emphasis on major historical figures; a central focus on a mediocre main character; and, most important of all, a depiction of the class struggle. Although some of these characteristics can be found in varying degrees in the novels I study, I believe that none expresses all three to the extent that Lukács would prefer. In particular, the class struggle in many of the novels I study has disappeared altogether; the traditional Marxist interpretive approach, as articulated by Lukács, leaves many questions unanswered when I consider the novels written by the seven authors I have chosen.

Nor do I associate these novelists with what Linda Hutcheon characterizes as "historiographic metafiction." They do not simply "problematize" the notion of historical knowledge; they are not *pasticheurs* espousing "a postmodern ideology of plurality and recognition of difference" (*Poetics* 114). Hutcheon's book *The Poetics of Postmodernism* remains a fine scholarly work, yet there is much in it with which I disagree. Although a thorough analysis of her theoretical observations lies beyond the scope of my study, I feel it necessary to mention certain of my objections so as to distinguish my approach to these contemporary works of fiction from hers.

I find serious problems with Hutcheon's characterization of the difference between modernism and postmodernism. The analogies between architecture and literature do not really hold. Although there may be many similarities between Charles Moore's Piazza d'Italia and J. M. Coetzee's *Foe,* there are far fewer between a structure by Mies van der Rohe and a novel by James Joyce. Indeed, Hutcheon's characterization of modernist literature rings false. When she asserts that modernism suffers from a "dogmatic reductionism," that it was "unable to deal with ambiguity and irony," and that it denied the "validity of the past" (30), we can recognize how faulty such observations are when we consider literature rather than architecture. One wonders if in fact Hutcheon has willfully forgotten Thomas Buddenbrook's visit to the dentist in *Buddenbrooks,* or the scene of the red slippers of Oriane de Guermantes in the *Recherche,* or the coin in the palm of Corley's hand in Joyce's "Two Gallants." Why else would she be so bold as to suggest that modernists, high modernists especially, were bereft of irony and hostile toward history?

Of equal concern to me is Hutcheon's assertion that postmodernism's salient features are "contradiction and a move toward anti-totalization" (42). Such pronouncements lose much of their persuasive power when we consider the totalizing effects of market forces that do much to commodify every postmodern work of art she enthusiastically describes. Finally, Hutcheon's emphasis on parody as the crucial form of critique offered by postmodern works raises serious doubts about its effectiveness. Parody, much like the carnivalesque, remains circumscribed by the existing power structures that in effect co-opt and commodify it. Put another way, it is unlikely that a film such as *Brazil* will topple Hollywood. Perhaps Fredric Jameson explains it best when he argues that, in our contemporary world, "parody finds itself without a vocation"; it is being replaced by pastiche, something Jameson refers to as "blank parody" (*Postmodernism* 17). It is this particular form of parody as pastiche or blank parody that Hutcheon describes in her work, and it is for this reason that I find her arguments about parody as critique in postmodern works so unconvincing.

I have purposely avoided spending much time discussing the concept of postmodernism precisely because I find it so muddled. Discussions of the concept and its relation to modernism will do little to illuminate the works of fiction I address here. The novelists I write about in my study have often been described as postmodernists by Hutcheon and others, but I will not burden them with this label. When Hutcheon writes that post-modernism "confront[s] and contest[s] any modernist discarding *or* recuperating of the past in the name of the future" and continues by asserting that postmodernism conducts a "re-evaluation of and dialogue with the past in the light of the present" (*Poetics* 19), I am tempted to ask, To what end? The novelists whose works I examine in the pages that follow are very much concerned with the future as well as the past; they do more than "dialogue with" the past. On the contrary, these novelists try to *think* history; that is, they see the novel as a form of speculative thinking that engages the poetic imagination in an attempt to construct, not discover, the truth of the past.

In the course of my study, I turn to the theoretical insights of Giambattista Vico and Friedrich Nietzsche. I use Vico's thought to explore how these novelists not only produce the knowledge of the historical period about which they write but also articulate oppositional voices to the abstract and rational descriptions of experience that characterize many forms of contemporary historiography. Similarly, Nietzsche offers me a theoretical framework and vocabulary with which I can discuss the role the novel plays in historical discourse.

Having said all this, I want to state directly that I am not relying on Vico and Nietzsche as authorities. I am not suggesting that Vico and Nietzsche understood everything I have identified in the novels under examination. Nor am I suggesting that all of our current debates about history can be solved if only we would read Vico and Nietzsche in certain ways. By the same token, I am not suggesting that the novelists whose works I examine have studied Vico and Nietzsche; some have, some have not. Rather,

I see in the writings of Vico and Nietzsche many elemental affinities with the novels I identify as presenting poietic history.

At this point, one might ask, Why Vico and Nietzsche? Why not rely on a host of contemporary theorists and philosophers who speak about these very same issues (e.g., Michel Foucault, Jürgen Habermas, Dominick LaCapra, Jean-François Lyotard, Edward Said, Hayden White, et al.)? To be sure, the work of these distinguished intellectuals appears in the pages of my study. Nevertheless, I have found that many of us in the scholarly world are prone to borrow the vocabulary of these thinkers without pausing to consider deeply the foundations of their thinking. My purpose in grounding this study in the writings of Vico and Nietzsche is to establish an intellectual foundation to the field of inquiry of which it is a part. Clearly theorists such as Foucault and White owe many of their insights to Nietzsche and Vico respectively. My contention is that we would do well to look closely at these two philosophers before we quickly adopt the contemporary vocabulary of popular theories. I have found the writings of both Vico and Nietzsche to be more fruitful and powerful than much of what is written today on the topics of history, literature, and postmodern culture. In this regard, I view the works of Vico and Nietzsche as a "Paideuma," something Ezra Pound referred to as "the gristly roots of ideas that are in action" (58). If ours is the period of the crisis of history (some claim it is coming to an end; others that it is coming to worldwide consciousness), then the two main philosophers we should turn to are neither Hegel and his epigoni, nor Heidegger, but Vico and Nietzsche. Another way of saying this would be that at the present moment we would do well to turn away from philosophers who concern themselves with epistemological and ontological investigations and focus our attention on philosophers who make axiological inquiries. The writings of Vico and Nietzsche contain sustained meditations on the formation of values, and their respective works have much to teach us when we consider what type of world we will choose to build, which itself will be an extension of a past that we must also choose.

My turn toward Vico and Nietzsche, therefore, makes it possible for me to set up a reciprocal reading of these two philosophers' works and the seven novels I examine. My intent is to illuminate certain aspects of the novels under discussion by referring to the writings of Vico and Nietzsche and, simultaneously, to show how the novels themselves illuminate, elaborate, or correct certain elements of these philosophers' works. I have found the philosophical vocabulary of both Vico and Nietzsche to be rich,

supple, and allusive when placed in dialogue with the novels I have chosen to study. For this reason, I have structured this study in such a way
that I move back and forth from philosopher to novelist in an attempt to
broaden our understanding of the poietic in both Vico and Nietzsche and
the novels under scrutiny.

In many ways, this study can be viewed as a meditation on three quotations. The first comes from paragraph 819 of Vico's *New Science*, which
reads, in part, as follows: "Hence memory is the same as imagination,
which for that reason is called *memoria* in Latin. . . . Memory thus has
three different aspects: memory when it remembers things, imagination
when it alters or imitates them, and invention when it gives them a new
turn or puts them into proper arrangement and relationship." The next
two quotations come from Nietzsche. In an early unpublished essay entitled "On Truth and Lies in a Nonmoral Sense" he writes: "The drive toward the formation of metaphors is the fundamental human drive which
one cannot for a single instant dispense with in thought, for one would
thereby dispense with man himself" (PT 88–89). In *Beyond Good and Evil*
he poses the following question: "Why couldn't the world *that concerns
us*—be a fiction?" (47). If, while examining the various literary works that
I have chosen, I manage to deepen the understanding of these three statements, then I will have accomplished my goal.

Our understanding of history becomes altered if we posit, as does
Nietzsche, that neither *Eros* nor *Thanatos* but the impulse to make metaphors constitutes the vital human drive. As a function of such a drive,
history would no longer be perceived to unfold according to a particular
logic that culminates in absolute knowledge; rather, history would be a
function of constructions in language. From this perspective, Nietzsche's
Will to Power becomes a Will to Metaphor or Figuration—the expression
of a competing narrative, which, like every living thing, "does everything
it can not to preserve itself but to become *more*—" (WP ¶ 688). Coupled
with Vico's observation that memory and imagination are the same, we
can see that history, something that clearly concerns us, should be regarded as a fiction, one that makes it possible for us to live.

To view history as a form of fiction does not mean that history is untrue. Memory, imagination, and metaphor congeal to form the various
narratives of history, but they in no way return us to the actualities of the
past. This is why the final quotation from Nietzsche mentioned above is
so important. It is instructive to view the sentence in German, because
the sentence—"Warum dürfte die Welt, *die uns etwas angeht*—nicht eine

Fiktion sein?"—contains the verb *angehen*, which can convey several meanings, including: to fit and be tolerable; to attack or tackle a problem; to charge, make a rush at, or go at something. In this regard, we must find a tolerable way to interact with the world even as it attacks or charges us with a response of some sort. Nietzsche's question, therefore, can be taken in two ways. One could read the question "rhetorically," in which case the implication is that we should regard the world as a fiction. Yet, if the question is taken literally, we see that Nietzsche is stating that the world is not a fiction and that we simply cannot view it as such *but that* our only tolerable response to the world as it charges or attacks us is to resort to fictions. In other words, we will never understand the world, but we can understand our systems of interpretation, the "fictions" that we ourselves have constructed. The world, and everything in it, lies beyond our ken. We must, therefore, respond with lies of our own.

The novels that I examine in this study extend the speculations of the philosophers while, at the same time, the philosophical writings help to illuminate the particular fictions I have chosen to study. In this regard, my approach to the question of the relation between literature and history differs from the approaches adopted by several contemporary critics. In the context of recent books about history and literature, I would distinguish my study from three exemplary scholarly works that examine many of the same issues that I address here. In his 1989 book *History and the Contemporary Novel*, David Cowart produces an admirable schema for analyzing contemporary historical novels. My study resembles Cowart's in that I analyze seven novels whereas he analyzes eight (we focus our attention on completely different works of fiction). Cowart identifies four categories that he claims are neither absolute nor definitive: (1) works that attempt to "recreate the past as vividly as possible"; (2) works that project a future based on "the conventions of fictions of the past"; (3) works that focus on a turning point and show how the present became the present; and (4) works that depict the present age "in the distant mirror of the past" (9–12). I, on the other hand, choose to develop my analysis using philosophical discourse rather than a personal schema.

In her 1991 book *Writing History as a Prophet: Postmodernist Innovations of the Historical Novel*, Elisabeth Wesseling chooses to determine the ways in which "postmodernist historical fictions comply with and diverge from the conventions of the historical novel" (2). Wesseling provides an excellent description of the origins and development of the historical novel and offers her own definition of postmodernist fictions. Unlike Wesseling, I choose not to stress the historical novel tradition, nor am I solely concerned with the so-called postmodern novel.

Perhaps the book that mine most closely resembles in terms of approach is *The Novel and the Globalization of Culture,* the 1995 study by Michael Valdez Moses. Using the philosophical writings of Hegel and his contemporary disciple, Francis Fukuyama, Moses analyzes five novels from the nineteenth and twentieth centuries so as to prove that the modernization and globalization of culture constitutes an irreversible and universal process. Like Moses, I analyze novels from both the "First" and "Third" worlds; and, although we do not examine the same works, we do share a common author—Mario Vargas Llosa. Similarly, I, too, rely on a philosophical framework to conduct my analysis. Yet this most important similarity is also the source of our greatest difference. I disagree with Moses when he argues that Nietzsche "relativize[s] the philosophic claims of modernity" (201). Rather than embrace the received idea that Nietzsche purveys a destructive moral relativism, I direct my attention to other, more important elements of his philosophy; namely, I examine Nietzsche's sustained meditation on the power of metaphoric projection and the creation of truth in language. To Moses I would respond that relativization occurs through global economic modernization by the means of capital. The danger of the relativization of values occurs not because of Nietzschean speculations on value formation. On the contrary, it is precisely the globalization of world culture by means of free market capitalism that has relativized all values. Everything, as the saying goes, has been reduced to "the bottom line"; perhaps Nietzsche has something to tell us about that particular metaphor.

In the study that follows, I choose to emphasize how both Vico and Nietzsche describe the methods by which we produce worlds via the imagination. The novels I examine express affinities with the philosophical insights of these two thinkers and provide me with a means to discuss how the key to understanding the past and creating a future lies in the imagination. In the introductory chapter, I describe how the novel functions as a discursive space between literature and history. In each of the subsequent chapters, I analyze a specific novel: Carlos Fuentes's *Terra Nostra,* Susan Daitch's *L.C.,* Salman Rushdie's *Midnight's Children,* Michel Tournier's *Le Roi des Aulnes* (The Ogre), Ishmael Reed's *Mumbo Jumbo,* Graham Swift's *Waterland,* and Mario Vargas Llosa's *El hablador* (The Storyteller). I conclude my study with a discussion of how these and other novels may be viewed as a form of praxis.

I begin with Fuentes because he has written on and spoken about both Vico and Nietzsche, and his lengthy masterpiece chronicles the beginnings of the Old and New Worlds. His novel allows me to establish both a model for the reciprocal reading of literature and philosophy and a trajectory for my entire book. By analyzing *Terra Nostra* first, I can discuss the specific aspects of Vico's and Nietzsche's writings that I will concentrate on in the chapters that follow. In addition, Fuentes's novel moves from the Old World to the New World and back, and I will follow this pattern of geographic alternation in subsequent chapters. Consequently, after the chapter on Fuentes, I move to Daitch's novel, which returns us to Europe, but this time we see Europe during the age(s) of revolution as figured in the experiences of women. From Europe of the nineteenth century I turn my attention to twentieth-century India, analyzing a culture that is both younger and older than the European one that colonized it. In choosing Rushdie, I touch on a transcultural writer who was educated as a historian and who has specialized in writing novels that focus on both historical events in the age of writing and contemporary politics. I then return to Europe, but this time I choose Europe of the twentieth century, as I focus on the origins of the Holocaust as described in a novel written by a trained philosopher, to determine what literature has to tell us about a historical event that is irrefutable yet escapes our understanding. From the ashes of the Holocaust, I go back to the New World as it is figured in *Mumbo Jumbo*. Reed's novel opens up an alternative mythic world, one that seeks to shake off the burdens of the European past and place us at the crossroads of Africa and the Americas. In Swift's novel we return to Europe, but we delve further into the mythic underpinnings of historical narrative as we witness the confrontation between a grand historical narrative of progress and a primordial mythic power of cyclical repetition. Finally, in Vargas Llosa's novel we enter the world of myth and imagination as expressed in the tales of a still-extant prehistoric tribe in the Amazonian jungle. The trajectory I trace, therefore, is one in which the particular authors are less and less familiar with the two philosophers whose works inform my study. In addition, I also move from novels that inscribe more traditional notions of history toward novels that increasingly concern themselves with myth.

When viewed together, the seven novels I will examine form three modalities of the poietic novel as I see it. Both Fuentes and Rushdie create the history of forgotten possibilities. With *Terra Nostra*, Fuentes reminds Spanish-speaking peoples that the vibrant multicultural world of

Spain before 1492 included Muslims, Jews, and Christians. According to Fuentes, we must recover this often forgotten past because it can provide a key to the future of our ever-increasing, multipolar world. By imagining that past, by experiencing, through fiction, the thinking that contributed to the dismantling of that world, we can understand the consequences of the choices that were made and avoid making similar choices in the future.

Similarly, Rushdie recounts the history of the creation of India and the tragic consequences that ensued when the establishment of both India and Pakistan separated Hindu and Muslim populations. What some might regard as Rushdie's utopianism is rooted in an understanding of the past that reveals itself to us through figurations of the imagination. Rushdie's poietic history allows us to rethink the past of the Indian subcontinent in the hopes of reconfiguring the future. By reminding us of forgotten possibilities, both Fuentes and Rushdie call attention to the fact that we are not condemned to repeat the mistakes of the past; the past contains paths that were not followed, and these untrodden trails can be followed now, in the present moment.

Daitch, Reed, and Vargas Llosa constitute a group of novelists who write novels in the second modality of poietic history, novels of countermemory and cultural critique. More so than the other four novelists under scrutiny here, these three construct narratives that overtly underscore the creation of the narrative itself. The self-reflexive narratives of Daitch, Reed, and Vargas Llosa provide creative paradigms whereby we may reconfigure the past through imaginative acts. All three novelists imply that the verifiability of the past is ultimately undecidable, but they do not stop there. Rather, they assert that we must decide for ourselves what the truths of the past will be so as to construct our future. The three novelists contend that we only have interpretations of the past, and it is through acts of imagination, acts through which we "figure out" the past, that we can make sense of our world. The novels that Daitch, Reed, and Vargas Llosa construct address themselves to questions of gender, race, and cultural interanimation respectively. The answers to these questions, which we will articulate in the years ahead, will be crucial to the survival of our culture, and poietic history as written by these three novelists will offer us paradigms for constructing values though narrating the past.

Finally, Tournier and Swift write novels of history as myth, the third modality of poietic history. Both novelists examine the mythic dimensions of all histories. *Le Roi des Aulnes* depicts the mythic underpinnings of fascist consciousness. Rather than present a model for the future, Tournier presents us with a warning. We see how the mythic structures that undergird all historical narratives can be configured in ways that will lead to destruction and violence. The poietic history Tournier constructs allows us to understand, from the inside, the workings of the totalizing, fascistic mind, and in doing so Tournier forces us to reconsider totalizing impulses we engage in ourselves.

Swift, like Tournier, studies the mythic dimension of history. More than any of the other six novelists, Swift sustains a provocative meditation on the structures of historical narrative, structures that he sees as emerging from myth, the origins of which remain forever obscure to us. At the same time, his novel suggests that we cannot escape these mythic dimensions, that in fact we must rely on them to understand and make sense of who we are, where we came from, and who we might become.

Once again, I will emphasize that I am not claiming that these novelists are intentionally drawing on the works of Vico and Nietzsche—some are and several are not. Rather, I am conducting a reciprocal reading of these novels with particular texts written by Vico and Nietzsche so as to foster a greater understanding not only of literature and philosophy but also of history and our relationship to it.

1

Making the Truth:
History, Fiction, and Philosophy

If philosophers have acknowledged that an ancient quarrel between poetry and philosophy has long been in existence, recent critics
have also recognized that a much more modern, yet no more amicable,
relation exists between the novel and history. In part, the fratricidal strife
between these two modes of discourse can be traced back to what literary theorists and historians alike deem their common source of filiation:
the epic. Both novelists and historians, it seems, want to claim the crown
that once adorned the epic and made it the dominant form of narrative
expression in its time. In so doing, these epigoni struggle to show that they
are the true heirs of a narrative form that clearly expressed the ethos of
an entire civilization and that their form of narrative discourse, *and theirs
alone,* can serve the same purpose in modern times.

Theorists of the novel often claim that the epic engendered the novel.
Georg Lukács, for example, sees the novel as the means by which modern authors attempt to recover the "totality of life" that epic authors perceived as naturally inhering in the ancient world. The condition of modern humanity, argues Lukács, is such that we suffer from a feeling of
"transcendental homelessness," and the novel serves as "the epic of an age
in which the extensive totality of life is no longer directly given" (*Theory*
56). The novel, therefore, functions as a totalizing form that seeks to recapture a transcendence that is no longer immanent.

Philosophers of history, by contrast, see the epic as the progenitor of
history. R. G. Collingwood, for one, thinks that Herodotus invented history and that, even though his writings contained many "legendary elements" common to the works of Homer and Hesiod, the "father of histo-

ry" distanced himself from his poetic forebears in that he "ask[ed] questions instead of repeating legends" (19). For Herodotus, history is an inquiry into the deeds of men; in other words, it reveals humankind to itself by recounting what humankind has done. This act of recounting deeds, therefore, has strong ties to the epic and the *res gestae* traditions.

Arguing from a less philosophical position, Georges May traces the filiation of both history and the novel back to the epic by noting that the Homeric poems contain historical and novelistic elements. During the Hellenistic age, novelists, according to May, based their Alexandrian fictions on the epic model, whereas writers such as Herodotus, Thucydides, and Polybius wrote narratives that differentiated themselves from the epic by being "mieux attestés" and "moins légendaires" (155). According to this view, the relationship between history and the novel grows through repeated patterns of divergence and convergence in which certain ages experience greater or lesser difficulty in determining a distinct difference between the two forms of narrative. At the end of the seventeenth century, for example, Europe was gripped by an epistemological crisis that, according to Paul Hazard, was popularly termed Historical Pyrrhonism. Historians were suffering from a triple assault mounted by Cartesians, who called for the application of the method to history; Jansenists, who distrusted the "everlasting itch for knowledge"; and freethinkers, who characterized historians as lackeys, ever willing to write untruthful narratives that pleased those in power (35–36). This devastating attack on the veracity of history proper, claims Georges May, took place at a time (roughly 1660–1730) when a series of biographies, memoirs, chronicles, and autobiographies effected a new fusion of history and the novel (156). History, it seems, was no longer believable because it resembled what one read in novels. Thus, it was the confluence of the two genres that produced the crisis, and, as May argues, it was not until around 1700 that the novel began to be "emancipated" from history. The emancipation would result from a foregrounding of imaginary detail and a reduction in the amount of realistic detail that individual authors would include in novels. As English Showalter points out, it was *La Princesse de Clèves* that, as early as 1678, first indicated the strength of this technique, because it appealed to a readership that took pleasure in recognizing that it was reading the work as art, not history (56). By the time we reach the nineteenth century, however, yet another stark divergence between the genres occurs. "After the French Revolution," writes Lionel Gossman, "the dominant ambition of historians was to make history—rather than fiction—the successor of epic as the repository of society's values and of its understanding of the world" (252).

As we know, these clear and distinct lines of demarcation between the two genres become blurred once again, not only in the nineteenth century, which witnessed the production of the great historical novels—*Waverley, I Promessi Sposi, Salammbô, War and Peace*—but also in our own time, which produces what Linda Hutcheon terms "historiographic metafiction." In response to the current interest in the breakdown between the two genres, critics such as Joseph W. Turner and Roger G. Seamon have attempted to categorize specific types of historical novels as well as discuss the theoretical implications of accepting or denying the distinction between historical and fictional narratives. This troublesome kinship between history and the novel has also been the focus of several contemporary theoreticians of the novel who have developed more sophisticated and nuanced explanations of the relationship. Walter L. Reed, in his *Exemplary History of the Novel*, believes that the novel "explores the difference between the fictions which are enshrined in the institutions of literature and the fictions, more truthful historically or merely more familiar, by which we lead our daily lives" (5). Michael McKeon, by contrast, contends that the most important narrative model for the novel was not another literary genre but "historical experience itself." "The distinction," he quickly adds, "is artificial: literary models both structure the way history is experienced and in turn take their 'own' shape from that experience" (238). Both Reed and McKeon recognize the impossibility of maintaining a strict dichotomy between the historical and the fictional; there exists a reciprocal—if not dialectical—relation between the two genres. As Gossman points out: "Fictional writing is constantly questioning existing fictional conventions, and for centuries it did so by appealing to history. But historical writing operates in the same way: every attempt to devise an order different from that of pure chronicle involved an appeal to the order of art—of fictional narrative or of drama" (241). This interweaving of the two genres, as noted by literary critics, has also not escaped the notice of contemporary historiographers and philosophers of history.

In his *Philosophy and the Historical Understanding*, W. B. Gallie produces one of the first contemporary reevaluations of the relation between history and fiction. History is a "species of the genus Story," claims Gallie. "Narrative is the form which expresses what is basic to and characteristic of historical understanding" (66). For Gallie, the key to this historical understanding lies in learning to read a story well. According to Louis O.

Mink, Gallie's analysis informs us that history resembles fiction in that it "essentially depends on and develops our skill and subtlety in following stories," but it differs from fiction in that it "is obligated to rest upon evidence of the occurrence in real space and time of what it describes" ("History and Fiction" 545).

Mink himself struggled with this issue throughout his life. His writings are among the most thoughtful, well-reasoned, and judicious inquiries into the idea of history and its relation to both philosophy and narrative. In his seminal essay "Narrative Form as Cognitive Instrument," Mink confirms that both common sense and historiographic practice presuppose that "everything that has happened belongs to a single determinate realm of unchanging actuality" (194). Yet this belief that the past is single and determinate contradicts the relational functions of narrative form, the primary means by which history is produced. Narrative, by its very form, offers innumerable combinatory relations that belie the notion that there exists a single ordering relation of "events." As Mink points out, an event is an "abstraction from a narrative." Particular narrative structures produce particular descriptions of events, and, for this reason, Mink insists that there exists no single, determinate past, no "untold story." On the contrary, "There can be only past facts not yet described in a context of narrative form" ("Narrative Form" 201).

The nature of facts also disturbs Dominick LaCapra. In "Rethinking Intellectual History and Reading Texts," he argues that although historians "may not invent [their] facts or references," they do "make use of heuristic fictions, counterfactuals, and models to orient their research into facts" (57). LaCapra rejects the idea that intellectual history consists of a reconstruction of the past. Such a "documentary conception is excessively restrictive," he writes (61). In its place he calls for a dialogue with the past, an approach in which the historian examines a "text" (or series of texts), which he defines as "a situated use of language marked by a tense interaction between mutually implicated yet at times contestatory tendencies" (26).

LaCapra's view grows out of his recognition of the false dichotomy that separates history and literature. The approach he calls for resembles the technique adopted by many contemporary literary critics who read against the grain of the literature they examine. For LaCapra, traditional solutions to historiographic problems—solutions such as determining the relation between the author's intention and the text, the relation of society and culture to the text, or even the relation of the text to the corpus of a writer—should be seen as problems of inquiry rather than as solutions to the problem of historiography. In LaCapra's view, "texts should be seen to address us in more subtle and challenging ways, and they should be carried into the present—with implications for the future—in a dialogical fashion" (63). When LaCapra argues that "what should be taken as a problem for inquiry is the nature of the relationships among various analytically defined distinctions in the actual functioning of language" (57), he implies that one of the most significant areas of investigation should be the actual narrative forms that obtain in historiographic writing.

The narrative form of historiography has also been the focus of Hayden White, perhaps the most famous practitioner of combining narrative theory and history. Ever since he published his tropological analyses of nineteenth-century historiography in *Metahistory*, White has persisted in probing the relations between history and narrative. For White, the historian engages in a poetic act by first prefiguring "as a possible object of knowledge the whole set of events reported in the documents" (*Metahistory* 30). White's tropological schema is, by now, well known. Nevertheless, the importance of his insights cannot be overlooked. By focusing attention on the irreducible tropological foundations of historical narratives and their various modes of emplotment, argument, and ideological implication, he redirects our attention to the very linguistic substance that makes up all narratives. White reminds us of something we so quickly overlook in our pursuit of determining "what really happened" when we write histories: namely, that all history is made; it is made of language; and, as such, it is allusive, ambiguous, contradictory, semantically abundant—in short, creative in every sense of the word. This is precisely what White means when he asserts that histories are "verbal fictions, the contents of which are as much *invented* as *found*" (*Tropics* 82).

For White, the opposition we commonly accept between history and fiction arose following the French Revolution. He claims that writers such as Voltaire and De Mably recognized that "many kinds of truth, even in history, could be presented to the reader only by means of fictional techniques of representation" (*Tropics* 123). For these historians, the key opposition was between truth and error, not fact and fiction. In the nineteenth century, however, writers began to "identify truth with fact and to regard fiction as the opposite of truth" (*Tropics* 123). This inversion (fueled no doubt by the ascendancy of positivism in the sciences) has led to the commonly held view, *the received idea*, that somehow history is based on fact, that historical language is transparent, and that the ultimate goal of historiography was best expressed by Leopold von Ranke in his assertion that history should describe the past *"wie es eigentlich gewesen"* (as it actually had been). It is precisely this common view that White seeks to discredit. His methodology directs our attention to the textual nature of history and emphasizes that the principal question is not "What are the facts? but rather, How are the facts to be described in order to sanction one mode of explaining them rather than another?" (*Tropics* 134). In this regard, White sees Paul Ricoeur as an ally in his struggle toward "disenthralling human intelligence from the sense of history" (*Tropics* 40).

As White himself has noted, Ricoeur's work "represents a considerable advancement over previous discussions of the relations between history and literature based on the supposed opposition of 'factual' to 'fictional' discourse" (*Content* 175). Ricoeur's hermeneutic approach emerges, in part, from the philosophy of Hans-Georg Gadamer, who acknowledges "the universal linguality of behaviour relative to the world" (*Hermeneutics* 65). Ricoeur stresses the narrative function of *all* historical explanations. In doing so, he develops a three-part argument in opposition to positivist interpretations of history. First, "there is more *fiction in history*" than positivists care to admit. Second, narrative fiction is more *mimetic* than positivists will allow. And third, there is the concept of "crossed reference" (*référence croisée*), by which Ricoeur means that the references of fiction and history "*cross* upon the basic historicity of human experience" (*Hermeneutics* 293–94). In other words, Ricoeur sees the two narrative modes of fiction and history as interweaving and thereby bringing historicity to language. This tripartite argument leads Ricoeur to conclude that *"the world of fiction leads us to the heart of the real world of action"* (*Hermeneutics* 296).

Such a hasty summary of Ricoeur's arguments does not do justice to the subtlety and ingenuity of his thought. His examination of fiction, mimesis, and cross-reference has resulted in the monumental critique *Time and Narrative*, in which he explores in much greater detail the relationship between history and fiction. According to Ricoeur, temporality is the irreducible constitutive element of human experience, and it is narrative—and narrative alone—that can respond to the "inconclusive rumination" that characterizes all aporetic "speculation on time" (*Time and Narrative* 1:6).

The key to realizing how narrative relates to time lies in understanding the concept of cross-reference. Ricoeur asserts that the interweaving of fiction and history can only be denied if we adopt a positivist outlook toward history that "would not recognize the aspect of fiction in its reference through traces" and an antireferential attitude toward literature that "would not recognize the importance of the metaphorical reference in all poetry" (*Time and Narrative* 1:82). For Ricoeur, these two forms of discourse—fictional and historical—continually "borrow" from one another in the course of their "concretization" (*Time and Narrative* 3:181). By this, Ricoeur means that the act of narrative construction makes concrete (in language) the intention of the discourse, and this constructive activity for both fiction and history is a function of what Ricoeur calls metaphoricity. Ricoeur claims we must move beyond a theory of metaphor as a method of word substitution toward an interaction theory that stresses the "discursive conception of metaphor" (*Rule* 66), a move that would focus attention on the sentence as the unit of discourse (*Rule* 68). Unlike signs, which merely point to other signs, discourse (and, by implication, the sentence) "points to an extra-linguistic reality which is its referent" (*Rule* 217). Metaphor, an operation in which one thing "stands for" another, makes possible a transference that establishes a tension. The metaphor constitutes a paradox that Ricoeur describes as the incision of the literal "is not" within the metaphorical "is" (*Rule* 255). Thus, metaphor, for Ricoeur, constitutes the modality of reference. Metaphor does not merely bring about a "simple transfer of words"; it conducts a "transaction between contexts" (*Rule* 80).

In light of our current discussion of the relation between fiction and history, we can see that both modes of discourse presuppose a referential realm (be it the "past" or the "imaginary") and, through narrative structurations, enact "standing-for" operations. In other words, historical discourse is "quasi-fictive" in that it places before the reader a narrative that stands for the past; whereas fictional discourse is "quasi-historical" in that "the unreal events that it relates are past facts for the narrative voice that addresses itself to the reader" (*Time and Narrative* 3:190). History and fiction are dependent on a narrative form in which the narrative function "stands for" events, the condition of temporal "events" to which the narrative refers, that lie beyond the narrative itself.

To explain more fully the relationship between narrative and the condition of temporality to which it refers, Ricoeur develops the notion of a threefold mimesis. To begin with, mimesis does not mean imitation in the sense of copying a preexistent reality. On the contrary, Ricoeur eschews the Platonic notion of mimesis in favor of mimesis as "creative imitation," an idea based on the Aristotelian concept of *muthos*, or emplotment. Ricoeur points out that the *Poetics* really discusses structuration, not structure; Aristotle emphasizes the organization of events or emplotment to distinguish "universals related to practical wisdom" from Platonic ideas. "A plot engenders such universals," writes Ricoeur, "when the structure of its action rests on the connections internal to the action and not on external accidents" (*Time and Narrative* 1:41). By ramifying this basic insight, Ricoeur is better able to understand the relation between human "experience" and narratives constructed to relate that experience to others. Simply stated, he believes that all understanding of the world stems from the fact that it can be narrated because we, as human beings, construct plots (an act he terms *configuration*) to mediate a practical experience (which is always *prefigured* in a given semantic field) and communicate it to others (who, in their act of reception, *refigure* it). These three terms—*prefiguration, configuration,* and *refiguration*—Ricoeur dubs mimesis$_1$, mimesis$_2$, and mimesis$_3$, respectively.

Prefiguration rests on the basic notion that "human action can be narrated . . . because it is always already articulated by signs, rules, and norms" (*Time and Narrative* 1:57). In other words, practical experience can only *be* experience because it is already constituted by various interrelated semiotic networks without which there would be no experience per se. We are born into and inextricably enmeshed in lexical and semiotic fields outside of which we cannot stand, think, "be." Mimesis$_1$, therefore, signifies the creative imitation of the "symbolic mediations and prenarrative resources of human acting" (*Time and Narrative* 1:81). Mimesis$_2$, by contrast, constitutes the configurational act, the structuring activity of plot production; it is the poetic act, the "kingdom of the *as if,*" the mediation of episodic events and story (*Time and Narrative* 1:64–66). With mimesis$_3$, we reach the stage of reception in the hearer or reader. The refigurational act "fulfills the work" in that each receiver unfolds the work in accordance with a unique field of semantic references. As Ricoeur writes: "The world is the whole set of references opened by every sort of descriptive or poetic text I have read, interpreted and loved" (*Time and Narrative* 1:80). Every refiguration through the act of "reading" potentially opens up new possibilities of experience in language. The threefold mimetic process, therefore, consists of tracing "the destiny of a prefigured time that becomes a refigured time through the mediation of a configured time" (*Time and Narrative* 1:54).

Ricoeur, Disclosure, and Proposed Worlds

The brief overview of some recent theories put forward by scholars in the literary and historical fields should leave no doubt that the boundaries between history and fiction are anything but clearly drawn and are the source of many disputes. I would agree with Mink: past actuality is not an untold story, it is a story too often told in accordance with some established, often veiled power structure; opposing voices are seldom, if ever, heard. I also agree with Hayden White: life "will be lived better if it has no single meaning but many different ones" (*Tropics* 50). Nevertheless, such ideas rarely see the light of day in public discourse. Genre-boundary indeterminacy is complicated by the fact that everyday language uncritically still preserves the history-fact/fiction-falsehood dichotomy. In other words, various theorists engage in heated debates about the issue while, at the same time, in daily conversations, the overwhelming majority of people who are not theorists continue to believe in the dichotomy. One gets the feeling that even if the views of Mink, White, and others were generally accepted by scholars, the average adult in Western society would still regard history as truth and fiction as a lie.

The approaches that I have surveyed do not seem to have an impact that extends beyond scholarly discourse because they have tended to present historiographic versions of the problem. Many of these theorists focus on a particular historical period to show the epistemological shifts that instigated the bifurcation of history and fiction (a method used by critics such as May, Hazard, and White, and perhaps made most famous by Michel Foucault) in the hopes of "unmasking" or "revealing" the constructed nature of the dichotomy. All of this unveiling is to no avail. Ricoeur, by contrast, pursues a philosophical line of inquiry that, paradoxically enough, may help scholars break out of what some would term a hermetic community of self-reflexive critical thinking.

Instead of focusing on unveiling, Ricoeur speaks of disclosure. "The sense of a text is not behind the text, but in front of it," he writes. "It is not something hidden, but something disclosed" (*Interpretation* 87). Writing and reading constitute *the* hermeneutical problem for Ricoeur. These two complementary acts initiate what Ricoeur terms a dialectic of "distanciation" and "appropriation" (*Interpretation* 43). Distanciation inheres in writing qua writing. By its very nature, "writing renders the text autonomous with respect to the intention of the author" (*Hermeneutics* 139). A sense of estrangement ensues when any text is read, and the interpretive act that every reader performs must be focused on the "proposed world" of the text, which is what Ricoeur refers to when he speaks of the sense of a text being in front of it. In other words, the reader "appropriates" a proposed world, "that which the work unfolds, discovers, reveals" (*Hermeneutics* 143). Now this proposed world is *not* the everyday world. In fact, the proposed world of the text constitutes a second-order distanciation that Ricoeur terms "a distanciation of the real from itself" (*Hermeneutics* 142). What is significant here is that, despite what Ricoeur himself claims, the second-order distanciation applies to fiction *and* history. The notion that history involves a first-order distanciation that is somehow linked to the "real," whereas fiction is removed one step further from the "real," strikes me as an odd sort of Platonism that weakens the power of Ricoeur's own arguments. The proposed world of a historian such as Johan Huizinga is just as estranged from the reader as is a novel by Umberto Eco. Both writers propose worlds that lie beyond the immediate experience of the reader. And the reader, according to Ricoeur, appropriates the text in the form of an interpretation that is nothing less than self-interpretation (*Hermeneutics* 158). Ricoeur admits that his term—appropriation—is his own translation of the German term *Aneignung*, which, in the verb form (*aneignen*) means "'to make one's own' what was initially 'alien'." This is important for Ricoeur because it marks the principal goal of all hermeneutics, namely, "to struggle against cultural distance and historical alienation" (*Hermeneutics* 185).

We must not lose sight of the fact that, by directing his attention at the sentence level of semantic production, Ricoeur preserves the notion of reference in the form of proposed worlds. The act of writing that constitutes a "standing-for" operation produces the proposed world that, in turn, is appropriated by the reader. The consequences of this theoretical move are enormous in that Ricoeur preserves the possibility of self-transformation through reading a text that is itself the product of the transformative power of metaphoricity. His approach avoids the intractable problem posed by the neoformalist practice that asserts that nothing lies beyond the text. By contrast, he also vigorously denies the strict dichotomization of history and fiction. For Ricoeur, both discursive forms posit a referential field via the configurational act that opens a world, proposes new possibilities, and offers to readers a means of refiguring, hence reinterpreting, the past. It is this reinterpretive act that offers the primary means toward emancipation (*Hermeneutics* 97).

In this regard, Ricoeur's theory possesses affinities with certain arguments offered by Richard Rorty. In *Contingency, Irony, and Solidarity*, Rorty calls for an end to traditional philosophical discourse and suggests that literature can best advance the cause of human solidarity and freedom. Although there are serious problems with Rorty's insistence on a distinction between the private and public spheres (83–95), there is something compelling about his argument that what "binds societies together are common vocabularies and common hopes" (86) and that "detailed descriptions of particular varieties of pain and humiliation" (192), as principally presented in novels, do more to forge this common vocabulary of social cohesion than any other form of discourse.

The concern with establishing socially cohesive vocabularies also appears in the writings of Ricoeur. In his third volume of *Time and Narrative*, Ricoeur emphasizes that history, forged of a "chain of memories," becomes a "we-relationship" (114). In other words, historical discourse creates a sense of communal identity, of shared experience, of a collective past. Fiction, by contrast, gives eyes to the memory of the horrible. Like Rorty in chapter 9 of *Contingency, Irony, and Solidarity*, Ricoeur sees the Holocaust narrative as a ground zero of historical representation. As Ricoeur bluntly states, "Either one counts the cadavers or one tells the story of the victims"; historical explanation lies somewhere between these two modes (*Time and Narrative* 3:188). In this sense, fictional discourse does not vitiate the veracity of the historical truth depicted; rather, fiction helps history realize the possibility of bringing into being a "standing-for" operation that broadens the horizons of the reader's understanding of the past. The fictional representations of the Shoah (one thinks of the crafted tales of Tadeusz Borowski) can do just as much (perhaps more) to deepen our understanding of the suffering of the victims than does a detailed study by Terrence Des Pres. One can see here a possible response to Walter Benjamin's assertion that adherents of historicism empathize with the victor (256). Novelists, Ricoeur would argue, need not empathize with the victors of history; in fact, as both Ricoeur and Rorty insist, novelists can give eyes and voice to the victims of history. They can open a second-order referential realm that examines and considers outcomes that were not realized; they can reimagine the past by reconstructing it, just as historians do, in order to speculate on the conditions of what those of us in the present accept as "what really happened" in that particular past.

The Philosophy of History: A Brief Review

The speculative activity that both Ricoeur and Rorty allude to traditionally falls under the domain of the philosophy of history, an area of philosophical endeavor that has largely fallen into disrepute. In no small part, this is due to the rejection of German Idealist interpretations of history and the subsequent conflation of scientific methodology and the verification of the historical past. Nevertheless, there is a long tradition in the philosophy of history, both critical and speculative, that it is best to recall. A complete review of the field lies beyond the scope of the present study, but a representative sampling will provide an overview of some general trends in the field.

One of the first Western philosophers to provide a detailed discussion of the relation between history and fiction was, of course, Aristotle. In book 9 of the *Poetics*, he declares that "it is not the function of the poet to relate what has happened, but what may happen,—what is possible according to the law of probability or necessity" (35). For Aristotle, the distinction is simple: poetry is more philosophical because it expresses the universal, whereas history merely expresses the particular. One need not be reminded that few, if any, people accept Aristotle's reasoning. This is not, however, to disparage the great philosopher. On the contrary, Aristotle's theory of mimesis, as interpreted by Ricoeur, will play a significant role in the development of the present study. Nevertheless, there is something familiarly unsatisfying with Aristotle's assertion that the historian "relates what has happened" whereas the poet relates "what may happen."

During the Middle Ages in Europe, the rise of Christianity brought with it an attendant philosophy of history, perhaps best expressed in Augustine's *City of God*. History, according to Augustine, is the unfolding of a divine plan. Irrespective of the injustices on earth, many of which he begins to enumerate in book 10, chapter 2, Augustine assures us that, on "the day of judgment," God's justice will prevail. It is the other world that is real; Augustine's is a teleological philosophy of history that sees all meaning in the spiritual realm beyond our mundane existence. Thus, with respect to the human realm, the Christian God is the cause of all historical processes, and humans carry out the will of God. Augustine flatly states: "so great is His wisdom and power, that all things which seem adverse to his purpose do still tend towards those just and good ends and issues which He Himself has foreknown" (811). After the Copernican Revolution, however, divine intervention in history is open to serious doubt.

In the eighteenth century, Immanuel Kant took up the challenge of explaining human actions in the face of a natural world as constructed by modern science. In his "Idea for a Universal History from the Cosmopolitan Point of View," Kant contends that history—which is to say, human actions—is "determined by universal laws" (*On History* 11). Kant insists that if we observe the human race as a whole, we will recognize that Nature drives humans, as a species, to develop reason fully such that it manifests itself in "a universal civic society which administers law among men" (16). Nature, it seems, has a "secret plan to bring forth a perfectly constituted state as the only condition in which the capacities of mankind can be fully developed" (21). The means by which Nature achieves this end is through the antagonism among individuals in society. In other words, Nature compels them to act irrationally, and these irrational, evil acts actually help spur the process by which humans become rational. Consequently, all forms of war, "purposeless savagery" (20), state conflicts, and institutional violence can be viewed as necessary steps on the road to enlightenment. "Thanks be to Nature," writes Kant (16). Suffice it to say, such a teleological view sends shivers down the spine of a person living in the late twentieth century.

In a similar vein, perhaps the most famous and least palatable philosophy of history for us, in this era "after Auschwitz," is that of G. W. F. Hegel. "World history in general is the development of Spirit in *Time*," Hegel writes. "Only the study of world history itself can show that it has proceeded rationally, that it represents the rationally necessary course of the World Spirit" (*Reason in History* 87, 12).

Equally perplexing is the critical philosophy of history of Wilhelm Dilthey. "The only complete, self-contained and clearly defined happening encountered everywhere in history and in every concept that occurs in human studies," writes Dilthey, "is the course of a life" (*Meaning in History* 97). For the father of *Geisteswissenschaften*, history can only be understood through the categories of life. Dilthey posits an isomorphism between the categories of human consciousness and historical categories. Autobiography serves as the best formal model for understanding life (85) and, by implication, for understanding history. Although Dilthey admits that the individual is "a point where systems intersect" (78), he does not recognize the inscriptive powers as well as the inscripted nature of these systems. In other words, he seems unwilling to admit that "life," as he terms it, is contextualized by a series of imbricated interpretations or "texts." These texts—systems, institutions, laws, myths, in short, discursive progenitors—constitute a particular *epistémè* at a specific moment in time, and it is the epistemic paradigm that gives to "life" its form that we perceive.

Also troublesome is Dilthey's insistence that the means by which we obtain knowledge of the physical world differs from the means we use to gain human knowledge. As Ricoeur has noted, this "ruinous dichotomy" between explanation and understanding has had dire consequences because it suggests that all explanation (i.e., *scientific* and *rational* explanation) is "naturalistic" and "causal" (*Hermeneutics* 92). By maintaining this strict dichotomy, Dilthey's philosophy inadvertently lends credence to those who champion scientific and "objective" methodologies in historiography *and* the philosophy of history. In fact, it could be argued that by formulating his "philosophy of Life," Dilthey made it easier for Karl Popper's and C. G. Hempel's covering-law model of historical explanation to become the focal point of theoretical debates concerning the philosophy of history. Notwithstanding the powerful refutation the covering-law model has received by William Dray in *Laws and Explanation in History,* the "objective" nature of "science" still grips the imagination of most readers of history and continues to instill latent feelings of inferiority among scholars in the "human sciences."

Despite the disappointment the tradition of the philosophy of history produces in contemporary readers, there are two philosophers who stand apart—Giambattista Vico and Friedrich Nietzsche. These two thinkers (who, in many ways, resemble one another) choose a different approach to the philosophical examination of history. Of the two, Nietzsche is by far better known to the community of literary theorists. For this reason, I will begin with a brief summary of Nietzsche's views on history and then offer an outline of Vico's theory of history.

In his famous second "Untimely Meditation," entitled "On the Uses and Disadvantages of History for Life," Nietzsche discusses in what ways history can help or hinder "life"—a concept to which we will return later. Nietzsche believes that to act we must be able to forget. Humankind must be able to "feel *unhistorically*," he argues, if it is to be creative and forge new, life-giving values. But, he is careful to add, "the unhistorical and the historical are necessary in equal measure for the health of an individual, of a people and of a culture" (UM 63). In other words, Nietzsche recognizes that in certain instances a historical perspective will be a hindrance, whereas in different circumstances a historical sense may be precisely what is needed; one must be able to discern which mode will best further life. With this basic dichotomy in mind, Nietzsche defines three forms of history (monumental, antiquarian, and critical), outlines the strengths and weaknesses of each type, and repeatedly stresses that, under certain conditions, each one of these types of historical activity can serve life.

Monumental history teaches us that the greatness of the past was "*possible* and may thus be possible again" (UM 69). It can inspire us to do great things; it can serve as a model for our courses of action in the present. Nevertheless, monumental history also has certain drawbacks. It "deceives by analogies," writes Nietzsche, and can inspire fanatical and foolish behavior. There is also a second, more pernicious problem with monumental history: it can be used by people to repudiate the powerful of the present age. The past can become an epic age that can never be matched, and the present can be perceived as a time of petty and insignificant actions.

Antiquarian history, by contrast, seeks to preserve traditions and pass them on to those that follow. This pietistic attitude, states Nietzsche, can further the interests of a community by forming strong bonds among communal members and thereby dissuading them from "the desire for expeditions and adventures" (UM 74). Antiquarian history, therefore, can preserve the tribe, but it can also render the tribe impotent. As Nietzsche himself points out, antiquarian history "knows only how to *preserve* life, not how to engender it" (UM 75). The difficulty for practitioners of antiquarian history becomes how to preserve tradition that is at the same time animated by the present. Failure to do so leads to a moribund society, a life that Nietzsche characterizes as mummified.

The third—and for late twentieth-century readers perhaps the most interesting—form of history that Nietzsche discusses is critical history, which, Nietzsche declares "is an attempt to give oneself, as it were *a posteriori*, a past in which one would like to originate in opposition to that in which one did originate" (UM 76). Simply stated, critical history is a form of revisionist history, a means by which a people can forge its own identity and liberate itself from characterizations that appear in dominant forms of historical representation. Critical history gives a free voice to those who want to make themselves anew and plot for themselves their own destiny. But, as Nietzsche warns, this is a most dangerous enterprise. Those who engage in critical history, an activity Nietzsche describes as taking "the knife to its roots," run the risk of failing to recognize that no one is free from the crimes of the past. To practice critical history in order to proclaim one's innocence would be a supreme act of bad faith. As

Nietzsche quite rightly affirms, "If we condemn these aberrations and regard ourselves as free of them, this does not alter the fact that we originate in them" (UM 76).

As we have seen, Nietzsche offers different perspectives on what history can be. He is careful to emphasize when history should be dispensed with as well as when a particular form of history should be used. He summarizes his position as follows: "If the man who wants to do something great has need of the past at all, he appropriates it by means of monumental history; he, on the other hand, who likes to persist in the familiar and the revered of old, tends the past as an antiquarian historian; and only he who is oppressed by a present need, and who wants to throw off his burden at any cost, has need of critical history, that is to say a history that judges and condemns" (UM 72). Common to all of these endeavors, it should be recalled, is Nietzsche's insistence that they serve life. What, then, does Nietzsche mean by life? To answer this question, it is best to turn first to one of his most profound and troubling interpreters: Martin Heidegger.

In his monumental interpretation of Nietzsche, Heidegger has much to say (and much not to say) about his most formidable precursor. On the question of what life means for Nietzsche, Heidegger is quite clear. Drawing support from paragraph 689 in *The Will to Power,* where Nietzsche writes, "Life, as the form of being most familiar to us, is specifically a will to the accumulation of force," Heidegger equates life with the will to power and the will to power with art (*Nietzsche* 1:69, 214–15). Heidegger contends, and I think quite rightly, that for Nietzsche, *"Art, as transfiguration, is more enhancing to life than truth"* (*Nietzsche* 1:217). If will to power is the overpowering of power—that is, the act of affirming values that compete with, oppose, and seek to overcome other values—then it is art that best effects this activity; it is art that creates new values, which for Nietzsche is what life is: creating values. "The will liberates," declares Zarathustra, "for to will is to create" (Z 206). As Heidegger himself asserts, "The highest value is *art,* in contradistinction to knowledge and truth. It does not copy what is at hand, does not explain matters in terms of beings at hand. But art transfigures life, moves it into higher, as yet unlived possibilities" (*Nietzsche* 3:81). Art affords us the principal means by which we can enact Nietzsche's perspectival philosophy. "Will to power interprets," writes Nietzsche (WP ¶ 643). Art, by its very nature, elicits various interpretations and valuations and offers none as given, true, correct.

Whereas discussions of Nietzsche's writings have become, by now, familiar (perhaps too familiar) to literary scholars, the second philosopher I will discuss, Giambattista Vico, presents formidable obstacles to the late twentieth-century mind. Unlike Nietzsche, who can be seen as a jester on the tragic stage of our era (and who, as Thomas Mann said of himself, was never more serious than when he was laughing), Vico appears to be so deadly earnest with his chronological table, indicating the exact date when God gave Moses the written law and when Cadmus founded Thebes, and so on, that he causes the reader immense embarrassment. One wonders aloud: Can he be serious? Vico's assertions that all civilizations emerge from three institutions (religion, marriage, and burial), that all cultures pass through three ages (divine, heroic, and human), and that history proceeds through a cycle, a course and recourse (*corso e ricorso*) that repeats endlessly through time strikes the modern reader as wild fabrication. *That,* however, is precisely the point. In his magnum opus *The New Science,* Vico writes a fable that is true; and in doing so, he instantiates his philosophy that, more than any other, underscores the notion that we, as humans, make our world.

Vico expresses his most important insight in his early treatise *On the Most Ancient Wisdom of the Italians.* Relying on a philological methodology, he observes that, "for the Latins, *verum* (the true) and *factum* (what is made) are interchangeable" (MAW 45). This leads Vico to declare that the ancient sages had attained an important insight that we have lost sight of; namely, that "the true is precisely what is made" (MAW 46). In other words, human beings make their own truths. What we do not make (Nature, for example), we cannot truly know.

As Leon Pompa points out, at the time he wrote *The Most Ancient Wisdom,* Vico did not believe that history could be a branch of knowledge. It was only when he came to write *The New Science,* Pompa argues, that Vico realized "that the men who are the agents in history are *in some sense* identical with the men who later write that history" (129). Through the process of identification, the historian can come to know the past. In other words, we can come to understand the motivations of certain individuals and groups of people in history by reconstructing in our own minds what it is they thought or felt. But this is not all that Vico says. At the end of book 1, Vico offers the philological proofs of his Science, of which number 6 reads: "The great fragments of antiquity, hitherto useless to science because they lay begrimed, broken and scattered, shed great light when cleaned, pieced together and restored" (NS ¶ 357). Herein lies Vico's persistent emphasis on the origin of human institutions, our understanding of which only comes through handling the fragments of the past that have survived in time. As Raffaello Franchini argues, the power of Vico's thought resides in his "philological-topological-critical method." Vico situates himself between a deductive and inductive historical methodology that preserves him from the pitfalls of either radical empiricism or abstract idealism (551). History, Vico tells us, because it is made by humans, can be known; and this knowledge is transmitted through the construction of narratives of the memory of the past.

The New Science describes what Vico terms "an Ideal eternal history traversed in time by the history of every nation in its rise, development, maturity, decline, and fall" (NS ¶ 349). He goes on to say that "he who meditates this Science narrates to himself this ideal eternal history so far as he himself makes it for himself by that proof 'it had, has, and will have to be'" (NS ¶ 349). History, therefore, is a narrative constructed in the minds of those who think the past; and this thinking rests in no small part on the memory, which, according to Vico, consists of three elements: "memory when it remembers things, imagination when it alters or imitates them, and invention when it gives them a new turn or puts them into proper arrangement and relationship" (NS ¶ 819). These three aspects—*memoria, fantasia,* and *ingegno*—comprise memory as a whole, which, Vico asserts, "is the same as imagination" (NS ¶ 819). Thus, history constitutes a creative mimesis, one that alters, invents, arranges. Human truths, writes Vico, "we shape (*fingamus*) for ourselves" (MAW 57). Through the handling of the material, the manipulation of the details, documents, and collective memories, we bring our experience to language and construct a fable, what Vico calls a true narrative (*vera narratio*) (NS ¶ 814).

According to Vico, the first fables actually contained civil truths (NS ¶ 198). Fables are the product of a metaphoric operation by which humans make meaning and thereby their world. Vico conjectures that primitive people "pictured the sky to themselves as a great animated body" (NS ¶ 377) whose thunder they called Jove. By naming the thunder Jove, these early humans—Vico calls them theological poets—constructed the greatest fable of all. The act of naming, the metaphoric enterprise par excellence, he says, involves the construction of an imaginative universal (*universale fantastico*), which he claims is the master key to *The New Science* (NS ¶ 34). Imaginative universals are not abstract generalizations; on the contrary, they are identical with that which they name. Donald P. Verene explains it best when he informs us that, for Vico, there does not exist an antecedent "empirical or historical order of events" that the poetic mind of the primitive human "rendered into fabulous form." "Events themselves," writes Verene, "are given form through fables" ("Vico's Science of Imaginative Universals" 303). It is the poetic, primitive mind that gives form to experience; without such forming, experience remains unintelligible.

Vico believes that all of civilization emerges from this initial poetic act. The institutions of religion, marriage, burial, forms of state—in short, all cultural institutions—grow out of the metaphoric structuration effected by imaginative universals that in and of themselves are fables. These fables, stories, and metaphors make up the *sensus communis*, the linguistic and semiotic network that connects people within a given culture; through these acts, which White calls acts of *metaphorical projection*, the human world comes to be. Vico's understanding of this process, White argues, led him to conceive of the fictive as the third ground between truth and fable that we popularly see as being opposed to one another (*Tropics* 145). The third ground, the fictive, as White calls it, is where I see Vico placing history—our modern "true narratives"—which we construct in order to understand our experience.

Vico and Nietzsche: An Analytic Framework

Up to this point, my juxtaposition of Nietzsche and Vico may appear to be little more than an act of desperate ex-centricity were it not for the fact that I am not alone. As David M. Parry reminds us, Isaiah Berlin, Edward Said, and Allan Megill, among others, have mentioned Vico and Nietzsche together. It is, however, the pioneering work of Parry himself that has brought to light the salient features of a comparative study of these two imaginative thinkers. In "Vico and Nietzsche," Parry begins by noting the obvious: both were philologists, both stressed the importance of institutions over ideas in determining culture, and both men were ignored in their lifetimes. He then goes on to discuss common areas of interest shared by the two. First, Parry argues, both Vico and Nietzsche used etymological methods to examine the origins of culture. Second, both men focused on the struggle between the nobles and the plebs, a struggle in which the plebs prevail. Third, both philosophers wrote autobiographies, which, Parry contends, enact their respective philosophies.

To Parry's line of analysis I would like to add two additional common themes that link the writings of Nietzsche and Vico. The first is their combined assault on science. The second is their mutual recognition that metaphor is the key to human creativity.

In one of the most famous passages in *The Will to Power,* Nietzsche declares: "Against positivism, which halts at phenomena—'There are only *facts*'—I would say: No, facts is precisely what there is not, only interpretations" (WP ¶ 481). Nietzsche waged a lifelong campaign against Truth, or the belief in immutable certainties. In Europe after Descartes, science was the main purveyor of such truths. Rather than appeal to a self-verifying method, Nietzsche continually questioned the grounds on which "objective" science is based. Physics, he declares in *Beyond Good and Evil,* is an interpretation (21). "One should use 'cause' and 'effect' only as pure concepts, that is to say, as conventional fictions for the purpose of designation and communication—*not* for explanation" (BGE 29). Again and again, Nietzsche emphasizes that it is we human—all-too-human—creatures who have invented the scientific method and with it the illusions that it provides.

In a similar fashion, as Yvon Belaval points out, Vico engaged in a protracted battle with Cartesianism throughout his adult life. As we have seen, Vico denies that truth is certain: the true is the made. We can only understand what we ourselves have made. In his *Autobiography,* Vico states that he "could not accept seriously or playfully the mechanical physics of Epicurus or Descartes because both start from a false position" (122). The false position to which Vico refers becomes the focal point of the *Ancient Wisdom* treatise, the entirety of which can be viewed as Vico's impassioned refutation of Descartes. Vico determines that Descartes errs when he begins with consciousness in the hopes of attaining certainty. Consciousness, retorts Vico, tells us only that we are conscious; it cannot give us knowledge. Equally disturbing to him is Descartes's rejection of the study of language, orators, historians, and poets (A 137). Such a move threatens the *sensus communis,* the very lifeblood of culture. As Verene points out in *Vico's Science of Imagination,* Cartesian method helps to bring into being the intelligible universal in contrast to Vico's imaginative universal. The intelligible universal creates conceptual language that drains expressions of their richness and ambiguity. Such conceptual language gives rise to technique, which in turn replaces the *sensus communis.* This loss characterizes the third age for Vico, a period in which the barbarism of reflection supplants poetic narration (193–221). Some 150 years later, Nietzsche would write: "Philosophy reduced to the theory of knowledge . . . is philosophy in its last throes" (BGE 123). Both Vico and Nietzsche see scientific method as the symptom of a dissipated culture.

One of the most interesting similarities between Vico and Nietzsche is their use of the word "science" and scientific terminology. In *The New Science*, Vico deliberately uses *Scienza* to reappropriate the word. His is a science in opposition to the positivistic science, the notion that immediately leaps to the modern mind when we hear the word. Similarly, Nietzsche entitles one of his most famous books *The Gay Science*, which he subtitles "la gaya scienza," implying that, for him, science is not a method but a joyful creating. In addition, he repeatedly plays on the word *Versuchen* (to attempt or experiment). For example, Zarathustra associates seekers (*Sucher*) with experimenters (*Versucher*) (Z 159). In *Daybreak*, Nietzsche asserts, "We are experiments: let us also want to be them" (191). And in *The Gay Science*, he calls "the idea that life could be an experiment of the seeker for knowledge" a "great liberator" (255). As Walter Kaufmann reminds us, "it is quite proper in German to speak of a scientist as making a *Versuch*" (85). Nietzsche, therefore, calls on us to try different perspectives, to attempt different interpretations, to live dangerously by calling into question epistemological assumptions that contribute to the construction of our perceptual field. In his very first book, Nietzsche calls for the destruction of science's "claim to universal validity" so as to bring about a rebirth of tragedy (BT 106). Vico as well calls his metaphysics experimental: "in this metaphysics we regard as true in nature that to which we make something similar in experiments" (MAW 109). Thus, both Nietzsche and Vico want to appropriate the language of science to propose their own philosophies, which they feel are superior to positivistic science.

In the place of science, Nietzsche and Vico emphasize metaphoric power. Perhaps Nietzsche's most often quoted line (excluding "God is dead") appears in a short essay entitled "On Truth and Lies in a Nonmoral Sense." The lines are familiar but worth recalling. Nietzsche asserts that truth is "a movable host of metaphors, metonymies, and anthropomorphisms"; we have forgotten that truths "are illusions"; they are "metaphors that have become worn-out and have been drained of their sensuous force" (PT 84). Nietzsche wants to leave no doubt: our world is constituted by means of a metaphoric operation. By insisting that this is the case, he echoes Vico's *verum-factum* principle when he writes: "We can comprehend only a world that we ourselves have made" (WP ¶ 495). Like Vico before him, Nietzsche perceives *the* struggle of the modern age as that between the creative imagination and philosophy seduced by a reflective dialectic. He characterizes this conflict as a struggle between Homer and Plato (GM 153–54).

For Vico, Homer is the supreme exemplar of poetic wisdom. Out of Homer comes Greek culture. Vico concludes that "the Greek people were themselves Homer" (NS ¶ 875). In other words, the interweaving of language, fables, customs, and symbols that comprise the Homeric epics fabricates the cultural cloth of ancient Greece. The wisdom of Homer, which Vico associates with a barbarism of the senses, is distinct from the barbarism of reflection that characterizes modern culture caught in the grip of scientific technology.

This common focus on metaphor results in both philosophers choosing related metaphors to figure their respective philosophies. As we have seen, Vico claims that by naming the thunder Jove, primitive people fashioned an imaginative universal. Prior to this moment, all human experience was a flux such that no two events could be seen as similar. After the Jove experience, humans had a starting point. Jove, being named, became a universal (i.e., each thunderclap was Jove). As Verene tells it, Vico conceived of primitive people as living in a world of "real words." He writes: "Vico asks us to imagine a beginning point of human experience in which all was body and bodily motion, in which meaning was an action between bodies and in which human thought was nothing more than the bodily act of sensation" (*Vico's Science* 85). Thus, thinking and sensing are coextensive for the theological poets, and thinking is a metaphoric operation.

Vico succinctly states that "every metaphor is a fable in brief" (NS ¶ 404). But the metaphoric operation to which he refers is not an act of substitution; rather, as Verene quite rightly argues, for Vico metaphor is a process of identification for the primitive person. The imaginative universal enfolds itself around *is* as a concept. The *is*, Verene informs us, "appears from the first moment with a double meaning—as *being* and as *copula.*" "In the imaginative universal," he continues, "something *is* for the mind . . . and something *is* 'in relation'" (*Vico's Science* 173). In other words, the imaginative universal is not a case of protonominalism; that is, the theological poets do not observe phenomena and then name them. Rather, by naming the thunder Jove, it becomes a phenomenon—intelligible, created, real. This, then, is the metaphoric underpinning of all reality for Vico, the thunder that *is* Jove.

In Nietzsche, lightning serves as the key image. For example, the Overman, declares Zarathustra, "is this lightning" (Z 14). He is "the lightning out of the dark cloud of man" (Z 20). One must be prepared for the lightning bolts of redemption, the lightning bolts that say yes and affirm all of life (Z 228). But in the *Genealogy of Morals*, Nietzsche offers his most detailed discussion of what the metaphor of lightning means for him. He writes: "the popular mind separates the lightning from its flash and takes the latter for an action. . . . But there is no 'being' behind doing, effecting, becoming; 'the doer' is merely a fiction added to the deed—the deed is everything. The popular mind in fact doubles the deed; when it sees the lightning flash, it is the deed of a deed . . . our entire science still lies under the misleading influence of language and has not disposed of that little changeling, the 'subject'" (45). What I find interesting here is Nietzsche's critique of the scientific explanation that sees the flash as a manifestation of lightning. Nietzsche's desire to dispose of the subject does not concern me as much as his understanding of lightning that *is* flash. In this respect, he echoes Vico in that when he criticizes a language that posits agency and strengthens notions of causality, he simultaneously suggests that a superior language would make the two—lightning and flash—coterminus. To my mind, this implied superior language resembles to a remarkable degree the metaphoric language of identity in which the *is* expresses *being* and serves as a *copula*—in this case the lightning *is* flash. I will even suggest that what Nietzsche seeks (in language) in his Dionysian experience is a return to the barbarism of the senses, a return to the metaphorical projections of "real words" from the body. As Vico affirms that the faculties of memory "have their roots in the body and draw their strength from it" (NS ¶ 819), so Nietzsche asserts that "there is more reason in your body than in your best wisdom" (Z 34–35). In a way, Nietzsche announces a new *corso* when he proclaims the Overman. He heralds the dawn of humans who create values for themselves and craft their lives as a work of art. Thus, the Overman may very well be the possessor of poetic wisdom.

At the end of his "Uses and Disadvantages" essay, Nietzsche states that we must endeavor to "organize the chaos" so as to recognize our "real needs" and break out of a cycle of repeating what we have heard, learning what is already known, and imitating what already exists. "To become masters of the chaos," he writes in *The Will to Power*, "one must compel one's chaos to become form" (¶ 842). The configurative act that Nietzsche calls for harkens all the way back to the origins of Greek philosophy, which, he claims, seeks to determine how "a chaos [could] become a cosmos" (PTA 107). This, then, is the Nietzschean project: to make of life a work of art.

For Vico, "wisdom itself is nothing but the skillful care of what is fitting" (MAW 61). By focusing our attention on what it is that we make, he reminds us that knowledge is not an abstract concept that occupies ideal space. On the contrary, human knowledge is precisely that—human; and Vico makes us aware that if we make the world we can also unmake it or remake it. By stressing the role metaphor plays in the construction of reality, Vico, like Nietzsche, underscores the irreducibly linguistic nature of our experience. Understanding can only be achieved through a combination of philosophical and philological methods.

The threefold memory that Vico describes, with its emphasis on *memoria, fantasia,* and *ingegno,* makes possible a creative history. In his "Uses and Disadvantages" essay, Nietzsche gives us three possible types of history. Using the philosophies of Vico and Nietzsche in tandem, I would propose a fourth: speculative poietic history. Such a history, I will claim, appears in the form of the novel. It is the novel that allows writers to explore the boundaries of the possible in the past and bring to our awareness in the present the potential for self and social transformation.

As I suggested in the introduction, novels of poietic history focus on the formation of values; they concern themselves with the future as much as with the past; and they emphasize the mythic underpinnings of all histories. The three modalities I discussed—the history of forgotten possibilities, history as countermemory of cultural critique, and history as myth—all emerge from imaginative speculations about the past that are figured in language. These novels of poietic history confirm Mink's observations that narrative structures produce the description of events and that facts arise only in a contextualized narrative form. The speculations these novels engage in give us pause to consider some other facts about the past. Similarly, novels of poietic history verify White's observation that facts serve as a means to sanction particular explanatory modes. Novelists of poietic history, however, permit us to sanction different modes of understanding by contextualizing facts in new and different ways.

As Michel de Certeau has observed, historical understanding predicates itself on what is forgotten (4). Every known historical phenomenon comes to light because some other phenomenon is pushed into the shadows. Novels of poietic history very often redirect our attention to those formerly obscured phenomena. This is not to suggest that what these novelists discuss is any less real than what one would find in conventional historiography. Once again, de Certeau reminds us that, when it comes to history, "the productive *activity* and the period *known* distort each other" (37). This reciprocal distortion that occurs between history qua history and history as writing receives repeated emphasis in novels of poietic history. Such novels make clear to us the meaning-producing capacity of all narrative constructions even as they specifically point out that the actualities of the past never return without the distorting activities of writing and narrative configuration.

To conduct my analysis of the novels I have chosen, I will use both Nietzsche's and Vico's philosophical writings in varying degrees so as to explore what each novel has to say about history. For example, in some instances I employ Nietzsche's three categories of history—monumental, antiquarian, critical—as forms of historical discourse that the novelists inscribe in their novels in opposition to their own poietic form of speculative history—that is, the novels they have written. In other words, some of the novels that I have chosen to examine contain within them versions of the Nietzschean categories of history, and the authors of these novels attempt to subvert these versions so as to advance their own speculative poietic history.

When I employ Vico's writings I often pursue other goals. In Vichian philosophy, the metaphor holds the supreme position; it is through metaphor that we construct the human world. In the novels I will analyze, the authors produce a metaphor or series of metaphors that mobilize their speculations. Vico's philosophy will best serve my purpose because it posits a threefold memory that contains simple recollection, creative imitation, and invention through new contextualizations. With this in mind, I see striking parallels between Vico's threefold memory and Ricoeur's threefold mimesis. These two thinkers offer powerful theoretical devices to examine and explicate both fiction and history. The prefigurative level of mimesis$_1$, which grounds itself on the always already existent cultural semiotic field, corresponds with Vico's notion of *memoria*, which he equates with simple remembering, for which the cultural semiotic remains the sine qua non. Ricoeur's mimesis$_2$, the configurational act, possesses strong affinities with Vico's *fantasia*, an imitation through alteration. It is configuration that structures plot for Ricoeur, and, for Vico, *fantasia* is the fable-making act. Finally, Ricoeur's refiguration, mimesis$_3$, the fulfillment of the work that occurs in each receiver's mind, resembles Vico's *ingegno*, the inventive act that gives memory "a new turn" or puts memories into a "proper relationship or arrangement" (NS ¶ 819).

The superimposition of Ricoeur's threefold mimesis onto Vico's threefold memory provides a theory of narrative with which to describe the speculative philosophies of history that some of the novelists construct. As such, it is purely a heuristic device. I do not wish to suggest that Ricoeur's theory is the same as Vico's philosophy; it is not even clear to me if in fact Ricoeur has studied Vico. What is far more important is that both men offer a vocabulary and a hermeneutics that can best explore the historical speculations occurring in the novels I wish to study.

I also see an associative link between Vico's notion of metaphor and Ricoeur's discursive conception of metaphor. As White points out, Vico's thought contains a "hermeneutical principle," one that suggests that "speech itself provides the key for interpreting cultural phenomena" (*Tropics* 203). I believe that Vico's contention that every metaphor is a fable in brief presages Ricoeur's own theory of the discursive conception of metaphor. Both thinkers, I would argue, want to move away from theories of sign substitution and toward an understanding of narrative constructions of the "real." Both men recognize that metaphoric structuration constitutes the "real" and informs historical narrative. The key to Vico and Ricoeur, therefore, is the metaphor; and it is by means of metaphor that one obtains access to the referential field we ordinarily call reality, that is, the cultural institutions that make up our world.

Taken together, the writings of Vico and Nietzsche offer a dynamic interpretive schema that can be used to examine the meaning-producing potential of novels that focus on forgotten possibilities, develop counternarratives to popular notions of history, and explore the notion of history as myth. These two philosophers provide both a powerful vocabulary and a rich conceptual field that can be combined in various ways to conduct detailed narrative analyses. In addition, both stress the importance of metaphoric structuration and emplotment and, in doing so, offer interpretive keys to understanding how truths are made in novels and in history proper.

The novelists I choose to study here—Carlos Fuentes, Susan Daitch, Salman Rushdie, Michel Tournier, Ishmael Reed, Graham Swift, and Mario Vargas Llosa—have each produced a novel that heightens the tension between history and fiction by pursuing a historico-philosophical line of inquiry. These novelists write the type of text that best exemplifies what Ricoeur terms the interweaving of fiction and history; they craft what I have called the novel of speculative poietic history. In their respective novels, the authors question the assumptions underlying our conceptions of a particular historical past (e.g., the Spain of Philip II and the conquest of the Americas, the rise of fascism in Europe, and the founding of India as an independent nation-state). These seven contemporary novelists interrogate the historicity of popular notions of the past, accounts that have been inscribed in the collective memory of the tribe, accounts that deny their significatory status by repeatedly appealing to a referent of the "reality" of the past. In contradistinction to this uncritically accepted referent, the authors I study open up a second-order referential field that is interpenetrated by and deeply enmeshed in historical detail that we ordinarily assume emerges from an "objective," "scientific"—in short, "historiographic"—methodology. By imbuing their works with historical detail, these seven novelists *are not* attempting to reduplicate the past. Unlike some of their contemporaries, who fashion what critics term a postmodern style, Fuentes, Daitch, Rushdie, Tournier, Reed, Swift, and Vargas Llosa in the seven novels to be examined—*Terra Nostra, L.C., Midnight's Children, Le Roi des Aulnes* (The Ogre), *Mumbo Jumbo, Waterland,* and *El hablador* (The Storyteller)—do not heed what Ricoeur derisively calls "the plea for a fragmented, inconsistent fiction" (to my mind an apt description of one type of postmodern aesthetic in literature). As Ricoeur points out, such attempts to reproduce the "chaos of reality" (even if it is the commodified world of late-capitalist culture) "returns mimesis to its weakest function," that is, copying the real (*Time and Narrative* 2:14). Instead of merely copying the "real," the seven authors under examination attempt to annihilate it by expanding the referential field in order to effect what Ricoeur calls a *mimesis* that is a *poiesis,* a creative construction that grounds the possibility of critique (*Hermeneutics* 180).

As Ricoeur himself admits, "fiction is the road to redescription" (*Rule* 239). The seven novels I have chosen offer their readers what Ricoeur terms a "proposed world." In so doing, they perform two functions. First, these proposed worlds that unfold in front of the text do not simply unveil the hidden power structures of history or reveal the institutional forces that shaped the past, nor do they seek to discover the slow evolutionary processes of history. Rather, these seven novelists seek to rupture the condensation of memory, myth, and worn metaphor that has become our historical "truth." Like Nietzsche, they believe that "truth is an error" (WP ¶ 493); that they write novels suggests that they reject the claims of some historians who rely on "scientific" methods to uncover the structures of everyday life. (The problem here is that, once again, a scientific epistemology undergirds the "histories" of scholars such as the Annalistes and reinforces the illusion of there being a truth.) In opposition to such historical positivism, these novelists practice an antiempirical historiography. They write novels that confirm Nietzsche's "History of an Error," which he entitles "How the 'True World' Finally Became a Fable" in his *Twilight of the Idols.* The seven novels to be examined here abolish the true *and* apparent worlds and thereby suggest the possibility of creating new values for the future. By writing novels, these seven writers verify Mink's observation that no determinate past exists; rather, narrative structures produce events. The novels that these seven authors write critique contemporary notions of the past by making us aware that the past is the "fictive" realm, what White calls the third ground between empirical "truth" and unbridled fantasy. Such a critique of contemporary notions of the past makes us additionally aware that our present is no less "fictive" in White's sense of the word.

The second task that these seven novels set out to accomplish can best be expressed by means of Rorty's theory that the novel enhances human solidarity. Fuentes, Daitch, Rushdie, Tournier, Reed, Swift, and Vargas Llosa create vocabularies that try to forge common hopes. They depict marginalized peoples who suffer immense pain and humiliation in order to attempt not only to elicit a reader's empathetic response but also to spur the reader's recognition of the need to change current conditions and attitudes. These seven novelists engage in a historico-political praxis that questions accepted notions of the real (either past or present) and proposes alternative ways of structuring it.

The speculative novel of poietic history also produces a philosophy of history. As such, it bridges traditions between two distinct modes of literary and philosophical discourse. As I hope to make clear, the seven novels I examine express a deep familiarity with these traditions. The seven authors try to *think* history; that is, they see the novel as a form of speculative thinking that engages the poetic imagination that itself is the source of all "histories." Each of these novels expresses a struggle on the part of the author to come to grips with meaning made through the writing of history. The novelistic mode affords them the opportunity to play out the construction of a particular history that also expresses what history is or can be for those of us who read it, write it, live it. By focusing attention on the second-order referential field, these seven novelists diminish the power of the referential field that traditional history lays claim to, a field no more "real" than the second-order field. In short, these seven writers philosophize about history, and their novels implicitly ask, What—or, more significantly—whose purpose does history serve? How are histories constructed? What does it mean to construct a history? What other histories are possible? How might they be useful?

The seven novelists I examine here would agree with de Certeau when he opines that "history is probably our myth" (*Writing* 21). If, as de Certeau argues, historians "can write only by combining within their practice the 'other' that moves and misleads them and the real that they can represent only through fiction" (*Writing* 14), then I would contend that novelists of poietic history are really superior historians. I take what de Certeau says to be true; namely, that "for the last four centuries, 'the making of history' has referred to writing" (*Writing* 5–6). Here, then, are writers who have "made" history through acts of the imagination.

By writing their novels, Fuentes, Daitch, Rushdie, Tournier, Reed, Swift, and Vargas Llosa hold reality up to a mirror, not the famous mirror on wheels of Stendhal, but Nietzsche's "glittering magic mirror of a *philosophical parodist*" (UM 108). Each of these novelists constructs a fabulous, imaginary landscape that reinscribes what we think we know about a historical period or event, all the while confirming Ricoeur's insight that "the world of fiction leads us to the heart of the real world of action" (*Hermeneutics* 296). These novelists engage in speculations that make possible a critique of the accepted versions of history, a critique that challenges us to refigure our images of the past and configure possible histories for the future. Their novels are "true narrations" in the Vichian sense; and, like Nietzsche, they ask, "Why couldn't the world *that concerns us*—be a fiction?" (BGE 47).

2

Imagining the Past:
Carlos Fuentes's *Terra Nostra*

Memory is the same as imagination.
—Vico, *The New Science*

All historians speak of things which have never existed except in imagination.
—Nietzsche, *Daybreak*

Terra Nostra is a *roman gourmand*, which is to say, it is a novel that seeks to incorporate many of the very best novels as well as several other specialized discourses between its covers. In this novel, Carlos Fuentes appropriates the writings of contemporary novelists such as Cortázar, García Márquez, Borges, Cabrera Infante, Donoso, Carpentier, and Vargas Llosa as well as the Spanish classics *Don Quixote, La celestina,* and *El burlador de Sevilla* and combines them with the historical studies of Américo Castro, the Cabala, and the writings of Giulio Camillo, to mention but a few. To summarize the plot of the novel is undoubtedly an exercise in futility: nevertheless, certain features can be described in a somewhat loose fashion.

The novel opens in Paris, 1999, where the one-armed Pollo Phoibee witnesses the miraculous birth of a child with twelve toes and a crimson cross on his shoulder. Pollo reads a strange message signed by "Ludovico and Celestina" that tells him what he must do with the mysterious child. Later, Pollo encounters Celestina on a Parisian bridge; he slips and falls into the Seine and simultaneously plunges the reader into a vortex of tales as Celestina bids the reader to listen to her story.

As readers, we are transported back to the court of Philip II, El Señor, who is presently building the magnificent monument to death, the Escorial. Through a series of several narrators, including El Señor himself, we learn many things: for example, three identical youths have appeared, each with twelve toes and a crimson cross on his back; as a youth, El Señor ran with a pack of renegades that included Celestina and Ludovico, a group El Señor eventually betrays; one of the three mysterious youths tells El

Señor about his fantastic voyage to the New World (a narration that constitutes nearly one-third of the novel); a workers' rebellion is savagely put down by El Señor's chief huntsman, Guzmán; a manuscript contained in a green bottle that is found near one of the youths describes the Roman court of the emperor Tiberius; El Señor dies and reemerges in the form of a wolf in present-day Spain; and, in the end, characters from famous novels by Latin American authors play a wicked card game based on the political violence and corruption of Latin American regimes while Pollo, safe in his apartment, makes love to Celestina such that they fuse and become a single hermaphrodite on the first morning of the year 2000.

Such a novel is not without its detractors. Distinguished critics such as Eduardo González, Lucille Kerr, and Roberto González Echevarría have complained bitterly about the length, style, structure, and tone of Fuentes's novel. The very length of the book and its complex narrative style is enough to intimidate many readers. Couple this with *Terra Nostra*'s encyclopedic scope of sixteenth-century Europe, and it is easy to see why Fuentes has received some rather pointed criticism.

These critics of *Terra Nostra* share two traits in common. First, they appear to be reluctant, if not unwilling, to grant an author the right to force his or her reader to struggle while reading. Second, these critics champion the ever-popular postmodern clichés of "indeterminacy" and "openness," and they oppose this idea of the novel of free play to what they feel is Fuentes's closed, "modernist" novel.

Unlike some of these critics, I believe that readers of novels understand that what Margaret Sayers Peden says of *Terra Nostra* applies to all novels: namely, a novel "is a work that poses, but does not answer, questions" (42). By its very nature the novel demands that we enter a world constructed by the human imagination. During the act of reading we are confronted with systems of representation and esoteric information that make the world we thought we knew appear strange. The novel does not seek to demonstrate a particular theory; rather, the novel conducts a questioning of the "real" and the means by which we experience and interpret the real in our daily lives. To my mind, *Terra Nostra* engages in just such a questioning of the real and therefore cannot be characterized as a closed work of art.

I concur with commentators such as Jaime Alazraki, Alexis Márquez Rodríguez, Alfred J. MacAdam, and Zunilda Gertel, who suggest that contained within this rich garden of intertextual delights there exists a series of proposals of hypotheses concerning the meaning and construction of history. As Candace K. Holt and Anna J. Gemrich argue, Fuentes is also concerned with defining a Latin American identity that emerges from its history. Fuentes, it seems, is intent on uncovering the philosophical foundations of history as discursive practice as well as articulating the complex relationships between cultural memory and history proper, all of which make it possible to understand the cultural identity of the people living in Latin America.

As Juan Goytisolo pointed out long ago, because *Terra Nostra* consists of multiple narrative voices that distort and contradict one another, this necessarily means that the reader "will participate in the process of construction of the novel by way of multiple contradictory readings." "The narrative space of *Terra Nostra*," he writes, "is a free space, open to dialogue and the intervention of the reader" (22). *Terra Nostra,* therefore, appears to be closed only for those not willing to be open to multiple readings that may in some cases require detailed and painstaking secondary reading.

In addition to Goytisolo, Carl Gutiérrez vigorously defends Fuentes's narrative technique. Gutiérrez points out that González Echevarría chooses to ignore the role that doubt plays in the novel. He does not seem to recognize that to accuse Fuentes of attempting to exert power over the reader implies that the novel posits a belief in an origin of some sort; and this, as Gutiérrez quite rightly argues, is what *Terra Nostra* works against. There is no originary narrative or voice in *Terra Nostra;* only manuscripts and partial interpretations exist. Gutiérrez also reminds readers such as Kerr that to expect an ending that explains it all for you is precisely what Fuentes is attempting to subvert. In this regard, Fuentes is questioning a type of "traditional history" that seeks a "ground that would maintain existing forms of power" (258).

I agree with Goytisolo and Gutiérrez. *Terra Nostra* is a pluridimensional text; its shifting points of view, myriad narrators, different geographical settings, and numerous temporal contexts make the novel a source of endless interpretive play. The idea of interpretive choice, however, remains an element of what I perceive to be the most significant philosophical aspect of the novel: Fuentes's meditation on history. Contained within the pages of *Terra Nostra* is a philosophy of history that grows out of a combination of Nietzschean and Vichian philosophy; and it is through a combinatory method of sorts that Fuentes constructs his novel to recast history in a different mold. Those critics who charge that Fuentes seeks out origins fail to see the similarities between his project and Nietzsche's genealogical project. As Alan D. Schrift correctly indicates in his book on Nietzsche, "the aim of the genealogical search for origins is not the discernment of truth but the deciphering of value" (*Nietzsche and the Question* 173). Fuentes seeks out the values that inform Hispanic culture, values that have had a tremendous impact on Latin American culture. By using elements of Nietzschean genealogy and Vichian threefold memory, Fuentes constructs a relativized history that offers new insights into the past and possibilities for the future.

Terra Nostra, therefore, constitutes a long meditation on the relation between imagination and the construction of historical truth. The novel presents itself as a garden of forking paths, but it does not fully circumscribe itself within the realm of the fantastic. Unlike Jorge Luis Borges, Fuentes engages historiography to bring about a change in the realm of politics as it is shaped by so-called historical truths. With all due respect to the Argentine master, one could say that Borges theorizes the relationship between imagination and historical truth, whereas Fuentes carries out a praxis. Michel Foucault, for example, claims that it was Borges who, in large part, was responsible for the creation of *The Order of Things*. Foucault's work, however, differs markedly from Borges's fiction. Foucault is engaged in a praxis; Borges theorizes different possibilities. The same is true of the relation between Borges and Fuentes. We should not forget that Borges, in his story "The Immortal," also has something to say about Vico (*Labyrinths* 105–18), but Fuentes adopts Vichian practices to affect the reception of ideas about Hispanic cultural history and suggest new political possibilities for the future.

Through his novel, Fuentes demonstrates his mastery of the materials—historiographic, literary, mythic, theological—and he writes various speculations on the narrative possibilities in the past. The speculative narratives Fuentes offers perform a double signification. First, they underscore the notion that all truths, including historical truths, are made—they are interpretations of events. Second, by engaging in imaginative configurations of past events, Fuentes emphasizes the creative power of the imagination in the conceptualization of the real world. To reconfigure the past repudiates the notion of a closed interpretive field that yields only one truth of what really took place, and it also shatters the feeling of inevitability in the context of contemporary political life and future expectations. It is this projection toward the future that marks the significance of *Terra Nostra* as a form of praxis. One can imagine the possibilities in the future as well as the past, and these possibilities are rooted in the imagination; they are never given. The question remains, then, How does Fuentes perform this feat in the pages of his novel?

I believe that Fuentes adopts the philosophical approaches of Nietzsche and Vico to write the speculative poietic history he entitles *Terra Nostra*. Fuentes incorporates Nietzschean perspectival philosophy in *Terra Nostra* to allow other voices from the past to speak in opposition to the universal narrative we have come to accept as history. In contrast to El Señor's monumental history, the chorus of voices within the novel offers, in part, a Nietzschean critical history. Fuentes's approach centers itself around the idea of Nietzschean tragedy—the idea that the tragic enacts a play of values that achieves no final, definitive resolution of closure. The preserved tension between the values expressed in the Nietzschean characterization of the tragic mode suspends resolution and thereby opens up a space for the inquiry performed by Fuentes's novel. In addition, Fuentes relies on a Vichian method in order to narrate his history. The Vichian approach provides Fuentes with not only a narrative structure but also a creative method: he employs Vico's threefold memory as a narrating principle that permits him to reconfigure the text of remembered history so as to refigure that past in the mind of his readers. By combining these two philosophical approaches in his novel, Fuentes constructs a poietic history, one that affirms the essential role played by the imagination in the construction of the historical past and our real worlds.

Nietzsche According to Fuentes

The significance of Nietzschean thought for Fuentes is no secret. Fuentes considers Nietzsche to be one of the most important influences in his life. In a 1967 interview with José-Miguel Ullán, Fuentes confessed that he suffered from "una adhesión intelectual esquizoide" (a schizoid intellectual adherence) to both Nietzsche and Marx. He went on to explain:

> En la lucha perpetua entre "episteme" y "doxa" Nietzsche ofreció el método de autocontradiccción para impedir el sistema del dogma: variar sin fin las perspectivas, criticar sin fin las certidumbres adquiridas, iluminar desde todos los puntos de vista: una filosofia escultórica de múltiples llaves, de multiplicadas hipótesis, que requiere de la contradicción para no petrificarse en el sistem. (12)

In the perpetual struggle between "episteme" and "doxa" Nietzsche offers the method of self-contradiction so as to hinder the system of dogma: to vary the perspectives endlessly, to critique acquired certainties endlessly, to illuminate from all points of view: a sculptural philosophy of multiple keys, of multiplying hypotheses, that requires contradiction so as not to become petrified in a system.

For Fuentes, Nietzsche offers a method by which we can combat dogma of any stripe. The perspectival philosophy that Nietzsche formulated, a philosophy of numerous hypotheses, multiple keys, and several points of view, defeats the system-building obsession that grows out of dogmatism, received ideas, and given truths and certainties. Readers of *Terra Nostra* should recognize that through his creation of multiple narrations, Fuentes employs a Nietzschean perspectival method that undermines the dogmatic beliefs of El Señor—beliefs that characterize Spain after 1492. A more detailed examination of the novel will show just how great a role Nietzsche plays in Fuentes's novel.

The most obvious Nietzschean component in *Terra Nostra* appears in the very activity of El Señor himself. By constructing the Escorial, Felipe practices an extravagant form of monumental history. The Escorial is as Fuentes has described it: "the central symbol of Spain" that "represent[s] honor and mortification" (MacShane 3). "Let the dead bury the living," the motto Nietzsche ascribes to monumental historians gone awry, becomes El Señor's unspoken credo (UM 72). Felipe is an exhausted leader, he shuns his wife Isabel, and he does not want to produce an heir. In the Nietzschean sense, he is diametrically opposed to any activity that furthers life. In this regard, the long procession of corpses that winds its way across the Spanish countryside epitomizes the image of the "masquerade" that Nietzsche uses to describe how monumental historians disguise their hatred of the present by focusing all their admiration on the past (UM 92). Executing a type of danse macabre reminiscent of the final tableau in Bergman's *Seventh Seal,* the Mad Lady Joanna leads the train of caskets containing the decomposed bodies of past monarchs and her own severed limbs. These physical fragments of the past, including Joanna herself, will be encased in the Escorial's monument to the ages, while Felipe longs for "a perpetual Mass for the Dead that will last until the end of time" (*Terra Nostra* 94).

Felipe's attempt at constructing a monumental history represents a particular pathology, but it is one that persists. When Felipe ascends the stairs and emerges in contemporary Spain, he finds himself near another product of monumental history: The Valley of the Fallen—a monument to Franco's Fascist soldiers. By placing El Señor in this specific setting, Fuentes confirms that he concurs with Nietzsche: monumental history is seductive, it can inspire fanaticism, and, in such cases, it does not promote life.

Fuentes's association with Nietzschean philosophy, however, does not end with his rejection of monumental history. Fuentes, like Nietzsche, believes that the modern age lacks a tragic dimension. "It is one of the great achievements of the human spirit to be able to understand life and recreate it in the tragic manner," said Fuentes in a 1988 interview. "But," he added, "perhaps we can't do that anymore" (Castillo 159). Whereas for Nietzsche, Socrates was the culprit who banished tragedy from the Greek stage, for Fuentes, it is history that effects this transition. In an interview published in *Diacritics* in 1980, Fuentes stated: "History's absolutism depends for its existence on one thing: the elimination of Tragedy." In the same interview, Fuentes discussed the relationship between history and tragedy, and he emphasized how history appeals to an empiricism based on the notion of causality. Fuentes is quite clear about his debt to Nietzsche in this matter: "I think it is a causal and Socratic thought, as Nietzsche sees it, that wants to establish a very clear relation between cause and effect, a relation absent in Tragedy." History's reliance on causality, argues Fuentes, obscures the "world of values" that exists "outside the purely causal and empirical and ethical world" (Tittler 51–52). In other words, Fuentes, like Nietzsche, pursues an axiological as opposed to an epistemological approach. For Fuentes, tragedy, and tragedy alone, circumscribes a world of conflicting values. The world of value conflict is one history shuns because in such a world "there are no guilty parties" (51). In other words, value-centered discourse such as tragedy does not recognize any absolute right and wrong. (Indeed, of what is Oedipus guilty? Do we blame Antigone? or even Creon?) History, on the other hand, seeks out its heroes and villains and inevitably champions one perspective over another. Tragedy, however, remains ambivalent. Fuentes sees in tragedy the same play of values that serves as the cornerstone of Nietzsche's perspectival philosophy.

Fuentes's phrase "guilty parties" serves as a shorthand expression for Nietzsche's famous genealogical investigations into the origin of good and evil. In *On the Genealogy of Morals,* Nietzsche argues that the categories good and evil replaced the categories good and bad when a weak, moralistic, and priestly class, fueled with resentment, overturned an aristocratic, noble class. As a result, the moralistic and now dominant groups can impose absolute moral categories on all activities; or, as Fuentes terms it, guilty parties can be blamed for any problem. Fuentes elucidates Nietzschean philosophy by explicitly discussing the relationship between *res-sentiment* and history. History, Fuentes implies, is the discursive practice of a culture of *ressentiment*, and it is such a culture that produces the In-quisition, the expulsion of the Moors from Spain, or the Shoah. Each of these activities grew out of particular types of historical explanations that assigned guilt to a specific group. The practice continues to this day, as many revisionist and reactionary historians seek out individuals, nations, or entire cultures to blame for horrific atrocities.

In a 1980 interview at UCLA, Fuentes explained in simple and direct terms what is at stake when cultures choose to base political decisions on historical paradigms fueled by *ressentiment*. Fuentes criticized U.S. foreign policy, saying: "The U.S. must stop thinking of its foreign policy in terms of friends and enemies. No such things exist. There are different nation-al interests, and these national interests must be perceived mutually, as valid, as honorable" (Oviedo et al. 9). The political element of Fuentes's Nietzschean perspective is quite clear: nations can choose to adhere to a worldview of strict dichotomies founded on universal right and wrong (a dichotomy that masks the interests of the parties that construct those moral categories), or nations can recognize global politics as a play of values wherein each participant has a legitimate claim to assert its values. The key here, for Fuentes, is how particular nations use and abuse histo-ry in order to maintain a bipolar vision of world politics. In this regard, history, in the case of the United States, for example, becomes a paradigm that is superimposed on succeeding situations in order to justify foreign policy decisions. When nations use history in this manner, they often seek out "guilty parties" that resemble other guilty parties in the past—the Jews, the Communists, Hitler, and so on.

In contradistinction to a history of guilty parties, Fuentes wants to erase the boundary between history and literature. The Mexican author states unequivocally: "I would like to see History relativized as much as litera-ture" (Tittler 51). Relativizing history would mean that there would be no truth, no single perspective from which to describe and assess human activity. Histories, such as Fuentes would like them to be, would, in cer-tain instances, become tragedies—or, in Nietzschean terms, the expres-sion of the play of values.

In order to regain a tragic vision, Fuentes indicates that it is necessary to redefine tragedy for the modern age. In an address before the Interna-tional Association of Poets, Playwrights, Editors, Essayists, and Novelists (P.E.N.) delivered at the time he was completing *Terra Nostra*, Fuentes opined that modern tragedy consisted of "the tragedy of a freedom that can err" ("Central and Eccentric" 90). One can easily see how *Terra Nostra* records the errors of the Spanish monarchy, errors that resulted in sterilizing a once-vibrant and multicultural society. In *Don Quixote; or, The Critique of Reading*, a scholarly study Fuentes published at the same time as *Terra Nostra*, which, as Lanin A. Gyurko demonstrates, is indispensable for understanding the novel (16–35), Fuentes asserts that the expulsion of the Moors and Jews from Spain dealt a catastrophic blow to the vitality of Spanish life. "The combined expulsion of Jews and Moslems," he writes, "meant that Spain, in effect, deprived itself of the talents and services it would later sorely need to maintain its imperial status" (*Don Quixote* 25). Human errors—the expulsion of the Moors and Jews in 1492 and the defeat of the *comuneros* in 1521—constituted the tragedy of Spanish history, a chronicle of self-mutilation. Fuentes, therefore, chooses these specific events, plus the death of Philip II in 1598 (which signals the apotheosis of the construction of the necropolis of the Escorial), as the settings for writing a Nietzschean version of Spanish history, a version that expresses the conflict of values.

The Nietzschean vision of tragedy is based on the well-known opposition of Apollo and Dionysus. Apollo is the god of sculpture and dreams. "Apollo," writes Nietzsche, is the "image of the *principium individuationis*," through which the "wisdom of 'illusion'" speaks to us (BT 36). The Dionysian, on the other hand, "is no longer an artist, he has become a work of art" (BT 37).

Consider the opening lines of *Terra Nostra*. "Incredible the first animal that dreamed of another animal" (9). Dream plays a pivotal role in *Terra Nostra*. (As a young boy, Felipe interprets the dreams of Pedro, Celestina, Simon, and Ludovico; the novel implies that the youth may have dreamed his entire voyage to the New World; Ludovico transports the bodies of the three youths throughout Europe while they remain inert in small coffins, each dreaming the lives of the other two; etc.) The novel suggests, moreover, that an opposition exists between dream and history. When Ludovico awakens the youths from their infinite cycle of dreaming, he states: "I am returning to them the freedom the dream took from them, I am returning them to history" (585). Yet Fuentes is not content to let the opposition stand, nor is he satisfied with proclaiming history superior to dream. On the contrary, Fuentes believes that history and dream inform each other; it is nearly impossible to disentangle one from the other and folly to try.

The relation between history and dream, as *Terra Nostra* shows, is exceedingly complex. To read the reports of the conquistadores and the first travelers to the New World, for example, is to read the record of wish fulfillment. The fantastic landscape, as both Eduardo O'Gorman and Antonello Gerbi have shown, satisfied the dreams of the first Europeans who came to the Americas. Similarly, the Aztecs took Cortés to be Quetzalcoatl, the Plumed Serpent, who was prophesied to return at that time. Dreams imagined and dreams fulfilled, suggests Fuentes, are the stuff history is made on; and this perceived relation between history and dream underscores the relationship between Fuentes and Nietzschean philosophy.

For Nietzsche, Apollo speaks to us through the veil of illusion or "symbolical dream image" (BT 38). The Apollonian is the image-making function, a form of artifice that expresses the striving of the individual. "Apollo," writes Nietzsche, "wants to grant repose to individual beings precisely by drawing boundaries between them" (BT 72). Fuentes expresses the Apollonian dimension through the various dreams and projects of the characters in the novel. Felipe's dream of the Escorial, Guzmán's visions of riches in the New World, the workers' dream of revolution, and even Pedro's dream of the commune represent instances of the singular, bounded field of vision that becomes, in some cases, a reality. In fact, Fuentes subverts the initial dichotomy of dream versus history by insisting that history, as we have come to know it, is, in many respects, the dream of those in power. It is the vision of the Escorial, just as it is the dream of the New World, that leads to the constructions of those separate, yet related, realities. In opposition to *this* conception of Apollonian dream *as* history, Fuentes posits the Dionysian narration *of* history. Just as in "song and dance man expresses himself as a member of a higher community" (BT 17) and thus becomes a work of art, the imbricated narrations that make up *Terra Nostra*—the polyphony of voices that confirm the novel's credo that many lives are needed to fulfill one personality—make of *history* a work of art, an activity that Nietzsche declared to be "the highest task and the truly metaphysical activity of this life" (BT 31–32). As Fuentes writes in his study *Don Quixote; or, The Critique of Reading:* "Art gives life to what history killed. Art gives voice to what history denied, silenced or persecuted. Art brings truth to the lies of history" (44). Fuentes, in other words, sees in multiple narrations a type of Dionysiac ecstasy, what Nietzsche describes as "the shattering of the individual and his fusion with primal being" (BT 65). The hermaphroditic union of Pollo and Celestina at the end of the novel clearly symbolizes the primal fusion that Nietzsche speaks of. Pollo's very name highlights the tragic moment of fusion, and the construction of *Terra Nostra* itself plays out the Nietzschean view of tragedy.

According to Nietzsche, "the *tragic myth* is to be understood only as a symbolization of Dionysian wisdom through Apollinian [*sic*] artifices" (BT 131). There exists in tragedy a tension between these two modes. In *Terra Nostra*, the same tension exists insofar as the spell of the individuated dream *historias* of Felipe, Guzmán, Ludovico, and others (many of which are based on historical documents) is broken by the sea of stories, the primal being of narration. As one of the youths tells Ludovico, "it is the narration, not the dream, that is infinite" (567). Thus, Fuentes's novel suggests that what we ordinarily view as history consists of the individuated dream constructions emanating from a particular point of view and, as such, offers a distorted representation of the past. On the other hand, tragedy, specifically Nietzschean tragedy, as Fuentes sees it, expresses the tension between individuated constructions of history and the infinite variations of narration that can articulate possible histories, other histories as well as histories of the Other.

The idea that multiple narrations of history grow out of Fuentes's own understanding of Nietzschean philosophy appears in *Terra Nostra* itself. In one of the most stunning intertextual inversions of the novel, Fuentes has El Señor reverse a famous passage from Nietzsche's *Gay Science* entitled "The Greatest Weight," in which Nietzsche describes a demon that approaches you and says that you will be forced to live "innumerable times more" your "life as you now live it" (273). In *Terra Nostra*, Fuentes has El Señor speak to Guzmán and say:

> Does a Devil never approach you and say, that wasn't how it was, it was not only that way, it could have happened that way but also in a thousand different ways, depending upon who is telling it, depending on who saw it and how he chanced to see it; imagine for an instant, Guzmán, what would happen if everyone offered their multiple and contradictory versions of what had happened, and even what had not happened; everyone, I tell you, Lords as well as serfs, the sane and the mad, the devout and the heretical, then what would happen Guzmán? (188)

What would happen would be the construction of *Terra Nostra:* our world.

The famous demon in *The Gay Science* represents the first articulation of Nietzsche's concept of the eternal return, an idea that, as Joan Stambaugh's study *Nietzsche's Thought of Eternal Return* details, has fueled a storm of controversy in Nietzsche studies for many years. To my mind, Gilles Deleuze has focused on the most significant element in the notion of eternal return when he writes: "As an ethical thought the eternal return is the new formulation of the practical synthesis: whatever you will, will it in such a way that you also will its eternal return" (68). Alan D. Schrift is even more explicit: "The doctrine thus asks: 'Are you living your life in such a way that you would will to live everything again the same way for all eternity?' It is in this sense that the eternal recurrence stands as the 'highest formula of affirmation' [the quotation comes from *Ecce Homo*], for to say 'Yes' to the eternal recurrence is to say 'Yes' to the entirety of one's existence" (*Nietzsche and the Question* 71). Both Deleuze and Schrift stress the ethical dimension of Nietzsche's thought. Nietzsche's demon inspires terror because it demands that you weigh an impending choice in such a manner that you imagine that you will be forced to repeat the act again and again, ad infinitum. "If this thought gains possession of you, it would change you as you are or perhaps crush you," writes Nietzsche, and he leaves it at that (GS 274). The power of the idea of eternal recurrence, its paralytic effect, is enhanced precisely because Nietzsche does not explain his ideas any further. Fuentes, however, takes us one step further—to the day after, so to speak.

The demon that Felipe describes is one that talks about action ex post facto. In other words, after you have taken a course of action and convinced yourself that you were justified in doing so, Felipe's demon inspires the same terror because he questions the veracity of the account you have *narrated* to yourself. Felipe's demon, therefore, is the demon of history; it sows the seeds of doubt and challenges the official explanations of any event, what many of us today would call the historical truth. We believe that such official explanations should be neither subjective nor opinionated; and, above all, they cannot be contradictory. But Fuentes, like Nietzsche before him, rejects the unitary vision of official history. As he wrote in his book on José Luis Cuevas, "understanding is everywhere and may never be conquered by one single vision" (*El mundo* 43).

Thus, both demons stress alternative possibilities—Nietzsche's before the act, Felipe's afterward. Fuentes, however, has thought through Nietzsche's eternal recurrence in a unique manner. In the novel, Valerio Camillo expresses this unique view when he says to Ludovico: "History repeats itself only because we are unaware of the alternate possibility for each historic event" (561). The notion of eternal recurrence becomes an inevitability *because* no one listened to the Nietzschean demon prior to taking action. Consequently, we are terrified by the demon Fuentes describes—a demon who underscores the ethical dimension of narrated history just as Nietzsche's demon emphasizes the ethical dimension of personal action. In both instances, the ethical component of life founds itself on choice, whether it be choosing to commit a certain act or choosing a specific narrative strategy to describe events that occurred in the past. Fuentes suggests that by having remained deaf to the demon who demands that we must consider all possibilities before acting, we are haunted by the voices of what could have been or what happened that we want to deny. Through Felipe's demon, Fuentes applies the Nietzschean ethic to the concept of narration; and in doing so, he confirms the central role narration plays in the construction of history. Like Nietzsche, Fuentes believes that any history, if it is worthy of the name, should further life; for Fuentes, this means all questions of history must ultimately come down to questions of narration.

In order to discuss the relationship Fuentes perceives between narration and history, we must turn to Fuentes's use and understanding of Vico. The narration of history Fuentes presents in *Terra Nostra* is one that opposes El Señor's "hierarchical and unified perspective," which leads to "a single reading of reality" (620). Fuentes's method of narration is Vichian; it acknowledges the interchangeable nature of that which is true and that which is made. To understand what role Vichian philosophy plays in *Terra Nostra*, we must first examine what Fuentes has said about Vico and then return to the novel itself.

Vico According to Fuentes

In a 1981 interview published in the *Paris Review*, Fuentes contended: "Our idea of time as a spiral, our basic historical vision, is derived both from Vico and from our everyday experience of times that coexist" (152). In a 1988 interview with Debra Castillo, he stated that "Vico told us that the first thing that the tribe creates is its language, and the first thing it creates with its language is its myths" (156). Undoubtedly, Fuentes sees in Vico a philosopher who understands the linguistic foundation of culture as well as the concept of human time.

In his 1990 book *Valiente mundo nuevo*, Fuentes discusses in greater detail what Vico means to him and what he should mean for Latin American thinkers in general. For Fuentes, Latin America would have been far better off had it embraced the teachings of Vico rather than Voltaire. The universalism of the Enlightenment was Eurocentric, and Fuentes contends that Vico recognized this and condemned it (*Valiente* 33). According to Fuentes, Vico's philosophy, which acknowledges the autonomy of individual cultures and the various stages cultures go through, is much more compatible with the Latin American world, "un mundo polycultural y multirracial en desarrollo" (a polycultural and multiracial world in development), than a philosophy based on universal reason (*Valiente* 35). Finally, it is Vico's emphasis on concrete variety and not abstract uniformity that makes him so important for the heterogeneous, polyglot culture of Latin America (*Valiente* 31).

Vico also appears quite openly in Fuentes's 1989 novel *Christopher Unborn*. We read, for example, the narrator imploring us, saying: "*please, Reader, course and recourse with me!*" (461). In a manner of speaking, the entire novel can be read as a *corso* in gestation. As the narrator relates: "I've known it for centuries, it's always the same and always new, the serpent of spiral sperm, the commodius vicus of history, narrow gate of vicogenesis" (132). Nods to *Finnegans Wake* aside, the important point to be gleaned here is that Vico is one of the central thinkers—if not the central thinker—for Fuentes. Vico offers a philosophy that acknowledges the linguistic base of all social institutions, grants an equal status to all cultures, serves as a rich source of literary creation (as in the case of Joyce), and returns us to the concrete particulars of human experience rather than abstract concepts of human history and time. Although Fuentes invokes Vico on many occasions and in different discourses, I believe that the Vichian influence on Fuentes's writing does not appear more productively and imaginatively than in the pages of *Terra Nostra*.

For readers of *Terra Nostra*, the most obvious indication that Vico plays a role in the novel appears in the very name of one of the principal characters: Ludovico. A first-year Latin student knows that *Ludo* in Latin means "I play" (from the verb *ludere:* to play). Thus, Fuentes clearly tells his readers, *Ludovico:* "I am playing Vico."

The tripartite structure of *Terra Nostra* also establishes another parallel between Fuentes and Vico. According to Vico, every nation develops through the successive ages of gods, heroes, and men (NS ¶ 813). This three-part development in turn generates eleven triadic unities among which are three kinds of customs, three kinds of governments, and three kinds of languages (NS ¶ 915ff). *Terra Nostra* also contains a series of triadic figures. First and foremost, there are the three youths who appear in different guises in three different ages. Three artists occupy El Señor's court—Toribio, Julián, and the Chronicler. There are also the thirty-three steps in El Señor's mausoleum, *three* steps more than El Señor requested be built. When El Señor ascends these steps and looks at his reflection in a mirror, he embarks on a Vichian *corso* of dissolution because he sees the reflection of his face grow old and decompose. After death, El Señor ascends these same steps and experiences a type of Vichian *recorso* as he emerges in the future in the form of a wolf, an animal associated with the mythic origins of his own family line. Finally, there is the one-eyed magus of Spalato who tells Ludovico of the three ages of man, three ages that roughly correspond to Vico's ages of gods, heroes, and men (547).

In the closing pages of *Terra Nostra*, Brother Julián, El Señor's palace iconographer, relates to the Chronicler one of the key ideas of the novel as a whole. "True history," he states, "is circular and eternal" (652). Julián's words express the central concept in paragraph 245 of *The New Science*, where Vico contends that there exists an "ideal eternal history traversed in time by every nation in its rise, development, maturity, decline, and fall." Some four paragraphs earlier, he states: "Men first feel necessity, then look for utility, next attend to comfort, still later amuse themselves with pleasure, thence grow dissolute in luxury, and finally go mad and waste their substance" (NS ¶ 241). These two quotations contain in brief the essence of Vico's celebrated notion of *corsi e ricorsi*, the cyclical theory of historical development. Vico's words accurately describe the multiple trajectories of various cultures depicted in *Terra Nostra*, where we read of the Spanish monarchy, which ends in dissolution and madness; the decline and fall of the Aztec civilization; Rome under the rule of Tiberius; and contemporary Western culture as envisaged in 1999.

Lois Parkinson Zamora, in her excellent book *Writing the Apocalypse*, focuses attention on the Vichian dimensions of *Terra Nostra*. She correctly observes that Fuentes concurs with "Vico's belief that the most imaginative texts are also the most real, and that history is to be heard in the voices of the poets" (152–53). It would be foolish for me to attempt to improve on Zamora's superb summary of Fuentes's "Vichian aesthetic" (as she terms it). Her work on and understanding of *Terra Nostra* is of the first order. With respect to Vico, however, Zamora's interpretation is flawed. She attributes to Vico a vision of history as a spiral of cycles. "There *is* a progressive movement inherent in Vico's spiraling history," she writes (162). Nowhere in *The New Science* does Vico speak of spirals, and the notion of progress is antithetical to Vico's explicit description of ideal eternal history in paragraph 245.

Zamora, however, does not seem to be aware of Vico's own quite lucid explanation of what he means by ideal eternal history. She adheres to a belief in spirals, as far as I can tell, for three reasons. First, as we have seen, Fuentes himself refers to spirals in Vico's thought ("Art of Fiction" 152). As we *shall* see, however, Fuentes's novel belies a notion of a spiraling history of progress. Perhaps Fuentes has intentionally mixed the idea of gyres in Yeats's poetic cosmology (which does involve spirals) with Vico's cycles. After all, one of *Terra Nostra*'s epigraphs consists of two lines from "Easter, 1916." Whatever the case may be, we must look to *Terra Nostra* itself to see what Vichian visions lie there. The next two reasons why Zamora believes in spirals are explicitly expressed in footnotes to A. Robert Caponigri's *Time and Idea: The Theory of History in Giambattista Vico* and Isaiah Berlin's *Vico and Herder: Two Studies in the History of Ideas*. Zamora rests her claim on these two rather dated interpretations of Vico's thought.

With respect to Caponigri, it is important to recognize that his book has been criticized by Vico scholars. In a 1957 review, Max H. Fisch, the English-language translator of Vico, wrote that Caponigri's "main thesis is mistaken" (648). Fisch correctly points out that ideal eternal history "is not the end toward which the temporal process moves but the uniform law of which the entire course of each nation's history is one instance" (649). In other words, there is no telos in Vichian history, no transcendental absolute toward which humankind is striving; there is plainly and simply what Vico says there is in paragraph 245: a cycle of rise, development, maturity, decline, and fall. With respect to Isaiah Berlin, a few years after he wrote his book on Vico and Herder, he conceded that a different interpretation of Vico's ideal eternal history was valid. It is to this theory that I must now turn.

In an essay entitled "Vico's Philosophy of Imagination," Donald Verene argues that there are two types of imagination or *fantasia* at play in *The New Science*. The first *fantasia*, described in the section on poetic wisdom, refers to the construction of imaginative universals—the Jove experience, wherein the first people attributed the name Jove to thunder and thereby created a universal (i.e., all thunder was Jove). The second form of *fantasia*, argues Verene, "functions as the medium through which the *New Science* itself gains recollective understanding of the human world" (27). Verene claims that the second *fantasia* consists of ideal eternal history itself, which is an imagining of time as a whole such that "time is seen as a drama in which there is an identity between origin and end" (28). Thus, the "ideal eternal history is the recollective imaginative universal through which any nation and consequently the human world can be grasped as a whole" (29). In other words, through recollection, humans apprehend themselves *in time*. Verene's notion of what he terms recollective *fantasia* was acknowledged by Isaiah Berlin to be a convincing interpretation of Vico because it explains how Vico, living after the age of poetic wisdom, came to understand and express the metaphoric operations enacted by the first humans ("Comment"). Ideal eternal history is Vico's metaphor, an analog to the Jove experience that gives him a method by which he can craft an image that expresses the relation of humans to temporal experience conceived of as a whole. Thus, it is by means of recollective *fantasia* that Vico creates *The New Science*.

As Verene points out in *Vico's Science of Imagination*, "the genius of Vico's recollective imaginative universal of ideal eternal history is its perception of the reality of ends. History is not tragic simply because it contains nothing but rise and fall. It is tragic because the movement of origins to ends opens the possibility of heroism within a cycle" (112). The key element here is the notion of tragedy, a notion that links Vico to Nietzsche and both thinkers to Fuentes. All three see tragedy as the essence of genuine human existence. Attempts to construct a reality by means of new metaphors in opposition to the given, the accepted, and the received metaphors that make up reality constitute the heroic act par excellence for humans; it remains the only means by which, in the words of Vico, we make our truths; or, in the words of Nietzsche, by which we lose our masters and find ourselves.

I have belabored this point on Vichian philosophy for two reasons. First, I want to clarify that despite what Fuentes claims about Vico and spirals, there are no spirals in Vico's philosophy, nor does it contain an idea of progress. Indeed (*pace* Zamora), there is no progress in *Terra Nostra* either. In the novel we witness the dissolution of the Roman empire under Tiberius, the beginning of the end of the Spanish monarchy, the destruction of the Aztec empire, even an imagined apocalypse at the next millennium. As opposed to progress, the novel records the possibilities of heroism within a cycle, to borrow Verene's phrase. Be it Felipe as a youth with Celestina, Ludovico, Simon, and Pedro; or Quetzalcoatl and the Aztecs; or Guzmán and the *comuneros;* or the unnamed guerrilla in the Mexico of the future—each of these imagined scenarios provides heroic possibilities that end in tragic failure. As Juan Goytisolo has discerned, *Terra Nostra* contains "two diametrically opposed ideas": "the necessity and the failure of revolution" (10). Thus, Vico's tragic theory of history represents the logical complement to the Nietzschean component that we also perceived in the novel; it also grounds Fuentes's belief in a continually renewed opposition to the established metaphoric structures that preserve particular networks of power.

The second reason for my long digression on what some might think is a rather esoteric point in Vichian philosophy is that I want to reiterate the supreme importance of the recollective or memory-driven process in Vico's thought. Vico's threefold memory remains the cornerstone of his philosophy, and I believe that his recollective *fantasia,* his emphasis on fable, and his concern with metaphor establish strong associative links with the writings of Paul Ricoeur.

Vico and Ricoeur

In "Discovery of the True Homer," the richest and most curious book of *The New Science,* Vico discusses memory. He states: "Memory thus has three different aspects: memory when it remembers things, imagination when it alters or imitates them, and invention when it gives them a new turn or puts them into proper arrangement and relationship" (NS ¶ 819). For Vico, memory is comprised of three parts: *memoria, fantasia,* and *ingegno. Memoria* simply consists of remembering that which occurred in the past. *Fantasia,* however, requires the active construction of images in pursuit of a mimetic or an expressive mode of re-presenting to the mind what took place in the past. And *ingegno* involves the placement of the constructed image in the context of a constellation of already constructed images. Thus, memory is a creative act, *the* creative act; for inasmuch as we are human, we come to know what we are by remembering what we were.

The Vichian concept of memory plays a major role in Fuentes's novel. Memory is a recurrent theme: El Señor recounts his memories of victory to his dog Bocanegra, the youth becomes the Lord of Memory in the New World, and Ludovico visits Valerio Camillo's Theater of Memory. Each of these narratives is constructed by a human imagination; none of the narrators can reproduce events as they actually were in the past. For Fuentes, both in his novel and in the minds of his readers, the Vichian threefold memory is constantly at work. As each narrative is told it must be assimilated, both by the characters in the novel and the readers of the novel, into the context of other narratives that have already been told. As readers, we must recall a particular youth who is washed ashore the Cabo de los Desastres, and we are constantly refiguring in our own minds which youth this may be as he, or perhaps one of the other two, appears in different guises throughout the novel. We must recall which youth this might be in a given moment, just as we must remember what the narrative means when, late in the novel, it refers to Ludovico standing in the shadows of the Cathedral (580) and thereby alludes to a scene that took place some five hundred pages earlier. In order to remember as readers, we must constantly reimagine past scenes and reconfigure them in the context of a narrative or series of simultaneous narratives that will alter the original impression we received.

As a novelist, Carlos Fuentes instantiates the Vichian threefold memory through the construction of *Terra Nostra* itself. *Terra Nostra* is the memory of the history—both real and imagined—of our world. Drawing on the various fictions and histories that he has read, Fuentes "alters" and "imitates" those narratives he remembers and "gives them a new turn" and "puts them into proper [his own] arrangement and relationship" (*NS* ¶ 819). In doing so, Fuentes draws on a fundamental concept that Vico first articulated in his early work *On the Most Ancient Wisdom of the Italians:* the true is the made. Vico writes: "For the Latins, *verum* (the true) and *factum* (what is made) are interchangeable, or to use the customary language of the Schools, they are convertible [*verum et factum convertuntur*]" (45). Vico's notion here is quite simple: humans can only know what humans make. We make our own truth; and for Vico the most fundamental act of making is the metaphor. For example, in *The New Science*, Vico describes the "first barbarians" making the first metaphor by identifying Jove with thunder (NS ¶ 377). From this act of metaphoric structuration springs the possibility of formulating imaginative universals, which in turn makes possible the creation of cultural institutions. In a certain sense, all of history rests on metaphor. Every metaphor, claims Vico, "is a fable in brief" (NS ¶ 404); and for Vico this means "the first fables . . . must therefore have been the histories of the first peoples" (NS ¶ 198).

Metaphor, the central element in Vico's philosophy, also serves as the cornerstone to the philosophy of Ricoeur. The most intriguing point of comparison to be made between Vico and Ricoeur, however, is the relation between Vico's threefold memory and Ricoeur's threefold mimesis. Such a comparison will serve as the means by which to discuss how Fuentes inscribes Vichian philosophy into his narrative.

For Vico, *memoria* quite simply refers to the act of remembering that which occurred in the past. For Ricoeur, mimesis$_1$ consists of "a preunderstanding of the world of action" as expressed through structural, symbolic, and temporal features (*Time and Narrative* 1:54). He believes that one must have "competence" in mastering these three conceptual networks in order to gain any type of understanding (55). Ricoeur is quite explicit on this point: in order to "understand a narrative," one must "master the rules that govern its syntagmatic order" (56). With respect to the symbolic network, he notes that "human action can be narrated . . . because it is always already articulated by signs, rules, and norms" (57). And, finally, there exists for us all a preunderstanding of "temporal features that remain implicit in symbolic mediations of action" (60). By combining Vico with Ricoeur at this first level, one can see that without an understanding of the structural, symbolic, and temporal networks, there would be no memory of any given event—such an experience would lie beyond the boundaries of language and therefore remain incommunicable.

In the context of an examination of *Terra Nostra*, there are three aspects to the *prefigurative* level of the narrative. First, there are the simple memories of the narrators themselves. In a chapter entitled "Victory," El Señor narrates the story of his military victory over the Adamites to his dog Bocanegra, and we read: "in his memory . . . arose tumultuous images of the devastating battle he had waged against heresy in the lowlands of Brabant and Batavia" (47). Similarly, in a chapter entitled "Prisoner of Love," La Señora narrates her life history to a mouse that nibbles on her hymen (162–68). Ludovico, Celestina, the Chronicler, and the youth, just to name a few, also narrate their separate pasts based on memories that in turn are filtered through specific structural, symbolic, and temporal networks. El Señor, for example, must understand the structures of orthodoxy and heresy before he can possibly narrate the events of a campaign based on opposition to the practices of a particular sect. El Señor's entire narration presupposes his understanding of the rules and norms of warfare, his knowledge of how his "remote ancestors had combatted and vanquished the Waldenses and Insabbatists" (47), and his clear recognition that these events he narrates to his dog took place in the past.

The second prefigurative aspect of the narrative consists of the memory of the readers of the text. We as readers bring to the text a preunderstanding of certain textual signifiers. We recall that the Aztec civilization was conquered and destroyed by the Spanish conquistadores in the sixteenth century, that Philip II built a magnificent monument called the Escorial, that the Jews were expelled from Spain in the fifteenth century. If we are better informed about Spanish culture, we may know about the expulsion of the Moors or the revolt of the *comuneros* in 1521. Certainly, some readers recognize characters from the works of Cervantes, Fernando de Rojas, and Tirso de Molina. In other words, Fuentes, as writer of the novel, presupposes a certain degree of preunderstanding of Spanish history, culture, and literature. A reader without this level of familiarity would simply be lost because such a reader would not understand the signs, rules, and temporal indices that are contained in the narrative.

The third prefigurative aspect of the novel consists of what I will term historical memory (as expressed in the writings of Américo Castro, Frances Yates, and Norman Cohn). Fuentes has made much of the enormous debt he owes to these historians, and he specifically mentions them as progenitors of *Terra Nostra* in his theoretical companion piece to the novel, *Don Quixote; or, The Critique of Reading*. The writings of these historians serve as the historiographic *memoria* of *Terra Nostra*. We should keep in mind, however, that as histories, these works themselves are configured and refigured in association with other texts and histories. There quite simply is no ground zero of a historiographic state of existence outside the conceptual networks that Ricoeur mentions as constitutive of mimesis$_1$.

The second component of memory for Vico is *fantasia*, or imagination, which "alters or imitates things" such that actions that occurred in the past are represented to the mind. This second stage corresponds to Ricoeur's mimesis$_2$, which he describes as an act of configuration. Mimesis$_2$, claims Ricoeur, serves as a mediating function: first, between individual events and a whole story; second, among heterogeneous factors such as "agents, goals, means, interactions, circumstances, and unexpected results"; and third, within the temporal dimensions of narrative as expressed in story and plot (or, to borrow structuralist terminology: *fabula* and *sjuzet*, or *fable* and *récit*) (*Time and Narrative* 1:65–67).

Taken together, Vico's *fantasia* and Ricoeur's configurational act point directly to the metaphorical foundations of all narratives. *Fantasia* is the essence of the poetic wisdom of the ancients for Vico, just as "grasping together," the basis of Ricoeur's act of configuration, makes emplotment possible. Without this fundamental operation, meaning is impossible. Just as Vico claims that no cultural institutions can be produced or even conceived of prior to the metaphoric operation of identifying Jove with thunder, Ricoeur reminds us that no meaning can be produced without an "arrangement that transforms the succession of events" into a whole (*Time and Narrative* 1:67).

Terra Nostra can be seen as a long meditation on the relation between imagination and configuration. Fuentes clearly expresses a philosophy of history analogous to Vico's own philosophy when, for example, Ludovico reads a passage from Aquinas, stating, "man can understand nothing without images" (555), or Ludovico equates memory and imagination by stating that he "believed that without eyes there would be no memory and consequently there would be no imagination" (636). But Fuentes perhaps best expresses the relation between imagination and configuration when he describes the Chronicler as one who "could no longer differentiate between what he imagined and what he saw, and thus he added imagination to truth and truth to imagination, believing that everything in this world, after passing from his eyes to his mind, and from there to pen and paper, was fable" (234). The allusion to Vichian thought is unmistakable. But by far the most significant aspect of this description of the Chronicler is the conclusion he reaches after he writes an exemplary novel: "this fictitious reality is the only possibility for being, for ceasing merely to exist." He continues, saying that "one must struggle boldly . . . as great heroes and the implausible knights-errant struggled . . . so that one may tell the world: this is my reality, the only true and unique reality, the reality of my words and their creations" (235).

The heroism of which the Chronicler speaks corresponds to the Vichian recollective *fantasia*, the poetic ordering of the past, the grasping together to make a whole narrative of what has taken place in time. Fuentes represents this struggle in the conversations between Ludovico, Celestina, and El Señor that take place over seven days and appear in the third section of the novel (589–628). In the chapter entitled "Third Day," for example, El Señor decrees that the New World does not exist; like a madman, he continuously interrupts Ludovico and reasserts his own vision of reality. On the fourth day, he hears about the adventures of Don Quixote and discovers to his horror that the tale of the mad knight was being reproduced by a printing press. This revelation upsets El Señor because he recognizes that the advent of the printing press means that "reality belongs to everyone, for only what is written is real" (605). The proliferation of texts undermines Felipe's ability to narrate a single story and superimpose his view of reality onto the construction of history. As he himself relates, "power is founded upon the text" (605), but many texts and many narratives threaten El Señor's univocal interpretation of events.

As Felipe's single narration contests the competing voices of Ludovico, Celestina, Guzmán, and the others, we as readers of the text are forced to balance the myriad voices and disentangle them in order to reconstruct a story out of the variously narrated events. At the level of novelistic construction, Fuentes has focused on what Ricoeur terms "the paradox of temporality" (*Time and Narrative* 1:66) in order to make the reader enact a process of narrative production. As in most sophisticated novels, *Terra Nostra* complicates the relation between story and plot, but Fuentes makes it impossible for the reader to achieve a total understanding of what really happened. What was dream and what was real in this fictional world? The reader will never really know. Fuentes uses this ambiguity in the fictional world in order to establish a homology between novelistic construction and historical reconstruction. In this regard, he invites readers to construct their own true readings of the novel just as he, Fuentes, constructed his own history of Hispanic culture in the form of *Terra Nostra*. Fuentes implies that the imagination required to make sense of novelistic events differs in no substantive fashion from the configurative act used to write a history. In *Terra Nostra*, Fuentes uses elements of traditional history in order to create metaphors that underpin a novelistic narrative of history in opposition to established historical explanations that maintain a single vision of the past.

The Novel as History

In constructing his tragedy of Spanish history, Fuentes relies heavily on the writings of Américo Castro. In his essay on *Don Quixote*, Fuentes explains how important Castro's writings were for him. For Fuentes, Castro's contention that Spanish genius resulted from a unique blend of Judeo-Islamic-Christian culture provides the Mexican author with a conceptual space in which he can explore the possibilities of refiguring the past to emphasize a cultural milieu that may be recoverable in the future. Fuentes does not seek to falsify the past; rather, he strives to show that historical changes occurred because those in power privileged certain interpretations over others. Fuentes, therefore, suggests other possible interpretations that would have led to different outcomes.

The voices that Fuentes creates to contest Felipe's narrative comprise a Nietzschean critical history that involves "an attempt to give oneself, as it were *a posteriori,* a past in which one would like to originate in opposition to that in which one did originate" (UM 76). The great blunder in

Spanish history, according to Castro, was the simultaneous expulsion of the Jews and the Moors in 1492, an act that destroyed the rich interanimation of distinct cultures that together made up the vibrant heterogeneity of Spanish life before the close of the fifteenth century. Fuentes shares Castro's interpretation of events, and *Terra Nostra* offers us not only a glimpse of what might have been (as well as what has been largely forgotten) but also what might yet be if the banished cultures were reintegrated into the story of Spanish life. In addition to accepting Castro's basic premises, Fuentes also culls from Castro's writings certain filaments from which he weaves some of *Terra Nostra*'s metaphors.

In his *España en su historia* (translated as *The Structure of Spanish History*), Castro rejects what he terms a rationalist approach to history, and he also rejects the notion of facts on the grounds that "human facts taken by themselves are unreal abstractions" (146, 221). Instead, Castro seeks out controlling cultural metaphors, linguistic and literary continuities, and what he calls historical features of a people. All cultures, argues Castro, possess what he terms a "dwelling-place" and a "functional structure." By this, Castro means that cultures may contain the same "furniture" (i.e., technology, governmental structures, school systems, etc.), but the vital "preferences" and "reluctances" and the modes people adopt to express those preferences are the product of a given people's values (33). The constitutive feature of the Spanish people, according to Castro, is what he calls "*vivir desviviéndose,*" from the verb *desvivirse:* "to roll back its own living process, to live in disagreement with its own self," a process he also describes as a "construction by destruction" (10–11, 193).

We can easily discern how Fuentes uses Castro's concepts in order to construct *Terra Nostra.* The Escorial corresponds to Castro's theoretical metaphor of the dwelling-place; it is a living metaphor out of which grow the many convoluted narratives that comprise the novel. By developing the Escorial as metaphor, Fuentes also seizes on the supreme expression of *vivir desviviéndose:* construction by destruction. As we know, the Escorial exhausted the Spanish treasury in order to commemorate the dead. No better symbol of the Spanish penchant for *desvivirse,* or unliving, can be found; and Fuentes develops this idea even further through his construction of El Señor.

As many critics have noticed, El Señor is a composite of several Spanish monarchs, most notably Philip II, Charles V, and Ferdinand II. Fuentes does not fuse different historical figures simply to flaunt his creative authority. Rather, Fuentes constructs the composite of the monarch for two specific reasons. First, El Señor embodies the central tenet of the novel, which is repeated several times: "One lifetime is not sufficient. Many existences are needed to fulfill one personality" (532). In this regard, El Señor expresses *the* personality of the Spanish monarchy, something Castro calls "personal absolutism" (123). Second, the creation of El Señor constitutes a type of pseudomorphism with the figure of Saint James. In the sixth chapter of his Spanish history, Castro argues that Spain cannot be adequately understood without a proper comprehension of Saint James and the pilgrimages to Santiago de Compostela. The saint venerated at Compostela was really a composite of James the Greater and James the Lesser, the brother of Christ. In the minds of the Spanish people, these two figures were one, and Spaniards' devotion to his memory galvanized the Christian believers against the armies of Islam. Thus, it was a fictional construction that girded the Spanish Christians, and this willingness to combine figures is precisely what Fuentes imitates when he constructs El Señor.

Fuentes appropriates Castro's writings and reconfigures them in such a way that he imagines a different narrative that presents the same *historia*. Having perceived history as another text that is made, Fuentes understands that it can be altered in such a way that new truths can be expressed. The primary Vichian principle—the true is the made—is not lost on Fuentes. From the pages of history come other stories that can be discerned between the lines, behind them, or in some cases within the lines read backward. In order to produce a new reading of history, one must disrupt the rigid vision of the whole of the past based on, in Nietzsche's words, "illusions which we have forgotten are illusions" (PT 84). Instead, like Fuentes, one must imagine new configurations that yield new interpretations and promise a new past for the future.

To engage in such imaginative activities leads to the third aspect of Vico's threefold memory—*ingegno*. Once the image has been constructed by means of *fantasia*, that new image enters a field of already constituted images and thus initiates a type of kaleidoscopic response. *Ingegno* signals the operation by which connections are made such that the newly established imaginative construct makes sense within the context of previously established images. Without *ingegno*, each product of *fantasia* would simply be a discrete image of the past that would remain incomprehensible. Just as the somatic response of a hysteric or the obsessive-compulsive behavior of a neurotic preserves the past but remains unintelligible without the aid of psychoanalytic explanation that puts the behavior in context, the products of imaginative construction cannot be understood without the contextualizing activity of *ingegno*.

The third Vichian element corresponds to Ricoeur's refigurative activity, which he calls mimesis₃. Ricoeur states that the third mimesis "marks the intersection of the world of the text and the world of the hearer or reader" (*Time and Narrative* 1:71). In other words, mimesis₃ refers to the reception of a given text into the field of texts that constitutes the world, the field of reference that is itself always already composed of texts, signs, and metaphoric structures. This is not to suggest that Ricoeur is arguing that there is nothing outside the text. On the contrary, he affirms that "language is oriented beyond itself"; he believes in an "ontological presupposition of reference" because of "our experience of being in the world and in time" (78). Therefore, language constitutes, and is constituted by, the temporal and ontological elements of human consciousness. As Ricoeur notes, "time becomes human to the extent that it is articulated through a narrative mode" (52). Thus, texts can transform experience because they themselves are products of experience, all of which can only be expressed in language.

With respect to *Terra Nostra*, Fuentes configures history in such a way that he makes the reader refigure the past of both human and literary history. For students of literature, the refigurative enterprise occurs most shockingly when Fuentes retells the story of Quixote. According to Fuentes, Quixote, as a young man, was a Don Juan figure who seduced Dulcinea and killed her father after the father had stabbed and killed Dulcinea. Late in his life, Quixote meets Ludovico and the three youths and recounts his tale. After he fled the murder scene, Quixote began to read. "Books were my only consolation," he tells Ludovico (575). But when, as an old man, he returns to the grave of Dulcinea and her father and invites the statue of her father to dinner (thus repeating the actions of Don Juan in *El burlador de Sevilla*), the statue gives a different response. "The statue only laughed," reports Quixote. "He told me he was condemning me to something worse, that my imaginings and my reading would become reality" (576).

Fuentes configures Cervantes's story in a new way. Consequently, readers must refigure the character of Quixote. To suggest that Quixote was Don Juan in his youth is a stunning *coup de maître* that opens up a wide range of interpretive possibilities that lie beyond the scope of the present study. Suffice it to say, Fuentes's rewriting of *Don Quixote* rivals the more famous rewritings offered by Kafka and Borges and suggests a series of

comparative historico-cultural readings that examine not only how, sep-
arately, Quixote and Don Juan inform Spanish culture and relate to one
another, but also how, if they are conceived of as one character, we must
reinterpret Spanish culture as a whole.

Just as Fuentes reconfigures *Don Quixote* and makes us refigure the text
and its relation to other texts, Fuentes also reconfigures history and makes
us aware of possibilities that existed in the past and have been forgotten.
Fuentes's configuration of history grows out of metaphor. As we have
seen, Fuentes employs the Escorial and even El Señor as metaphors. As
Ricoeur has argued, metaphor theory "shows how new possibilities for
articulating and conceptualizing reality can arise through the assimilation
of hitherto separated semantic fields" (*Interpretation* 57). In the case of
Terra Nostra, Fuentes mixes historical and fictional semantic fields in order to create new meanings in history by making us refigure what we take
to be history.

Among the many metaphors that exist in *Terra Nostra*, the richest, as
Margaret Sayers Peden has observed, may very well be the mirror (47).
In *Terra Nostra*, the mirror metaphor expresses the very activity Fuentes
engages in when he configures history as novel. Mirrors can be found
throughout the novel: El Señor carries a mirror as he ascends the stairs,
Pedro the shipbuilder brings one to the New World, the youth in the New
World is called Smoking Mirror (which is a phrase later used to describe
television screens), and there are mirrors in the cell where Don Juan and
Inés are imprisoned. In *Terra Nostra*, the liberating possibilities inherent
in the experience of recollective *fantasia* express themselves through the
image of the mirror.

As Robert A. Parsons has noted, in *Terra Nostra* "the mirror functions
both as a critical metaphor for the work's structural features and as a
means to explore hidden facets of the identity of characters" (77). For
Parsons, the mirror reveals "hidden aspects of the image reflected" (83)
and, as such, is used in the novel "to create conscious awareness of repressed or unperceived dimensions of characters' identities" (86). For
Dorita Nouhaud, however, the mirror "prolonge en écho narratif le thème
du Jumeau, du double, que Fuentes, fidèle aux sources mythiques, asso-
cie toujours à Quetzalcoatl" (19; extends through narrative echoing the
theme of twinship, of the double, which Fuentes, faithful to the mythic
sources, always associates with Quetzalcoatl). Although both Parsons and
Nouhaud make valid points, I believe that the mirror signifies more than
the return of the repressed and the theme of twinship. For me, the mir-

ror emblematizes the operative enactment of the Vichian threefold memory. In the context of the novel, the mirror reflects not only the constructed nature of cultural memory but also the constructed nature of individual memory.

The use of the mirror and its link to a collective and an individual memory is quite common in Fuentes's works. In *The Death of Artemio Cruz*, for example, the mirror serves as a recurrent symbol of individual recollective consciousness as Cruz sees himself reflected in revolving doors, sequined purses, pools of water, and actual mirrors. Such mirrorings signify the manner in which memories enact a reflective mode in the mind such that the individual who remembers tries to create the truth of the past through simultaneously recalling an image of the past and embellishing or altering that image in order to express the truth of the past. Perhaps the most famous expression of this linkage occurs when Cruz and his lover Regina invent the memory of seeing one another reflected in a pool of water. Their shared memory is an act of the imagination—in point of fact, such an event never occurred, but it nonetheless expresses the truth of their experience of love (76–77).

In *The Buried Mirror*, however, Fuentes extends the use of the mirror motif beyond an individual consciousness and employs it as a cultural metaphor to describe the bifurcated experience of the Hispanic world. From the black pyrite mirrors at the pyramid of El Tajín to Cervantes's Knight of the Mirrors, from the mirror in a Velásquez painting back to the "smoking mirror" of Tezcatlipoca, Hispanic culture has projected and reflected images of itself back and forth across space and time, distorting and obscuring even as it preserves and memorializes what it was and is. In this regard, the mirror symbol enacts at the cultural level what occurs at the individual level in *Artemio Cruz*. As Fuentes himself asks, "is not the mirror both a reflection of reality and a projection of the imagination?" (*Buried Mirror* 11). This dual capacity of reflection and imagination that Fuentes ascribes to the mirror occurs both at the individual and the cultural level in *Terra Nostra*; and, in this novel, Fuentes most fully expresses the multifariousness of the mirror image and its significance in making understandable the relationship between memory and history.

We usually associate mirrors with reflection. In the context of a historical novel, this would suggest a strict mimetic mode of representation. Ever since Stendhal used the mirror in *Le Rouge et le Noir* as a metaphor to explain that he was reflecting what existed in society, novelists have been troubled by this notion. Referring to Stendhal's mirror in the *Paris Review* interview, Fuentes stated that literature could not be content with being a mirror of reality. "I think literature creates reality or it is not literature at all," he stated. "The mirror is also a way to augment reality," he continued; "it augments reality or it does nothing" (155–56).

By calling for an augmentation of reality, Fuentes echoes one of Ricoeur's most important themes: *mimesis* as *poiesis*. Mimesis, argues Ricoeur, "does not mean a duplication of reality; *mimesis* is not a copy: *mimesis* is *poiesis*, that is, construction, creation" (*Hermeneutics* 180). For Ricoeur, we make meaning by emplotment, by making fables of sorts; and, as Vico reminds us, every metaphor is a fable. This constructive activity augments (Fuentes) or refigures (Ricoeur) reality as we understand it and makes it possible for us to change our world. By drawing attention to the Latin origins of the word for mirror, Fuentes highlights the multiple significatory capacities of all metaphors, which, as metaphors, possess a power to negate and preserve simultaneously.

Fuentes is right to return to the Latin origins of the word mirror. *Speculum*, derived from *specere*, means to look at. But good Vichian methodology requires that etymologies be explored further, and we see that *specere* is also the root for *specula*, or watchtower, which in turn informs *speculari*, meaning to spy out, watch, or observe, the root of our English word speculation. I engage in this bit of Vichian proof to stress how Fuentes engages in a speculative enterprise when he writes *Terra Nostra*, just as Vico does in writing *The New Science*. For Vico and Fuentes, history is not given, it is made, and it is human beings who make it. To call on the novel to describe events as they actually happened in the time of Philip II is to appeal to some method of narrative composition that is other than human. Rather than attempt to construct narratives that depict how it actually was in the past, Vico and Fuentes prefer to construct true narratives. True speech (*vera narratio*), claims Vico, stems from the fable, which in turn refers to the *logos* (NS ¶ 401). For Fuentes, this means that the true speech of his novel, which depicts the past, must be composed of the countless oral and written narratives—the rumors, the documents, the icons, the medallions, the paintings, and the fictions from the past—which he then circulates within the novel.

By writing *Terra Nostra*, Fuentes speculates on history and succeeds in constructing a poietic history. Fuentes signals this fact to the reader in his description of what happens when the Chronicler sings his poem about the shepherd lad who loves La Señora. Unbeknownst to the Chronicler, La Señora is in fact having an affair with the boy Mihail-Ben-Sama, and the truth that the poet reveals results in the boy being falsely accused of having committed acts of sodomy with another shepherd, which in turn leads to his summary execution. As Julián states, the Chronicler "was convinced that he had read us the poetic truth, he hadn't the least intimation that he had repeated aloud to us the secret truth" (238). Here Fuentes suggests that the difference between the truth made in poetry and the truth made in life is, at times, indistinguishable. Both truths are made, and both impinge on one another and affect what we commonly refer to as the real world. Fuentes underscores this irony by having Mihail-Ben-Sama killed for the wrong reason: the truth of the liaison is revealed in a fiction and is preserved in the realm of the imaginary, whereas the boy is killed because of a fiction believed to be true.

But Fuentes is after more than delicious irony. He employs both Vichian and Nietzschean philosophies of history for a specific purpose. Like Hayden White, he acknowledges the tropologic foundation of any history; and, like Edward Said, he feels that the Vichian project seeks understanding "in terms of a collective fate" (*Beginnings* 352). To these two interpretations, Fuentes adds one of his own. If the true is indeed the made, he suggests, then we can choose our own past in order to shape our future. This is not to say that we falsify accounts, ignore events, or deny narratives that constitute the dominant historical representation of a given past. On the contrary, by choosing our past, we actively assess the various interpretations available and determine the consequences of having accepted a particular interpretation. What is done *can* be undone to the extent that we in the present can reject what Walter Benjamin terms the document of barbarism—history—in favor of the other voices that speak to us, however muted, from the past.

Fuentes's poietic history acknowledges the constructed nature of all histories. Like the unnamed scribe of the court of Tiberius, Fuentes reminds us that "true history perhaps is not the story of events, or investigation of principles, but simply a farce of specters, an illusion procreating illusions, a mirage believing in its own substance" (699). Thus, it is the dogma of a true history, one that claims to describe events "as they actually happened," that the novel, the modern form of heresy, challenges. As El Señor himself recognizes, heresy "reveal[s] the infinite possibilities for combining our holy truths" (240). Similarly, the novel reveals infinite possibilities for combining secular, human truths.

As we have seen, Fuentes interpolates both Nietzsche and Vico into *Terra Nostra* in order to write his poietic history. By incorporating Nietzschean philosophy, Fuentes affirms his belief that any history must further life, that all histories are tropologic constructs, and that the ethical choices made by the historian that determine narrative strategies are just as great as the ethical decisions made by actors in the past. By "playing Vico" in his novel, Fuentes affirms the possibility of recreating our own historical fate. And this act of re-creation is brought about through the combined activities of Vichian memory—*memoria, fantasia,* and *ingegno.*

Thus, poietic history seeks an axiological rather than an epistemological ground. As such, it configures, by means of metaphoric structuration, a narrative of the past that describes history as tragedy, as an ever-recurring play of values that does not achieve some ultimate goal or state of consciousness. Rather, poietic history, as practiced by Fuentes, is a form of heretical discourse with respect to most contemporary historiography. In *Terra Nostra,* Fuentes confirms an observation made by Borges, who writes: "we must suspect that there is no universe in the organic, unifying sense inherent in that ambitious word. If there is, we must conjecture its purpose; we must conjecture the words, the definitions, the etymologies, the synonymies of God's secret dictionary" (*Borges: A Reader* 143). The conjectural or speculative enterprise in which Fuentes engages resurrects a countermemory of the past and lets us hear the forgotten dreams, interpretations, and possibilities from that past; it may also open new possibilities for the future of our world.

3

Experiencing the Past: Susan Daitch's *L.C.*

But in the thick darkness enveloping the earliest antiquity, so remote from ourselves, there shines the eternal and never failing light of a truth beyond all question: that the world of civil society has certainly been made by men, and that its principles are therefore to be found within the modifications of our own human mind.
—Vico, *The New Science*

If you are to venture to interpret the past you can do so only out of the fullest exertion of the vigour of the present. . . .
—Nietzsche, *Untimely Meditations*

One of the standard clichés that circulate in fiction writing workshops is the sage advice to "write what you know about." Implied in this statement that we can best express what we ourselves know is the notion that we know best what we ourselves have experienced. This emphasis on experiential knowledge has also been the focus of much historiography of late. The once-popular monumental histories that offered readers a portrait of the past through the life of a "great" historical figure, be it Alexander, Peter, Frederick, or Catherine, have given way to equally popular histories of the lives of common people. History lived by the ordinary folk, it is thought, will provide us with a better understanding of what really occurred in the past. The notion that the intentions of kings, queens, and courtiers determine the course of events has given way to the belief that history is the narrative of narratives—that is, the sum total of accumulated stories of the past—and that the stories we have ignored up to this point are the daily observations made by average people in their letters, diaries, and notebooks. Werner Sollors expresses just such a view in his introduction to Hamilton Holt's *Life Stories of (Undistinguished) Americans*, where he writes: "Life stories—especially autobiographies—do indeed form a rich and unsurpassed resource for an understanding of the inward experience of how social and individual forces may interact" (xi).

Put another way, we could say that there are those who hold that intentionality is secondary to what we might term experientiality. For many current historians and documentary filmmakers, the truth boils down to this: the experiences of individual participants in history, often recorded in their own words, present us with the best means of reliving the past. A cursory examination of typical history book club selections reveals books ranging from collections of letters written by U.S. Civil War participants to collections of interviews of Nazi death camp guards and executioners. In several instances, the focus of these historical accounts is on the statements produced by everyday individuals who participated in historical events.

The Turn to Common Experience in Historiography

In the realm of distinguished scholarly production, one of the most celebrated examples of the turn toward the examination of the life of a common individual is Carlo Ginzburg's *Cheese and the Worms,* a fascinating examination of the life of a sixteenth-century Italian miller named Menocchio. As Ginzburg notes in his introduction: "In the past historians could be accused of wanting to know only about 'the great deeds of kings,' but today this is certainly no longer true. More and more they are turning toward what their predecessors passed over in silence, discarded, or simply ignored. 'Who built Thebes of the seven gates?' Bertolt Brecht's 'literate worker' was already asking. The sources tell us nothing about these anonymous masons, but the question retains all its significance" (xiii). In his historical study, Ginzburg contends that "an investigation initially pivoting on an individual, moreover an apparently unusual one, ended by developing into a general hypothesis on the popular culture (more precisely, peasant culture) of preindustrial Europe" (xii). And so we are treated to the testimony of Menocchio, who, among other things, declared that an original chaos of mixed elements—which resembled cheese—produced worms—which in fact were angels (6). Ginzburg goes on to trace the thinking of Menocchio back to particular books and popular interpretations of books, but he is careful to add that "Menocchio didn't parrot the opinions or ideas of others" (50). Rather, what Ginzburg sets out to prove is that Menocchio's thinking was an outgrowth of the convergence of the popular and intellectual cultures of his time.

In a similar fashion, Jonathan Spence's *Question of Hu* examines the life of "an exasperating and apparently unprepossessing man" (xvii). Spence points out that "Chinese biographical tradition" preserved an abundance of material on scholars, statesmen, philosophers, poets, and even merchants and soldiers; but "Hu was none of those things" (xvii). However, Hu's experience in eighteenth-century France, claims Spence, offers us a better means to understand the confrontation between two cultures.

Moving from the large scale of the clash of cultures to the much smaller scale of the community, we learn about the behaviors of fourteenth-century French village folk in Emmanuel Le Roy Ladurie's *Montaillou*. In this work, Le Roy Ladurie examines court records and testimony given by peasants to Jacques Fournier, bishop of Pamiers and supervisor of the Inquisition. According to Le Roy Ladurie: "In the process of revealing their position on official Catholicism, the peasants examined by Fournier's Inquisition, many from the village of Montaillou, have given an extraordinarily detailed and vivid picture of their everyday life" (vii). What we then read is a remarkable assemblage of revelatory confessions about the peasants' daily activities in various aspects of life—the conduct of shepherds, conceptualizations of time and space, typical sexual practices—that holds together the general narrative Le Roy Ladurie has written. In doing this, he reveals the ethos of an entire community.

Natalie Zemon Davis adopts much the same approach in her historical account *The Return of Martin Guerre*. In her introduction she asks: "But how do historians discover such things about anyone in the past? We look at letters and diaries, autobiographies, memoirs, family histories" (1). Once again, the focus is on individual experience as articulated by the individuals themselves; and, in the case of *Martin Guerre*, the lives of a few individuals—as recorded in their testimony before courts of law—make it possible for us to understand an entire class or community of people, in this case the sixteenth-century French Languedoc village of Artigat.

Even the televisual media have adopted the experiential approach when it comes to historical documentaries. Gone are the days of the disembodied, magisterial voice explaining what took place in the past while the camera pans paintings of battle scenes. Instead, we have programs such as the enormously popular U.S. television documentary *The Civil War*, directed by Ken Burns, much of which is voice-over narration of the excerpts of letters and diary entries of people who witnessed and experienced myriad aspects of the American Civil War.

In its more sophisticated versions, the experiential approach can provide great insight into what we thought was the past. The words of the participants, *as interpreted* by historians such as Ginzburg or Spence, provide us a better means of making sense of what these people thought had happened or thought they were doing as much as it tells us what really happened. In other words, it provides us with a glimpse of what means of interpretation these people invoked in their own time. In its less sophisticated forms (and there are moments of this in the Burns documentary), the idea seems to be that the words of the participants—their experiences as recorded in language—are transparent. Thus, we need only read (or hear) their words and these words can stand alone, nothing more need be said, they speak for themselves.

The Problem of Experience

But is this necessarily the case? Can any person speak for herself or himself *tout court*? Can we convey our experiences directly through language? Consider any occurrence in our lives that we might try to relate to an interlocutor. One of the first things we try to do is determine if the listener has had a similar encounter. At this point, we have already reached a philosophical conundrum because neither we (through repetition or memory, so it seems) nor anyone else can experience the exact same situation. Nevertheless, we ignore these philosophical niceties and press on, trying to establish some ground of mutual understanding. If the interlocutor has not participated in or been witness to a similar situation, we switch to analogy or metaphor, hoping eventually to gain a handhold on the imagination of the person to whom we are speaking.

For example, if you are describing a rather long wait in line at the local bank, you might ask me if I use the same bank or if I have also stood in a long line at a bank. If I say yes to either or both of these questions, the joy in your storytelling comes from developing the unique aspects of your particular bank episode (the appeal to hyperbole is obvious here) and allowing my responses (from incredulity to one-upmanship) to contribute to the construction of the narrative through the dialogical act of narrating. But what of those cases in which I have no similar frame of reference? What of those cases in which you struggle to find the proper analogy or the right metaphor, and language somehow fails you? How can you go about relating your experience to me?

In her critically acclaimed book *The Body in Pain*, Elaine Scarry examines the limits of language that become evident when it comes to conveying the most incontrovertible experience any of us can have: physical pain. As Scarry points out, pain is the ultimate locus of certainty in the life of a human being. "For the person in pain," she writes, "so incontestably and unnegotiably present is it that 'having pain' may come to be thought of as the most vibrant example of what it is to 'have certainty,' while for the other person it is so elusive that 'hearing about pain' may exist as the primary model of what it is 'to have doubt'" (4). We do not doubt the pain we feel; however, when called upon to relate that feeling to someone else, we are at a loss. Language fails us. Very often we cannot find the words to express what we feel, and this makes it nearly impossible for others to understand what has happened to us. "Physical pain," writes Scarry, "does not simply resist language but actively destroys it" (4).

Scarry explores the ramifications of this phenomenon and discusses, for example, how physicians must rely on a series of analogies and key words (throbbing, burning, flickering, etc.) to obtain a general idea of the sort of pain a patient is enduring. These words, which form a type of asymptotic lexicon, help physicians make effective diagnoses, but rarely do the patients feel as if they have conveyed what has happened to them physically.

By far the most disturbing part of Scarry's analysis has to do with torture. Victims of torture become disarticulated. Their extreme experiences cannot be conveyed in language (especially if they have survived torture that has left few visible scars); therefore, their credibility is at stake when they try to testify as to what happened to them. Those administering torture are well aware of this. Thus, the effectiveness of this form of political terror rests on the simple fact that the truth of the victims' reality (i.e., what has actually happened to them) is irrefutable but incommunicable. The tortured have been silenced through the certainty of their experience, the torturers vindicated through doubts about their culpability. Both positions are secured by the limits of language.

The importance of Scarry's insight to historiography cannot be overemphasized. For Scarry, the problematic of the relationship between language and pain can be summed up as follows: "It is precisely because it takes no object that it, more than any other phenomenon, resists objectification in language" (5). When we consider some of the extreme circumstances that humans have endured in history, we begin to appreciate just how difficult it is for participants and witnesses to describe what happened in a believable fashion. And when we consider the paltry number of extant objects that we can point to when we read chronicles, narratives, and accounts of the past—particularly the ancient past—we see that Scarry's observation about language vis-à-vis pain can be extended to historiography in cases that lie even beyond instances of painful events in history. Perhaps the most recent, famous, and controversial example of this

very problem has been the continuing debate over the veracity of Holocaust accounts. Without delving into the particulars of the *Historikerstreit*
in Germany in the 1980s, controversies surrounding the authorship of
Anne Frank's diaries, or pronouncements made by Jean-François Lyotard,
it is safe to say that the enormous events most often signified by the word
"Auschwitz" raise serious questions about what constitutes evidence, what
can serve as an object for historical investigation, how written accounts
are verified, and how humans relate the truth of their experience.

In his excellent study *Writing and Rewriting the Holocaust*, James E.
Young provides us with one of the best analyses of Holocaust writing as
discourse that has been produced thus far. Of particular importance to
Young is the very means by which people structured their narrative accounts of various aspects of the Holocaust. Young argues that each of these
narratives depends on certain discursive conventions, storytelling proto-
cols, and antecedent narrative paradigms that make it possible not only
for the writers to construct their narratives but also for the readers to
understand them. "Far from transcending or displacing the events of the
Holocaust," writes Young, "the governing mythoi of these writers are actually central to their experiences. For the 'poetics' of literary testimony
not only framed the writers' experiences as they unfolded, shaping their
understanding and responses; but the language, tropes, and selected details of their texts ultimately shape our understanding of events afterwards" (10). Thus, Holocaust writers and their particular audiences share
a certain repertoire of readings and allusions. The manner in which these
writers convey their experience is constrained by specific discursive parameters—a strategy Young describes as "generic form"—that structure
testimony. Common wisdom suggests that it is the immediacy of the diary form that lends it its authority, that renders its factuality irrefutable.
But, as Young notes,

> while the exigencies of time and memory may weigh heavily on the factuality
> of a given report, they are in other ways no less mediational than the linguis-
> tic, cultural, and religious patterns of mind and expression that frame a writ-
> er's narrative moment by moment, during or after the Holocaust. For even the
> diarists themselves—once they enter immediate experience into the tropes and
> structures of narrative—necessarily convert experience into an organized,
> often ritualized, memory of experience. (25)

The ritualistic manner in which two writers record the same event may
differ markedly, but in no way does this undermine the veracity of each

writer's account. Every writer, no matter what the topic, falls under the domination of discursive practice as well as a shared sense of the past with a particular group to whom the writing is addressed. This explains why two witnesses of the same event may produce very different accounts: no two writers share the exact same mental library.

Extended beyond the boundaries of Holocaust studies, Young's observations provide us with an important reminder of how historical narratives are circumscribed by narrative convention. One could go even further and say that the very thing we call experience itself is so circumscribed. Joan W. Scott, in her powerful critique of the turn toward experience as a foundation for historical analysis, contends that historical truth emerges from a process of interpretive engagement with significatory systems, none of which can be used as an interpretive ground. "Experience," she writes, "is at once always already an interpretation and something that needs to be interpreted. What counts as experience is neither self-evident nor straight-forward; it is always contested, and always therefore political" (797).

Another way of saying this is that there exists no experience that is unmediated. Our comprehension of events we witness or participate in occurs because we possess signifying systems—language, metaphors, concepts, and so forth—that make us make sense of disparate phenomena. Without these systems of signification, the world would be quite literally incomprehensible. We would be akin to Vico's first humans, who viewed each phenomenon as a discrete act. Thus, the crash of thunder was a shocking, explosive sound. The next crash of thunder was also a shocking, explosive sound, but it was not perceived to be similar or related to the first crash of thunder. It was only when the *bestioni* expressed the first imaginative universal by declaring the thunder to be Jove that it was possible to make sense of the world (NS ¶ 377). The capacity to universalize through concepts permeates our encounters with the myriad phenomena that surround us; even as we undergo an experience, we are enmeshed in signifying systems that will always constitute the field of meaning for us. As Scott says, there is no ground zero. We are engulfed by signifiers and, as such, cannot appeal beyond them. Nietzsche put it best: for us there exist "only interpretations" (WP ¶ 481).

Scott's second point—that is, the inescapable political nature of all experience—must not be overlooked. In fact, when it comes to historiography, this may be the most significant point she makes. Readers have long been familiar with the notion that every historian practices some sort of politics, that it is actually impossible to write a genuinely objective history. But seldom do we as readers of history pause to think about the motivations of individual historians—both famous and not so famous. What led to the different interpretations of the French Revolution produced by Burke and Michelet? Was each historian pursuing some other goal perhaps unknown even to him? How does the pursuit of such unconscious objectives color the history that becomes written?

The recent controversy surrounding two interpretations of Captain James Cook's death in Hawaii offers us a telling example of the political dimension of any interpretation of a historical event. Two distinguished cultural anthropologists, Gananath Obeyesekere and Marshall Sahlins, have produced accounts of Cook's encounter with the Hawaiians that reach very different conclusions about how the Hawaiians interpreted their experience. In 1982 and 1983, Sahlins delivered a series of lectures at Princeton University that focused on the Polynesian War and Cook's death in Hawaii. With respect to the sea captain, Sahlins argued that Cook arrived on the island in 1778–79, during the Makahiki celebration period that commemorates the fertility god Lono. According to Sahlins, Cook arrived in the right place and at the right time to be taken as a manifestation of Lono himself. He even departed at the proper time; but when he was forced to return to the island to make repairs to his vessel, the Hawaiians saw this as a crisis in the very structure of the order of their world, and their logical response was to kill Cook and put their world aright.

Obeyesekere rejects this view in *The Apotheosis of Captain Cook*, claiming that Sahlins's interpretation is a form of mythmaking on the part of Europeans. For Obeyesekere, the idea that the "Natives" regarded Cook as a god is a myth invented by eighteenth-century Europeans themselves. "To put it bluntly," he writes, "I doubt that the natives created their European god; the Europeans created him for them. This 'European god' is a myth of conquest, imperialism, and civilization—a triad that cannot be easily separated" (3). Obeyesekere views the Hawaiians as being much more pragmatic; Sahlins, he contends, prefers to look on them as irrational primitives, an interpretation that helps to support the cultural imperialism of the West. The evidence Sahlins adduces in support of his interpretation, claims Obeyesekere, includes the following arguments: (1) the Hawaiians viewed Cook's ship as a manifestation of Lono's canoe; (2) when the English sailor Watman died and was buried, the Hawaiians perceived him as the victim that was required to be sacrificed as

part of the Makahiki festival; and (3) when the English sailors dismantled the Makahiki shrine and used it for firewood, the Hawaiians interpreted this as part of the ritual dismantling of the shrine that occurred
every year. Obeyesekere's response to this is as lucid as it is terse:

> I think it quite improbable that the Hawaiians could not make a distinction
> between the physical shape of Lono's tiny canoe that is floated at the conclu-
> sion of Makahiki and Cook's great ships, or that for them the corpse of Wat-
> man was a sacrificial victim, or that marines dismantling the palings of the
> shrine for firewood was a ritual dismantling of the sort practiced by their own
> priests. One has to balance the facts of physical perception with cultural real-
> ity and what I have called "practical rationality." (60)

In *How "Natives" Think*, Sahlins presents a devastating and sometimes
acrimonious rebuttal to Obeyesekere's critique. Accusing Obeyesekere of
adopting an "inverted ethnocentrism" that ends in "an anti-anthropolo-
gy" (151), Sahlins contends that the "central critical vision of Obeyesekere's book" yields the following: "the Hawaiians are endowed with the
highest form of Western mentality, while Western scholars slavishly repeat the irrational beliefs of their ancestors" (9). Sahlins takes Obeyesekere to task for "presuming that as a native Sri Lankan he has a privileged
insight into how Hawaiians thought" (1). As a result, in Sahlins's view,
Obeyesekere's "underlying thesis is crudely unhistorical, a not-too-implic-
it notion that all natives so-called (by Europeans) are alike, most notably
in their common cause for resentment" (5).

In a chapter entitled "Historical Fiction, Makeshift Ethnography," Sahlins argues that Obeyesekere "fail[ed] to consider the Hawaiians' theological doctrines" (122); instead, he produced an analysis in which "Hawai-
ian theology is understood on the basis of (alleged) Sri Lankan notions
of gods and their worldly forms" (120). In short, Sahlins asserts that by
"selectively ignoring or misrepresenting the primary documents, he
[Obeyesekere] constructs an implausible history out of a habitual combination of commonsense realism and pop anthropology" (117).

Both of these respected anthropologists amass evidence in support of
their arguments, and both offer eloquent defenses of their respective positions. The political implications of each of their positions are quite obvious, and we as readers are left to choose. The truth about Cook in Hawaii, it seems, is a matter of interpretation. The debate between Sahlins
and Obeyesekere, however, underscores Scott's major point: that inter-

pretation based on experience (in this case the experience of other peoples as interpreted by anthropologists) is never transparent and is always inflected with a deeply political dimension.

A Novel Response to Experience

The problems surrounding historical interpretation based on experience lie at the heart of Susan Daitch's first novel, *L.C.* Daitch's novel provides an ideal ground to examine central problems associated with the writing of history because *L.C.* presents an interpretation of competing readings of a history based on experience. Specifically, Daitch's novel enacts the process of Nietzschean genealogy, an approach that puts into play philological interpretation and, in Alan D. Schrift's words, perspectival, "creative textual appropriation" ("Between" 105). Thus, *L.C.* gives readers an intimate view of how historians construct history to promote cultural as well as individual goals. At the same time, the novel underscores the Vichian notion of the mythic dimension of all history. Through its very structure, *L.C.* provides us with a superb example of Vico's concept of *ingenium*, the ability to bring together what appear to be unrelated elements to make new configurations of the past. In short, *L.C.* makes us cognizant of the irreducible metaphoric dimension in all historical narratives and reminds us that they are a fabling forth of actualities.

At this point, one might object and say that contemporary historians have acknowledged many of these same issues. Hayden White, of course, made his fellow historians acutely aware of the tropological underpinnings of every historical narrative. But White has never produced a historical narrative as such; his contributions have been strictly theoretical, very often in the form of metanarrative. Natalie Zemon Davis, by way of contrast, does produce historical narratives; and, in the case of *The Return of Martin Guerre*, she focuses specifically on individual experience. Nevertheless, her seamless narrative, which she admits "is in part my invention" (5), does not display a contestation of interpretations. Despite two closing chapters of the book—"Histoire prodigieuse, Histoire tragique," which discusses the two earliest and most substantial versions of the Martin Guerre tale written by Jean de Coras and Guillaume Le Sueur; and "Of the Lame," which describes Michel de Montaigne's critique of Coras's judgment—Davis does not focus her primary attention on the different ways in which the tale has been interpreted. Instead, in the bulk of her book, she produces her own eloquent, eminently readable prose, which provides us with a single (but not totalized) interpretation of the incident in Artigat. Even though the tale "retains a stubborn vitality," Davis characterizes herself as a "historian who has deciphered it" (125).

Perhaps *I, Pierre Rivière*, edited by Michel Foucault, provides us with the best example of a contemporary form of historiography that attempts to accomplish what I claim Daitch's novel succeeds in doing. Daitch and Foucault demonstrate how interpretation constitutes an act of poetic creation. Foucault's book, which examines the account of a nineteenth-century peasant who murdered his mother, sister, and brother, includes witness statements, medical and judicial reports, a narrative written by the accused himself, as well as analytical papers produced by eight members of a seminar conducted by Foucault at the Collège de France. The focus here is necessarily on discourse and its relation to truth. As Foucault admits in the foreword, "I think the reason we decided to publish these documents was to draw a map, so to speak, of those combats, to reconstruct these confrontations and battles, to rediscover the interaction of those discourses as weapons of attack and defense in the relations of power and knowledge" (xi).

By reading this text, we learn that one medical examiner, a Dr. Bouchard, felt that the accused showed "no sign of mental derangement" (124), whereas Dr. Vastel was "deeply and fully convinced that Rivière was not sane" (125). Armed with these and other contradictory observations made by the principal participants in the trial, Foucault's fellow seminar members draw some interesting conclusions of their own. Jean-Pierre Peter and Jeanne Faveret interpret Rivière's act as one of rebellion against the social order such that he felt he was "slaughtering a tyrant" (191). The institutions of social order, the authors argue, declared Rivière insane precisely because they wanted "to reduce the significance of his act; since it was aimed at the social order, the order of the contract, it could only be something done by a beast or a madman, the opposite of a man" (193). By granting Rivière a reprieve because he was insane, the authorities depoliticized his act. Interpreting the Rivière case in light of fly sheets, Foucault contends that these popular narratives of the time, describing acts of crime and punishment, commemorated "history below the level of power, one which clashed with the law" (205). Rather than focus on popular forms of discourse, Blandine Barret-Kriegel places the Rivière case in the realm of legal discourse. She examines the Rivière trial in the context of the regicide trial of Fieschi and argues that the Rivière verdict was affected by the Fieschi trial itself. Philippe Riot, however, examines the competing legal and medical discourses that make up part of the actual legal proceedings and concludes that the account of Rivière's life was used by doctors to demonstrate the accused's state of "mental deficiency" and that this same account was used by the judges and prosecution to show that Rivière had never been mad (232). For his part, Riot observes a particular "break" in the Rivière narrative that makes it possible for the doctors and lawyers to produce their conflicting accounts (235). Ultimately, Riot contends that the competing legal and medical accounts required that one disregard the memoir written by the accused himself.

In its entirety, the case of Pierre Rivière, as presented by Foucault, does touch on many of the elements I discussed earlier: perspectivism, interpretation as an act of creation, and language as the medium of historical truth production. It does not, however, focus specifically on the concept of experience, nor does it provide any detailed discussion of the relation between literature and history. Rather, *I, Pierre Rivière* offers an examination of some of the problems raised by Nietzsche, Scott, and Schrift at the level of institutional discursive practice.

Rather than rely on historians for a thorough understanding of the complexities associated with contestatory interpretations, the limits of experiential knowledge, and the grounds of truth, it is incumbent upon us to turn to literature, for it is literature that allows us to examine these issues in a space that Wendy Steiner describes as a "virtual realm tied to the world by acts of interpretation" (8). As Paul de Man said, literature "is the only form of language free from the fallacy of unmediated expression" (17); and, as such, it provides us with the perfect ground for investigating the very concept of interpretive mediation via linguistic expression. In this regard, *L.C.* is the ideal narrative to conduct our investigation of these matters.

L.C. concerns itself with the writing of history as based on individual experience—specifically women's experience in history and feminist historical practice that records, celebrates, and critiques that experience. Surprisingly, the novel has received scant critical attention. Linda Hutcheon has offered a handful of illuminating pages on *L.C.* in two books on postmodernism and what she terms "historiographic metafiction," and a special 1993 issue of the *Review of Contemporary Fiction* devoted four articles to Daitch's work. Aside from this, little has been said about this novel, which is unfortunate because it is a wonderfully complex and superbly crafted piece of fiction.

Very much a novel about writing, translation, and history, *L.C.* at first glance appears to be a type of historical novel that presents itself as a genuine historical artifact containing both the journal entries of Lucienne Crozier, a participant in the revolution of 1848 in Paris, as well as an introduction and explanatory notes provided by the translator of the journal, Dr. Willa Rehnfield. Lucienne's diary, as translated by Rehnfield, records the impressions of a young woman who had an affair with the painter Eugène Delacroix, joined the revolutionary group 14 Juillet, and—after the failure of the 1848 revolution—eventually escaped to North Africa with one of the group's leaders, Jean de la Tour, only to succumb to tuberculosis and die.

About one hundred pages into the novel, a second editor, a certain Jane Amme, provides six additional explanatory notes, two of which critique the Rehnfield translation and two more that seek to clarify what Rehnfield has written. The reader next discovers that Jane has a particular story to tell that is independent from, yet intimately related to, the Crozier story and that *L.C.* itself is much more than a novel disguised as a historical document. Jane offers an "Epilogue" in the middle of *L.C.* that explains how Rehnfield obtained the journal and how she, Jane, became an editorial assistant to Rehnfield and eventually the executor of Rehnfield's will.

Jane Amme, it turns out, is the *nom de guerre* of a former 1960s revolutionary who survived the battles of Berkeley (1968–72) and was forced to go underground after she killed a man who had raped her. The alleged rapist, Luc Ferrier, was also an industrialist who had reaped huge profits from the sale of war matériel used during the Vietnam War. When Jane kills Ferrier with a firebomb, the press concludes that antiwar activists murdered him. To avoid arrest, Jane travels east and begins to work for Rehnfield; she later learns that Luc Ferrier was the person who helped Rehnfield obtain the Crozier diary when he bought some Delacroix paintings on the black market and had them smuggled into the United States.

Daitch's novel then takes yet another surprising turn when Jane offers her own translation of the last few months' entries in the Crozier diary. Jane's translation differs markedly from Rehnfield's and conveys Amme's repudiation of Rehnfield's historical methodology, her political ideology, and her understanding of the French language. Taken in its entirety, therefore, *L.C.* records the experiences of three women: a rebel during the revolution of 1848, a student radical of the 1960s, and a traditionally trained historian. By presenting her readers with two translations of a historical document—one by the traditional historian Rehnfield and the other by a 1960s radical—Daitch's novel produces an interpretive contest between a historian who is dependent on what we might term a *grand récit* and a person practicing Nietzschean genealogy.

History/Genealogy/Literature

Nietzsche's position with respect to history and its purposes was perhaps best expressed in the title of his second untimely meditation, "On the Uses and Disadvantages of History for Life"; his concern was to "learn better how to employ history for the purpose of life" (UM 66). In other words, Nietzsche sought to determine under what circumstances one should employ a certain type of history to make a truth that would enhance the "health of an individual, of a people and of a culture" (UM 63).

For most of us, history consists of a larger vision beyond the level of the individual, a vision that attempts to make sense of the collective experience of nations, groups, and entire races. As a form of intellectual inquiry, history is called upon to articulate the truth of the past. In the modern era, most historians believe that the key to uncovering historical truth lies in distinguishing stories about the past that are true from those that are false. This dichotomy of true and false, the common way of distinguishing the real and the fictive that undergirds the typical understanding of human experience, served as the focal point of Nietzsche's philosophical investigations. Rather than accept the standard dichotomy of true/false, Nietzsche, in an activity he termed genealogy, turned his attention to the constitutive properties and the concomitant outcomes of this and other dichotomies. In Nietzsche's estimation, to declare a judgment false does not automatically imply a rejection of that judgment. "The question," writes Nietzsche in *Beyond Good and Evil*, "is to what extent [the judgment] is life-promoting, life-preserving, species preserving, perhaps even species cultivating" (11).

Thus, in responding to the problem of history, truth, and expression in language, Nietzsche offered genealogy as the means by which we *make* the truths of history to meet certain political, social, or cultural needs in the present and for the future. Nietzschean genealogy, as Schrift points out, emerges from the tension produced between Nietzsche's philosophy of perspectivism and his adherence to principles of philological practice. "Perspectival interpretation seem[s] to allow for an unbounded play of creative textual appropriation," writes Schrift, but "philological interpretation seems to call for methodological rigour and meticulous attention to the text itself" ("Between" 104). It is this opposition that makes genealogy possible, such that it "appears to occupy a space between the interpretive demands of philological attention and perspectival creativity" ("Between" 108).

Because the enhancement of life is the most important criterion governing genealogical practice, there are no correct interpretations; rather, there are those that either enhance or diminish life. The task of the historian, therefore, is to produce an interpretation that organizes different perspectives while at the same time employing philological rigor in pursuit of making a truth that will promote the life of the present culture.

Nietzsche's emphasis on the enhancement of life, however, is not limited to his history essay. On the contrary, the focus on life constitutes the central concern of his writings. But life, for Nietzsche, is inextricably bound to the concept of art; indeed, it is the highest manifestation of the creative drive—we cannot separate the two. From his early declaration in *The Birth of Tragedy* that "it is only as an aesthetic phenomenon that existence and the world are eternally justified" (BT 52) to his late characterization of the "world as a work of art that gives birth to itself" (WP ¶ 796), Nietzsche offers us a sustained examination of the relationship between living and creating, between being an artist and being alive. In his lengthy study of Nietzsche, Heidegger points out that it is precisely because art possesses a transfigurative capacity in contradistinction to the fixed quality of truth that Nietzsche sees in art its fundamental life-enhancing capability (*Nietzsche* 1:216–17). For Nietzsche, truth constitutes a "fixation of semblance"; art, however, "opens life up for creation of more life" (Schrift, *Nietzsche and the Question* 50). As Alexander Nehamas explains it, "Nietzsche's model for the world, for objects, and for people turns out to be the literary text and its components; his model for our relation to the world turns out to be interpretation" (90–91).

Nietzsche's insistence on the centrality of art and its relationship to truth is one of his most profound philosophical legacies. As an intellectual heir of Nietzsche, Scott pursues the line of analysis that focuses on the complex relation between truth and art. In her essay on "The Evidence of Experience," Scott calls for a type of reading that "would grant to 'the literary' an integral, even irreducible, status of its own." But she adds the following proviso: "To grant such status is not to make 'the literary' foundational, but to open new possibilities for analyzing discursive productions of social and political reality as complex, contradictory processes" (793–94).

For Scott, the literary serves as a locus of examination that affords us the opportunity to establish the interactive lines of filiation, cross-fertil-ization, and communication as well as to enact the processes of negation, condensation, appropriation, contradiction, and displacement that come into being when we *figure out* history in the form of a narrative. Scott emphasizes that this process of literary figuration, like the process of ex-perience, is necessarily political, and she thereby implies that the literary has value in that it is aware of its own figurative status, whereas neither experience nor other forms of discourse self-consciously acknowledge that they themselves emerge from antecedent chains of figuration. As de Man argues, "fiction is not myth, for it knows and names itself as fiction. It is not a demystification, it is demystified from the start" (18). Or, as Nietzsche said much earlier and much more directly: "art treats *illusion as illusion;* therefore it does not wish to deceive, it *is true*" (PT 96).

Although Scott's argument echoes much of Nietzsche's philosophy, she stops short of collapsing the distinction between fact and fiction. Even so, her declarations that "experience is a subject's history" and "language is the site of history's enactment" lead her to conclude that the literary may be an indispensable site of historical interpretation because historical expla-nation cannot afford to separate experience from language (793). Her pur-pose is not to promote what she calls "linguistic determinism"; rather, she wants "to insist . . . on the productive quality of discourse" (793). In other words, she seeks to engage in a critical examination of how competing dis-cursive practices impinge on, limit, support, further, thwart, explain, shape (and themselves constitute) human experience; literature, she suggests, provides us with the best means to conduct such an examination.

Taken together, then, Scott's call for a type of reading that grants the literary a special status finds its philosophical roots in Nietzschean gene-alogical practice; and the tension between philology and perspectivism that Schrift identifies as being the force field of genealogical production offers us a way of understanding Scott's proposed reading practice. Nietz-sche and Scott suggest that the literary, by its very nature, enacts an in-terpretive activity that affords us the best opportunity to analyze the con-tentious discursive production of reality, the play of forces that genealogy exposes as being constitutive properties of the real. It is my contention that *L.C.* illustrates precisely the kind of genealogical method initiated by Nietzsche and promoted more recently by Scott.

Historical Interpretation and the Production of Truth(s)

The first translator of the Crozier diary, Dr. Rehnfield, represents a member of a growing body of historians who look to the particulars of everyday life to learn "what really happened" in the past. She resembles those historians who, according to Scott, issue a "challenge to normative history" by resting their "claim to legitimacy on the authority of experience" to correct "oversights resulting from inaccurate or incomplete vision" (776). Precisely because a diary contains the language of personal experience, a language she uncritically accepts as being wholly transparent, Rehnfield believes that such a document can make a positive contribution to our understanding of the past. In other words, Lucienne's experience becomes foundational for Rehnfield; but it in *no way challenges the larger view of the past.* For Dr. Rehnfield, historical truth is *found,* and it is corroborated by supporting evidence gathered from the past, but this evidence constitutes elements of a larger historical pattern that is already understood. Her entire interpretation is bounded by certain meaning-producing, grand narratives of the nineteenth century that are received wisdom from the fields of sociology, political science, epidemiology, and demography. Thus, Lucienne's times, according to Rehnfield, were shaped by figures such as Daumier, Balzac, Napoleon, Talleyrand, King Louis-Philippe, and Guizot. In Rehnfield's hands, therefore, Lucienne becomes a metonymic exemplar of what we already know about nineteenth-century experience as produced by social, economic, and political discourses.

Rehnfield thinks she is producing knowledge that is objective and in the service of advancing understanding through scholarship. She believes she is making available to her readers "the private thoughts of a woman who witnessed a revolution and vanished several years later, an indirect casualty of its aftermath" (1). Ignorant of other potential motivations for her translation, Willa succumbs to the accepted notion of historical research as being a project of discovery, that is, historians find the truths of the past.

For Jane, however, historical truth is not found; it is made. She would agree with Nietzsche's observation about truth in reason in his essay "On Truth and Lies in a Nonmoral Sense." He writes: "When someone hides something behind a bush and looks for it again in the same place and finds it there as well, there is not much to praise in such seeking and finding. Yet this is how matters stand regarding seeking and finding 'truth' within the realm of reason" (PT 85). Historical truths, like all truths according to

Nietzsche, are made through the interpretive act, and Jane's truth emerges from her act of translating the diary as she begins to understand Lucienne's experience in 1848 through her own encounters with the revolutionary movements of the 1960s. Jane sees her own life as a repetition of Crozier's within a radical movement. Both the revolutionaries of 1968 and the *Quarante-huitards* of 1848 fought for social equality but refused to extend equal rights to women within their own groups. The parallels between the two movements cannot be denied. Indeed, the central feminist thrust of the novel hinges on the reader's recognition that if the old French adage "plus ça change, plus c'est la même chose" still holds true, it remains true with respect to the position of women in society in general, and in revolutionary movements in particular, *because* the position of women has been stabilized through social fictions (what Foucault would term discursive practices) taken to be true or natural. Jane's translation of the Crozier diary and the narration of her own experiences—which echo Lucienne's— serve as a genealogical critique aimed at uncovering (or destabilizing) the social fictions that have governed the representation of women's experiences in history.

By offering her own footnotes and translating a portion of the Crozier diary herself, Jane constructs a perspective in opposition to Rehnfield's. First, she employs philological rigor and points out how Rehnfield would often make errors in translation by employing anachronistic expressions. For example, Jane indicates that Rehnfield uses the concept of the picket line before it came into existence (114). Similarly, Rehnfield claims that the 14 Juillet group was making dynamite a full eighteen years before Alfred Nobel invented it (220).

As she continues to study the Rehnfield translation of the Crozier diary, Jane "began to consider what the translator skipped, blanched at and erased, or forgot to include altogether, as if by accident. It's a lacuna the eye ignored because the overall pattern was taken for granted—suddenly the gap stood out and became the whole text, the whole story" (164). In other words, Rehnfield approached the diary with a preconceived "overall pattern," a *grand récit* of sorts, that determined the perspective that emerges from the translation. Rehnfield sought to "enlarge the picture," as Scott would say, but her horizon of interpretive possibilities is limited by the received ideas of narratives of nineteenth-century history. By appealing to the experience of Crozier as a confirmation of the historical narrative, Rehnfield's approach suffers from a fundamental flaw because, as Scott points out, "the project of making experience visible precludes critical examination of the workings of the ideological system itself, its categories of representation. . . . its premises about what these categories mean and how they operate" (778).

Jane's approach toward the diary differs dramatically from Rehnfield's. Language, which Scott calls "the site of history's enactment" (793), serves as Jane's primary field of investigation as she produces her own translation of the Crozier diary. "Translation," Jane correctly observes, "is a filter, there is always some refraction" (171–72). With this in mind, Jane rejects Rehnfield's interpretation and selects her own filter by attending to the particularities of language to articulate her own perspective, a perspective that seeks to enhance, in Nietzschean fashion, the life of her culture.

In her most stunning deviation from the Rehnfield translation—and one that directly challenges Rehnfield's method—Jane reads Lucienne's diary figuratively rather than literally. In an entry dated 5 August 1848, Lucienne describes what she calls her "quarantine" in North Africa (272). Complaining bitterly that Jean de la Tour's "ideas exist and thrive exclusive of female contribution," Lucienne decides that, rather than accept Jean's invitation to meet S., she would prefer to "remain in quarantine." Unlike Rehnfield, who accepts language as being contextualized in an already articulated narrative of the past (i.e., any use of the term quarantine refers to the larger pattern of the nineteenth-century outbreak of tuberculosis), Jane chooses to read the passage figuratively. Jane's Lucienne does not suffer from tuberculosis; rather, she is a victim of the repressive society of North Africa that forbids women to go freely out-of-doors.

Only by dressing as men can she and her friend Pascale see the society that has welcomed Jean de la Tour and the other exiled revolutionaries. In the context of the passages translated by Jane, phrases such as "remain in quarantine" and "I'm treated like a chronic invalid" (269) serve as metaphors to describe what Lucienne felt like when she was denied permission to move freely in North African society. For Jane, Lucienne employs an illness metaphor to describe her personal condition and the chronic ailment of her culture—that is, inequality between the sexes. Jane's figurative reading receives confirmation at the end of the diary when Lucienne shows her conscious use of sickness metaphors by concluding the 13 November entry with the following lines: "Sickness is ensured, I have been exposed to contagion, in this case fear of arrest and prison" (281). The repressive society, not biological disease, triggers Lucienne's play of language. Jane's method of reading the diary figuratively confirms Nietzsche's dicta that all language is "a movable host of metaphors" (PT 84) and that "the world with which we are concerned is false, i.e., is not a fact but a fable and approximation on the basis of a meager sum of observations" (WP ¶ 616).

The Political Is the Personal

In addition to the focus on social history, it is important to consider *L.C.* in light of the specific elements of Nietzsche's pronouncements and examine the Crozier diary with an eye toward the "health of an individual." Such an analysis raises some very interesting questions about the relationship between the two translations and the lives of the writers who produced them. As Esther Allen has noted, Rehnfield and Amme "see and depict [Lucienne] as an image of themselves" (119). It can hardly escape the notice of most readers that Rehnfield, the sickly academic who dies an invalid attended to by a cook, a nurse, and her assistant, depicts Lucienne as a victim of tuberculosis who dies in quarantine; whereas Jane Amme, the 1960s activist who lives in hiding, portrays Lucienne as a feminist pamphleteer who is sequestered by the customs of Algerian society and pursued by the French police.

The tension between these two interpretations of Lucienne's life accounts for some of the major theoretical issues raised by the novel as a whole, issues focused on the concepts of writing, translation, and interpretation. On the very first page of the novel, which consists of Willa's introduction to the journal, the scholar sows doubt in the reader's mind when she wonders "if we can believe what diarists write about themselves" (1). Rehnfield's observation has crossed the minds of most diary readers because a diary by its very nature is predicated on its unique status as a document that expresses the most intimate thoughts of its writer; yet we can never verify the truth of what is being said because such thoughts supposedly have never been expressed to anyone else. In reading any diary, we confront the possibility of self-fashioning as well as self-deception; the diarist may in fact be inventing a self as much as reflecting one. Thus, the act of writing the self in a diary sets up an opposition between the self reflected on in writing and the self that acts in the everyday world. It is precisely this type of dichotomy that Daitch explores in *L.C.* when she considers the two meanings of history (i.e., a series of past events *and* a narrative of past events), which I will return to later.

Rehnfield complicates the picture further by admitting that in her translation she "regularizes" certain passages so as to put them in a "logical narrative sequence" (5). At this point, we reach a second and equally troubling difficulty. Even if we accept the honesty of the writer of the diary, how do we know that we can trust the translator? This is the very issue Jane raises in her comments on Rehnfield's translation. According to Jane, "Dr Rehnfield pressed her passages over the lines" of Lucienne's diary, thereby producing a "blurry palimpsest" (163). Jane asserts that Rehnfield approached her project with certain historical paradigms in mind, that she filtered her interpretation through a type of grand narrative that colored her understanding of Lucienne's words. In the Rehnfield translation, "the overall pattern," Jane writes, "was taken for granted" (164). From Jane's perspective, the reason for this is simple: "Willa believed the fewer keys the better" (165). By accepting certain paradigms, the historian need not trouble herself over contradictory information contained in the journal, instances of ambiguity, or certain fissures or moments of semantic slippage in the text itself. Jane summarizes her critique of the Rehnfield translation by contending that Willa's "prejudices were invasive of her translation and she felt both weighted and compelled by them" (168). Most readers may be persuaded by Jane; after all, Willa obtained the diary from Luc Ferrier, who may or may not have been a rapist and was an arms profiteer and an art smuggler. Willa's association with such a character may raise doubts in some readers' minds about her political sympathies as well as her judgment. By aligning herself with Ferrier, Rehnfield appears to be a part of the status quo; so, for readers who prefer a more progressive politics, the Amme translation has greater appeal.

But does Jane Amme manage to avoid the same trap into which she accuses Rehnfield of having fallen? As William Anthony Nericcio succinctly phrases it: "The only thing that may well make us trust 'Jane' is the way she does not trust Willa" (106). There is nothing to suggest that Jane herself has not altered the journal. Perhaps in her case a phrase she uses to describe Willa's translation technique can be applied to Jane's translation as well: "her framing intrudes into the picture" (163). Indeed, what are we to make of the haunting homologies that we can establish between what Jane describes as her experience in a revolutionary group and Lucienne's in 14 Juillet? One could argue that Jane's friend Win is similar to Jean de La Tour; that Jane's need to "even the score" (252) with her rapist mirrors Lucienne's desire to "even the score" (178) with Jean; that the character Maria Farouk, who only appears in Jane's translation, may have some association with Jane's revolutionary cohort Mary; and that the final tableau of the novel, which has Jane hiding in her apartment with her shades drawn, is inscribed in the Amme translation of the journal, which has Lucienne stating: "I expect to be arrested soon" (281).

By constructing her novel in this manner, Daitch calls every interpretation into question. An aura of suspicion hangs over the novel as a whole and underscores the fundamental ambiguity that surrounds all acts of translation. For in addition to the two competing written translations of the journal, the novel explores the larger question of the translation or transformation of the self, and this emerges most clearly in Lucienne's own reflections on the act of writing. Setting aside for a moment the notion of the two translations of the journal, one can see that no matter which translation one accepts, the journal in both versions records the transformation of a young woman from bourgeois wife to sharp cultural critic. Early on, Lucienne asks the profound question (and this may be the central question of the novel): "How is a book like a life?" She then admits that this is a "riddle whose solution escapes me, a riddle I thought I ought to answer before I sat down to write" (17).

At first blush we might think that the question is backward, that is, that she should ask how a life resembles a book. Lucienne, however, proceeds from the notion that a book, unlike life, is constructed and therefore can only imitate a natural or given state of affairs. In the case of a book or diary that records the specific events of a life, however, an additional dilemma arises. The problem, as Lucienne recognizes, is where to begin. Even if she starts to write in her journal about the activities on that very day (4 January 1847), she still feels "some explanation or introduction is necessary." The Lucienne C. of many years later, she fears, will not remember what these observations are referring to. "It's a question of doubting continuity," she writes (17), and herein lies the key to the riddle that haunts Lucienne and the reader as well. The continuity of a book, from Lucienne's perspective, cannot be disputed: books begin and end, they are completely contained between two covers, and the very notion of their readability is contingent on a semantics that grows out of established syntactical arrangements. For Lucienne, life is somewhat different. The disparate events that make up the actualities of everyday experience appear to have no continuity—they unfold in a random, haphazard pattern. Only individual human consciousness guarantees a flow of continuity, but that consciousness falls prey to doubt, lapses of memory, sensory deceptions, and unacknowledged repressions.

Lucienne's meditation on writing considers some of these difficulties in the following manner: "As far as diary writing and inconsistent memory goes, it's not enough to list a day's actions: packing, boarding, driving, travelling. A life doesn't begin on page 1. This train ride began when we received news of my father's drowning and only my mother and I breathed the truth to each other. History, background information, pattern of cause and effect leading up to the present moment, a cold afternoon, four days after New Year's. Why do I write all this down? To put a present to use?" (17). Lucienne recognizes that the chain of events leading up to her present moment on the train can be traced back to years earlier, when she was a girl and learned of her father's death. The idea here is that there exists a pattern of causes and effects that in the aggregate could lead to a series in infinite regress. Yet she also notes that simply to record a list of activities is insufficient; something other than the act of categorizing must guarantee continuity over time. Lucienne assumes that books, unlike life, begin at the beginning, on page one. But as Flaubert teaches us in *Sentimental Education*, this is not necessarily the case. In the aftermath of current narrative theories of intertextuality offered by Bakhtin, Barthes, Kristeva, and Foucault, we realize that this is not even the norm. Indeed, the book has given way to the notion of the text that consists of an endless chain of signifiers, a continually unfolding semiosis that reveals to us how books, and works of literature specifically, often presumed to be closed and finished products, are in fact open matrices of textual elements culled from other books and other discursive forms.

Lucienne's characterization of the book recalls what Barthes has to say about the work, or *oeuvre*, as opposed to the text. For Barthes, the work is closed; it is "a fragment of a substance," something that "can be held in the hand" ("From Work" 156–57). The text, by contrast, is open, it "is held in language, only exists in the movement of a discourse" ("From Work" 157). The text, unlike the work, is "plural"; it constitutes "an explosion, a dissemination" ("From Work" 159). If the metaphor for the work is "*organism*," the metaphor for the text is *network* ("From Work" 161). In other words, the text is the flow of discourse in a continual state of transformation and flux that is not bounded by any interpretive field or genre.

So the answer to Lucienne's question would be: a book is *not* like a life, but a text is. This is the principal lesson that Lucienne teaches us. Why does she "write all this down?" She realizes that to make sense of her experience, she must make of her life a text; the continuity of experience can only be maintained through textualization, through narrativity. Lucienne does this; her narrative constitutes her experience, and we as readers of the journal can only acknowledge Lucienne as having been real through the text that survives her.

As readers of *L.C.*, we learn that we have nothing but texts—several of them—to work with. In addition to the two translations of the journal itself, the novel is shot through with references to Flaubert and Marx, Proudhon and Saint-Simon, Rosa Luxemburg and Emma Goldman, whose works inform our overall reading and offer us potential keys to our interpretations. "The things we leave behind us, the clues," writes Lucienne when she stumbles across the scattered calling cards of Hippolyte Phébus in the carnage of the barricaded streets of Paris (126). The clues, of course, are linguistic in nature, and what Lucienne teaches us is that experience consists of a textualization of actuality. Without the turn to textualized narrative, we would be left to "list a day's actions," which simply is "not enough."

Of critical importance is the second question Lucienne poses when she wonders if she writes merely to "put the present to use." Such a remark returns us to considerations of Nietzsche's analysis of the truth of history. If, as Nietzsche states, it is possible to write a history that promotes the health of an individual, one can argue that Lucienne's act of writing is an attempt to promote her individual well-being. Clearly, both translations of the journal indicate that she is struggling to forge her own identity in opposition to many of the cultural and social constraints that dominate her life.

One can also argue that the two translations of the Crozier diary constitute an attempt on the part of the two translators to promote their own self-understanding and personal health. Each translator finds in the journal elements of her own life. In writing their translations, Rehnfield and Amme produce a history that uses the past. Each translator configures Lucienne's reflections so as to help make sense of her own experience and the choices she has made. Jane Amme states this quite emphatically when she addresses the reader, saying: "My epilogue is a Book II, a running commentary in the margins of the diary. This space, these margins, Dr Rehnfield would probably claim were hers by virtue of the acts of translating and introducing, but I think she's wrong because Lucienne's story and mine run in tandem, then mine keeps going where hers leaves off" (220).

With remarkable candor, Amme articulates the Nietzschean principle of making effective use of history. Her rejection of Rehnfield's appropriation of interpretive space only highlights her own claim to authority. By asserting that her life parallels Lucienne's and then positing that her life picks up where Lucienne's "leaves off," Amme shows us how we establish continuity through narrativity. The two women historians occupy "this space" and inscribe themselves in "these margins" of the text of another woman who herself is occupying a space on the margins of another text, the text of her time. Amme's declaration indicates how we must use the past to live in the present and project ourselves into the future. We cannot do otherwise. Put differently, what Michel de Certeau says about Freud and the writing of *Moses and Monotheism* can be said of Amme and Rehnfield as well: "The *place* from which Freud writes and the *production of his writing* enter into the text along with the *object* that he is taking up" (312).

Daitch admitted as much in an interview in which she indicated that her "impulse to use history has something to do with storytelling itself, the need to create comparisons. History as a kind of ready-made that can be reinterpreted, misinterpreted, and translated" (McCaffery 80). In the case of the two translators in Daitch's novel, each uses Lucienne's journal as a ready-made to construct the narrative of her own experiences as refracted through the writings of a nineteenth-century woman. This act of appropriation through translation allows each translator to understand her own life in historical terms. Such acts on the part of historians are not unusual. As de Certeau reminds us, "history endlessly finds the present in its object and the past in its practice" (36). In terms of their specific acts of writing, Rehnfield and Amme see themselves as participants in larger historical events. But for the former, the heroic struggle manifests itself against a terminal illness; whereas for the latter, the struggle takes the form of political resistance. Thus, the experience of each translator makes itself manifest through the act of retextualizing already textualized experiences in Lucienne's journal, which itself is composed of antecedent texts.

Perhaps some mention should be made here of the Nietzschean term "health." Clearly, we cannot argue that Willa, who succumbs to an illness, or Jane, who lives on the run, lead physically and psychologically healthy lives (much the same could be said for Nietzsche himself). Rather, the two women craft translations that make it possible for them to accept the fate that has befallen them. Like Nietzsche's Zarathustra, each woman, through the act of translation, says yes to the life she has led—this does not mean such a life is filled with happiness, but joy comes in affirming the tragic condition of life, accepting what we have chosen, and saying yes to that choice. In constructing these translations, Willa and Jane have given voice to their choices and—in a modest, yet important, way—affirmed their individual lives.

The Stories of History

As we have noted, Jane's translation technique rests heavily on exploiting the metaphoric richness of words. But Jane's emphasis on the figurative should not surprise us once we pause and reconsider what Lucienne consistently says throughout the diary—even in the portions of it translated by Rehnfield. The diary opens with Lucienne recalling an eccentric woman named Mlle Pitou, who told a fable about three shepherdesses in perpetual mourning: one longed for the past, one for the present, and one for the future. Lucienne then details a conversation she had many years later, on board a train, with an old woman who reminds her of Mlle Pitou. The old woman relates the story of the railroad bridge that is haunted by the spirits of two women and a man who were mysteriously murdered there during the Reign of Terror. Lucienne sees in the story of the three murder victims the fable of the three shepherdesses. "The bridge murders become travelling spirits," she writes, "and before too many years they are the three desperate shepherdesses" (15).

The story the new Mlle Pitou relates is full of rumors. No one knows the identities of the victims. Consequently, speculation abounds: one of the women came from a wealthy family from the Nord; there was kidnapping involved; she was avoiding an arranged marriage. There were even purported sightings of the victims, before and after their deaths (14). On hearing this, Lucienne reflects meditatively that "one acquires a more complex identity as one ages"; but, in this instance, the "accretions of memory" dissolve, and we are left with "a life gone without record" (15).

From this encounter with the storyteller, Lucienne concludes: "Over the generations the history turns into tales" (15). But is this necessarily the case? Is it not the other way around? The peculiarity of Lucienne's interpretation that history turns into tales stems from her tendency to employ a euhemeristic approach: she seeks a rational explanation of inexplicable things. The enigmatic tale of the three shepherdesses, according to Lucienne, must be a distorted version of the actual deaths of three people. Yet the text of the novel belies such a notion. First, it is Lucienne herself who offers this interpretation; there is no corroborating evidence in the novel to suggest that other people saw a connection between the fable and the crime. Second, the novel itself is structured in such a way that fables *precede* what we might term the historical account of Lucienne's life. Finally, Lucienne herself announces what she is doing by invoking a repeated refrain throughout the novel, the phrase "going backwards."

We first encounter the phrase "going backwards" in the second, italicized introduction written by Willa Rehnfield. In this instance, it constitutes a two-word, one-sentence paragraph that comes on the heels of a
description of the violent protests of the late 1960s. In this context, Willa
could mean that the country was slipping into an earlier form of political
violence that twentieth-century America had supposedly left behind. She
could also mean that she herself—in this reflective, almost diary-like piece
of prose—was signaling that her thoughts were turning to an earlier time
(which in fact occurs—the next paragraph talks of the circumstances
under which she obtained the Crozier diary). Then again, Willa could be
unconsciously expressing what she (and every historian) does when writing historical narratives. Historians quite literally go backward and, in
doing so, they often read back into events what occurs in the present.

This third way of interpreting the "going backwards" phrase receives
greater support when we encounter it in Lucienne's journal. In her first
entry, she writes: "I am on a train travelling south, the illusion is that I'm
being projected forward, an old woman entered my compartment, said
'Let me tell you a story', and I'm taken backward" (18). The paradigmatic
image of the train, symbol of nineteenth-century movement through time,
becomes linked to the idea of narrative that pulls in an opposite direction.
The train takes us forward, toward the future. Narrative pushes us backward, toward the past. This temporal contradiction appears again when
Lucienne describes the train ride she and Jean take as they escape France:
"The motion of the train projected us forward. The train consumed track
the way my eye followed words on a page, one right after another in sequence without skipping. Railroad ties as they passed under us and sentences as I read them were perceived as units of time, the hours of travelling. My seat faced backwards while Jean faced ahead. I wanted to change
places with him but he had fallen asleep" (149). Here, the paradox of narrative temporality receives its fullest expression. As we read forward
through a historical narrative, we are carried backward. There is nothing
particularly remarkable about this observation. We need only recall Kierkegaard's assertion that we live life forward and understand it backward
to realize that such notions have been around for some time. However,
Lucienne's description of the railroad ties in the context of the novel causes
the reader to remember the story that Lucienne had heard of the three
murder victims on her first train ride, a story described in her journal.
Communal fables haunt this description of an actual and rather mundane
occurrence in the life of the narrator and thereby establish *in the mind of*

the reader a link between historical narrative (Lucienne's backward facing position clearly marks her as a historian) and fables as such. The fact that Lucienne claims she "mourn[s] for the present" (15) reinforces the idea that she occupies the historian's position in that she is seeking to make sense of her present experience by coming to grips with rendering it as a historical narrative. The key factor to keep in mind in all of this is that the power and significance of the fable escape Lucienne's understanding, but they do not escape the novel's readers. It is not until Lucienne confronts the power of Delacroix's art that she cognizes the precessive function of fabular form to make sense of the actualities of her day.

It is my contention that by opening her novel about the construction of history through narrative with references to fables, Daitch draws attention to the mythic foundations of all historical discourse. The fable of the three shepherdesses announces the major theme of temporality within the novel as well as the relationship between time and narrative, but it also recalls Hesiod, whom Vico quotes, saying: "we make bold to affirm that he who meditates this Science narrates to himself this ideal eternal history so far as he himself makes it for himself by that proof 'it had, has, and will have to be'" (NS ¶ 349). The idea that we as humans are immersed in time, that we make sense of the phenomenal world through acts of storytelling that themselves are constrained by notions of past, present, and future, takes on a dimension of inevitability in Vico's philosophy of divine Providence. Placed within the context of narrativization, however, the notion of inevitability becomes associated with structuration, that is, the method of narrative figuration will dictate a determinate interpretation. With respect to Daitch's novel, for example, the methodology each translator employs, as we have seen, determines different interpretive possibilities of the Crozier journal.

Daitch's use of fables to begin her novel also underscores one of Vico's most important philosophical insights; namely, "all the histories of the gentiles have their beginnings in fables" (NS ¶ 51). The common stories of the people—which are the source of their common sense, something Vico defines as "judgment without reflection, shared by an entire class, an entire people, an entire nation, or the entire human race" (NS ¶ 142)—constitute expressions of the barbaric wisdom of human experience that record cultural memories as rendered in image-producing language. As Stephen Daniel points out, "cultural memory is not a rational reconstruction of events. It is the communal cognizance of the sensible or figural forms of meaning expressed by and on the surface of poetic language" (136).

L.C. contains these fables so as to remind us of the fabular foundations of human history. According to Daniel: "Fables as such do not *describe* the world, as if the fabular construction were distinct from a meaningfully organized world. Rather they constitute or give origins to the world as meaningful and epistemologically accessible. As the sense-bound narrative expression of the world, fable certifies reality as meaningfully accessible" (153). The two fables at the beginning of *L.C.* make available to us, *as readers* of the novel, the means by which we can discern what Daitch says about the constructions of histories. Of course, the fables are obscure. As Vico points out: "The fables in their origin were true and severe narrations, whence mythos, fable, was defined as vera narratio. But because they were originally for the most part gross, they gradually lost their original meanings, were then altered, subsequently became improbable, after that obscure, then scandalous, and finally incredible" (NS ¶ 814). Even though fables undergo this process, it is possible to make sense of the fables in *L.C.* to some degree. As we have already noted, the fable of the three shepherdesses signals the inescapable temporality that governs all narrative. Similarly, one could argue that the fable of the three murder victims signifies the nature of history as being governed by inexplicable violence. These two fables make it possible for us to understand what is at stake when Lucienne, as well as Willa and Jane, attempt to narrate a history. All three writers must construct their respective tales in accordance with temporal parameters and, at the same time, privilege one period (i.e., mourn for the past, present, or future). Clearly, Lucienne chooses the present—she declares as much (15). But I would argue that Willa mourns for the past and Jane for the future, inasmuch as Willa truly believes she is resurrecting the experience of a woman from the past, and Jane's major concern appears to be to help bring about a revolution that avoids the gender-biased mistakes of the past. All three writers must also contend with the violence of history, and each confronts this actuality in her own way—Lucienne by rendering the raw sensuality of the streets, Willa by offering place-names and elliptical comments, Jane by providing analytical descriptions of confrontations between students and the California National Guard. Thus, the fables of the novel provide us with the narrative foundation on which Daitch builds her multilayered text.

We should also recognize that when Lucienne observes that the "Mademoiselle Pitous of the world . . . carry on the private history of each department of France" (15), she signals the traditionally established dichotomy of private and public history, wherein the former is either marginalized (e.g., everyone remembers the Reign of Terror, but no one knows the truth about these three people) or made to serve as a distorting lens such that we never really gain access to the actualities of the past that are themselves not fully explained away by the larger, public historical narratives. The Pitou vignettes announce a central theme of the novel: the private history of Lucienne will be related to the larger story of the events of 1848; and, depending on what perspective (or translation) one adopts, Lucienne's private history will either confirm the larger narrative of history or critique and contradict it.

By declaring her preference for mourning for the present, Lucienne expresses not only her concern for living in the here and now but also her interest in what Nietzsche terms the formation of values. Nowhere is this more clearly expressed than in the diary passages that reflect on or describe certain art and artists. As we shall see, Lucienne—largely through her exposure to the powerful images of art, particularly the art of Eugène Delacroix—learns how history and our understanding of historical actualities founds itself on the fabular and mythic dimensions of culture.

Art as the Means of Interpretation

As her diary repeatedly indicates, Lucienne views the interpretive schemes adopted by artists with grave suspicion because what informs those interpretations is never fully articulated. "I'm not impressed by mirrors of nature," Lucienne writes (24). The typical painting of still life does not reveal a truth; rather, it presents what is always already known. Such re-presentations of the given reproduce already accepted descriptions of the real and confirm an ontology predicated on an unacknowledged epistemology. The focus of such art is on a state of being rather than a moment of becoming. It is little wonder, then, that the French refer to still life as *la nature morte*. As viewers of such art, we already know what we are looking at; our preconceptions are confirmed, the interpretation foreclosed. These so-called mirrors of nature depict the world as having reached a final state. But, as Nietzsche argues, the world "does not aim at a final state" (WP ¶ 708); rather, the world is in a state of becoming.

Lucienne's interest in becoming rather than being attracts her to the work of Delacroix. When she first sees his painting of a Turk about to spear a leopard, she is struck by the lack of resolution in the scene. The action is suspended; the Turk may kill the leopard or the cunning animal may in fact kill the Turk. In her first attempts to interpret the canvas, Lucienne calls on her familiarity with depictions of St. George and the dragon. Her initial reflex is to superimpose an already articulated Western narrative similar to, but not identical with, the one she encounters. This method of interpretation, however, does not work. "St George is the historic victor," she writes, "but with regard to the little Turk it's not clear" (24). In what ultimately can be construed as an Orientalist perspective, Lucienne nevertheless sees in Delacroix's canvas a supratemporal moment that paradoxically captures a state of becoming; no prior narrative can offer the viewer an interpretive grid because the scene Delacroix presents is in flux, whereas the interpretive paradigm of St. George is self-contained, closed off, or—in Lucienne's words— "historic." The image of the Turk is mythic; it lies outside of time and provides a paradigmatic image of the human condition in time. It is precisely from just such actual human endeavors performed by ordinary people that the singular moment of St. George becomes commemorated *in history*. In countless hunts antedating St. George's encounter with the dragon, men slew what were often purported to be fantastic creatures. It is only later that St. George became absorbed into history and the legend of the slain dragon achieved its fame. The mythic encounter of man and beast, however, preceded the legend of St. George. Thus, the meditation on the relation of myth and history is contained in this image of St. George. As described in Daitch's novel, we see the mythic element of the Delacroix painting resisting Lucienne's interpretive strategy of reading history back into myth or fable; and, for the first time, Lucienne begins to see how so-called reality—as commemorated in history—grows out of mythic foundations. It is at this point that she begins to admire the power of Delacroix's art.

Lucienne's preference for Delacroix's approach receives confirmation when she views the work of Rémy Gommereux, a practicing "new realist." Gommereux claims his realism is "all inclusive." But, as Lucienne points out: "His realism isn't simply an all-inclusive mirror. There are schemes of elimination, the encyclopaedic impulse is often only a glib repetition of ideas that are in the Parisian air" (86). Put simply, Gommereux leaves things out; he embellishes his paintings with received ideas. His documentary impulse and his obsession with drawing never fill the lacunae inherent in his representations of the real world. It is no accident that his name, Gommereux, contains the word for eraser (*gomme*).

History as Erasure

Gommereux's name also contains a clue about one of the major
themes of *L.C.*: the notion of erasure. In fact, the word "erase" in its various verbal forms appears repeatedly throughout the novel. We first encounter it early on when Lucienne discusses the tale of the three corpses.
In her journal, Lucienne records what the Mlle Pitou on the train was
saying about the dead bodies. This Mlle Pitou quotes a curé who told her
about the incident and remarked that it "'makes you wonder how people
can live their lives, then be completely erased from the face of the earth
as if they were no more than a smudge on a page'" (15). This early journal
entry contains several of the key thematic elements of the novel. Initially, we recognize in the fable of the three victims the focus on the mythic
origins of history, origins that, as the quotation suggests, are under erasure. Additionally, the curé underscores one of *L.C.*'s recurrent ideas: the
textualization of the actualities of the past. Finally, there is the complex
nature of this recorded speech. The statement about erasure appears in a
translation of a journal whose original text no longer exists. In the (translated) journal, Lucienne recounts from memory the statement of a woman who herself is recalling what someone else said to her much earlier.
Thus, the actual speech is at several removes from us as readers, and this
practice of narrative distancing enacts what takes place in the construction of most historical narratives. The actual people of the past have been
erased by time; only signs of their existence remain, and very often these
signs are interpreted for us by others whose comments we, as historians
and researchers, must take into account. The past, then, can only be perceived through a glass darkly, and the reflective surface of this glass consists of the layers of recorded, ultimately written, speech.

Textualization of the actualities of the past achieves one of its most striking expressions when we next encounter the concept of erasure. After
witnessing the street battles during the February days of the 1848 revolution, Lucienne writes: "The barricades are now abandoned, the felled trees
and sentry boxes are slippery and bright in the rain. Not indelible, the trail
of blood will wash away by tomorrow. Some future history book can map
the sites of street fighting in a more permanent ink" (128–29). Although
the word erase does not appear here, the concept of erasure dominates
Lucienne's remarks. The striking image of the "not indelible" blood replaced by permanent ink confirms that the ephemeral lives of humans only

endure in language. The artifacts—barricades, weapons, clothing, furniture, calling cards, vestiges of lives lived—are literal metonyms of the embodied experience of the past. We cannot, like Odysseus, pour out blood and hear the voices of the dead; we can only spill ink.

Ink, the blood of consciousness, persists in time. The experience of a person such as Lucienne consists of the language she uses and abuses as she writes in her journal to make sense of the phenomenal world that surrounds her. It is through her language that we can gain access to her as an individual *in time*. Focusing on Lucienne's expressions as part of a larger pattern of discourse in a given period, as does Willa Rehnfield, only gives us access to her *in history*. Amme raises this very point when she writes: "It never occurred to either Luc Ferrier or Willa that what was valuable about the Lucienne Crozier diary was the woman who wrote it, not the fact that it documented her affair with a man whose paintings were worth enough to contribute to a corporate business venture 120 years later" (185–86). Yet, even if we escape the contextualizing power of grand narrative constructions, we fall prey to our own language and interpretive paradigms, which are embedded in their own significatory schemata. Even as we write the past, the act of articulation necessarily enacts an erasure. Willa, Jane, and even Lucienne herself erase part of the assemblage of disparate phenomena (what some might term "the whole story") so as to have a story to tell. Michel de Certeau describes the process historians go through (and these three "historians" are no exception) as one of "breakage," the scission between the present act of interpretation and the object of the past as organized in a series of representations. "In the past from which it is distinguished," writes de Certeau, "[the 'labor designated by breakage'] promotes a selection between what can be *understood* and what must be *forgotten* in order to obtain the representation of the present intelligibility" (4). In other words, without erasure, there would be no history; we would be left with random description, non sequiturs, and uninterpretable utterances, a form of history that, in Barthes's words, does not "signify," a discourse "limited to a pure unstructured series of notations" ("Discourse" 137). Ultimately, we as readers engage in erasure as well, as we occlude certain elements of the text in the hopes of producing a coherent interpretation. No interpretation can achieve complete totalization or exhaustion. The question of erasure is fundamental because what is erased will determine what is produced. In Jane's estimation, Willa erases Lucienne and discovers what was already known about society in this period of history. Jane, by contrast, erases the metanarrative and discovers a Lucienne who helps her cope with late twentieth-century society.

The tension that exists between history and actuality receives its clearest expression in Lucienne's own journal, where she describes how she returned to reading books in late August 1848. She briefly discusses Germaine Necker de Staël's book on Napoleon Bonaparte and then makes the following comment: "A luxury: maintaining the advantage of reviewing history rather than facing it" (208). In a moment of respite from the confusions of revolutionary activity, she immerses herself in the reflections of a woman who herself witnessed revolutionary and repressive times. Lucienne recognizes that daily activities are chaotic—much like the scenes she tries to describe in all their immediacy when she moves through the barricaded streets of Paris. Written history organizes these actualities and makes a narrative of them. However, history in no way reproduces the actualities of the past—these phenomena remain forever ephemeral, like the blood washed away in the street.

The idea of erasure occurs several more times in the novel. Jean de la Tour twice declares that the impending revolution will erase history (132, 145). This idea becomes transformed when Jane mocks Win for thinking he has a monopoly on believing in the capability of "rectifying history's erasures" (248). When Jean mentions the idea of erasure, he speaks the language of revolution. The violent overturning of the social order will utterly destroy what had once been taken to be natural. In this regard, the old order is false and illegitimate because it was created by men; but, through the revolution, it will be replaced by what is truly natural, a social order based on inherent rights. Thus, the revolutionaries arrogate to themselves the mantle of natural authority. This affinity with nature achieves full expression when Lucienne writes that Jean is "convinced social change will only take place in Europe after earthquakes, cataclysms and revolutions enough to erase all of it" (145). The association of erasure with nature receives its most direct expression when Lucienne offers her description of the simoon, the sandstorm of the African desert that is capable of "erasing roads as if there had never been any" (203). Revolution in the mid-nineteenth century, it seems, appears to those promulgating it as a natural process that performs a necessary and inevitable erasure of the social script of inequality. By the time we reach the late twentieth century, however, the idea of erasure and its relationship to revolution undergoes a profound change.

Jane's barbed retort to Win about his arrogance in thinking he alone has a monopoly on trying to rectify "history's erasures" indicates that the revolutionaries of 1968 do not so much see themselves as agents in a natural process of erasing the social order as did the revolutionaries of 1848; rather, they conceive of themselves as agents attempting to make amends for what history has erased of the past. Like Walter Benjamin, the Berkeley students see history as the story of the victors, a document of barbarism. The transformation over the 120-year period signals a shift from the belief in the instrumentalism of language promulgating the natural and inevitable erasure of socially constructed institutions to the conviction about the irreducible nature of language and the necessity for resurrecting obscured or lost counternarratives to the regulative narrative of history. In Jane's time, the revolutionary does not so much serve nature as she serves a story in opposition to the dominant story of her culture, society, and time.

Jane speaks explicitly about the erasures of history when she criticizes the Rehnfield translation. As we have already noted, Jane "began to consider what the translator skipped, blanched at and erased, or forgot to include altogether, as if by accident" (164). Willa's preoccupation with compartmentalizing Lucienne's life in the larger context of nineteenth-century French history, just as she compartmentalized her notes and marginalia in her files, leads Jane to remark that "in the path of her drive to label and annotate lay the fear of discovery" (165).

All of these references to erasure in the novel raise questions about the relationship between history and memory, between history and textuality. With regard to erasure and memory in history, Daitch's novel adds to our understanding of Nietzsche's description of how to produce histories that serve life. Early on, we noted how Nietzsche argues that history should be crafted in such a way to serve the health of an individual, a culture, or a people. The quotation in its entirety reads as follows: "This, precisely, is the proposition the reader is invited to meditate upon: *the unhistorical and the historical are necessary in equal measure for the health of an individual, of a people and of a culture*" (UM 63). One cannot simply invoke a historical sensibility and hope to serve life; one must also know what should not be included. For Nietzsche, "*there is a degree of sleeplessness, of rumination, of the historical sense, which is harmful and ultimately fatal to the living thing*" (UM 62). Put simply, some things are worth forgetting. To write and carefully construct the life-promoting historical narrative is only half of the process, according to Nietzsche; the other half consists of forgetting, of leaving out, of *erasing*, as Daitch might say, that which is not life-promoting.

The unhistorical sense, a notion that at times can be obscure in Nietzsche's essay, achieves greater clarity in Daitch's novel when we consider memory in a textual sense. If, as I have argued, the genealogical method helps to produce those counternarratives that help rectify "history's erasures," this process also will require us to forget certain aspects of the narrative we seek to overturn. Ultimately, if the counternarrative prevails, the former hegemonic narrative may become forgotten entirely. To consider the Nietzschean project for a moment, if Western culture in general were to follow Nietzsche's philosophy on the issue of good and evil, it would go beyond such concepts, and the day would come when we would forget such notions as good and evil. Thus, the unhistorical, although closely aligned with a basic animality (as Nietzsche argues), can also be seen as the conscious act of the person who must craft history and so choose not to write about a certain subject. This act of forgetting becomes the unhistorical in that it remains the unwritten.

With respect to the art of historiography, *L.C.* indicates that those historians who seek to reproduce the past through narrativization in hopes of reproducing the real (i.e., adopting a type of literary realism) are simply deluded. Long ago, Barthes reminded us that realism is really an "effect" produced through the careful selection and presentation of verbal expressions that conjure, through mimesis, the world as we already see it. "In 'objective' history, the 'real' is never anything but an unformulated signified sheltered behind the apparent omnipotence of the referent," writes Barthes ("Discourse" 139). Such a realism tells us nothing new, it only repeats what we accept as being true. Thus, realism, ostensibly an unmediated form of mimetic reproduction, does in fact emerge from a mediative process—the realist text grows out of other texts that offer up to us schemes we already understand.

Within the novel itself, Lucienne perceives the limits of the so-called realist technique. Lucienne's recognition that a realist technique based on former narratives does not offer valid representations of the real world parallels Jane's rejection of Rehnfield's interpretive approach, one that could be characterized as both realistic and dependent on former narrative truths. Nietzsche himself characterized all attempts at capturing the real world as the work of "we spiders" who sit in our net. "Whatever we may catch in it," writes Nietzsche, "we catch nothing at all except that which allows itself to be caught in precisely *our* net" (D 73). From Jane's perspective, Rehnfield spins a web of meanings that catches what she is looking for: an individual who embodies the grand narratives of the nineteenth century. But the key to Jane's response to Rehnfield lies in her understanding of Lucienne's recognition of the truth of art, the supratemporal art of Delacroix.

Just as Lucienne looked on the Delacroix painting and engaged in a creative interpretive act by rejecting the St. George paradigm offered by her culture, Jane rejects the interpretive grids offered by established history and chooses to read the Crozier diary creatively. Through her translation, Jane creates her own past and establishes the continuity between Lucienne's experience and her own. Her goal is to examine the ideologies that determined her experience. Unlike Rehnfield, who simply admits that the *Quarante-huitards* were sexists and leaves it at that, Jane wants to uncover what assumptions led to the repeated failure of revolutionary movements. For Jane, the answer is quite clear: to this day, so-called revolutionaries adhere to ideologies that conceive of women as being subservient. The attitude of the men of 1848, an attitude that led to the immediate rejection of Pascale's ideas during clandestine meetings in Paris, repeats itself in 1968 when Win, a Berkeley radical, regards Jane as a submissive sex partner, a nursemaid, and a typist. In other words, both sets of revolutionaries failed to see gender as a power relation.

When we compare Amme to Rehnfield, we see that she, too, attempts to promote the health of her culture as well as her own health. As I noted earlier, both historians inscribed themselves in their respective translations and thereby came to terms with how best to promote their individual lives through interpreting their experiences via the translation of the Crozier diary. In addition, I acknowledged that Rehnfield assumes she is serving her culture by offering an objective history of the experience of a woman who lived in the past. Similarly, Amme promotes the life of her culture by offering a critique of the past. In short, one can say that Rehnfield's translation preserves the status quo while Amme's critiques it. Another way of saying this is that Rehnfield practices a form of antiquarian history (in the Nietzschean sense), whereas Amme produces a critical history.

The Discourse of History

Through her juxtaposition of two perspectives on history within the boundaries of a novel and through her emphasis on the importance of philological attentiveness, Daitch creates an interpretation of history that simultaneously shows us how historical reality results from contradictory discursive production processes. Thus, the two temporal planes (1848 and 1968) under scrutiny in Daitch's novel are represented in two ways. They are traditionally represented through already understood historical narratives that reduce the semantic possibilities available to readers of historical texts. As we have seen, when Rehnfield limits her understanding of "quarantine" to the semantic field of illness, she thereby occludes the tropic potential of the word. Similarly, the journalistic explanation of the bombing of Luc Ferrier appeals to the grand antiwar narrative that obscures the story of Jane's rape. Yet, in its presentation of counternarratives, the second manner of historical representation, Daitch's novel underscores the necessity of a philological rigor, one that does not so much seek to unmask the truth or the essence of history as it does to contribute to life. "La philologie rigoureuse," writes Sarah Kofman, "dévoile l'interprétation comme interprétation au nom d'une autre interprétation qui ne prétend pas saisir l'essence l'être mais qui donne une lecture révélatrice d'une volonté affirmative de la vie" (*Nietzsche* 204; rigorous [strict] philology reveals interpretation as interpretation in the name of another interpretation which does not claim to grasp the essence of being but which yields a revelatory reading of an affirmative will to life). Daitch's novel leaves us with nothing *but* interpretations; we do not read the original French journals of Lucienne. We do not even know if such manuscripts exist in our (the reader's) world. Nor would it matter.

For Daitch's novel suggests that when it comes to history, there are only interpretations. Like Nietzsche, she believes that we must choose interpretations that contribute to the health of our culture. Daitch also confirms Scott's claim that the literary is a key locus for understanding historical reality. *L.C.* performs the very analysis of the "discursive productions of social and political reality" that Scott calls for and shows them to be "complex, contradictory processes" (794).

L.C. demands a reevaluation of revolutionary politics and points to a reconceptualization of such politics to bring about substantive change. The title itself signals this call to the reader. The homonymous reading of the title in French would signify, in addition to the letters of the alphabet, a terse declarative sentence: "Elle sait" (she knows). But herein lies the irreducible ambiguity of the novel and, concomitantly, history, particularly history based on experience. For in truth who is "she"? And in fact, what does she "know"? The answers to these questions can only emerge through the interpretive act, one that involves the interplay of philological rigor and perspectival free play even as it acknowledges that such acts are always contested and always political.

One could say that "she knows" some of the principal lessons Vico has taught us. *L.C.* demonstrates what Stephen Daniel claims to be one of Vico's greatest insights. For Daniel, Vico teaches us that "events cannot be either true or false; truth and falsity are reserved for the rational constructions of history. To make history, therefore, is to apply principles of interpretation to events that are assumed to have occurred because they are already found in commonplaces (topoi) of the community" (136). Clearly *L.C.*, through its very construction, compels its readers to apply "principles of interpretation" to events found in the commonplaces of the Eurocentric community. In addition, one can argue that Daitch's novel provides readers with a stunning example of the Vichian notion of *ingenium*, which Daniel characterizes as "the possibility of novel figuration inherent in, and on the surface of, human language" (140). Daitch's multilayered text, which interpenetrates temporal planes even as it imbricates narrative elements, provides us with a superb example of how memory as *ingegno* makes new historical meaning and understanding possible. In this regard, Daniel once again provides us with a useful explanation. "Ingenium," he writes, "does not cut things apart: rather it cuts through the artificial rational divisions that separate topics. In short, ingenuity concerns itself less with the restrictions of truth (which assumes rational, critical discrimination) than with the presumption of the unity and harmony throughout nature, which permits the ingenious person to bring together things that, 'to those lacking this faculty, seemed to have no relation to one another at all'" (148). The passage quoted here, which is taken from Vico's "Polemiche," points to one of the key features of Daitch's technique. The "presumption of unity" that informs *L.C.* makes it possible for us to bring together the disparate elements of the text and make a history that holds together the narratives of three women in such a way that we better understand the past.

A second way of interpreting "elle sait" returns us to Nietzsche. In *Beyond Good and Evil,* Nietzsche discusses the danger of grammatical habits. In a famous passage, he argues that "it is a falsification of the facts of the case to say that the subject 'I' is the condition of the predicate 'think.' *It* thinks; but that this 'it' is precisely the famous old 'ego' is, to put it mildly, only a supposition, an assertion, and assuredly not an 'immediate certainty'" (BGE 24). Rather than posit agency in the form of a subject, Nietzsche calls for the recognition of the power of language itself to mean. Perhaps this, too, is what *L.C.* teaches us. Following the innovatory move of Monique Wittig, who, in *Les Guérillères*, uses the feminine pronoun "elles" (against standard idiomatic French usage) to indicate "they," we could argue that "elle sait" signifies (following Nietzsche) "it knows." Daitch's novel certainly highlights the metaphoric power of language to yield particular meaning; and, in this case, it is not so much the historians but the language itself that produces these meanings. Both the Vichian and Nietzschean interpretations are possible, and neither is mutually exclusive.

In *L.C.*, Daitch enacts the problematic of producing a history. In this regard, she allows her readers to better understand the definition of history offered by de Certeau, who writes: "I mean by 'history' this practice (a discipline), its result (a discourse), or the relation of the two in the form of a 'production.' To be sure, in current usage 'history' connotes both a science and that which it studies—the explication which is *stated*, and the reality of *what has taken place* or what takes place" (21). Daitch's entire novel inscribes and produces discourses that result from particular interpretive practices. The Rehnfield interpretation grows out of a tradition of the grand historical narrative, whereas the Amme interpretation is a counternarrative in the Foucauldian sense. To her readers, Daitch makes available the process by which history is made. Once again, de Certeau provides the best definition when he contends: "History finally refers to a 'making,' a 'doing,' which is not only its own ('making history'), but also that of the society which specifies a certain scientific production" (47). As we have seen, Rehnfield and Amme reflect particular societies (professional academics for the former, revolutionary activists for the latter) and adhere to the scientific norms of each group (scholarship and revolutionary politics, respectively).

But *L.C.* does even more than this. Offering a slightly different definition of history, de Certeau writes: "The word 'history' vacillates between two poles: the story which is recounted (*Historie*) and what is produced (*Geschichte*). . . . In a word, historians create absences. From these documents . . . they reproduce a past that is taken up by but never reduced to their new discourse" (288). *L.C.* instantiates the notion of an absence created through the vacillation or tension produced by the opposition between a story recounted and a story produced. In what sounds like a variation on the structuralist opposition between *fable* and *récit*, de Certeau reminds us that the actualities of the past will remain beyond our grasp. Through the production of history (*Geschichte*), we recount the story of the past (*Historie*), but between the two lies a gap. In the case of *L.C.*, that gap is Lucienne Crozier herself. We will never know her; and no translation of the journal, not even the journal itself, will give us access to her. The experience of this woman has been (as it must always be) mediated by language, and our (hi)stories about her will be forms of discourse that will be already subject to interpretive schemes.

Like Scott, Daitch acknowledges that no ground exists, least of all experience, on which one can build a history. The somber, some would say ominous, ending of the novel underscores the realization that the interpretive process never reaches a final state, never escapes contestation, and always remains within the field of politics. In some sense, however, Jane Amme fails to understand what de Certeau is quick to point out: "History is not a substitute for social praxis, but its fragile witness and necessary critique" (48). Jane's production of her own translation, in conjunction with her withdrawal from the everyday world, signals either a profound resignation to the hopelessness of promulgating political change or a somewhat smug feeling of having done the only thing we can do (i.e., offer an interpretation). As William Anthony Nericcio sees it: "Were one to translate Daitch's view, there remains something antithetical between analysis and action, history and resistance, the challenge being to produce the analysis that would not restore the status quo. How does one craft a representation that is not always already working to undermine *eventicity*" (111). In response to Nericcio, I would say that perhaps he mistakes Daitch's view for Jane's. Jane has withdrawn from the world and given up on action and resistance. Daitch, however, has produced a novel that may in fact spur readers on to take action. Clearly, Jane's translation offers a critique; but as history, in de Certeau's estimation, it cannot involve social praxis. *L.C.*, however, is not history; it is a novel. As such, it can be seen as a form of praxis that makes available to the imagination new possibilities of the real.

Daitch's novel has much to teach us about the uses and limitations of history. Like Nietzsche, Daitch recognizes that certain types of history are necessary if a culture is to survive. In this regard, Jane's translation offers some hope for interpreting the past so as to affect the future and improve the position of women in society. Like Vico, Daitch discerns the fabular foundations of all history and acknowledges that the truly great interpretive enterprises involve *ingenium*, the capacity to bring together seemingly disparate phenomena to make new configurations of the past and thereby build a future.

With respect to feminist historical practice, *L.C.* articulates a more direct response. When Daitch the novelist has Rehnfield confine sexist behavior to the past, contextualize Crozier's language in the already-given grand narrative of nineteenth-century France, and base her research on documents obtained from a rapist and industrialist who embodies the controlling political power structures of the present age, she presents a damning indictment of contemporary historians—even historians of so-called women's history—who still cling to the notion that historiographic methodology based on evidence obtained through experience reveals the truth. Such an approach, Daitch suggests, is simply misguided and in many ways remains complicitous with the very power structures that perpetuate social inequalities that persist to this day. It is Jane's approach that allows her to *make* her own truth and, in doing so, further life.

Through her novel, Daitch reveals the constitutive discursivity of the real. She allows readers to feel the effects of what Barthes calls the "paradox which governs the entire pertinence of historical discourse (in relation to other types of discourse)." As Barthes notes: "fact never has any but a linguistic existence (as the term of discourse), yet everything happens as if this linguistic existence were merely a pure and simple 'copy' of *another* existence situated in an extra-structural field, the 'real'" ("Discourse" 138). Daitch's fiction recapitulates the figuration of all forms of history and echoes Nietzsche's understanding that we "must organize the chaos within [us] by thinking back to [our] real needs" (UM 123). Daitch, like Scott, refuses to separate experience and language. *L.C.* shows us the conflicts, contradictions, and multiple meanings produced by competing discourses and, in so doing, confirms Scott's notion that "the literary" can "open new possibilities" for analyzing history.

4

Critiquing the Past:
Salman Rushdie's *Midnight's Children*

It is noteworthy that in all languages the greater part of the expressions relating
to inanimate things are formed by metaphor from the human body and its parts
and from the human senses and passions.
—Vico, *The New Science*

This is a parable for each one of us: he must organize the chaos within him by
thinking back to his real needs.
—Nietzsche, *Untimely Meditations*

With the publication of *The Moor's Last Sigh*, many readers breathed
a sigh (of relief) of their own, as if to say: "At last, Rushdie is back." The
years of exile had silenced him, in a way, and no number of short stories,
essays or an allegorical children's book could dissuade readers from believing that in fact the fatwa had worked. But with the *Moor*, Rushdie returned to familiar ground. Here was another "big" novel about India filled
with politics, magic, and wicked parody that so endeared Rushdie to an
English-speaking audience when *Midnight's Children* first appeared in 1980.
Indeed, Aadam Sinai, a character from the 1980 Booker Prize winner, also
appears in *The Moor's Last Sigh*, and the links between the two novels do
not end there. Like its predecessor, the *Moor* focuses on a character who
experiences a miraculous birth—in this case, Moraes Zogoiby is born at
four and a half months, ages twice as fast as normal humans, and possesses
a strange physical defect in the form of a club-like hand. Like *Midnight's
Children*, Rushdie's 1995 novel also focuses on Bombay, describes the complex genealogies of two families, and presents a scathing critique of Indian politicians. An important difference in this last matter appears to be
that, rather than attack politicians directly, as he did the Gandhi family
in *Midnight's Children*, Rushdie chose to disguise his target, much as he
masked the Ayatollah Khomeini in *The Satanic Verses*. Thus, Bal Thackery,
an actual leader in the Shiv Shena Party, appears in the novel in the guise
of Raman Fielding, an extremist ideologue of the Hindu movement.
   Despite the strong similarities between *The Moor's Last Sigh* and *Midnight's Children*, I believe that there exists a significant difference between

them as well. Although both novels present pointed criticisms of contemporary Indian politics, it is *Midnight's Children* that specifically looks at the notion of history and its effects on a nation and various peoples. Critics often chart a trajectory of Rushdie's novels, noting that he moves his foci from India (*Midnight's Children*) to Pakistan (*Shame*) to England (*The Satanic Verses*) and now back to India (*The Moor's Last Sigh*). But of these four major novels, it is *Midnight's Children* that presents Rushdie's most sustained examination of history as a concept, and it is for this reason that I choose to focus my attention on the 1980 novel rather than his more recent or more notorious books.

It is important to recall that Rushdie was not professionally trained in Western philosophy; nor does he quote the philosophical texts of Vico and Nietzsche directly in his novels. His style is much more allusive when it comes to the Western tradition, and that tradition, for Rushdie, is much more literary than it is philosophical. This, of course, may raise a theoretically significant objection in the reader's mind. There exists the problem of using Western philosophy to explicate a novel that owes as much to Eastern traditions as it does to Western ones. In short, I run the risk of being accused of adopting a limiting, Eurocentric interpretive strategy.

To this inevitable criticism I respond that my purpose is neither to champion the traditions of Indian culture nor to trace the many Eastern literary and religious traditions that are contained in Rushdie's writing. This has been admirably done by many critics who are far more knowledgeable about these matters than I. Rather, I see as part of my purpose the necessity to explain Rushdie to a *Western* audience, one that is far more familiar with Nietzsche and possibly Vico than with the Qur'an, the Hadith, the Purana, or even the *Tales from the Thousand and One Nights*. I say this for two reasons. First, in light of the controversy surrounding Rushdie, it is clear that his views and intentions have been misunderstood and misrepresented by readers and commentators in both the East and West. I believe that a reading of Rushdie in the context of Western philosophy would make his intentions for his Western audience quite clear. Second—and to me this is the most significant reason for my approach—Rushdie most often addresses himself to a Western audience. Several readers of *Midnight's Children* have noticed how Rushdie will explain various Indian traditions and allusions in the course of the narrative but will remain silent with respect to allusions to Western traditions. For example, the reader of *Midnight's Children* is told about the god Ganesh but is expected to pick up on all the allusions to *Tristram Shandy*. Rushdie's ideal reader, it seems, is Western educated. It appears that Rushdie hopes to promote change in the mind of the Western reader; he does not want to produce an exotic portrait of India. By reading Rushdie through Nietzsche and Vico, I hope to avoid the aura of exoticism that could result from my attempting to speak for traditions and practices with which I am much less familiar.

Having said all this, I would like to point out a trend in Rushdie criticism that I find most disturbing. Many critics go to great lengths to demonstrate the "Indianness" of Rushdie's writing. Dieter Reimenschneider claims that Rushdie's novel concerns itself with "the crucial question of Indian philosophy and the Indian mind" (196). Similarly, Joseph Swann and Richard Cronin argue that Rushdie's drive to include the whole in his narrative is peculiar to Indian writing. And Ron Shepherd asserts that Rushdie's novel expresses a "characteristically Indian view of the world" (52). Just what each of these critics means by "Indian" is not entirely clear. Nevertheless, to suggest that Rushdie's attempt to express the whole is unique to Indian writing ignores a long and popular tradition of encyclopedic fiction in the West (think of Rabelais, Melville, Joyce, even Pynchon). Furthermore, to talk about an "Indian" view of the world runs counter to Rushdie's own understanding of his native country. "India," he said in an interview, "if it means anything, means plurality" (Brooks 64). Rushdie does not believe in—nor can he articulate—a single "Indian" perspective. It is a plurality of perspectives and cultures that Rushdie seeks to give voice to in his fiction. As Una Chaudhuri has argued, Rushdie is performing a new type of writing—"trans-cultural writing" ("Writing" 35). Unfortunately, there are few if any transcultural readers. Rushdie is far ahead of the majority of his audience, and it remains for us Western readers to learn to read Rushdie first within the context of our own cultural traditions and then within the context of other traditions. Only then will we begin to read him well. I view my approach to reading Rushdie in tandem with Nietzsche and Vico as a positive first step in developing the transcultural expertise that Rushdie's rich and imaginative fiction requires.

Midnight's Children offers its readers a poietic history that presents a counternarrative of the accepted notions of history that, among other things, focuses on the forgotten possibilities of the past. In *Midnight's Children*, Rushdie does not directly refer to Nietzsche and Vico, as does Fuentes in *Terra Nostra*, nor does he use Nietzschean concepts to create an aesthetic object that mirrors the historical period that it represents, as does Tournier in *The Ogre*. Rather, Rushdie constructs an entire counternarrative to the history of modern India that articulates a Nietzschean form of critical history through Vichian metaphoric constructions and imaginative recollection. There does not exist, however, a direct relationship between Rushdie's novel and the writings of Nietzsche and Vico. In the case of Rushdie, the philosophical texts, like Wittgenstein's infamous ladder, will provide me with a means of reaching my goal: to show how human truths are made through the act of narration. I will, for example, use the three historical modes that Nietzsche discusses in his essay on history as a means of arguing that Saleem Sinai, the narrator of the novel, employs a critical mode of historical writing that opposes the antiquarian and the monumental modes of history. In a similar fashion, I adopt a Vichian vocabulary to discuss how Rushdie's novel grows out of the complex interplay of metaphor, memory, and imagination.

The Nietzschean Dimension of *Midnight's Children*

Although we may not be able to find exact quotations from Nietzsche's writings in Rushdie's novel, some of the German philosopher's basic ideas are nonetheless reflected in Rushdie's prose. As Syed Amanuddin observes, "Rushdie's modern world view rests on the premise that both God and tragedy are dead" (43). Such a worldview places Rushdie in perfect accord with Nietzsche. With respect to Nietzsche's writings on history, principally in his essay "On the Uses and Disadvantages of History for Life," the accord between Nietzsche and Rushdie becomes even more noticeable. In the final paragraph of his essay, Nietzsche writes: "This is a parable for each of us: he must organize the chaos within him by thinking back to his real needs" (UM 123). Nietzsche argues that we can make sense of human experience and make that experience useful "for life" only if we organize the disparate and ephemeral events that comprise human experience in accordance with one of three particular modes that he believes serve specific purposes. As Nietzsche conceives of it, the person who "wants to do something great" will appeal to monumental history; the person who wants to preserve tradition will espouse an antiquarian history; and "only he who is oppressed . . . has need of critical history" (UM 72). All three of these approaches allow the practitioner to "organize the chaos," and it is this drive to configure with an eye toward coherence that connects Nietzsche's philosophy with Saleem's narrative in *Midnight's Children*.

In the second paragraph of the novel, Saleem expresses feelings of extreme urgency. "I must work fast," he writes, "faster than Scheherazade, if I am able to end up meaning—yes, meaning—something. I admit it: above all things, I fear absurdity" (4). Saleem's "absurdity" corresponds to Nietzsche's "chaos." Saleem's narrative constitutes the struggle to make meaning in a world bereft of a preestablished transcendental meaning that is revealed to humankind. At the beginning of the sixth chapter, Saleem muses on the notion that if "everything is planned in advance, then we all have meaning, and are spared the terror of knowing ourselves to be random" (89). Yet this is precisely the terror that Saleem and his fellow citizens of the new states of India and Pakistan must face, because on 15 August 1947, the people of this region became de jure members of a community of independent, secular states that derived their raisons d'être from a constructed history of their origins and experiences. The problem for Saleem, and for readers of the novel as well, becomes one of determining not only what story to tell but also how to tell it. In other words, it becomes a problem of form.

The answer, for Saleem, lies in the "chutnification" of history—an approach that, as we shall see, is a type of Nietzschean critical history as expressed through Vichian imaginative principles. At the very close of the novel, Saleem describes this culinary art of the historical chronicle in the following manner: "The art is to change the flavor in degree, but not in kind; and above all . . . to give it shape and form—that is to say, meaning. (I have mentioned my fear of absurdity.)" (549–50). By reminding us, once again, of his fear of absurdity, Saleem confirms the Nietzschean necessity to give form to chaos. In addition, when he later proclaims that his pickles of history "possess the authentic taste of truth" and that "they are, despite everything, acts of love" (550), he echoes Nietzsche's affirmation of the creative element within the historical modes: "for it is only in love, only when shaded by the illusion produced by love, that is to say in the unconditional faith in right and perfection, that man is creative" (UM 95). *Midnight's Children*, however, does not simply echo Nietzschean phrases. Rather, Rushdie explores the various historical modes that Nietzsche describes, and he offers a particular critical version in hopes of serving life in India. Saleem best expresses this when he tells Padma, his audience of one, that he is writing the story for his son Aadam. "I'm telling my story for him," he says to Padma, "so that afterwards . . . he will know" (252–53).

The three modes of history that Nietzsche discusses in "On the Uses and Disadvantages of History for Life"—the antiquarian, the monumental, and the critical—can be used as a means to discuss how Rushdie's novel depicts the struggle between various truths about India's history

that have been constructed by different groups. The three modes roughly correspond to three specific characters that Rushdie creates in *Midnight's Children*. These characters embody many of the traits that Nietzsche assigns to the three historical modes. In Rushdie's fictional world,
William Methwold practices a form of antiquarian history; the Widow
is a proponent of monumental history; Saleem is a critical historian, and
his writing, the narrative that comprises *Midnight's Children*, is a critical
history that only realizes itself completely in the minds of readers of the
novel. For Nietzsche, all three modes are capable of either serving or
thwarting life. Nietzsche firmly believes that moments exist when antiquarian and monumental as well as critical history can further the cause
of life. Nietzsche is at pains to point out, however, that "each of the three
species of history which exist belongs to a certain soil and climate and only
to that: in any other it grows into a devastating weed" (UM 72). In his
novel, Rushdie depicts both the antiquarian and the monumental modes
of history as devastating weeds—monstrous growths that choke out the
living foliage on the Indian subcontinent. Only the third mode, critical
history, appears as having the potential to contribute to life.

William Methwold, the last scion of the Methwold family and propri-
etor of the Methwold Estate, is a practicing antiquarian historian par
excellence. He expresses antiquarian desire, the desire "to preserve for
those who shall come into existence after him the conditions under which
he himself came into existence" (UM 73), most clearly through the perverse conditions under which he sells his enormous estate to Ahmed Sinai, Homi Catrack, the Ibrahims, the Dubashes, the Sabarmatis, and Dr.
Narlikar. "Methwold's Estate," Saleem informs us, "was sold on two conditions: that the houses be bought complete with every last thing in them,
that the entire contents be retained by the new owners; and that the actual transfer should not take place until midnight on August 15th" (109).
By transferring his entire estate, a veritable *Europa intacta*, Methwold preserves and reveres the past and looks back with piety on the Raj.

According to Nietzsche, the antiquarian looks about himself and says,
"Here we lived." "With the aid of this 'we'," writes Nietzsche, "he looks
beyond his own individual transitory existence and feels himself to be the
spirit of his house, his race, his city" (UM 73). Nietzsche continues: "The
antiquarian sense of a man, a community, a whole people, always possesses an extremely restricted field of vision" (UM 74). As Methwold expresses
it to Ahmed Sinai: "You'll admit we weren't all bad: built your roads.
Schools, railway trains, parliamentary system, all worthwhile things"

(109–10). Methwold's "we" is necessarily restrictive; he views the British as the quintessentially civilizing influence on the Indian subcontinent. Methwold is simply unable to acknowledge the existence of any culture other than his own, including one that predates his by several centuries. There is nothing on the estate that would even suggest that anything other than European culture exists. The architecture of the buildings, "durable mansions with red gabled roofs and turret towers in each corner, ivory-white corner towers wearing pointy red-tiled hats," and their very names, "Versailles Villa, Buckingham Villa, Escorial Villa and Sans Souci" (108), signal simultaneously a repudiation of indigenous architectural traditions as well as a desire to superimpose historical European paradigms on the Indian landscape and consciousness. "The history of [the antiquarian's] city," writes Nietzsche, "becomes for him the history of himself; he reads its walls, its towered gate, its rules and regulations, its holidays, like an illuminated diary of his youth and in all this he finds again himself, his force, his industry, his joy, his judgement, his folly and his vices" (UM 73). As Methwold confesses to the incredulous Ahmed Sinai, "you'll permit a departing colonial his little game? We don't have much left to do, we British, except to play our games" (109).

As we have seen, the game that Methwold plays concerns not only objects but names as well. The names of the houses on his estate are, of course, the names of famous European palaces either built at the height of absolute monarchism in Europe or expressive of a nostalgia for that same absolutist power. These names carry a history, an entire tradition of the rights of kings and centralized authority. The preservation of tradition through naming appears most pointedly, however, in Methwold's own name. Saleem indicates that Methwold is named after William Methwold, the East India Company officer who, in 1633, was the first to envision Bombay as a British stronghold and a future city. The word "Methwold" itself signifies the conceptualization of British colonial expansion—a *myth* world, as Uma Parameswaran terms it—of projected desire ("Handcuffed to History" 45). Both things and words, therefore, are at play in Methwold's game, but the words are not enough. When Amina Sinai fears that it will be dangerous to bargain with the "loony" Englishman, Ahmed rebukes her, saying: "Mr. Methwold is a fine man; a person of breeding; a man of honour; I will not have his name . . ." (110). By leaving this utterance unfinished, Rushdie makes its meaning plural. The reader can perceive the utterance as either an incomplete sentence or a declarative statement. In the context of the litany of positive attributes that Ahmed assigns to Methwold, the incomplete sentence suggests that Ahmed will not have Methwold's name impugned. Viewed as a complete sentence, however, the utterance portends *to the reader* that Sinai will not succumb to Methwold's antiquarian strategy— that is, he will reject Methwold's name and, with it, British traditions.

Methwold seeks to preserve the traditions of the British Raj through the very materiality of his estate. His hope is that the objects will affect the new occupants in such a way that the traditions of the past will be preserved. "My notion," he tells Ahmed Sinai, is to "select suitable persons . . . hand everything over absolutely intact: in tiptop working order" (111). Methwold presumably assumes that the order will continue to work long after he has departed.

Methwold adopts a method (and it should not be overlooked that his very name contains the word "method") described in detail in Nietzsche's essay. In his discussion of the antiquarian, Nietzsche describes how the "possession of ancestral goods" changes the antiquarian soul (UM 73). But this "possession" results from a dynamic relation between the antiquarian soul and the revered objects. The ancestral goods "acquire their own dignity and inviolability" because "the preserving and revering soul of the antiquarian man has emigrated into them and there made its home" (UM 73). The emigration of which Nietzsche speaks, therefore, is reciprocal; the antiquarian man imbues the objects with dignity, and these objects, in turn, possess the antiquarian man. The word Nietzsche uses for emigrate, *übersiedeln,* which literally means "to settle over," accurately conveys the very process Methwold and the British have enacted in India. The British names and architecture have *settled over* India, and it is antiquarians such as Methwold who want to ensure that this reciprocal emigration between cultural objects and consciousness continues. Methwold trusts that the material substance of the past that he has revered and preserved with such fetishistic fastidiousness will effect a reciprocal emigration on the new owners. In this case, Methwold's antiquarian ethos would "emigrate" and possess Ahmed Sinai and his compatriots, thereby preserving the imperial traditions of the British Raj. At first, such a tactic seems to work, inasmuch as Saleem admits that "Methwold's estate is changing them" (i.e., the soon-to-be owners). We learn that the Indians "slip effortlessly into their imitation Oxford drawls" (113) when Methwold joins them at cocktail hour. Similarly, we are told that Ahmed's voice changes in the presence of an Englishman; "it has become," Saleem writes, "a hideous mockery of an Oxford drawl" (110). But Methwold's influence will not endure. As Saleem indicates, it is Methwold's presence more than anything else that elicits the imitative response among Ahmed and his friends. Once Methwold leaves the scene, the traditions he hopes will endure slowly crumble to dust.

The second Nietzschean mode of history that Rushdie recreates in his novel is monumental history, a mode that Nietzsche claims responds to the "demand that greatness shall be everlasting" (UM 68). The character in *Midnight's Children* who openly embraces the monumental approach to history is the Widow—Indira Gandhi. The Widow is a member of what Saleem terms "the ruling dynasty of India" (512); she is the daughter of Jawaharlal Nehru, the first Prime Minister of India (1947–64), is herself a Prime Minister (1966–77 and 1980–84), and is the mother of two sons— Sanjay, the leader of the Youth Congress during the "Emergency" (1975– 77) and as such "the second most powerful figure in India" at that time (Wolpert 401); and Rajiv, a future Prime Minister (1984–89). It is Indira who makes herself and her family larger than life.

In an introduction to Tariq Ali's book *An Indian Dynasty: The Story of the Nehru-Gandhi Family*, Rushdie describes how that family "has set about self-mythification with a will" (xv). The will to myth reached its height in 1975, when Indira Gandhi's campaign slogan was "India is Indira and Indira is India," a historical fact Rushdie includes in the pages of his own novel. In *Midnight's Children*, Rushdie constructs a countermyth to the one Indira offered, a countermyth that clearly exposes Indira Gandhi's political maneuvers as being part of a monumentalizing strategy with respect to history.

According to Nietzsche, the past suffers harm when the monumental mode predominates. "Whole segments of [the past] are forgotten, despised and flow away in an uninterrupted colourless flood, and only individual embellished facts rise out of it like islands," writes Nietzsche (UM 71). As Rushdie indicates in his introduction to Ali's book, the island facts that have arisen about the Emergency Indira Gandhi declared in 1975 are those she herself proclaimed to a Western audience that wanted to believe her and "saw that a rehabilitated Mrs Gandhi would be of great use" (*Indian Dynasty* xv). These island facts ignore the suffering and hardship inflicted on those who endured the Emergency. As Inder Malhotra, former correspondent of the *Statesman* and editor of the *Times of India*, points out: "According to Amnesty International, 140,000 Indians were detained without trial in 1975–76" (178). Zareer Masani, a biographer of Indira Gandhi, believes that she resorted "to measures more Draconian than those used by the British Raj" (305). And in the words of the Shah Commission Report on the Emergency: "Thousands were detained and a series of totally illegal and unwarranted actions followed involving untold human misery and suffering" (qtd. in Ali 186). These forgotten segments of history were swept away by the flood of monumentalism that Indira Gandhi released in her quest to retain power. In *Midnight's Children*, Rushdie explicitly pits the monumentalism of the Widow against what we shall perceive to be the critical historicism of Saleem; and, in doing so, Rushdie improves on Nietzsche's own critique of the monumentalist approach.

In his essay "On the Uses and Disadvantages of History for Life," Nietzsche offers an example of the destructive potential of monumental history. In the world of art, argues Nietzsche, inartistic people turn their weapons against "the strong artistic spirits," the people that Nietzsche believes are the only ones able to learn from the history of art and transform what they have learned into a "life-enhancing" practice (UM 71). Unlike Nietzsche, Rushdie does not consign the artist to a special realm where he or she must contend solely with the "monumentalist history of the artists" (71). Rather, Rushdie places the artist in opposition to all historians— political, social, and cultural—as well as art historians. As Rushdie expressed it in a 1983 interview with Una Chaudhuri, artists and politicians are "natural rivals" who "fight for the same territory." Both the writer and the politician seek to make reality "in their own image." In short, said Rushdie, "they're doing the same thing" ("Imaginative" 47). In the context of a history of India, Rushdie perceives an inevitable antagonism between artists (who seek to explore the myriad dimensions of past experience) and politicians (who seek to preserve the historical truth). In *Midnight's Children*, Rushdie represents the conflict between artistic and political rendering of history by focusing on the rivalry between the Widow and Saleem. As Saleem admits: "Mother Indira really had it in for me" (502).

The monumentalism of the Widow appears most forcefully in the descriptions that Saleem offers of her. The Widow first appears in a terrifying dream that Saleem has during a fever. Here she takes the form of a huge, voracious monster who gathers children in her hands, rips them apart, and rolls them into little green balls that she hurls into the night. Saleem describes her as having green and black hair; her "arm is long as death its skin is green the fingernails are long and sharp and black"; and the "children torn in two in Widow hands which rolling rolling halves of children roll them into little balls" (249). The Widow in this guise most closely resembles the goddess Kali the Black, who represents "Death and the Destroyer." In pictures, Kali the Black, "with protruding tongue, garland of skulls and hands holding weapons and severed heads, stands stark naked upon the prostrate body of—her beloved consort Shiva" (Hinnells 52–53). It should be noted that Kali is but one manifestation of the Mother-goddess in Hindu iconography. She is also known as Uma, Durga, Devi, even Parvati (Hinnells 52). To readers of *Midnight's Children,* this should come as somewhat of a shock, inasmuch as the character Parvati saves Saleem and gives birth to Aadam Sinai, a member of the new generation of India's children and a ray of hope for the future. Nevertheless, readers of Rushdie's novel should recognize the complex relationship between myth, history, and politics that he examines in novelistic form.

Through his narrator, Saleem, Rushdie clearly indicates how the Widow, Indira Gandhi, conflates her own image with that of the traditional Mother-goddess. At the same time, however, Rushdie wants to show the consequences of performing just such an act. The Widow, Saleem declares, "was not only Prime Minister of India but also aspired to be Devi, the Mother-goddess in her most terrible aspect, possessor of the shakti of the gods" (522). By seeking possession of the shakti, or spiritual power of the Divine Mother, the Widow enacts a monumentalist strategy through which she constructs what Nietzsche describes as a deceptive analogy that uses "seductive similarities" to inspire "foolhardiness" and "fanaticism" (UM 71). Saleem's characterization might at first seem extreme; surely Indira Gandhi did not conceive of herself literally as a mother-goddess. Irrespective of her own self-perceptions, however, it is clear that she was perceived in this fashion by many Indians. Dom Moraes, for example, in his flattering and apologetic biography of Indira, relates how the famous Indian artist M. F. Husain painted a triptych of her during the Emergency depicting her as "Durga or Kali, the goddess of death and renewal, riding bloodily across India" (224); Inder Malhotra confirms this story (175). The point to be made here is not that Indira Gandhi went about proclaiming herself as Devi the Mother-goddess; rather, her swift and cruel actions during the Emergency were perceived to be analogous with the actions of Devi, and this was a role that "Mother Indira" did not repudiate.

In addition to the analogy to mythic figures, Indira, through her very family lineage, conjures up the greatness of her father Jawaharlal Nehru and her grandfather Motilal. This monumentalist association is so obvious that it is almost always taken for granted. (Citizens of the United States might understand this idea better if they thought about the mystique of the Kennedy family.) Saleem himself quickly summarizes the life of Indira Gandhi at the close of the chapter entitled "A Wedding," and it is assumed that everyone knows about the Nehru clan and its dynastic aura. But what is also indicated in Saleem's biographical sketch—and never omitted in any discussion of Indira Gandhi with which I am familiar—is the disclaimer that Indira is "not related to 'Mahatma' M. K. Gandhi" (501). What is interesting about this repeated refrain in writings about Indira Gandhi is that by denying a familial tie to the Mahatma, she is nevertheless associated with him (if only syntactically) and thereby elevated to his position of importance in the history of India. Thus, taken as a whole: by being Nehru's daughter, Indira embodies the glory of past leadership; by a fortuitous twist, her name, Gandhi, associates her with one of the few truly deified humans in modern times; and finally, by living in a country with the long and deeply rooted traditions of Hindu iconography, she is, in the minds of millions of Indians, linked with the figure of the Mother-goddess. In the hands of a politician, such semiotic power can prove to be a very potent weapon. The appeal to the great figures of the past, as Nietzsche reminds us, implies that "the greatness that once existed was in any event once possible and may be possible again" (UM 69). Indira Gandhi, it seems, knew this quite well. At the conclusion of the Indo-Pakistani War of 1971, she wrote to U.S. President Richard Nixon, saying: "there are moments in history when brooding tragedy and its dark shadows can be lightened by recalling great moments of the past" (Batia 260). A more lucid expression of Nietzsche's concept of the monumental attitude would be difficult to find.

To align the Widow with the monumentalist approach, Rushdie places the greatest emphasis on her association with the Mother-goddess. He does this because the projected supernaturalism of the Widow complements the preternatural powers of Saleem and the Midnight Children's Conference, thus making them natural antagonists. By establishing this mythopoetic sphere of confrontation, Rushdie can explore the reasons for the serious setback of democracy in India and trace this failure to the repeated willingness of the people, as well as the politicians, to adopt a monumentalist approach toward history. Rushdie is able to conduct such an exploration of this phenomenon through the fictional Saleem because he has established a series of correspondences between Saleem and Indira Gandhi herself.

On the occasion of his birth, Saleem receives a letter from Jawaharlal Nehru, in which the prime minister writes: "We shall be watching over your life with the closest attention; it will be, in a sense, the mirror of our own" (143). Late in the novel, Saleem suspects that the Widow might have read the letter that Nehru wrote to him when he was a baby, a letter in which "her own sloganized centrality was denied" (510). Saleem fears that the Widow will view him as a usurper—a person who will displace her from her future position in the pantheon of monumental leaders in history. Nehru's letter marks Saleem in such a way that he cannot escape his destiny. He *is* India; his future is India's future—or at least this is what he has been led to believe.

Letters, it seems, also played a prominent role in the development of Indira Gandhi. Indira and her father conducted a famous correspondence for many years, much of which has been published. Like Saleem, Indira was marked by her father and designated as a special person in India. In a letter written to Indira on her thirteenth birthday, Jawaharlal Nehru wrote:

> Do you remember how fascinated you were when you first read the story of Jeanne d'Arc, and how your ambition was to be something like her? Ordinary men and women are not usually heroic. They think of their daily bread and butter, of their children, of their household worries and the like. But a time comes when a whole people become full of faith for a great cause, and then even simple, ordinary men and women become heroes, and history becomes stirring and epoch making. Great leaders have something in them which inspires a whole people and makes them do great deeds. (Nehru 2)

Three years later, he would write Indira and send her George Bernard Shaw's *Saint Joan*, saying, "the story is a great one and it bears reading and re-reading" (Gandhi 81). As Zareer Masani points out, Nehru's letters were to Indira what those mysterious voices were to Jeanne d'Arc. Masani even relates the anecdote of the young Indira telling her aunt: "someday I am going to lead my people to freedom as Joan of Arc did." This repeated emphasis on the Maid of Orleans, argues Masani, led Indira to develop a St. Joan syndrome (28, 16). Whether or not Indira ever suffered from such a syndrome is beside the point. What is certain is that Nehru relied on a monumental approach to history, instructed his daughter in this fashion, and made it possible for Indira to look to a great figure in the past such as Jeanne d'Arc to accomplish great deeds in the future.

With respect to Rushdie's novel, the importance of the Nehru-Indira Gandhi correspondence cannot be overlooked. For Saleem, the burden of history is too great. On the novel's very first page, Saleem confesses: "I had been mysteriously handcuffed to history, my destinies indissolubly chained to those of my country" (3). Saleem and his conference will fail. But the failure is not Saleem's alone; and it is through a series of eerie echoes and correspondences between Indira and Saleem that Rushdie indicates how the burden of monumentalism in Indian politics leads to a repeated pattern of authoritarianism and subsequent collapse.

I have digressed into the personal history of Indira Gandhi to show more fully the intricate interweavings of fact and fiction (as we ordinarily use those terms) that Rushdie enacts in *Midnight's Children* and through which he demonstrates how the great traditions of the past, when used to measure the present and construct the future, often lead to the problem that Nietzsche foresees for the practicing monumentalist—that is, "the dead bury the living" (UM 72).

The lost opportunity of the Children of Midnight occurs because the monumentalist approach is used by the fledgling, independent Indian government to preserve its hold on power. Rushdie's novel, in part, is an examination of the consequences of choosing such an approach. As Rushdie admitted in an interview: "If *Midnight's Children* had any purpose . . . it was an attempt to say that the thirty-two years between independence and the end of the book didn't add up to very much, that a kind of betrayal had taken place, and that the book was dealing with the nature of that betrayal" (Haffenden 249). One of the main traitors was, of course, Indira Gandhi. In Rushdie's words, she used "the power cult of the mother—of Hindu mother-goddess symbols and allusions—and of the idea of shakti" (Ali xiv) to remain in office. In doing so, she simultaneously destroyed the democratic institutions of independent India and reinforced the notion that the repetitive cycle of destruction and regeneration that obtains in Hindu teaching can also be used to describe modern political processes (something Rushdie returns to in *The Moor's Last Sigh*). This explains why, in the novel, the generation that follows Saleem's Children of Midnight, the generation represented by Aadam Sinai, is symbolically born of the traditional gods—the great figures of the past who are part of the cycle of destruction and regeneration as expressed by the mother-goddess. This also explains why Kali and Parvati, two names for the same goddess, can engage in two distinct activities in the novel. Kali the Widow drains the Children of Midnight of their hope, whereas Parvati gives birth to the next generation. Thus, the cycle of destruction and regeneration, preserved in the monumental traditions of the past, continues in the present when those same traditions are called upon to justify contemporary actions. Saleem refers to this cyclic view of history when he writes: "I remain, today, half-convinced that in that time of accelerated events and diseased hours the past of India rose up to confound her present; the newborn, secular state was being given an awesome reminder of its fabulous antiquity, in which democracy and votes for women were irrelevant . . . so that people were seized with atavistic longings, and forgetting the new myth of freedom reverted to their old ways, their old regionalist loyalties and prejudices" (294).

In an attempt to throw off the burden of cyclical monumentalism, Saleem employs the critical mode of history and writes a counternarrative that expresses the "new myth of freedom." Nietzsche succinctly describes the goal of the critical mode in these words: "It is an attempt to give oneself, as it were *a posteriori*, a past in which one would like to originate in opposition to that in which one did originate" (UM 76). Nietzsche's words aptly describe Saleem's strategy in *Midnight's Children* in that Saleem sets out to narrate the history of India in the form of an autobiography. But Saleem's is no ordinary tale of development from childhood to maturity. Rushdie himself has commented on this aspect of his novel; he originally conceived the novel as a Proustian project of sorts—a search for and recovery of lost time; but, during the course of writing the novel, he discovered that his subject changed and became "the way in which we remake the past to suit our present purposes, using memory as our tool" (*Imaginary* 24). In this regard, Rushdie sees the novel and writing as means to bring about change. Unlike many practitioners of poststructuralist theory, Rushdie firmly believes and has flatly stated: "Books are about things which are outside of books" (Brooks 56). Using language that echoes Fredric Jameson's call for the "invention and projection of a global cognitive mapping" ("Postmodernism" 53), Rushdie asserts that the goal of fiction is to "draw new and better maps of reality and make new languages with which we can understand the world" (*Imaginary* 100). In the essay "Outside the Whale," from which the previous quotation is taken, Rushdie pleads for writers to abandon the current retreat from the political that characterizes so much of their writing today. The reason for this is clear to Rushdie; in a 1984 interview, he complained: "I don't think that there has ever been a time when the truth has been so manipulated, because the weapons of manipulation are now so sophisticated" (Brooks 68). The power of governments to manipulate images and information is so immense and the reservoir of the cultural semiotic so deep that the writer remains one of the few people who can construct an entire narrative in opposition to the unidimensional, simplistic, reductive, slogan-laden messages offered up by governments and free market advertising. Rushdie explained this in an interview recorded by Bandung File and broadcast by the BBC: "One of the things that a writer can do is say: Here is the way in which you're told you're supposed to look at the world, but actually there are also some other ways. . . . One of the reasons for writing, I believe, is to slightly increase the sum of what it's possible to think" (Appignanesi 23). By writing his narrative, Saleem augments the truths we have accepted about India's history, and his very style makes it possible for us to think in new ways.

But just what sort of history does Saleem present? When he writes in *Midnight's Children* that "Europe repeats itself, in India, as farce" (221), he clearly echoes Marx. And when he refers to his narration as a *"Grundrisse"* (354), he raises expectations that his will be an interpretation based on historical materialism. One can further point to the fact that, at a 1983 lecture given at the University of Aarhus in Denmark, Rushdie stated: "If you ask me about my politics, my politics would be broadly speaking Marxist" (*"Midnight's Children* and *Shame"* 17). In *Midnight's Children*, however, Rushdie seeks to distance himself from all established historiographic methods, including the Marxist one. Mary Pereira's belief that her act of switching the baby Saleem with the baby Shiva (the child of poor parents with the child of rich parents) constitutes a revolutionary act that pays homage to her lover Joseph D'Costa may indeed give us a reason to believe that Rushdie and even Saleem have sympathies with Marxist thought, but such an approach will not express the truth that Saleem's narrative hopes to create. As Keith Wilson points out, Rushdie "does not presume a reader who believes that the stock in trade of written history is incontrovertible objective fact that lies beyond the appropriateness of interpretation" (34). Should there be any doubt in the reader's mind, Rushdie dispels this notion through his creation of Saleem's uncle, Hanif Aziz.

After a short period of success in the Bombay film industry, Hanif becomes "the only realistic writer" working in Bombay, and he tries in vain to sell his "story of a pickle-factory created, run and worked in entirely by women" (292). Hanif wants to depict the working conditions in contemporary Indian industry as realistically as possible. His cinematic version of the Condition of the Working Class in Bombay, however, is never accepted as a script, and eventually Hanif succumbs to suicide. Hanif's vision is too limited, too narrow in scope, to interest the film magnates of Bombay. And it is equally too limited for Saleem's purposes, for the realistic-materialist approach can only offer a partial interpretation. Nevertheless, Hanif's approach is included in Saleem's narrative. After all, at the end of the novel, we realize that Saleem works in a pickle factory run by his old ayah, Mary Pereira. The story of the workers is there—but such a story can never take into account the entire sprawling and oftentimes fantastic proportions of Indian history, and it is just such a history, complete with Nietzschean critical dimensions, that Saleem sets out to write.

When Saleem describes his tale as a "web of . . . interweaving genealogies" (495), he indicates the Nietzschean characteristic of his project. Aruna Srivastava, in her article "'The Empire Writes Back': Language and History in *Shame* and *Midnight's Children*," is the first critic to have perceived the Nietzschean and Foucauldian dimensions of Rushdie's project. Her purpose is to show how Mahatma Gandhi's "mythical view of history" is superior to the views of both Nietzsche and Foucault and how all three appear in Saleem's narrative.

Srivastava's understanding of Nietzsche is derived from her reading of Foucault's essay "Nietzsche, Genealogy, History." She connects Rushdie and Nietzsche by reproducing the passage in which Foucault discusses the relation between the body and history, where he asserts that genealogy's task is to "expose a body totally imprinted by history and the process of history's destruction of the body" (148). Foucault goes on to explain that the focus on the descent or emergence of an idea, practice, or value-producing system of oppositions will identify the "accidents" and "errors," the "deviations," and the "faulty calculations" that made themselves manifest during an extended "interaction" characterized by a struggle of forces that enacts the "endlessly repeated play of dominations" (*Language* 146–50).

Foucault's characterization of Nietzsche's views on history, however, rests on his desire to see in Nietzsche's own thought *a progressive continuity* in which the three modes of history discussed in the *Untimely Meditations* become "metamorphosized" into the genealogical method of Nietzsche's treatise on morals. Such a teleological interpretation of Nietzsche's thought appears to me to be antithetical to the very spirit of Nietzsche's perspectival philosophy. I prefer to look at critical history as Nietzsche defined it without recourse to a later perspective he adopted in a work he wrote over a decade after publishing the *Untimely Meditations*.

By far the most fruitful way to argue for a genealogical method in *Midnight's Children* would involve a careful examination of the role played by Mian Abdullah, the founder of the Muslim splinter group that does *not* want an independent Islamic state. Abdullah is murdered and India is partitioned, but the spirit of Abdullah haunts Saleem's entire narrative, and his vision is a lost opportunity, a path India did not pursue. As such, it constitutes one of those critical junctures Nietzsche discusses when he describes how genealogy uncovers those moments from the past that are repressed and forgotten. Unfortunately, Srivastava never discusses Abdullah's role. Instead, she argues that Saleem practices a form of Foucault's notion of "effective history." I, however, believe that Saleem is employing Nietzsche's form of critical history.

We should, therefore, reexamine the very purpose of the critical mode as Nietzsche defines it. The person practicing the critical form of history must, in Nietzsche's words, "employ the strength to break up and dissolve a part of the past" (UM 75); this past must be "condemned" by the critical historian, who "takes the knife to its roots" (UM 76). In addition, as we have already noted, the critical historian tries to choose a past in opposition to the past from which he or she originated.

Saleem, without a doubt, practices the critical mode of history. One past that he seeks to break up and dissolve is the mythico-religious past preserved in Hindu tradition. At one point he writes: "Think of this: history, in my version, entered a new phase on August 15th, 1947—but in another version, that inescapable date is no more than one fleeting instant in the Age of Darkness, Kali-Yuga, in which the cow of mortality has been reduced to standing, teeteringly, on a single leg!" (233). Saleem recognizes that the traditional, religious, cyclical view of history opposes his own version of events in the twentieth century. But, as we have already noted, the Widow uses this tradition as a bulwark against political opponents; and, behind it, she is able to construct an official version based on facts about the Emergency, a version that Saleem also opposes. Thus, Saleem's critical weapon must be turned against a religious traditionalism that posits a repeated pattern of destruction and regeneration and against a modern form of governmental manipulation of the cultural and political semiotic that produces objective truth.

As Nietzsche warns, to exercise the critical mode "is always a dangerous process" (UM 76). Saleem takes the risks implicit in using a critical approach and adopts a strategy whereby he combines the fabulous with the factual. We should be mindful that Saleem describes his narrative as "this source-book, this Hadith or Purana or *Grundrisse*" (354). He arrogates to himself the traditions of Qur'anic revelation and the utterances of the Prophet, ancient Sanskrit legends and lore as well as contemporary historiographic methodology to produce an entire counternarrative that re-jects the sterility of the antiquarian approach of Methwold and exposes the duplicity inherent in the Widow's monumentalism. Perhaps the most striking and dangerous critical practice that Saleem engages in occurs when he cuts up newspaper headlines to send an anonymous note to Commander Sabarmati to inform him about his wife's infidelities. Saleem refers to this practice as the "cutting up [of] history to suit my nefarious purposes" (311). By tearing out portions of the newspaper to construct his own truth, Saleem wields the Nietzschean knife of critical history. Saleem takes the very material of the record of everyday life (i.e., the language of the newspapers) and rearranges it so as to tell a tale about adultery. He does this to communicate (indirectly) with his mother and warn her of the consequences of being unfaithful to her husband. By sending this let-ter, Saleem, like Nietzsche's critical historian, sits in judgment and con-demns the past (in this case his mother's love of her former husband, Nadir Kahn). As a result of this critical exercise, Homi Catrack is killed, Lila Sabarmati wounded, Commander Sabarmati imprisoned, and Sal-eem's mother terrified out of her wits.

As a critical historian, Saleem attempts to give himself a past that con-sists of three elements. First, Saleem's past is one that acknowledges the importance of the traditions of democratic and representative forms of government—one of the few positive British influences in India (Saleem is, after all, the son of Methwold). Second, his past acknowledges the teeming millions of the Indian populace that are forgotten in most histo-ries of India, which prefer to focus on the great figures of history. Third, and most important of all, Saleem's past affirms the creative power of the imagination to construct our reality; it is imagination, specifically meta-phoric construction, that permits us to structure our world and make true narratives, in the Vichian sense of the term.

The past Saleem constructs places great emphasis on the need for his-tory to represent the will and desires of all the people. The true spirit of India, according to Saleem, is embodied in a person such as Mian Abdul-lah, the Hummingbird, founder of the Free Island Convocation, an orga-nization of Muslim splinter groups that opposes the Muslim League. The Muslim League hopes to partition India after independence to obtain a separate Muslim state. In the words of the Rani of Cooch Naheen, the League consists of "landowners with vested interests to protect." "They go like toads," she says, "to the British and form governments for them" (47). The Muslim League, of course, prevails, and Pakistan becomes a sep-

arate state. Even so, in the Hummingbird, Saleem sees the hope of organizing a widely diverse society composed of different religious groups and
social classes. The murder of Mian Abdullah at the hands of Muslim
League assassins marks a lost opportunity; but the hope of a religiously
and socially heterogeneous Indian society reappears in the form of Picture Singh, the snake charmer and leader of the magicians' ghetto, who
"spoke of a socialism which owed nothing to foreign influences" (476).
"Picture Singh," writes Saleem, "would follow in the footsteps of Mian
Abdullah" (477). Just as Fuentes, in *Terra Nostra*, revealed the opportunity lost when the Jews and Muslims were expelled from Spain, so does
Rushdie reveal the unfulfilled possibilities of a heterogeneous society, one
possible future lost when the partition occurred. By focusing on the Hummingbird and Picture Singh, Saleem sees at the originary moment of India the path that was not pursued, and he selects the vision of Mian Abdullah and Picture Singh as possibilities for India's future, a future that
would reject religious factionalism and dynastic rule and embrace a society that respects cultural difference and allows all points of view to be
represented.

In his critical history, Saleem also acknowledges the millions of diverse
groups that make up India's population. He attempts to accomplish this
task by recording the many voices and perspectives that are seldom included in most historical accounts of India. "To understand just one life,
you have to swallow the whole world," he states (126); and, in his writing, Saleem spews out the undigested bits of human experience that are
not absorbed into the body of historical writing. He avoids the historical
approach that places primary emphasis on the great figures. Mahatma
Gandhi, for example, a person one would expect to find in a novel about
the making of modern India, hardly appears at all. Similarly, the members
of the Nehru-Gandhi family appear only briefly and oftentimes in fantas-
tically altered forms. Instead, Saleem records the daily activities of different common people and reproduces their wonderful language and idiosyncratic locutions. One of the most singular commoners is Tai, the
boatman, whose chatter is "fantastic, grandiloquent and ceaseless" (9).
Perhaps the most memorable character of all is Saleem's own grandmoth-
er, the Reverend Mother. Her use of the term "whatsitsname," which she
inserts haphazardly into her speech, makes for some of the most comic
utterances in the entire novel. The many characters in the magicians'
ghetto imbue the city with a carnivalesque atmosphere and point toward
the intermingling of languages and social practices that include both high

and low culture. Similarly, the war in Bangladesh is filtered through the experiences of Ayooba, Shaheed, Farooq, and Saleem—common soldiers who witness the atrocities committed by the Pakistani forces. In each of these instances, the focus is on the common, everyday experience of average people, and it is their experience, in Saleem's estimation, that comprises a true history of India.

Finally, there is the element of the imagination, which is essential to Saleem's critical method. Saleem's account grows out of the voices he hears of the Midnight Children's Conference. The 1,001 children born during India's first hour of independence can all communicate with Saleem telepathically. When he first hears these voices, Saleem compares himself to great figures in both Eastern and Western religions. "Like Musa or Moses, like Muhammad the Penultimate," he writes, "I heard voices on a hill" (192). Years later, he compares himself to scorned prophets: "At every turn I am thwarted; a prophet in the wilderness like Maslama, like ibn Sinan!" (471). By comparing himself with these religious figures from the past, Saleem establishes the homology between heretical expression within the context of sacred writing and heretical writing in the context of historical representation. In other words, just as Moses and Muhammad heard voices that led them to articulate religious interpretations in opposition to the dominant religious practices of their milieux—Egypt and Mecca respectively—Saleem offers us an interpretation that runs counter to accepted notions of historiography. The homology between the sacred and the secular becomes even more acute when we consider Saleem's Muslim background. "God is the supreme Plotter" we read in surah 3:54 of the Qur'an. Saleem, in his own way, becomes a master plotter of history; "the feeling had come upon me that I was somehow creating a world," he writes (207). Saleem tells a tale of human experience, but the truth of his tale emerges not from objective facts but, rather, from the manner in which he configures his story.

Rushdie calls attention to the transition from the sacred to the secular on the second page of his novel. Here, Saleem describes the day his grandfather, Dr. Aadam Aziz, rejected religion. While bowing to Mecca in prayer, Aziz hits his nose on the frozen ground and suffers a nosebleed. At that moment he resolves "never again to kiss earth for any god or man" (4). The consequences of this resolution are enormous; for, as Saleem indicates, this decision "made a hole in him, a vacancy in a vital inner chamber, leaving him vulnerable to women and history" (4). As Rushdie himself has admitted, the "hole" becomes the dominant "leitmotif" of the novel (*"Midnight's Children* and *Shame"* 4). For example, Dr. Aziz is forced to examine the body of Naseem Ghani by looking through a hole in a sheet that is held over her body to preserve her modesty. Dr. Aziz only gets to see bits and pieces of Naseem over time, but this does not prevent him from imagining her as a whole person and eventually marrying her. Whereas Carol Ann Howells views the sheet as a "warning against the narrator's attempts and the reader's desire to discover total meaning" (199), and Keith Wilson sees in the perforated sheet an imaging of Saleem's own attempts to "see the whole picture" from his own "limiting vantage points" (31), I contend that, viewed in the context of the entire novel, the hole relates to the gaps in narration that plague Saleem—and that plague all historians. Just as Dr. Aziz must piece together an image of Naseem, so too must Saleem piece together the entire story of his narrative.

The metaphor of the hole itself serves as the image that relates the loss of religious faith (i.e., the hole in Aadam Aziz) and the gaps, or semantic lacunae, in historical narratives. Saleem's quest to make meaning through narration indicates that the writing and rewriting of history never really end but that the provisional meanings that we make from history necessarily result from a coherence achieved through the configuration of inscripted and imagined materials. The historian, much like Saleem, must fill in the narrative gaps, gaps that had been previously bridged by transcendental meaning supplied by faith.

Every narration, of course, is an interpretation. Yet early on, Saleem declares, "I seem to have found from somewhere the trick of filling in the gaps in my knowledge, so that everything is in my head, down to the last detail" (15). Saleem's "trick" is the trope. Metaphor, the dominant trope of *Midnight's Children*, serves as the cornerstone to Saleem's critical history. "Reality can have metaphorical content," Saleem writes; and, he adds, "that does not make it less real" (240). In fact, readers of the novel recognize that metaphor may, at times, be the only way to express a particular reality. I have already discussed the perforated sheet as the central metaphor of the novel that emblematizes the fragmented nature of all historical narratives. In addition to this, Rushdie figures his history with several other metaphors such that his novel presents history as a performance of narration as opposed to a re-presentation of events that took place in the past. Saleem's truth grows out of a series of metaphors that metamorphose and generate new metaphors, and this verbal mobilization allows Saleem to continue narrating.

Narrating Metaphors: A Vichian Perspective

One of the best examples of what I will call narrating metaphors (something we will see again in Swift's *Waterland*) is the image of the finger as it appears in *Midnight's Children*. When he was an infant, Saleem's crib rested beneath a picture whose focal point was a fisherman's pointing finger. For Saleem, the finger literally pointed to the framed newspaper photo taken at his birth and the letter from Nehru that was hanging on the opposite wall, thus serving as a constant reminder of the burden of history he had to shoulder for being the first child born in independent India. The finger also reminds Saleem of his own index finger, the tip of which was cut off in a school accident. The blood test taken at a hospital following the injury revealed that in fact Saleem was not the biological child of Amina and Ahmed Sinai. In other words, the finger points toward a troubled genealogy. Finally, the finger points beyond the Sinai household, out to the sea. It is "an accusing finger," in Saleem's words, "which obliged us to look at the city's dispossessed" (144). With the finger metaphor, we have the narrative in brief: a tale of the Midnight Child, born of a heterogeneous and richly diverse culture, who tries to give voice to the forgotten folk of history. At the same time, however, the finger also signifies Saleem's own process of fashioning his story, linking his personal catastrophes with the public and political fiascoes of independent India. The finger in the painting points to the personal—Saleem's genealogy— and the public—the dispossessed—and it is by shaping his story that Saleem establishes the relation between the two and expresses the truth of his times.

The finger, therefore, is a metaphor that generates the narrative. Like the hole metaphor, the finger begins as an image and ends by reflecting back on the process of narrating itself. Rushdie does much the same thing with the nose metaphor. Saleem's large nose allows Rushdie to describe the geography of the region as well as make it possible for him to record the various voices of the Indian people (it is Saleem's stuffed sinuses that make his mind a telepathic receiver). In addition, Rushdie extends the metaphor: Saleem becomes a great sniffer and, as such, serves in a Pakistani tracking unit deployed in Bangladesh. Thus, by extending the nose metaphor, Rushdie can investigate a seldom-discussed aspect of recent Indo-Pakistani history, all within the confines of a coherent narrative that refuses to omit those historical events that official histories willfully overlook.

To express his truth, Saleem must continue to narrate; like Scheherazade, he must forestall the silence, and he succeeds in doing so by unfolding his metaphors and following the logic of their figuration. Saleem refers to his narrating process as the chutnification of history—a metaphor Saleem uses to describe how his writing resembles the pickling process. "What is required for chutnification?" asks Saleem. He answers: "eyes . . . which are undeceived by the superficial blandishment of fruit, . . . fingers which, with the featheriest touch, can probe the secret inconstant hearts of green tomatoes; and above all a nose capable of discerning the hidden languages of what-must-be-pickled" (548–49). He describes his "special blends," which include "memories, dreams, ideas." Chutnification involves "a certain alteration, a slight intensification of taste." "The art," he writes, "is to change flavor in degree, but not in kind; and above all . . . to give it shape and form—that is to say meaning," which will produce the "taste of truth" (549–50). Saleem's description of the chutnification process emphasizes the necessity to make truths, truths that are sensed through the body. The eyes, the fingers, and the nose are sensing organs that help shape and form the very story that we narrate to ourselves and declare to be true.

Through his emphasis on metaphor, the body, and the shaping of narrative truths, Rushdie touches on many elements one finds in Vico's philosophy of history. In *The New Science*, for example, Vico points out how humans think through the body and craft metaphors that express the world around them (NS ¶ 405). Wisdom, for Vico's first humans, consisted of a body-based sensibility, a form of thinking that verifies the *verumfactum* principle that he first articulated in his treatise *On the Most Ancient Wisdom of the Italians*. In this treatise, Vico writes: "The true is precisely what is made (*Verum esse ipsum factum*)" (46). Human wisdom is *made*, not discovered or revealed.

Rather than convey the notion that Rushdie somehow confirms Vichian philosophy, I want to adopt a Vichian vocabulary to examine more carefully the process by which Rushdie narrates his historical truth. Just as I earlier employed Nietzsche's three categories of history to examine how Saleem articulates a critical history in opposition to popular and official histories of India, I will now employ certain Vichian concepts to discuss how Rushdie constructs his narrative.

As we have already noted, Vico believes that historical truth, like all human truths, is made. For Vico, "those truths are human truths, the elements of which we shape (*fingamus*) for ourselves, which we contain within ourselves, and which we project ad infinitum (to infinity) through postulates; and when we combine them we make truths that by combining them, we come to know" (MAW 57). Vico's use of the verb *fingo* (to form, shape, fashion) clearly conveys the notion that we as humans make truths by engaging in a wide variety of creative acts. With respect to writing, we fashion our truths in language by giving form to our narratives. Viewed from a Vichian perspective, Saleem *makes* his truth by writing a history based on narrating metaphors that unfold and can be extended to give the narrative shape and, in Saleem's words, "meaning." To give shape to his story, Saleem must rely on memory and imagination, and Vichian philosophy provides the most effective means of describing how these two elements work together in Saleem's chutnified narrative.

Rushdie himself has defined *Midnight's Children* as a "book about the nature of memory" (Chaudhuri, "Imaginative" 40). Saleem confirms this notion when he writes: "Morality, judgment, character . . . it all starts with memory" (253). For Vico, memory becomes a central concept around which he builds *The New Science*. "Memory," writes Vico, "thus has three different aspects: memory when it remembers things, imagination when it alters or imitates them, and invention when it gives them a new turn or puts them into proper arrangement" (NS ¶ 819). Saleem gives his own version of the Vichian concept of threefold memory when he tells Padma: "I told you the truth . . . Memory's truth, because memory has its own special kind. It selects, eliminates, alters, exaggerates, minimizes, glorifies, and vilifies also; but in the end it creates its own reality" (253). Saleem's description of "memory's truth" corresponds to Vico's definition of the threefold memory. Saleem's narrative, in effect, performs the Vichian project of making truth based on memory that cannot but "alter," "imitate," or give a "new turn" to "things" and thereby produce "a coherent version of events." The chutnification of history, therefore, develops from a creative memory that makes the truth of the past.

Consider, for example, the tragicomic episode of Commander Sabarmati and his wife, Lila. Lila Sabarmati is having an affair with Homi Catrack, and Saleem reveals this to Commander Sabarmati to chastise his own mother. Saleem feels that if Lila's infidelities are exposed, his mother will be too frightened to continue her own illicit relationship with Nadir-Qasim. Saleem's scheme works; his letter spurs Sabarmati to kill Homi Catrack and seriously wound Lila. In the trials that follow, Sabarmati goes through an appeal process that eventually leaves his fate in the hands of the president of India. The people of India agonize over Sabarmati's fate. Saleem asks, "is India to give her approval to the rule of law or to the ancient principles of the overriding primacy of heroes? If Rama himself were alive would we send him to prison for slaying the abductor of Sita?" (317). Saleem perceives Sabarmati as a modern-day Rama—the hero of the *Ramayana* who killed Ravana, the abductor of his wife. In his lecture on *Midnight's Children*, Rushdie reminded his audience that the Sabarmati episode was based on the famous Commander Nanavati murder trial of the 1950s. Rushdie was perplexed as to why the entire nation of India was so obsessed with the fate of a military man who had shot his wife's lover; "why," he asked himself, "did it go so deep? And then I had this awful and blasphemous notion which I became convinced was true, which is that the Nanavati case was like a kind of re-staging in the 20th century of the *Ramayana* story." In other words, the *Ramayana* provided the perfect cultural paradigm for many people living in India. "What was happening," Rushdie went on to explain, "was that in the 20th century India was being asked to decide between two definitions of itself. One was . . . the rule of heroes, . . . the other was the rule of law" ("*Midnight's Children* and *Shame*" 12).

At this point, the language that Paul Ricoeur uses to discuss his concept of the threefold mimesis will better explain what Rushdie accomplishes in the Sabarmati episode. Rushdie takes the Nanavati story and *configures* it as part of Saleem's narrative; Nanavati becomes Sabarmati, a friend of the Sinai family. But after further reflection, Rushdie realized that the entire Nanavati scandal was in fact *prefigured* in the cultural myth of the *Ramayana*. The tension produced between the cultural prefiguration and Rushdie's fictional configuration brings about the *refiguration* of the story in the contemporary cultural context of the struggle between heroic and jurisprudential thinking.

Viewed from a Vichian perspective, one could say that, in his own way, Rushdie employs the threefold memory as described by Vico in paragraph 819 of *The New Science*. As an author, Rushdie employs imagination (*fantasia*) in that he alters and imitates the Nanavati case. But the remembrance (*memoria*) of the *Ramayana* in conjunction with the product of Rushdie's *fantasia* yields the invention (*ingegno*) of a new understanding of a particular historical event.

Memory is but one element in Saleem's chutnification process; the second element consists of imagination. Much like Vico, who states that "memory is the same as imagination" (NS ¶ 819), Rushdie suggests that memory and imagination are, by and large, identical. Perhaps the most striking episode that demonstrates the use of what could be called *fantasia* occurs in book 3 of the novel, in which Rushdie describes the Pakistani invasion of East Bengal in 1971.

A typical historical account of the Pakistani invasion of East Pakistan (now Bangladesh) appears in Stanley Wolpert's *New History of India.* According to Wolpert, the conflict grew out of the aftermath of the "first nationwide popular election" held in Pakistan in December 1970. In the election, Mujibur Rahman's Awami League won a clear majority in the East; Ali Bhutto's Pakistan People's Party won a definite majority in the West. In March 1971, the two sides conducted talks to reach some sort of compromise, but on 25 March, Bhutto and Yahya Khan, the outgoing president of Pakistan, broke off the talks. At that point, East Pakistan proclaimed itself Bangladesh; in response, West Pakistani troops positioned in Dacca opened fire on students and unarmed civilians and arrested Mujib. What followed was a campaign of systematic slaughter. By December 1971, ten million refugees had flooded into India, and "guerrilla bands of 'Liberation Forces' (*Mukti Bahini*)," made up of Bengali youths, fought against the Pakistani army. India's pleas with the United Nations to intervene and put an end to the suffering were to no avail; and, after being attacked by Pakistani forces on 3 December, India retaliated, attacked both East and West Pakistan, and liberated Bangladesh when the Pakistanis surrendered on 15 December (Wolpert 386–90).

Wolpert's account of the war omits any mention of the nature of the atrocities committed by the Pakistani army during its nine-month occupation of Bangladesh. To understand better the magnitude of the crimes against humanity that were committed, one has to turn to *The Genesis of Bangladesh,* a book by Subrata Roy Chowdhury, a senior advocate of the Supreme Court of India and High Court of Calcutta. In this book, written shortly after the liberation of Bangladesh, Chowdhury presents a carefully documented case that establishes a three-part structure: first, the legal precedents concerning genocide and war crimes that were expressed during the Nuremberg Trials and by the Geneva Conventions; second, the nature of the crimes committed by Pakistani forces as reported by eyewitnesses; and third, the initial response of the Bangladeshi government and its future obligation to prosecute war criminals.

Chowdhury's book makes for mind-numbing reading. Through his investigation, he establishes that the Pakistani government planned a deliberate genocidal campaign against the Bangladeshi people. He includes numerous eyewitness accounts of mass executions, rape, pillage, internment, and wanton destruction (76–187). All told, during the nine-month occupation, over one *million* Bangladeshis were killed, two million were left homeless, and ten million fled to India (viii). The genocidal campaign carried out in Bangladesh, which Chowdhury compares to the Nazi Holocaust, lies beyond the boundaries of rational explanation. No discussion of the plans of the Pakistani high command or the theory of terror can adequately explain how such acts could be committed by human beings. Similarly, even after reading countless reports of these events, it is difficult to imagine them actually occurring. Chowdhury himself admits: "It defies human imagination to visualize the patterns of killings, ghastly tortures and cruel atrocities stated to have been perpetrated by the Pakistani troops in East Bengal" (105). The magnitude of the horror is so great that there seems to be no means by which to record and thus make historically true those crimes that were committed in Bangladesh.

Just as Tournier expresses the horrors of fascism through the experiences and the consciousness of his protagonist in *The Ogre*, Rushdie's account of the Bangladeshi war is filtered through the experience of Saleem and three fellow trackers in the Pakistani Army. For Rushdie, the imagination *can* express the horror of the indiscriminate violence that was inflicted on the people of Bangladesh, but this imaginative construction must function in a particular way. Like Tournier, Rushdie recognizes that traditional historical methods cannot articulate the truth of extreme and traumatic events. As Saleem says: "Futility of statistics: during 1971, ten million refugees fled across the borders of East Pakistan-Bangladesh into India—but ten million (like all numbers larger than one thousand and one) refuses to be understood" (427). The "truth," in other words, lies beyond statistics; it cannot be articulated through dispassionate prose that feigns objectivity. Rushdie, of course, includes the grisly reportage of atrocities being committed. During the war, we are told of the burning of villages, mass arrests, and mass migrations. At the very end of the conflict, when Saleem enters Dacca, he tells us: "Shaheed and I saw many things which were not true, which were not possible, because our boys would not could not have behaved so badly; we saw men in spectacles with heads like eggs being shot in side-streets, we saw the intelligentsia of the city being massacred by the hundred, but it was not true because it could not have been true" (449). Saleem does provide details that one can find corroborated in the reports included in Chowdhury's book, and his disgust with the official denials offered by the Pakistani government is clearly audible through his sarcastic repetition of those same denials. Nevertheless, the primary method by which Rushdie conveys the truth of wartime experience is through a particular imaginative exercise that resembles Vico's concept of *fantasia.*

At the beginning of the war, Saleem becomes a tracking "dog" for the Pakistani army's Canine Unit for Tracking and Intelligence Activities (CUTIA). He goes by the name of buddha (which in Urdu means old man) and accompanies Ayooba, Shaheed, and Farooq as they ferret out members of the Mukti Bahini. The buddha, however, takes his compatriots south, deep into the heart of the Sundarbans jungle, because "incapable of continuing in the submissive performance of his duty [he] took to his heels and fled" (431).

Rushdie presents the Sundarbans chapter as a hallucinatory journey. Saleem describes the flight into the jungle as a "flight into the safety of dreams" (431). He and his companions "rushed wildly forward into the jungle to escape from the accusing, pain-filled voices of their victims" (437); Ayooba, Shaheed, and Farooq stuff their ears with jungle mud so that they will no longer be haunted by the voices of the dead and dying (438). Desensitized to the violence around them, they stumble on the remains of a Hindu temple and encounter four sari-wrapped women whom they first take to be houris. The four women turn out to be real, or so it seems, and the four men and women live in a timeless world of lovemaking and delight. The men, however, begin to become transparent, and in the end the women are reduced to "a small, blackened, fire-eaten heap of uncrushed bones" (440). Afterward, the four soldiers are swept out of the jungle by a tidal wave and returned to their unit.

The Sundarbans chapter demonstrates Rushdie's masterful use of the imagination. Here, he engages in imaginative exercises that closely resemble the concept of *fantasia* that Vico describes in his discussion of poetic wisdom. In this regard, I believe that Rushdie employs the poetic logic of the imagination that Vico speaks of in that his metaphor of the jungle "is a fable in brief" (NS ¶ 404).

In the novel, Saleem also invokes the imagination when he discusses the "modes of connection" that linked him to history. Saleem conceives of this as "two pairs of opposed adverbs" that produce four modes: actively-literally, passively-literally, actively-metaphorically, and passively-metaphorically (285–86). He offers examples to Padma to explain what he means. Active-literal refers to all actions that Saleem directly effected, such as the way he gave the language marchers a slogan on the day he crashed into columns of marchers on a bicycle he could not steer properly. Passive-metaphorical refers to the "socio-political trends and events" that affected him, such as the manner in which he and the nation grew and matured at the same rapid rate. Passive-literal refers to national events that "had a direct bearing" on the lives of Saleem and his family, such as the time when his father's (and all other Muslims') assets were frozen. Finally, the active-metaphorical "groups together those occasions on which things done by or to [Saleem] were mirrored in the macrocosm of public affairs"; Saleem argues that the blood he lost from his severed finger mirrored the blood spilled during the early years of independence (286).

James Harrison dismisses Saleem's analysis as "Polonius-like in its absurdity" (404), and Ron Shepherd finds Saleem's explanation to be "deliberately nonsensical" (52). I, however, see a method in Saleem's madness, one that relates to Vico's notion of metaphoric construction through acts of the imagination.

History for Saleem must be expressed in language; and, in this repect, Saleem's historical method reflects Vico's theory of representation that, in Mary B. Hesse's words, "is based on the ideal as well as the fictional, on imagination as well as cognition, and on the rhetorical as well as literal and argumentative uses of language" (197). The four opposed elements—active, passive, literal, metaphorical—ordinarily serve as linguistic terms: one can employ the active or passive voice; the language one uses can be unadorned or figurative. By asserting that he was "linked to history" by these linguistic elements, Saleem expresses his method of constructing his plot. At each point in his story, he must invoke one of the modes to connect one event to another. Emplotment, according to Ricoeur, "dynamizes every level of narrative articulation . . . . It is what brings about the transition between narrating and explaining" (*Time and Narrative* 1:168). For Saleem, the tetralogical schema he has devised will allow him to emplot events and construct his historical narrative. In other words, the fourfold scheme represents a particular narrating metaphor; it allows Saleem to continue narrating. Saleem concocts his tetralogical schema to develop other dimensions of his story and give it wholeness.

For Rushdie, metaphor, memory, and imagination serve as the constitutive elements of his novel. Rushdie presents a poietic history in *Midnight's Children* that articulates a Nietzschean form of critical history through Vichian metaphoric constructions. As Ricoeur argues, the relation between narrative and a course of events is metaphorical. "The reader is pointed toward the sort of figure that likens the narrated events to a narrative form that our culture has made us familiar with" (*Time and Nar-*

rative 3:154). By interweaving history and fiction, Rushdie helps us to realize how emplotment in language not only stands for—but also constitutes—historical experience. As Rushdie himself explains it: "We live in ideas. Through images we seek to comprehend our world. And through images we sometimes seek to subjugate and dominate others. But picture making, imagining, can also be a process of celebration, even of liberation. New images can chase out the old" (*Imaginary* 146–47). *Midnight's Children* is Rushdie's attempt to chase out the old images by structuring liberating metaphors and narrating to us the truths that we have made.

5
Redeeming the Past:
Michel Tournier's *Le Roi des Aulnes*

It is impossible for anyone to be at the same time a sublime poet and a sublime metaphysician, for metaphysics abstracts the mind from the senses, and the poetic faculty must submerge the whole mind in the senses; metaphysics soars up to universals, and the poetic faculty must plunge deep into particulars.
—Vico, *The New Science*

History amounts to a compendium of factual immorality.
—Nietzsche, *Untimely Meditations*

Michel Tournier is quite literally a philosopher manqué. Unlike Carlos Fuentes, Susan Daitch, Graham Swift, Mario Vargas Llosa, and others, Tournier began writing novels relatively late in life because his first ambition was to become a philosopher. He describes his unfulfilled aspirations in his intellectual autobiography *Le Vent Paraclet*, noting: "s'il fallait dater la naissance de ma vocation littéraire, on pourrait choisir ce mois de juillet 1949 où dans la cour de la Sorbonne Jean Beaufret m'apprit que mon nom ne figurait pas sur la liste des admissibles du concours d'agrégation" (163; if it were necessary to date the birth of my literary vocation, one would have to choose that month of July 1949 when in the courtyard of the Sorbonne Jean Beaufret informed me that my name did not appear on the list of candidates for the agrégation). Having failed his *agrégation,* Tournier turned to radio broadcasting and translating as a means of securing an income. Philosophy—and with it, his supreme ambition, "faire un grand système métaphysique à la Hegel" (Koster 149)— disappeared from the horizon of possibilities in 1949, only to reappear transformed eighteen years later in the first of a series of novels that would gain him a loyal and enthusiastic readership as well as a stormy critical reception.

In an interview, Tournier admitted that his problem was "trouver un passage entre la philosophie et le roman. Entre la vraie philosophie et le vrai roman (philosophie à la Hegel, roman à la Zola) en rejetant le 'roman philosophique' (Voltaire) qui est faux roman et fausse philosophie" (Brochier 11; to find a path between philosophy and the novel. Between genuine philosophy and the genuine novel [the philosophy of Hegel, the novel of Zola] while systematically rejecting the philosophical novel [Voltaire] which is a false novel and false philosophy). As a novelist, Tournier hoped to furnish his readers with "l'équivalent littéraire de ces sublimes inventions métaphysiques" (the literary equivalent of those sublime metaphysical inventions) such as the Cartesian *cogito*, Leibnitzian monads, and Husserlian phenomenology (*Paraclet* 179). In the course of his apprenticeship as a writer, Tournier discovered what for him would be the solution to his problem. "Le passage de la métaphysique au roman," he writes, "devait m'être fourni par le mythe" (*Paraclet* 188; The passage from metaphysics to the novel was furnished to me by myth).

It would seem, then, that myth, not history, is Tournier's primary concern. Each of his novels grows out of a foundational myth of some sort: *Vendredi* (translated as *Friday*) is a retelling of the Robinson Crusoe myth, *Le Roi des Aulnes* is based on the *Erlkönig* legend, *Les Météores* is informed by myths of twinship, *Gaspard, Melchior, et Balthazar* recounts the legend of the Magi, and *La Goutte d'Or* echoes Andersen's fairy tale "The Snow Queen." In the case of *Le Roi des Aulnes*, however, history plays an equally important role in the construction of the novel. In fact, in this, his most celebrated novel, Tournier goes to the greatest lengths to express the relationship between myth and history.

In *Le Roi des Aulnes* (translated as *The Ogre*), Tournier offers us the story of Abel Tiffauges, a simple automobile mechanic who grows up in 1930s France and ruminates on his early childhood experiences at St. Christopher's Catholic school for boys. Abel becomes obsessed with the memory of his schoolmate Nestor and develops an elaborate hermeneutic based on the concept of *phoria*, the act of carrying. Abel proceeds on a journey that takes him from his garage to a signal unit in the French army, to a German labor camp, to Goering's game reserve at Rominten, to his final destination at Kaltenborn, where he is employed as a recruiter-kidnapper of children for the Hitler Youth indoctrination program. It is only when he meets Ephraim, a Jewish child escaped from Auschwitz, that Abel learns the truth about the regime he serves.

The publication of *The Ogre* earned Tournier the Prix de Goncourt by unanimous vote of the jury, but it also plunged him into a heated controversy. Tournier received harsh criticism from readers who felt he was not only minimizing the culpability of the Nazis and their collaborators but also aestheticizing evil. Tiffauges, according to these critics, is guilty of collaboration; but, they hasten to add, Tournier's novel redeems Abel in the end and thus trivializes the historical facts (i.e., that millions of truly innocent people were murdered and that a great number of individuals made these murders possible). When writers such as Jean Améry and Saul Friedlander criticize Tournier's novel, we as readers feel uneasy and begin to wonder why he would craft an aesthetic object out of such historically volatile material.

To answer this question fairly, one must first acknowledge that any historical material (including information related to the Shoah) can be used in the construction of novels. Second, one must concede that the truths that novels provide are not circumscribed by the limited and limiting horizons of empirical science or historiographic methodologies that aspire to become a similar type of science. I agree with most critics; the notion of redemption is crucial to an understanding of the novel. Many readers feel that, in spite of all his shortcomings and his acts of clear complicity with his Nazi masters, Abel is redeemed in the end. The overt Christian symbolism in the novel persuades critics such as Susan Petit, Judith Ryan, and Josette A. Wisman that Abel is redeemed through an act of grace and that Ephraim is the Christ child. Undeniably, such an interpretation receives abundant textual support. But to accept a strictly Christian reading of *The Ogre* leaves the reader in a rather awkward—if not untenable—position with respect to the Shoah. When Jean Améry quotes the last line of Tournier's novel and writes, "Michel Tournier schrieb ein sowohl politisch als auch ästhetisch gefärhliches Buch" ("Ästhetizismus" 79; Michel Tournier wrote a politically as well as an aesthetically dangerous book), he is correct only if we read the novel as some sort of Christian allegory that enthralls the reader with the horrors of the death camps (appropriating the experience of Jewish suffering in the process) and offers reassurances through salvation offered by Ephraim. However, read philosophically, *The Ogre* appears in a much different light, and the notion of salvation, unmistakably there, is nonetheless radically transformed into a Nietzschean concept of redemption.

In the case of *The Ogre*, readers must be attuned to the fact that Tournier has written a philosophical novel, one that offers a philosophy of history even as it attempts to express an *understanding* (not an explanation) of a specific historical period. Tournier's deep and thorough meditation on fascist consciousness reflects elements of Nietzschean and Vichian philosophy within the body of his novel. Unlike *Terra Nostra*, *The Ogre* does not provide us with an example of how we today might reconfigure the past to shape our future. Rather, *The Ogre* provides us with a negative ex-

ample of the power available to those who recognize the irreducible mythic dimension (myth, as related to *muthos,* meaning structuration or emplotment) of all histories. Tournier employs Nietzschean philosophical
concepts and crafts a totalized aesthetic object—his novel—that expresses
the aestheticized politics of the fascist state. By turning to Paul Ricoeur's
theory of threefold mimesis to explain how Tournier crafts his novel, we
can see how Tournier configures prefigured elements from the past and
brings about a refiguration of ideas about fascism in the minds of his readers. In addition, Tournier adopts what could be viewed as a Vichian strategy by developing his novel from foundational myths and cultural symbolic structures. He also shares with Vico a profound mistrust of the
mathematized, abstract rationalism of the modern era. Both Vico and
Tournier seek wisdom that grows out of the constructed true stories, what
Vico calls *vera narratio,* that we as humans create.

The Ogre is composed of several philosophical components that both
form and inform the novel's structure, which in turn expresses Tournier's particular attitude about the relationship between myth and history.
At the end of his book-length study on the works of Tournier, Colin Davis
remarks: "Tournier's dilemma is his inability to make a definitive choice
between Hegel and Nietzsche, between the warm comfort of synthesis and
the cold wind of scarcity" (206). Unfortunately, after offering this brilliant
philosophical insight, Davis fails to develop it. He suggests that Tournier
has somehow managed to position himself between an older generation
of French scholars who looked to Hegel as a philosophical mentor and a
current generation of French thinkers who see Nietzsche as an intellectual precursor. As to what this might mean or how Hegel and Nietzsche
specifically inhere in each of Tournier's works, Davis has little to say.

Davis does provide some quotations from Tournier's essays in which
Tournier mentions Hegel's name, and Davis does quote the extended passage in *The Ogre* that gives a textbook definition of *Aufhebung:* "Tiffauges
had always thought the fateful significance of each step in his career was
fully attested only if it was not merely surpassed and transcended, but also
preserved in the subsequent stage" (262). However, much more could be
done. For example, one could argue that Tournier's *Ogre* resembles Hegel's *Phenomenology of Spirit,* structurally and thematically.

In terms of structure, both Tiffauges and the Hegelian phenomenal
consciousness travel on the "Highway of Despair"; Abel experiences a slow
evolution from consciousness to self-consciousness like the Hegelian subject of the *Phenomenology.* Abel also resembles the Hegelian subject in that

he proceeds step by step, from the sense-certainty of eating and defecating to the moment of self-consciousness, until he recognizes the true nature of his totalizing worldview. And like the Hegelian subject, Abel preserves the knowledge he has attained at earlier levels of consciousness. Finally, one could even claim that Tournier constructs a dirempted text, one that mirrors the *Phenomenology*'s dirempted consciousness, in that the novel alternates between a first-person and an omniscient third-person narrator.

In addition to the structural correspondences between *The Ogre* and the *Phenomenology*, certain thematic correspondences exist as well. Tournier expresses the theme of lordship and bondage through the myth of St. Christopher, the guiding force of Abel's life. Hegel's concept of *Aufhebung* and Abel's concept of phoria constitute the second thematic link between Tournier's novel and the *Phenomenology*. Daniel Bougnoux first indicated the correspondence between the two concepts in his essay "Des Métaphores à la phorie"; he reminds us that the German verb *aufheben* means not only to preserve and cancel but also to lift or to raise.

Tournier also expresses three other Hegelian themes. The concept of *verkehrte Welt* appears through Abel's writings on malign inversion. The notion of the Unhappy Consciousness, "the consciousness of self as a dual-natured, merely contradictory being" (*Phenomenology* 126), perhaps best describes Abel, particularly after he talks to Ephraim. Even the Hegelian Absolute appears in the final pages of Tournier's novel. At the end of the *Phenomenology*, Hegel discusses the "Calvary of absolute Spirit" (493), where history and the Sense of Knowing are comprehended as one. In the final moments of Tournier's novel, Tiffauges sees the three boys—Hajo, Haro, and Lothar—impaled on the Kaltenborn swords, a scene the narrator describes as "the Golgotha of boys" (368). The image of the impaled children symbolizes the self-destructive nature of self-knowledge attained through service to the historical movement of National Socialism in Germany. Thus, Abel's final act of simultaneously physically sinking and metaphorically rising echoes Hegel's notion of the raising up of the Spirit from the depths.

A complete discussion of the Hegelian elements in *The Ogre* lies beyond the scope of the present work. Nevertheless, I have engaged in this short inventory to emphasize the supreme significance of Davis's insight. As Davis has discerned, Tournier has inscribed *both* Hegelian and Nietzschean philosophy in *The Ogre*. Although Davis does not examine the relation between Nietzsche and Tournier in any detail, I will conduct an analysis of the Nietzschean dimensions of *The Ogre* and then discuss what role the philosophy of Nietzsche plays in Tournier's novelistic expression of a philosophy of history.

Nietzschean Philosophy in *The Ogre*

To discern the Nietzschean features of *The Ogre*, perhaps we must look at the final paragraph of the novel and ask ourselves in all serious-ness if the slowly turning, six-pointed star does not allude to Zarathus-tra's comment that "one must still have the chaos in oneself to be able to give birth to a dancing star" (Z 17). Admittedly, this may appear to be bold speculation; the textual allusions to Nietzsche in the novel are few: Nestor is described as resembling Silenus, the tutor and devoted follower of Di-onysus (20); Nestor compares the architectural unanimity of the boys' choir to "the wild Dionysiac unanimity that rises from a playground" (49); and, at the Louvre, Abel picks up the boy Etienne, and they imitate the pose of a sculpture of a satyr who carries the infant Dionysus on his neck (87). One could even draw a parallel between Abel's recurrent pronounce-ments that he is Nestor, the *Erlkönig*, Rasputin, Don Juan, and Atlas and Nietzsche's disclosure in a letter to Burkhardt that "at bottom I am all the names of history" (qtd. in Haar 34–35). Finally, one could point to the fact that Tournier quotes Nietzsche's lines about the dancing star in *Le Vent Paraclet* (199–200). These fragments, however, are hardly enough to sup-port the claim that *The Ogre* contains a Nietzschean dimension.

Aside from Davis, only Martine Gantrel has noticed a Nietzschean ele-ment to Tournier's novel. She notes a slight similarity between Abel's dis-cussion of benign and malign inversions and Nietzsche's theories on val-ues described in *Genealogy of Morals*, and then she quickly dismisses the importance of such a comparison (283). Nevertheless, it is Tournier him-self who has supplied the most suggestive clue. At the end of a 1971 essay entitled "Comment j'ai construit *Le Roi des Aulnes*," Tournier describes how the French writer Léon Bloy claimed that he, Léon Bloy, was responsible for the sinking of the *Titanic*. Bloy was an outspoken opponent of conspic-uous consumption, and the passengers on the *Titanic* symbolized every-thing he despised. Tournier approves of Bloy's outrageous pronouncements because he sees in them a "mélange de sérieux, de lyrisme, d'humour, de sens cosmique" (melange of the serious, of the lyrical, of humor, of cosmic meaning). This combination of the cosmic and the comic is summed up in Tournier's final line: "Il s'agit de Nietzsche, lorsqu'il écrit: 'Pour accou-

cher d'une étoile qui danse, il faut avoir un chaos en soi'" (89; It is the matter of Nietzsche when he writes: "To give birth to a dancing star one must
have a chaos within oneself"). There is, it seems, some connection between
Abel's final glimpse of the turning star and Nietzsche's Dionysian ecstasies.
To understand this connection better, we must take into account the structure of Tournier's text with an eye toward Nietzsche's own views on aesthetics.

Both Susan Petit and Arlette Bouloumié have argued that *The Ogre* possesses a musical structure. Although Petit stretches credibility when she
claims that Tournier inscribed his name as the major structural thematic
of the novel (much as Bach did in his *Art of the Fugue,* a work Tournier himself discusses in *Le Vent Paraclet*), both she and Bouloumié argue quite con-
vincingly that the novel's structure can best be described as a musical score
and that we, as readers, encounter various leitmotivs in the course of our
reading. As Bouloumié notes, "le sujet du *Roi des Aulnes* est la phorie. Comme le sujet de la fugue, c'est le thème générateur de l'oeuvre" (*Michel Tournier* 74). *The Ogre* consists of a central theme offered in different voices that
vary, transform, augment, repeat, and imitate one another in a tightly or-
chestrated fashion. The repeated imagery and its subsequent transformations in the novel—the russet and silver pigeons metamorphose into the
red- and silver-haired boys; Nestor the coprophage becomes Goering the
interpreter of animal droppings; Nestor and Abel on the playground become transfigured as Abel and Ephraim in the swamp; and so forth—become a type of contrapuntal system in a narrative structure that prescribes
a specific course of action. It is this musical structure of the novel that war-
rants the consideration of Nietzschean philosophy.

In *The Birth of Tragedy,* Nietzsche contends that it is music that gives
birth to myth and that "music strives to express its nature in Apollinian
[*sic*] images" (103). According to Nietzsche, Apollo embodies the dream
experience and remains "ruler over the beautiful illusion of the inner
world of fantasy" as well as "the symbolical analogue of the soothsaying
faculty" (35). He is "the glorious divine image of the *principium individuationis,* through whose gestures and eyes all the joy and wisdom of 'illusion,'
together with its beauty, speak to us" (36). The Apollonian mode, Nietzsche tells us, images the Dionysian symbolic intuition and, in doing so,
seeks order, unity, balance, and harmony.

Abel Tiffauges's psychic constructs constitute a type of Apollonian
dream work in which every sign (be it person, object, animal, or text)
is made to fit into Abel's peculiar semiological field of desire. As Stephen

Houlgate observes: "Apolline art thus involves consciously and creative-ly falsifying a life which we know to be terrible" (187). Abel perceives the phoric act he experienced with Nestor as the pivotal moment in his life, and he reinterprets everything around him in relation to the con-cept of phoria. Consequently, Abel sees himself as a St. Christopher figure, a modern Albuquerque, an Atlas, a Hercules, and a type of *Erlkönig* who gathers children. Throughout his entire life, Abel engages in inter-pretive acts involving strategies of displacement, condensation, and secondary revision that provide him with a coherently reconstructed, delusional world.

Abel's internalized dream work persists up until his encounter with Ephraim reveals the awful truth about the Nazi masters whom he serves. But Abel's drive for semiotic totalization, his desire for a unified, balanced, integrated experience that conforms to his personal interpretive strate-gy, is taken up by the text and undergoes a wickedly parodic twist when the three boys are impaled on the Kaltenborn swords. Abel is drawn to the gruesome scene after he hears a cry—"the cry," as the narrator tells us. This cry, perhaps the most significant leitmotiv in the novel, recurs at least eight times. When Abel writes that "all is sign. But only a piercing light or shriek [une lumière ou un cri éclatants] will penetrate our blunt-ed sight and hearing" (5), we as readers sense that it portends a revelato-ry moment. In the end, the cry signifies the destruction of Abel's objects of desire, signals the utter annihilation of his totalizing semiological sys-tem, and confirms his recognition of the malign nature of the Nazi sys-tem when he gazes on this demonic Golgotha.

In the context of the musical structure of the novel, however, the cry signals those "piercing shrieks" that Nietzsche claims express the Diony-sian tragic vision (BT 46). "At the very climax of joy," writes Nietzsche, "there sounds a cry of horror or a yearning lamentation for an irretriev-able loss" (BT 40). For Nietzsche, the cry expresses both horror and joy, and for *The Ogre*, this final cry marks the textual turn from the Apollonian dream world of Abel's solipsistic consciousness to the chaotic, frenzied world of Dionysian ecstasy. After seeing the impaled children, Abel is swept up as in a vertigo. Losing his glasses, he staggers "like someone shipwrecked in mid-ocean, who swims by instinct, without any hope of being saved" (369), following the directions shouted by Ephraim. In the midst of ma-chine-gun fire, billowing smoke, exploding antitank rockets, and the pul-verizing cannon fire of tanks, in this vortex of violence, Abel surrenders himself to the will of Ephraim. Abel's act of service to Ephraim differs from his other acts of service to the pigeons, the children, Nestor, Jeannot, and others in that these earlier acts were made manifest through his own web of desire. In serving Ephraim, Abel annihilates himself and empties his self of the Apollonian will to order and instead becomes absorbed in the chaotic current that leads to his eventual dissolution. As Nietzsche writes, "by the mystical triumphant cry of Dionysus the spell of individuation is broken" (BT 99). It is this terrifying and joyful experience that constitutes for Abel the Dionysian tragic ecstasy, which Nietzsche terms "the shattering of the individual and his fusion with primal being" (BT 65).

The tragic Dionysian vision, however, is not the only Nietzschean component to Tournier's novel. Nietzsche's persistent critique of scientific thinking and its reliance on cause-and-effect relationships receives equal emphasis in *The Ogre*. Nietzsche refers to cause and effect as "pure concepts." They are, he says, "conventional fictions for the purpose of designation and communication—*not* for explanation" (BGE 29). In *The Gay Science*, Nietzsche conjectures that "such a duality probably never exists" (173); rather, we pick out isolated points on a continuum of motion and infer causal relationships. In *The Ogre*, Abel himself calls the idea of causality into question. When speaking to a physician about the dent in his chest and his difficulty in breathing, Abel wonders if a relationship between the two exists. He conjectures that perhaps a cause-and-effect relationship does not exist. "But," he asks, "what about one of symbol and symbolized?" (69). Abel rejects a reductive, linear, causal explanation in favor of a semiotic harmonics of relatedness. In fact, the entire novel can be read this way. Tournier has written:

> il ne faut pas demander *qui* à la fin du roman a empalé les trois enfants—Haïo, Haro et Lothar—sur les épées monumentales scellées dans le garde-fou de la terasse du château. Qui? Mais tout le roman, bien sûr, la poussée irrésistible d'une masse de petits faits et notations accumulés sur les quatres cents pages qui précèdent. (*Paraclet* 129)

> One must not ask *who* at the end of the novel has impaled the three children Hajo, Haro, and Lothar on the monumental swords on the parapet of the terrace of the castle. Who? But the whole novel, of course, the irresistible thrust of a mass of little accumulated facts and notations on the preceding four hundred pages.

These accumulated notations and mass of facts recall Nietzsche's notion of a continuum in motion that is a whole that cannot be explained through methods of segmentation and selective observation.

The Ogre also dramatizes Nietzsche's critique of science through parody. The hunters at Kaltenborn subscribe to hilarious pseudoscientific systems of classifying deer antlers; the genetic experiments of Dr. Essig, the fatuous explanations of Professor Keil, and the racist, ideological scientism of Blaettchen constitute a sinister parody of the scientific method. Tournier's entire novel can be seen as a warning against scientific interpretations of human experience, interpretations that are reductive, abstract, and easily manipulated for malign purposes. It is worth remarking that Tournier also attacks science in *Le Vent Paraclet*, where he comically debunks mathematics by showing how simple equations elide the real world. He argues that $3 + 6 = 9$ only under certain circumstances. If we are talking about 3 toms and 6 cats, that total may be 33 (i.e., 24 kittens). On the other hand, $3 + 6$ ice cubes in the warm sun will equal 0 (*Paraclet* 46).

Perhaps the most significant Nietzschean element is the theory of eternal recurrence that appears repeatedly throughout the text. On the very first page of the novel, Abel writes: "When the earth was still only a ball of fire spinning [tournoyant] around in a helium sky the soul that lit it and made it spin [faisait tourner] was mine" (3). Abel thus suggests that he is somehow linked to a primordial cosmic process. Abel's persistent allusions to his mythological origins—his claim that he is a monster; his belief that his fate is linked to the legends of St. Christopher, the giant Atlas, and the biblical Abel; his allusions to "the great tribulation"; his claim that he has a "special relationship with the springs of the universe" (63)—reinforce the reader's intuitive feeling that, at the end of the novel, when Tiffauges sinks slowly into the mud, he returns to the mythic Prussian soil and thus to *Das Ur-Eine*, a state of primal unity. And there is the sense that he will return again as part of a continuing cyclical manifestation of some primordial state of being. Whether we choose to believe Abel in this matter is irrelevant; what must not go unnoticed is that the text reinforces this notion of cyclic return. Even Abel's childhood friend, Nestor, figures in the theme of Eternal Recurrence; the name Nestor means "the one who always returns" (Lampert 211).

Consider the next-to-last sentence of the novel: "He had to make a superhuman effort now to overcome the viscous resistance grinding in his belly and breast, but he persevered, knowing all was as it should be (sachant que tout était bien ainsi)" (370). In *Ecce Homo*, Nietzsche offers his formula for greatness in the expression *amor fati*. Persons who embrace this doctrine want "nothing to be different, not forward, not backward, not in all eternity." They do "not merely *bear* what is necessary, still less conceal it . . . but *love* it" (238). I emphasize the word "bear" because this is what Nietzsche refers to as "the greatest weight" (*Das Schwere*) in *The Gay Science* (273). The idea of weight plays a crucial role in Tournier's novel and signals Abel's acceptance of his destiny as he shoulders Ephraim and wanders into the murky swamp. Tournier explicitly mentions *amor fati* when he writes about the importance of the concept of fate (*destin*) in both *Le Roi des Aulnes* and *Les Météores*. Both novels, he claims, reveal a correspondence between a cosmic order and the development of an individual. Such a novelistic construction signals that "le *fatum* devient *amor fati*," writes Tournier. He continues: "Le véritable sujet de ces romans, c'est la lente métamorphose du destin en destinée, je veux dire d'un mécanisme obscur et coercitif en l'élan unanime et chaleureux d'un être vers son accomplissement" (*Paraclet* 242; The actual subject of these novels is the slow metamorphosis from fate into destiny, or I would say from an obscure and coercive mechanism into a complete and fiery momentum of a being toward its fulfillment). It is this *amor fati* that enables one to accept the terrifying concept of the Eternal Recurrence.

Nietzsche offers one of his clearest discussions of Eternal Recurrence in *The Gay Science,* where he relates the parable of the demon who confronts you and asks with respect to each and every thing in your life: "Do you desire this once more and innumerable times more?" (274). Such a burden is practically unthinkable; each action must be carried out with the intent that we will ourselves to do this again and again. This is the terrible burden the Overman must carry, and it is what allows the Overman to go beyond Good and Evil. Each individual must will Eternal Recurrence. Ironically, this willing or rewilling, as Pierre Klossowski correctly observes, signals a renunciation of "being myself once and for all." In such an act, "I am capable of becoming innumerable others" (109). In the case of Abel, he annihilates the desiring self that produced the semiotic system and thereby renounces it at the very moment he affirms his responsibility for employing it throughout his life.

Only by willing Eternal Recurrence, by affirming one's destiny, can one's life be redeemed in the Nietzschean sense. Abel's actions and thoughts best express what Nietzsche meant when he characterized redemption as the act through which one will "re-create all 'it was' until the will says, 'Thus I willed it! Thus I shall will it'" (Z 198). Like Zarathustra, Abel looks on his life and says: "Was *that* life? Well then! Once more!" (Z 157). He wants "to have what was and is repeated to all eternity, shouting insatiably *da capo*" (Z 68). Like Ezra Pound's Herakles—who says, "Splendor it all coheres," when he recognizes his fate at the end of *Women of Trachis*—Tiffauges resolutely carries out his final act in accordance with his own will.

The Nietzschean dimension of *The Ogre*, therefore, signals that human history is fundamentally tragic. The recognition of life's tragic dimension and the drive for a return to an irretrievable unity is a hallmark of Nietzschean philosophy. Dionysiac ecstasy is achieved at the price of dissolution; Nietzsche's tragic hero affirms a self-annihilating fate. The despair of which Nietzsche speaks finds its expression in Tournier's own myth of the creation that he includes in *Les Météores*, in *Gaspard, Melchior, et Balthazar*, and in *Le Vagabonde immobile*, as well as in *Le Roi des Aulnes*. Following Plato's myth in *The Symposium*, Tournier conceives of the original human as an androgyne. As Tiffauges himself argues, "if there is a fall of man in Genesis, it is not in the episode of the apple. . . . No, the fall consists in the breaking into three of the original Adam, letting fall woman and child from man, and thus creating three unfortunates" (17). The myth of the original Adam serves as Tournier's method of expressing despair over a lost unity, an irretrievable wholeness.

Both Nietzsche and Tournier's notion of lost unity has its analogue in the narration of history itself. The whole sought by humans takes the form of a narration we call history—an explanation of what occurred in reality. The structures of these narratives, however, come from myth. The longing for the irretrievable unity characterizes the anguish of the post-Rankean historian who still harbors a nostalgia for objective truth. History as narration is tragic because, as language, it is the medium of representation of actual events, and it cannot be otherwise. History, in other words, must accept its fate like a tragic hero in a classical drama; it is of and in language, as are the events it represents. Any attempt to step outside of the linguistic system of representation in hopes of obtaining a true, unmediated past will end in failure. History essays to return to that original moment, and its heroic effort to recover the past ends in tragic failure.

Tournier's novels indicate the relationship between myth and history. *The Ogre* in particular shows us that the tale of human history carries out the logic embedded in the very mythic narratives that serve as structural paradigms for our own true histories. Truth, as Nietzsche contends, is an army of metaphors. Tournier accepts this definition but rejects the idea of worn currency in favor of a circulation of metaphors based on restructuration through mythological narration. Tournier stresses not semiotic currency but semantic recurrence, the "esthétique de l'antisuspense" of children (*Paraclet* 34) or, in the words of Abel, "a repetition without monotony" (113).

In *Le Médianoche amoureux*, Tournier once again returns to the theme of repetition. Tournier ends the book with the fable of "les deux banquets," where two chefs compete for the title of being the caliph's chef. The second chef reproduces exactly the sumptuous meal that the first chef had offered on the first day. In the end, the caliph observes, "le sacré n'existe que par la répétition, et il gagne en éminence à chaque répétition" (268; the sacred exists only through repetition, and it gains prominence with each repetition). This is what Nietzsche characterizes as man's maturity: "the seriousness one had as a child, at play" (BGE 83). In Tournier's hands, Nietzsche's Eternal Recurrence becomes the retelling of the tale already told, again and again. In each of his works, Tournier demonstrates, with consummate skill, that the act of narration—metaphoric creation through emplotment and structuration—becomes the common ground of history and myth.

As a means of explaining more fully how Tournier structures his novel, I will turn to the theories of Ricoeur. His schema of the threefold mimesis will elucidate how Tournier sees in the conflation of myth and history the royal road to an understanding of human experience. In *The Ogre*, there are at least three aspects to the prefigurative level. One aspect stems directly from the experience of the protagonist, Abel; the other two elements emerge from a common cultural field of experience shared by Abel and the reader.

Ricoeur's Threefold Mimesis in *The Ogre*

The first prefigurative element, the one that relates to Abel and his horizon of experience, consists of the memories that Abel has of his youth. In a very literal sense, Abel's childhood experiences prefigure his life as an adult. Nestor, the interpreter of his own excrement, becomes Goering, the Master of the Hunt, who reads animal droppings; the fire and explosion that destroy part of St. Christopher's reappear in the apocalyptic flames that destroy Kaltenborn; and the childhood game in which Nestor picks up and carries Abel on his shoulders recurs through countless acts of Abel carrying a coworker, pigeons, and children and culminates in Abel bearing Ephraim on his shoulders as they escape from Kaltenborn. These are among the many examples of events in Abel's early life that foreshadow experiences he has in later life.

The second prefigurative element in *The Ogre* is composed of the many myths that inform the story. First and foremost, there is the Goethe poem "Der Erlkönig," from which the novel draws its title (*Le Roi des Aulnes*). Then there is the story of St. Christopher, taken from *The Golden Legend* of Jacques Voragine. There are also the legends and stories of Albuquerque, Baron des Adrets, and Plato's myth of the original androgyne, all of which are told in the novel itself.

Finally, there is what most readers would consider the most crucial prefigurative element in the novel—the sociohistorical context of Europe 1939–45. It is this third element that disturbs readers, because Tournier provides a meticulously detailed description of French society, German work camps, and the special Hitler Youth schools—the Napolas—all within a narrative dominated by the redemptive fantasies of a profoundly disturbed protagonist. Tournier is quite proud of the research he conducted in preparing to write the novel. In his essay "Comment j'ai construit *Le Roi des Aulnes*," Tournier describes how he pored over books and manuscripts produced by East Prussian émigrés who settled in Munich after the Second World War and tried to keep their memories alive by publishing books of humor, photo albums, and calendars. He tells how he interviewed Baldur von Schirach on his release from Spandau prison; how he located Auguste Heissmeyer, the onetime director of all the Napolas in the Reich and the postwar distributor of Coca-Cola in Württemberg; and how he spoke with former students of the Napolas. In a visit to a French lycée, Tournier told students how he used a radio transcript of the memories of an Auschwitz survivor who had entered the camp at ten years of age to construct Ephraim's description of the camp (Bouloumié, "Tournier Face" 24). In an interview with Jean-Louis de Rambures, Tournier claimed that he thoroughly examined the forty-two volumes of the Nuremberg Trials, as well as German tracts on hunting and military pamphlets on the use of carrier pigeons (164). Even at the end of the novel itself, Tournier includes extended footnotes that indicate where he obtained information that helped him produce representations of this historical period.

The problem, of course, is not that Tournier uses information obtained from other sources to write his novel. Rather, the problem revolves around what Ricoeur calls mimesis$_2$, the configuration of material. Configuration refers to the process of emplotment, which itself possesses a mediating function. Emplotment mediates individual events with the story as a whole; it "brings together factors as heterogeneous as agents, goals, means, interactions, circumstances [and] unexpected results"; it also mediates time. It is this final mediating function that is crucial for Ricoeur, inasmuch as emplotment mediates the temporal relation between episodic events and the whole story, which itself can only be conceived from an "end point" (*Time and Narrative* 1:65–67). Ricoeur contends: "To understand the story is to understand how and why the successive episode led to this conclusion, which far from being foreseeable, must finally be acceptable, as congruent with the episode brought together by the story" (*Time and Narrative* 1:67).

In the case of *The Ogre*, Ricoeur's theory must undergo serious modification not because there is no ending as such, but because everything *is* foreseeable and at the same time morally unacceptable. The correspondences between Abel's system of signification and Nazi Germany are overdetermined: three pigeons—two russet and one silver—that are skewered and roasted become three boys—two red haired and one with white hair—impaled on swords; Abel's childhood dream of Canada, inspired by Oliver Curwood's novel, becomes the "Canada" of Auschwitz; Abel's communal showers with the children parallel the Nazi gas chambers; and so forth. As the narrator tells us through Ephraim, Tiffauges learns about "an infernal city remorselessly building up which corresponded stone by stone to the phoric city he himself had dreamed of at Kaltenborn" (357). As readers of the novel, we cannot help but know what will happen because we live "after Auschwitz." So one does not ask whether the conclusion is acceptable or congruent, but rather, what does such a rigid correspondence reveal particularly when we keep in mind the prefigurative historical events?

One might be tempted to say that *The Ogre* enacts an overwhelming if not belabored irony. Certainly, such an interpretation can be supported. The novel hinges on a dramatic irony of sorts in that we know the historical circumstances of which the protagonist is unaware. Nevertheless, despite the many Flaubertian elements in *The Ogre*, Abel Tiffauges is no Frédéric Moreau, and the scorn we feel for a Homais, for example, does not resemble in any way the mixture of horror and pity we feel for Tiffauges. The distance necessary to establish an ironic mode collapses under the moral weight of the evidentiary material. As many commentators on the Shoah have remarked with respect to representing the events that took place in the death camps, traditional tropes have proven to be inadequate to the task. For an author and reader to retreat to a position of ironizing consciousness would imply a moral superiority to the person in question. In the case of the Shoah, however, such moral ground is simply untenable; or, to put it in Conradian terms, Abel Tiffauges is "one of us." Through an excessive repetition of correspondences and an overt parallelism between Abel's significatory system and the fascist political apparatus that he serves, Tournier effectively exhausts his readers and does not permit them the comfort of ironic distance. Bereft of the ironic heights, we, too, are carried along on Abel's journey and are forced to contend with this truly fearful symmetry.

The point at which readers experience a paralysis of judgment occurs when they ask, on concluding the novel, what we are to make of the relationship between Abel and his masters. Why has Tournier established these complex and rigid correspondences? At this point, we have entered the realm of refiguration. Mimesis$_3$, what Ricoeur calls "the intersection of the world of the text and the world of the hearer or reader" (*Time and Narrative* 1:71), serves as the locus of meaning production. Armed with the prefigurative notions of the world, the reader must confront the configurative construction that is the text and, through the interplay of these two elements, refigure the field of forces to bring about a new balance of power. In other words, prior to the appearance of the text, the reader's understanding rests on the support of prefigurative significatory systems that include individual experience mediated through social signs; history as transmitted orally, textually, and imagistically (i.e., through artwork, photographs, film, and video); and customs, social conventions, and beliefs. The appearance of the text on the field of play disrupts the array of prefigurative forces and necessitates a realignment. Even if the text is rejected outright, the phalanx of prefigurative forces must put more stress on one element as opposed to another (e.g., a reader may object that a historical novel is filled with technological anachronisms based on an appeal to empirical evidence).

In *The Ogre*, prefigurative understanding of fascism is completely overturned by the detailed representations of Abel's personal semiotic and his ogreish behavior. The most important idea in Abel's mind is that of ingestion, and the single most important act in Abel's world is phoria, the act of carrying. Therefore, the refigurative process that each reader must undertake has to align the myth of the ogre and the idea of phoria with fascist activities.

Tournier develops what might be termed the semiotics of the ogre to explore the psychological foundation of fascism itself. As Winifred Woodhull has argued in her superb essay "Fascist Bonding and Euphoria in Michel Tournier's *The Ogre*," Abel's activities relate directly to fascist ideology. She points out that by focusing on Abel's obsession with signs, Tournier compels the reader to take into account the "symbolic, affective, and erotic forces" that fascism "mobilizes, and then binds in authoritarian institutions." She continues: "Tournier's novel suggests that if fascist cultural institutions such as education, science, religion, art and political propaganda successfully bound subjects to an oppressive regime, it is because they expressed and partially satisfied needs and desires repressed by capitalist society and dismissed by the political left as irrelevant to the struggle for social transformation" (82–83). As Woodhull correctly points out, the theories of Freud—particularly his *Group Psychology and the Analysis of the Ego*, with its emphasis on the oral phase and the process of identification—as well as Melanie Klein's theories on pre-Oedipal, partial object identification—which involve notions of swallowing or being swallowed—explain the psychological underpinnings of the ogre motif and its relation to the fascist state (101–2). For Woodhull, "the ogre functions as a figure for fascist bonding" (100).

The ogre motif, therefore, affirms what Freud, Bataille, and others have said about fascism. Namely, fascist group behaviors grow out of libidinal ties through which group members identify with an authority figure who enacts a dynamic of passive-aggressive, sadomasochistic behaviors, thus legitimating the libidinal sacrifice called for to maintain an organized fascist state (Bataille, *Visions* 137–60).

With respect to phoria, Tournier goes beyond the psychological component of fascism to explore its mythic and linguistic foundations. Tournier has insisted that phoria is the one true subject of the novel (*Paraclet* 55, 124; Fischer 9). If the "moteur premier" of the novel is the fact that Tournier is a *Germanist* (and with the abundant allusions to Leibniz and Kant as well as Hegel and Nietzsche, this is plausible), then perhaps we should take Tournier seriously when he claims: "Toute lecture qui ne se centre pas sur la Phorie est en tachée de contre-sens" (Fischer 9; Any reading that does not center itself on phoria is marred by a misconception). A reading of *The Ogre* based on the concept of phoria requires an emphasis on elevation, carrying, and picking up—in other words, metaphor. Since the time of Aristotle, the gift of metaphor has been acknowledged as the supreme gift; and, according to Ricoeur, "metaphor is the rhetorical process by which discourse unleashes the power that certain fictions have to redescribe reality" (*Rule* 7). Metaphor involves "submission to reality *and* fabulous invention, unaltering representation *and* ennobling elevation" (*Rule* 40). Metaphor's "genius stroke" marks the philosopher as well as the poet (*Rule* 27).

Metaphor, Phoria, and Fascist Thinking

Earlier, I pointed out how many commentators on the Shoah have argued that narrative representations of what occurred in the death camps ultimately fail because they necessarily resort to tropologic strategies. Tournier, it may be argued, appears to have committed a terrible error in choosing metaphor as his principle narrative trope for *The Ogre*. But as James E. Young has argued in *Writing and Rewriting the Holocaust:*

> to leave Auschwitz outside of metaphor would be to leave it outside of language altogether: it was known, understood, and responded to metaphorically at the time by its victims; it has been organized, expressed and interpreted metaphorically by its writers; and it is now being remembered, commented upon, and given historical meaning metaphorically by scholars and poets of the next generation. If carried to its literal end, an injunction against Auschwitz metaphors would place events outside of language and meaning altogether, thereby mystifying the Holocaust and accomplishing after the fact precisely what the Nazis had hoped to accomplish through their own—often metaphorical—mystification of events. (91)

Young describes how witnesses of the Holocaust based their written testimonies on literary paradigms to describe their experience. By comparing the diaries of Moshe Flinker and Anne Frank, for example, Young demonstrates that their respective diaries grow out of different sociolinguistic and religious traditions that directly affect the types of images, metaphors, and turns of phrase each diarist uses. In essence, Young wants to disabuse us of the notion that historical facts can be rendered in language that is not already in some way figured. I would argue that, in his own way, Tournier does much the same thing. His novel centers itself on the phoria metaphor (what could be derisively termed a metametaphor) because he recognizes, as does Joan W. Scott, that by its very nature, language is always already figured through the various myths, legends, and vocabularies that constitute the total semantic field in which we find ourselves.

By emphasizing the metaphoric foundations of language, Tournier calls into question the very idea of history that posits itself in opposition to myth. In *Le Vent Paraclet*, Tournier writes that with respect to *The Ogre*, "les vrais ressorts du roman ne sont pas plus psychologiques et historiques que les pistons et les bielles des petites locomotives électriques des enfants ne font vraiment avancer la machine" (129; the true springs of the novel are no more psychological and historical than the pistons and rods of a child's little electric train are responsible for its movement). Such a pronouncement sounds strangely similar to the train metaphor Tolstoy uses in *War and Peace*. For Tolstoy, historical explanations can be compared to the various explanations used to describe the movement of a locomotive: for the peasant, the devil makes the train move; for another observer, the wheels set it in motion; for a third man, the cause can be found in the smoke coming out of the engine (1320). In the end, Tolstoy admits defeat; no interpretation can be offered that will adequately explain a historical event. Instead, we are left with metaphors that promote understanding. I believe that Tournier has taken Tolstoy's insight one step further in that he abandons any attempt to discover an explanatory mode. In essence, he argues that his novel is about metaphor because that is precisely what history is.

For Ricoeur, metaphor grows from a semantic, not a semiotic, level of discourse. He eschews a substitution theory of semiotic monism for an interactive theory of semiotic and semantic dualism (*Rule* 102–3). Metaphor stems from Aristotelian *muthos*, or emplotment. "The fundamental trait of *muthos*," writes Ricoeur, "is its character of order, of organization, of arranging or grouping" (*Rule* 36). Metaphoricity, therefore, "consists in describing a less known domain—human reality—in the light of relationships within a fictitious but better known domain—the tragic tale" (*Rule* 244). Consequently, mimesis no longer refers to a Platonic copy but to a "redescription"; *mimesis* becomes the "metaphoric reference" (*Rule* 244–45). According to Ricoeur, the notion of metaphor inheres in a narrative structuration that escapes the self-referentiality of the semiotic level and achieves a semantic level of reference to extralinguistic reality. In *The Ogre*, we witness Abel's escape from his own self-enclosed semiotic system to a referential semantic system of signification—an escape that results from the sum of Abel's experiences.

Thus, by inscribing his novel with Nietzschean elements that enact the tragic play of Apollonian and Dionysian forces along the lines of a musical score, Tournier produces a consummate aesthetic object founded on metaphoric structuration that best expresses the totalizing, aestheticized politics of the fascist state. Abel's overdetermined semiotic system culminates in an apocalypse of self-annihilation. In this regard, Tournier does what Philippe Lacoue-Labarthe contends Heidegger was attempting to do throughout his career; namely, he *thinks* Nazism. Lacoue-Labarthe's words aptly describe Tournier's project in that the novelist succeeds in "thinking through [Nazism's] stunning success, its power of seduction, its project and its victories" (127). He shows us the terrifying logic of the fascist mind and signals the terrible consequences we suffer if we choose to ignore the profound kinship between myth and history.

Although the fascist consciousness depicted by Tournier provides us with a negative example of the configurative process of structuring the past to reshape the future, it nonetheless signals the fundamental role this process plays in the construction of all historical projects. The incorporation of Nietzschean philosophy into his novel allows Tournier to underscore the aesthetic dimension inherent in all acts of human endeavor. But the Nietzschean philosophical component is not limited to the structural level of the narrative. Through a precise configuration of historical materials, Tournier refigures in our own mind the seductive power of the aesthetic component of fascist thinking. With a subtle and sophisticated irony, Tournier makes possible a transference of Nietzschean thought from the level of the text to the mind of the reader. As readers, we totalize the various symbolic and semiotic levels of the narrative; and, like Tiffauges, we must seek a Nietzschean form of redemption by means of a tragic affirmation of our totalizing reading of the novel. In other words, through a process of refiguration, we, too, are culpable of fascist totalization and must affirm our responsibility for having engaged in such activity.

The Vichian Dimensions of Tournier's Novel

The Ogre, however, provides not only a penetrating analysis of the fascist mind but also a profound meditation on history. In this regard, I see strong affinities between Tournier's philosophical project as it appears in the form of the novel and Vico's philosophical system in *The New Science.* Unlike Carlos Fuentes, Tournier makes no mention of Vico in his novels, essays, and interviews. Although trained as a philosopher, it is uncertain if, in fact, Tournier has ever studied Vico. Tournier's philosophic interests are centered in the German tradition of Leibniz, Kant, Hegel, and Heidegger. The two other main philosophers in Tournier's pantheon are Plato and Spinoza. Nevertheless, Tournier's emphasis on myth and his recourse to metaphor indicate that the philosophy of history expressed in *The Ogre* can be called Vichian.

There are four main ideas common to Tournier and Vico. First, both see history emerging from myth. When reading Tournier, one should always recall that he studied at the Musée de l'Homme when it was under the direction of Claude Lévi-Strauss, as he discusses in *Le Vol du vampire* (397–400). The similarities between Lévi-Strauss's structural anthropology and Vichian philosophy have been widely recognized, most notably in an article written by Edmund Leach, "Vico and Lévi-Strauss on the Origins of Humanity." Perhaps these similarities can best be expressed by quoting Lévi-Strauss himself. "Un mythe," he said, "est une histoire qui se passe à une époque où animaux et hommes n'étaient pas réellement distincts et pouvaient passer indifféremment de l'un à l'autre" (qtd. in Bouloumié, *Michel Tournier* 26; A myth is a story that occurs in a time when animals and men were not really distinct and were able to cross over freely from one to the other). The indeterminate status differential between humans and animals recalls Vico's original barbarians (the "first men," as he calls them), who "not being able to form intelligible class concepts of things had a natural need to create poetic characters; that is, imaginative class concepts or universals, to which, as to certain models or ideal portraits, to reduce all the particular species which resembled them" (NS ¶ 209).

As we have already noted, Vico's poetic universals are based on identification. The appellation of Jove for thunder enacts a process of identification whereby a universal class is established such that all thunder is Jove and Jove is all thunder. In *The Ogre*, the metaphoric operation of identification occurs most clearly when Abel identifies with Nestor. "I am Nestor," Abel writes (127), and he even adopts Nestor's verbal mannerisms. When they were children, Nestor would often refer to Tiffauges as "M'Abel," meaning either "my Abel" or "my pretty." When he is writing in his journal, Tiffauges often refers to himself as "M'Abel" (36, 99, 121).

It is through this process of identification, this act of the poetic imagination, that Abel is able to construct his elaborate mythology of phoria. In a way, Nestor serves as Abel's Jove experience. Nestor is described as having preternatural powers. At St. Christopher's, he is immune from punishment; he holds all the keys to the school; he makes cryptic remarks that Abel cannot understand; and, most godlike of all, he holds in his hand, just as God would hold the world, a gyroscope, "a cosmic toy." Nestor, therefore, signifies a superhuman, extratemporal power, and Abel clearly expresses this idea when he writes, "It is not surprising that Nestor, from whom I undoubtedly derive, should, like me, escape the measure of time" (18–19).

The Vichian view of the mythic origins of history first appears in the second paragraph of the novel, in which Abel claims he was the spirit that made the helium ball of fire that was the earth turn in the sky. Here we see the primordial moment when there was no differentiation between man and nature—Abel is quite literally the flame that ignites an imaginative universe that comes into being. In addition, Vico's concept of the *corso e ricorso* is also inscribed in the novel. Earlier, in the discussion on Nietzsche's Eternal Recurrence, we noted how the novel's structure reinforces the idea that Abel the *Erlkönig* can return. The exhumation of the Walkenau man, for example, presages Abel's fate within the novel and also warns the reader that the evil the *Erlkönig* represents can return. Seen through the Vichian perspective, Abel's journey constitutes a single *corso*—moving from mythic origins through heroic action to dissolution—and the beginning of a new cycle, a *ricorso*, as signified by the slowly turning star. Just as Vico states that "all the histories of the gentile nations have had fabulous beginnings" (NS ¶ 361), *The Ogre* indicates that Abel's particular *histoire* has fabulous beginnings as well. The fable of St. Christopher and the *Erlkönig* serve as the foundational myths of the narrative. The additional myths of St. Albuquerque and Atlas and the story of Baron des Adrets ground all of Abel's experiences and yield what he calls a "Nestorian truth," one "which infinitely surpasses the truth of fact" (47). Abel's pronouncement echoes Vico's axiom 48, in which he writes: "poetic truth is metaphysical truth, and physical truth which is not in conformity with it should be considered false" (NS ¶ 205). Just as Vico discerned that the mythic origins of culture yield the truths of the *sensus communis*, the reader of *The Ogre* recognizes that fabulous beginnings yield the truths of Abel's system.

The similarity between the methodologies used by Vico and Tournier constitutes the second major idea that is common to both writers. In paragraph 331 of *The New Science*, Vico complains that philosophers waste their time when they try to understand nature, because only God can know it. Vico argues that philosophers should study the civil world because men have made it. The entire *New Science* argues against rationalist philosophies of the concept and in favor of a philosophy of language that acknowledges the linguistic or etymologic underpinnings of what we perceive to be social reality. Commenting on his own work, Tournier remarked: "Certains romanciers se plaisent à dire que leurs personnages leur échappent et qu'ils se contentent de les suivre—chez moi, c'est différent, c'est le mécanisme mythologique et symbolique qui est si contraignant qu'il détermine entièrement l'action des personnages" (de Rambures 166; Certain novelists are pleased to say that their characters escape them and they are content to follow their characters—for me, it is different, it is the mythological and symbolic mechanism that is so constraining that it entirely determines the action of the characters). For Vico, history results from the archaic language that comprises the *sensus communis*. The *vera narratio*, the true speech that is articulated in the fables, the metaphoric structuring of experience, makes cultural institutions, hence history, possible. In a similar fashion, the fables embedded in *The Ogre* make possible a story that could not be otherwise. The correspondences between Abel's system and the fascist regime should be perfectly comprehensible at this point. Whereas earlier we saw how the correspondences reflected the psychological structure of fascism in particular, now, from the Vichian perspective, we can perceive how Tournier's novel indicates that human history in general is constrained by specific myths and fables.

Tournier has ingeniously inscribed both of these notions in the single metaphor of phoria. As he himself stated: "Le fond de la phorie est équivoque et rejoint le drame humaine de la *possession . . . servir* c'est *asservir:* on *serre* toujours ce que l'on *sert*" ("Treize clés" 22; The foundation of phoria is ambiguous and is connected to the human drama of possession. . . . to serve is to subjugate: one always seizes what one serves). Here we see the linguistic foundations of the mythic structure that informs the narrative. The homonym *sert/serre* expresses the irreducible *différance* that inheres in the structures of language and its attendant myths. Contained within the Christ-bearer is the *Erlkönig*, and this is a truth that Tournier's metaphor expresses so powerfully. Tournier's metaphoric-mythic approach points toward the realization that the history we make is shaped by cultural institutions that in turn emerge from mythic structures of thought. The fatalistic tenor of *The Ogre* results not so much from the recognition that the setting is 1940s Europe but that the cultural myths that established Europe up to that point made such a history inevitable. This is not to argue that Goethe was responsible for the Shoah. But the amalgam of cultural and social myths that contributed to the creation of Germany—myths consciously used, transformed, and exploited by the Nazis—was a constitutive element of the historical event we call the Holocaust.

The third major correspondence between Vico and Tournier centers itself on the single most difficult concept in Vichian philosophy: Providence. For those of us living after "the death of God," Vico's pronouncements may seem unsettling. Many Vico commentators pass over his concept of Providence, preferring instead to concentrate on Vico's contribution to contemporary notions of history (e.g., Edward Said and Hayden White). Providence, however, plays a prominent role in *The New Science*.

The most intelligent discussion of Vichian Providence comes from Vittorio Mathieu; in his essay "Truth as the Mother of History," Mathieu provides a reading that is commensurate with contemporary sensibilities. Mathieu believes that Vico's conception of Providence is closer to Plotinus's notion of *prónoia*—a divine unity that leaves behind imperfections—rather than what we often think of as biblical Providence. In Mathieu's view: "If providence is so conceived, history becomes a sequence of inadequacies through which providence shines (like Luther's God) *abscondita sub contrario:* right is born of violence, profit is the result of avidity, and technical progress of avarice, while truth is born of illusion" (118). In other words, good can come from wrong actions.

With respect to *The Ogre*, Vichian Providence is most evident in Abel's final acts. Tiffauges does rescue Ephraim; his act grows out of the sequence of past behavior, much of which served malign purposes. At the level of narration, illusion *does* offer us the truth. Abel's illusory hermeneutic does in fact express the truth of fascist psychology, as well as the mythic underpinnings of all historical narratives. The strong religious symbolism at the end of the novel suggests a providential aspect to history that Vico perceived more clearly than any other modern philosopher. As Mathieu writes: "Only when mythified can history reflect, in its infinite variety, an unchanging truth; conversely, an unchanging truth cannot become history unless it is expressed in mythical form" (114–15). Writing a history through myth is exactly what Tournier succeeds in doing in *The Ogre*.

Tournier repeatedly returns to the central myths of Western culture because he sees in them a source of wisdom. And it is the focus on the concept of wisdom that constitutes the fourth major idea common to Tournier and Vico. *Le Vent Paraclet* ends with a chapter entitled "Les Malheurs de Sophie" in which Tournier laments the loss of wisdom—sophia, *sapientia*. In his meditation on wisdom, Tournier echoes many of Vico's themes. "Nous vivons sous le terrorisme d'un savoir abstrait," he writes, "mi-expérimentale, mi-mathématique, et de règles de vie formelles définies par la morale" (283; We live under the terrorism of an abstract knowledge, half-experimental, half-mathematical, and of rules of life formally defined by morals). Tournier claims that our concern for wisdom disappeared because of three things: the advent of mathematical physics, the divorce between action and knowledge, and the absence of initiatory practices in the formal education of children. These three developments achieved their combined victory over wisdom at the close of the eighteenth century, argues Tournier. For Vico, of course, the defeat of wisdom occurred much earlier, in the seventeenth century, with the advent of Cartesianism. Despite their apparent disagreement over exactly when Western culture abandoned a pursuit of wisdom, these two writers agree on many fundamental points.

In paragraph 1106 of *The New Science*, Vico describes the barbarism of reflection that makes humans "more inhuman" than the barbarism of the senses that characterized the first humans. The barbarism of reflection obtains in the third Vichian age, the age of men, which follows the ages of gods and heroes. Reflection, Vico argues, is "the mother of falsehood" (NS ¶ 817); it opposes the poetic imagination and culminates in a Cartesian world of abstract conceptualization and alienating technologies. The world without wisdom that Tournier laments is precisely the world that Vico describes as existing in the third age. In fact, the three factors discussed by Tournier in "Les Malheurs de Sophie" also appear in Vico's treatise *On the Study Methods of Our Time*.

Vico voices many of the same complaints that Tournier makes about the modern mathematized world when he writes that "the principles of physics which are put forward as truths on the strength of the geometrical method are not really truths, but wear a semblance of probability" (SM 23). For Vico, plane geometry "accepts its truth from metaphysics" and "generates human truth" (MAW 75, 94), whereas analytic geometry, as championed by Descartes, yields an abstract world removed from common human experience. Similarly, Tournier's disgust over the separation of action from knowledge describes the problem Vico's entire philosophic project attempts to solve. In the seventh chapter of the *Study Methods*, Vico contends that "the greatest drawback of our educational methods is that we pay excessive amount of attention to the natural sciences and not enough to ethics" (33). Vico's point is that we believe that truths come from an investigation of nature because "nature seems unambiguous" to us (33). Human conduct, on the other hand, is ignored because clear and distinct ideas cannot be applied to an analysis of human actions.

Finally, Tournier's criticism of contemporary education, which he describes as nothing more than "un véhicule d'information utiles aux carrières professionelles" (*Paraclet* 288), echoes Vico's observations about education in his own time. *On the Study Methods of Our Time* is Vico's philosophy of education; it is his response to the rapid assimilation of the

Cartesian method into standard pedagogy—a practice that persists today. Vico wants to teach the whole of culture by focusing on the rhetorical arts—poetry, myth, even jurisprudence—rather than specialized fields of study. The description he offers of the students of his time (a description even more apposite today) is as follows: "although they may become extremely learned in some respects, their culture on the whole (and the whole is really the flower of wisdom) is incoherent" (SM 77).

Vico and Tournier uphold the poetic imagination in opposition to the abstract rationalism of the modern world. They feel a sense of loss for *sapientia* in the modern world, and they offer their writings as antidotes to the prevailing philosophies of their times. Thus, with respect to *The Ogre*, Vichian philosophy best explains the methodology Tournier adopts to demonstrate how history grows out of myth. The various myths that gird the totalizing consciousness of Abel Tiffauges parallel the totalizing fascist consciousness that configures the various foundational myths of European culture in pursuit of a politics of violence, exclusion, and self-destruction. The affinities Tournier shares with Vico do not end with a recognition of the mythic foundation of all history. As we have seen, Tournier also distrusts the mathematized, abstract rationalism of the modern world. Like Vico, Tournier perceives the inherent danger in conceiving of the world strictly along rationalist principles. We should never forget that concomitant with the fascist propensity for resurrecting a mythic past was an equally strong drive for the development of state-of-the-art science and technology. The Nazi Germany that looked back with nostalgia on the fallen of Tannenberg was the same society that produced the first jet aircraft, developed the most sophisticated mechanized war machine of its time, and nearly created the first atomic bomb. It is precisely this drive toward abstract rationalism—which achieves its highest expression in scientific endeavor and which Vico terms the barbarism of reflection—that made the conception of the Final Solution possible. Although Husserl glimpses the consequences of the positivist reduction of the idea of science and the subsequent mathematization of nature in *The Crisis of European Sciences and Transcendental Phenomenology*, the relationship between science and the advent of fascist thinking is a phenomenon that has yet to be fully explored. Nevertheless, Vico had warned of that danger; and in *The Ogre*, Tournier suggests that the links between the two are stronger than we are willing to admit.

Vico, of course, wrote a *new* science, one that challenged the Cartesian science of the eighteenth century. His is a science of human institutions based on a philological philosophy. Vico is not concerned with consciousness (*coscienza*), which verifies what is certain; rather, Vico pursues knowledge (*scienza*), which produces truth. As he writes: "Men who do not know what is true of things take care to hold fast to what is certain, so that if they cannot satisfy their intellects by knowledge [*scienza*], their wills at least may rest on consciousness [*coscienza*]" (NS ¶ 137). This, then, is Vico's project: the new science, *scienza nuova*.

Tournier has said: "Every important literary work is *true* science fiction: that is, it concerns the future, it predicts, it opens perspectives on to the future" (Heuston 403). Like Vico, Tournier sees science as a means to make truths, not as a means to discover certainties. The concern for the future that Tournier perceives in "important literary work" may give readers the impression that Tournier has condemned his own writings because he so often rewrites myths—stories linked to the past. But Tournier sees a very constructive potential in myth, a type of Nietzschean creation by destruction that only myth provides. In this regard, he differs somewhat from Vico, who at the end of *The New Science* expresses a pervading sense of resignation. It cannot be otherwise, *The New Science* seems to say. We happen to live during the era of the barbarism of reflection, and "so it goes." With Tournier, however, the myth possesses an ability to disrupt the social (i.e., those very human institutions that trace their origins back to myth). In an interview, Tournier distinguished between the national myths that are unifying and what he termed myths that are antisocial: "myths are rather destructive. I mean, myth is almost always the exaltation of an antisocial hero. . . . I have the impression that everything in society tends toward order and that myth is a means for the individual to escape from an order that suffocates him, by means of a hero who is revolting against the established order" (Daly 409). "La mission suprême d'un romancier," writes Tournier, "c'est peut être de ne pas se contenter de créer des personnages de roman, mais de vouloir lancer des mythes" ("Comment" 83; The supreme mission of a novelist is perhaps not to be content to create characters but to want to spawn myths). The novel, Tournier claims, possesses a "biological function" that serves "to foster, vitalise and modify the sensibility of the members of that society and future generations" (Heuston 403). Embedded in these Tournier statements is the idea that myth—even today—possesses a transformative power that can challenge existing social norms. Rather than accept the popular notion that myth necessarily reinforces the established sociopolitical structures, Tournier sees in myth the potential to alter those very same structures. If, as Vico tells us, myth makes the world, Tournier suggests that myth can unmake it. By constructing certain metaphors, the novelist is able to open up semantic possibilities that will unfold through the process of narration. Of course, in the case of *The Ogre*, Tournier offers us a negative portrait of the potential of mythic structuration. In no way is he suggesting that we should emulate the totalizing drive of Abel Tiffauges. Nevertheless, Tournier does point to the possibilities of mythic structuration and underscores its constitutive role in the development of all histories.

In paragraph 401 of *The New Science*, Vico contends that logic comes from *logos*, "whose first and proper meaning was *fabula.*" Vico goes on to argue that, in Greek, the fable was also called *mythos*, which in turn became defined as true speech (*vera narratio*). This first language, Vico writes, "was not a language in accord with the nature of things it dealt with"; rather, it "was a fantastic speech making use of physical substances endowed with life." The metaphoric language of Vico's theological poets lies at the heart of narration itself. Language cannot not be metaphoric; thus, each history unfolds in accordance with a logic that creates its own truth. Tournier himself speaks of "une logique profonde" that supports the architecture of *The Ogre* (*Paraclet* 129). For Vico and Tournier, therefore, the logic of the narrative results from the metaphorical language that achieves its supreme expression in myth.

Just as Vico returns to the mythic origins of Western culture, Tournier returns to the originary cultural myths to structure his narratives. Ideal eternal history, which serves as the controlling metaphor of Vico's philosophy, has its analogue in Tournier's metaphor of phoria. This is not to argue that phoria signifies ideal eternal history. On the contrary, these metaphors imply different things. They are similar, however, in that both writers have conceived of these master metaphors through which they generate their respective narratives. As Vico claims, every metaphor is a fable in brief (NS ¶ 404); and, from their respective metaphors, Vico and Tournier offer a true narration of history. Tournier, however, succeeds at something Vico deemed impossible. In paragraph 821 of *The New Science*, Vico asserts that one person cannot be both a sublime poet and a sublime metaphysician, because the former must look to the particulars, whereas the latter reaches up to the universals. In *The Ogre*, Tournier has written a novel that offers the concrete particulars of a specific historical period as well as a universal philosophy of history.

6

Improvising the Past:
Ishmael Reed's *Mumbo Jumbo*

Since they were unable to express this force abstractly, they represented it in concrete physical form as a cord, called chorda in Greek and in Latin at first fides, whose original and proper meaning appears in the phrase fides deorum, force of the gods. From this cord . . . they fashioned the lyre of Orpheus, to the accompaniment of which, singing to them the force of the gods in the auspices, he tamed the beasts of Greece to humanity.
—Vico, *The New Science*

I hope that the significance of history will not be thought to lie in its general propositions . . . but that its value will be seen to consist in its taking a familiar, perhaps commonplace theme, an everyday melody, and composing inspired variations on it, enhancing it, elevating it to a comprehensive symbol, and thus disclosing in the original theme a whole world of profundity, power and beauty.
—Nietzsche, *Untimely Meditations*

In paragraph 357 of *The New Science*, Vico figures antiquity as a heap of fragments that "lay begrimed, broken, and scattered," and he argues that these shards of history can only illuminate the past if they are "cleaned, pieced together, and restored." Such an image brings to mind the jigsaw puzzle; indeed, the activities of jigsaw puzzle enthusiasts have often been invoked when describing the work of a historian. For most puzzles, the player is given a complete picture of what should be constructed once all the pieces are properly placed together. Thus, one is presented with a picture of Notre Dame de Paris and is expected to reproduce this image after painstakingly placing disparate pieces together in an organized pattern.

This paradigm of construction, however, becomes strained when we pause to consider the difference that separates the puzzler from the historian. Historians are rarely given a picture of what they are looking for (or, in puzzle parlance, what they should piece together); at least that is what many of them claim. Rather, objective historians pick up the pieces of the past and create an image or narrative of what they think was there. Thus, to return to the jigsaw puzzle example, the very pieces that ostensibly make up Notre Dame de Paris may, in fact, in the hands of a historian, be used to construct the Bastille.

One can quickly object that, in most cases, the historian comes armed with a preestablished picture to be completed (this is most readily apparent in Whiggish, Marxist, and nationalist histories that so often come under attack for being ideologically biased). As discussed in the chapter on Daitch's *L.C.*, critics such as Joan W. Scott have argued persuasively that each historical interpretation is in some ways always already interpreted; or, to maintain the analogy, any attempt to construct a history depends on preconceived semantic structures that make it possible to complete a picture of the past. The idea that the same materials can be used to make a different picture—a strategy invoked by Daitch in *L.C.*—characterizes the practice of novelist and poet Ishmael Reed, but Reed advances the strategy by playing on variations of this theme.

Put another way, one could say that if history is a canvas, a writer such as Fuentes perceives it as a palimpsest, a surface of images that obscure other, often older, images that present a different picture of the past. Thus, *Terra Nostra* is the work of a craftsman who removes the varnished paints that make up the surface of the past to reveal the hidden images and stories that exist beneath the surface on that same canvas. Reed, by way of contrast, does not remove surface images. Instead, he takes that same series of images and makes of it something different—the Bastille of Notre Dame or *Guernica* of *Les Demoiselles d'Avignon*. This appropriation of the given series and the subsequent rearrangement of that series are what I see as Reed's jazz aesthetic, one that plays on the narrative of history and offers its readers something new.

Perhaps the most significant and enduring of Ishmael Reed's many famous and infamous works may very well be *Mumbo Jumbo*, a novel that describes the culture of the Jazz Age in 1920s America, presents a veiled critique of the Harlem Renaissance, and offers a scathing analysis of dominant white culture under the guise of a cartoon-like detective fiction, complete with voodoo rites, immortal beings who were original members of the Knights Templar, and a mythico-historical account of the origins of Western civilization traced back to ancient Egypt. Since its publication in 1972, Reed's novel has generated a host of critical responses. Robert Elliot Fox, for example, sees Reed in a triangular relationship with Amiri Baraka (LeRoi Jones) and Samuel R. Delany in which each writer, through his fiction, examines the limits of freedom and the problem of slavery in the past, present, and future. Kathyrn Hume, by way of contrast, argues that Reed—like Acker, Burroughs, Mailer, and Pynchon—responds to American forms of cultural control but differs from the others in that he offers the vision of an alternative social structure that stresses the cultivation of certain pleasures. In his book-length analysis of Reed, Reginald Martin focuses his attention on the Black Aesthetic tradition, especially as articulated in the writings of critics such as Addison Gayle, Houston Baker, and Baraka, and determines that Reed opposes any prescriptive attempts to make literature socially responsible or socially uplifting. Henry Louis Gates, in an essay and subsequent book, now become famous, declares that Reed's works are "the grand works of critical signification" ("'Blackness'" 723), by which he means that Reed "signifies," that is, repeats and inverts (parodies) the writing styles of his African-American predecessors. Reed, according to Gates, "tropes" or plays on the writings of Hurston, Wright, and Ellison.

One common feature unites these four critics: they all seek to place Reed's work within a literary tradition. In other words, they see Reed responding to literary forebears or working in relation to contemporary postmodern writers. I have chosen not to follow these lines of analysis, in part because this scholarly work, though exemplary and thorough, lies largely outside my scope of inquiry. In addition, I have also chosen not to follow the postmodern line of investigation because, like Appleby, Hunt, and Jacob, I believe that "there can be no postmodern history" (237). I will clarify my position on this in my last chapter; for now, suffice it to say that, in my estimation, Reed is not a postmodernist precisely because he creates new values through improvisation and variation on established themes rather than relativizes all values.

In the pages that follow, I will examine an area that most Reed commentators have ignored—namely, the philosophical tradition from which Reed's work stems. Whereas the previously named critics provide an aesthetic analysis—or, more properly, an analysis of aesthetic traditions vis-à-vis Reed's work—I will explore the philosophical current within Reed's narrative. I will argue that Reed's novel presents a critique of the stultifying tradition of the West that is strikingly similar to the one Nietzsche articulated. To my mind, Reed's philosophical project is precisely the one Nietzsche called for (i.e., the transvaluation of values), but Reed goes beyond Nietzsche's philosophical investigations of the Dionysian spirit in that he locates the proper medium for expressing the life-affirming dimension of human experience in the jazz idiom. In addition, Reed's novel ramifies the basic insight Vico offers into the creative process. Vico's understanding of the centrality of metaphoric structuration, its relation to the body, and his assertion that culture emerges from communal artistic (poetic) acts all receive brilliant expression in Reed's work.

Mumbo Jumbo describes the outbreak of Jes Grew, an antiplague that sweeps America in the 1920s. In short, Jes Grew is jazz music and dances associated with it, the spirit of African-American culture and its aesthetic manifestations. The novel is structured as a detective story in which two groups—the Mumbo Jumbo Kathedral (led by PaPa LaBas, a voodoo or, more correctly, HooDoo *houngan* who recalls the trickster figure of Yoruban mythology, Esu-Elegba) and the Wallflower Order (Ivy Leaguers and nondancers)—try to find the Book of Thoth that is the source of Jes Grew. At the very end of the novel, during a typical clichéd detective fiction scene, the Mumbo Jumbo Kathedral's PaPa LaBas narrates the events leading up to his discovery of the location of the book; but to do so, he must first explain the origins of the "jes' grew" phenomenon. According to LaBas, it all begins with the struggle between Osiris—the spiritual leader of the "theater of fecundation generation and proliferation" (161), who "became known as 'the man who did dances that caught on'" (162)—and Set—who, claims LaBas, "went down as the 1st man to shut nature out of himself. He called it discipline. He is also the deity of the modern clerk, always tabulating, and perhaps invented taxes" (162). Set hated everyone dancing and singing and felt that, when it came to Egypt, "there was hard work to be done, countries to invade, populations to subjugate" (163). Eventually, Set murders Osiris, gains control of Egypt, and outlaws dancing, music, even sex. But Osiris's mysteries lived on in the book that Thoth wrote, which recorded the music and dance steps, and through Dionysus, an Osirian disciple who carried these mysteries to Greece. Set, however, established a new monotheistic religion—Atonism (a term that connotes atonement, atonality, nonpigment), and this later devolves into the Judeo-Christian culture that dominates Western Europe. This struggle between the spirit of Osiris and Set repeats itself in the 1920s battle between the forces of HooDooism and the Wallflower Order.

The Nietzschean Connection

Anyone familiar with Nietzsche's writings—particularly *On the Genealogy of Morals, Twilight of the Idols, The Anti-Christ,* and his various works on Wagner—will recognize some astonishing parallels between Nietzsche and Reed's myths of origins, their focus on dance, and their devotion to music. Both clearly reject Christianity and its effects on culture, and both offer fables to explain the rise of Christian morality. In this regard, Set can be described as the man of *ressentiment,* the proponent of the ascetic ideal that Nietzsche describes in *On the Genealogy of Morals.* In Nietzsche's fable, the class of nobles who declared good that which was strong, robust, and powerful and bad that which was weak, impotent, and insignificant was overthrown by a weaker plebeian class. Etymologically, claims Nietzsche, the word "good" originally signified noble and aristocratic, and "bad" was simply its opposite. But an inversion of these values occurred when a priestly class, suffering from *ressentiment,* which Nietzsche characterizes as "the *need* to direct one's view outward instead of back to oneself" (GM 37), conceived of evil and equated this with the actions of the nobles. This transformation of values resulted in a moral conceptual world centered on guilt, conscience, and sacredness of duty (65). In Reed's novel, an inversion of values occurs when Set triumphs over Osiris, and the vibrant, life-affirming values of Osirian dance are replaced by the values of work, militarism, and repression.

Similarly, it is the Atonists who, like the Christians, opt for a single god, or what Nietzsche terms "the pitiable God of Christian monotono-theism" (AC 139). And, just as Nietzsche writes that "the Church . . . falsified even the history of mankind into the prehistory of the Christian Church" (AC 165), Reed describes "Atonist scholars" being "up to their old yellow journalism" when they converted Osiris into Pluto and transformed Isis into the Virgin Mary (170).

Nietzsche and Reed see in Christianity a malevolent, life-denying force. Nietzsche declares that Christianity is more harmful than any vice because it "has made an ideal out of *opposition* to the preservative instincts of strong life" (AC 127). As depicted by Reed, the Judeo-Christian (Atonist) culture promotes death and denies pleasure. For example, the narrator describes the Wallflower Order headquarters as follows:

> You have nothing real up here. Everything is polyurethane, Polystyrene, Lucite, Plexiglas, acrylate, Mylar, Teflon, phenolic, polycarbonate. A gallimaufry of synthetic materials. Wood you hate. Nothing to remind you of the Human Seed. The aesthetic is thin flat turgid dull grey bland like a yawn. . . . The Atonists got rid of their spirit 1000s of years ago with Him. The flesh is next. Plastic will soon prevail over flesh and bones. Death will have taken over. Why is it Death you like? Because then no 1 will keep you up all night with that racket dancing and singing. The next morning you can get up and build, drill, progress putting up skyscrapers and . . . and . . . and . . . working and stuff. You know? Keeping busy. (62–63)

This, of course, is Max Weber's nightmare updated for our times, his iron cage recast with high-tech materials. By offering us a vision of this synthetic, Pynchonesque world, Reed, like Nietzsche, underscores the connection between the cult of death and Christian beliefs.

Reed's more explicit critique of Christianity in his poem "Neo-HooDoo Manifesto" echoes many of the pronouncements in Nietzsche's *Twilight of the Idols*. In his manifesto, Reed identifies Christianity as the "Cop Religion" and Christ as a "landlord deity"; Jeho-vah is "a party-pooper and hater of dance," a "dangerous paranoid pain-in-the-neck a CopGod from the git-go" who was "the successful law and order candidate in the mythological relay of the 4th century A.D." (24). In short, Jeho-vah is "the God of punishment." As Chester Fontenot characterizes it: "Reed feels that the worst facet of Christianity is that it attempts to negate all other modes of thought and to insist upon the singularity of moral and ethical vision" (22). In his own work, Nietzsche is equally blunt. "Christianity," he writes, "is a hangman's metaphysics" (TI 63).

Just as both writers identify the same source of the problem, they propose similar alternatives. For Nietzsche, Dionysus embodied the principles he espoused. "Affirmation of life even in its strangest and sternest problems, the will to life rejoicing in its own inexhaustibility through the *sacrifice* of its highest types—*that* is what I called Dionysian . . . beyond terror and pity *to realize in oneself* the eternal joy of becoming—that joy which also encompasses *joy in destruction*" (TI 120). The turn to Dionysus—the god of music, dance, and, above all, frenzy—provided Nietzsche with the perfect metaphor for the antidote to the decadence of his age. Two key elements to Nietzsche's Dionysian thinking were the body and dance. In *The Gay Science*, for example, Nietzsche wonders if "philosophy has not been merely an interpretation of the body and a *misunderstanding of the body*" (34–35). In many ways, Nietzsche's entire oeuvre can be read as a rejection of philosophy as an expression of rationalism and its Platonic antecedents. For Nietzsche, Socrates is the villain because he rejects the body and elevates the mind to the sole source of truth. The abolition of poetry from the Republic, the rejection of eroticism, the limitation of the locus of truth to the psychscape of interior dialogues—these are the salient features of Platonic Socratism that Nietzsche deems dangerous. Rather than escape into the world of the idea, Nietzsche prefers to refocus attention on the corporeal.

"The body is a great reason," writes Nietzsche, "a plurality with one sense." He concludes this section of *Zarathustra* by saying: "There is more reason in your body than in your best wisdom" (34–35). The body, its densities, rhythmicities, potentialities, even its frailties offer an alternative to the philosopher. Understanding obtained via the abstract realm of ratiocination produces mummified knowledge, a desiccated corpse of consciousness preserved in time. Understanding achieved through the body, however, is knowledge in motion. In the volatile world of genuine philosophical thought, thinking itself is in flux, it is not static, finished, or complete; nor does it move to achieve a final resting point of absolute knowledge. Like an organism responding to and reflecting the myriad stimuli that affect it, the philosopher envisioned by Nietzsche is one whose body speaks. As Nietzsche himself expressed it: "I, too, who 'know' am dancing my dance" (GS 116).

As the emblem of Nietzsche's philosophy, the dancer provides him with the perfect figure, combining the physical, musical, and gestural. Rather than accept the dichotomy of mind and body (as do most modern philosophers), Nietzsche chooses to see the body in the mind. Whereas the overwhelming majority of philosophers privilege the mind, Nietzsche prefers to figure the body as a way of thinking, one characterized by temporal rhythms, speed, balance, and grace. One could say that much of Nietzsche's style—which expresses the swiftness of aphoristic utterance, the rhythms of the German language, and a delicate balance between what cursory readers might term poetic utterance and philosophical argument—comprises a type of dancing discourse. We recall that Nietzsche's supreme dancer, Zarathustra, must dance with both Wisdom and Life, who are one and the same.

Nietzsche's emphasis on the body and dance is in perfect accord with Reed's approach in *Mumbo Jumbo*. Jes Grew is a dance craze that sweeps America—its effects manifest themselves in the body. As one white official describes it, people infected with Jes Grew "were doing 'stupid sensual things,' were in a state of 'uncontrollable frenzy,' were wriggling like fish, doing something called the 'Eagle Rock' and the 'Sassy Bump'" (4). White authorities want to do away with Jes Grew because this logic of the body disrupts the ordered stability of a reason-centered society. Thus, Nietzsche's intuition that a frenzied, body-centered wisdom that feeds on musical (bodily) rhythms most threatens to destabilize the decadent culture of his time is confirmed in Reed's narrative of the Jazz Age. It is precisely this type of aesthetic phenomenon that will overturn the value structure of the period.

But why, one might ask, must this be so? How is it that sustained bodily activity, a focus on one's corporeal being, and the cultivation of bodily logic would disrupt if not overturn modern society? For this, one must look to Vico and explore how he sees the connection between the very activity of thinking and the body. Here, too, Reed's novel elaborates and confirms Vico's philosophical insights just as it expresses Nietzschean philosophy.

The Vichian Connection

We recall that the development of imaginative universals as posited by Vico stems from the projection of images of the body (NS ¶ 405), what Joseph Mali calls "thinking in anthropomorphic similes" (186). Thus, we have worn metaphors such as legs of chairs, eyes of needles, and bowels of the earth. In addition, Vico argues that the faculties of memory "have their roots in the body" (NS ¶ 819), thereby linking acts of the imagination with the reconstructive impulse necessary for the writing of history (i.e., knowing the past by imagining it). "The human mind is naturally inclined by the senses to see itself externally in the body," writes Vico, "and only with great difficulty does it come to understand itself by means of reflection" (NS ¶ 236). But it is precisely this reflective capacity, what Vico terms the "barbarism of reflection," that characterizes the thinking of the third age, the modern era of scientific methodology and purposive rationalism. Diametrically opposed to this manner of thinking is that which prevailed in the first age, something Vico called the "barbarism of the senses." What we see in Reed's narrative, therefore, is the juxtaposition, some might say the struggle, between these two modes of thinking.

Reed is not unique in doing this. In chapter 8, I will show how Mario Vargas Llosa contrasts two cultures even more widely separated than that of African-American and white American culture. Nevertheless, the cultural contrast as expressed in modes of thinking is key to understanding what Reed attempts to say about the viability of a culture, and Vico's philosophy offers us a superb way of grasping the full dimensions of Reed's account. As the earlier description of the Wallflower Order confirms, white America has succumbed to the barbarism of reflection. The frightening, technological, instrumentalizing vision of Western, post-Enlightenment thinking governs the scene. However, the Jes Grew phenomenon represents what one might call a form of poetic wisdom, a style of thinking Vico attributes to the "theological poets" and describes as "not rational and abstract" but "felt and imagined" (NS ¶ 375). In this regard, the *houngan* becomes a theological poet offering new ways of imagining the real, or what Vico would call "the true."

Obviously, Reed points out that the United States has a choice as to which form of thinking to espouse. In this regard, he appears to part company with Vico in that the unfolding of cultural development is not inevitable precisely because the culture of the United States is not homogeneous. The stakes are quite high. One could choose the barbarism of reflection and, as Vico describes it (and Reed's narrative implies), the people would "finally go mad and waste their substance" (NS ¶ 241). Or one could choose the poetic wisdom of the barbarism of the senses, in which case we would witness a Vichian recourse (*ricorso*), a phenomenon described in book 5 of *The New Science* that can roughly be equated with a return to the barbarism of the senses and the beginning of a new historical development of a culture.

I will address the theoretical ramifications of the contemporaneous clash of Vichian ages in chapter 8. In the meantime, I want to consider the significance of the Jes Grew epidemic as a form of poetic thinking. As Mali reminds us, Vico "perceived poetry in socio-political, not in merely aesthetic, terms" (171). For Vico, the focus is on the community, not individual expressions of genius or abstract conceptualization. Thus, poetry is a form of knowledge that differs from what we take to be scientific knowledge. Cecilia Miller remarks that Vico made a distinction between "knowledge (*scientia*, which was systematic and learned) and consciousness (*conscientia*, which was intuitive)" and placed "emphasis on the intuitive and communal aspect of mental activity" (51). Observed in this light, Jes Grew becomes an intuitive form of communal knowledge, one that is based in the senses.

One of the signal characteristics of the communal aspect of intuitive knowledge remains its indissoluble connection with oral culture. And in book 4 of *The New Science*, Vico shows how one can only understand the ancient Greeks by coming to terms with the oral tradition as commemorated in the Homeric poems. Similarly, *Mumbo Jumbo* stresses the oral tradition within the African-American community as exemplified through the movement of Jes Grew, which passes by word of mouth but is never written down. Reed underscores the primacy of the oral tradition by placing the grand summation scene in the Villa Lewaro, located at Irvington-on-Hudson. As Henry Louis Gates notes, Lewaro is an anagram for "we oral" (*Signifying* 225).

The poetic wisdom of Jes Grew achieves its articulation through dance and music; but in the confines of the novel, readers cognitively learn of it through the narration offered by PaPa LaBas at the end of *Mumbo Jumbo*. For many readers (particularly white ones), the myth of Osiris and Set will appear amusing if not preposterous. In the Vichian context, however, PaPa LaBas's tale is a *vera narratio*, a true narrative or myth; its truth, according to Mali, "consists not in its modes of cognition or representation of reality but rather in its mode of *narration* of it" (203). As Cecilia Miller confirms, myths for Vico were neither false statements nor true abstract metaphysical expressions; rather, they were "representative of the time in which they were created" (37). Thus, Reed offers us a mode of thinking in poetic logic expressed through a narrative of the manner in which a minority community thinks about its experience. This is not to suggest that every or even most African Americans believed in Osiris, Set, and the spirit of Jes Grew. On the contrary, the narrative expresses the truth of the belief in the struggle between Set and Osiris that serves as the metaphoric expression of the struggle between the African-American and white American cultures.

Perhaps the best way to place *Mumbo Jumbo* within a Vichian interpretive orbit is to point out that, as a whole, Reed's novel offers us a clear example of Vico's notion of *fantasia*. Cecilia Miller offers the most complete and succinct definition of this key Vichian term. According to Miller, *fantasia* has three meanings. First, it constitutes "the attempt by primitive peoples to make sense of their physical and social environments" (120). Here, of course, Miller refers to the *bestioni* Vico describes in his portrait of the first age. Clearly, the African-American culture depicted by Reed is not synonymous with Vico's first humans. Nevertheless, Reed signals emphatically that the manner in which the followers of the Mumbo Jumbo Kathedral and Jes Grew conceive of their world predates the scientific rationalism that dominates the contemporary culture of the United States. And, as already noted, the body-centered orientation of Jes Grew thinking exemplifies the thinking associated with the first age. Miller's second meaning of *fantasia* revolves around "the spirit of a particular age," by which she means "the composite mentality of the people of a particular civilization at a particular time" (120). In this case, Reed has reproduced the thinking of various groups within the African-American community; and it is through the true narrative, as mentioned above, that readers come to understand how the cultural struggle was (and is) conceived. Third, writes Miller, *fantasia* refers to "the function we must ourselves employ to unlock the minds, the consciousnesses, of these past civilizations to reconstruct patterns of past cultures" (120). In reading *Mumbo Jumbo*, we are forced to invoke *fantasia* ourselves as Reed challenges us to comprehend his rollicking and disorienting narrative. The very style and structure of the novel pose a problem for readers who rely on certain traditional European forms of narrative construction. To enter the minds of Reed's characters requires this third form of *fantasia* and constitutes the key to understanding just how Reed wishes to make known the profound cultural difference that obtains between the African-American and white communities in the United States as well as the power and effects of the different form of poetic wisdom that opposes the rationality of the dominant white culture.

Thus, a poetic wisdom expressed through the body would challenge the hyperrationalism of modern consciousness in that it would allow us to imagine other ways of organizing our real world. The form of poetic wisdom Reed relies on is musical in nature. The reasons for this are rather obvious: African-American culture has long been associated with music. More significant than this facile association, however, is the recognition that music is central to the African-American experience. As W. E. B. Du Bois noted, "a haunting echo of these weird old songs" lingers in the souls of all black folk (204). This is confirmed by LeRoi Jones (Amiri Baraka), who, in *Blues People*, argues that by conducting a socio-anthropological analysis of the music of the Negro, "something about the essential nature of the Negro's existence in this country ought to be revealed, as well as something about the essential of this country, i.e., society as a whole" (x). In his follow-up book, *Black Music*, Baraka notes that the blues, the progenitor of jazz music, expresses the racial memory of African Americans (183). Reed is well aware of these facts and consequently makes music the focus of his novel, whereby he can offer his cultural critique in the form of a true narrative. The mode of narration Reed chooses to use in his *vera narratio* can best be explained by returning to Nietzsche's philosophy because Nietzsche, much more so than Vico, saw music as central to understanding culture.

The Solution Found in Music

Although Nietzsche and Reed seek their solutions in music, it is Nietzsche who never discovers the music he needs to help bring about the revaluation of values. Early in his career, Nietzsche is the champion of Wagner, the veritable hero of *The Birth of Tragedy*, whose Bayreuth "signifies the morning consecration of the day of battle" (UM 212). But at the end of Nietzsche's life, Wagner is, in Nietzsche's words, "merely one of my sicknesses" (CW 155), a person associated with "the Christian concept, 'you ought to and must *believe*'" (CW 161). In *Nietzsche contra Wagner*, Nietzsche describes what he characterizes as his "physiological objections" to Wagner's music, music that saddens his entrails and upsets his stomach and circulation (664). The Wagnerian approach to music, writes Nietzsche, results in "the complete degeneration of rhythmic feeling" (NCW 666).

In the end, Nietzsche completely rejects Wagner. But herein lies a problem. Having distanced himself from Wagner, the artist he once thought embodied the spirit of Dionysus, Nietzsche loses his way—he never finds an exemplar or a form that best expresses the Dionysian. Michael Allen Gillespie has noted that Nietzsche attempts to express his repudiation of his former idol in a musical form. *Twilight of the Idols*, he argues, follows the sonata form (exposition, development, and recapitulation framed by an introduction and a coda). Gillespie is probably right. *Twilight of the Idols* is a sonata; but, as such, it is hardly the formal expression of Dionysian frenzy.

Nietzsche's pronouncement that "for any sort of aesthetic activity or perception to exist, a certain physiological precondition is indispensable: *intoxication*" (TI 518) and his definition of the Dionysian as "an urge to unity, a reaching out beyond personality, the everyday, society, reality, across the abyss of transitoriness: a passionate-painful overflowing into darker, fuller, more floating states" (WP ¶ 1050) sound more like descriptions of jazz than the sonata form of classical European music. Indeed, in his history of *Early Jazz*, Gunther Schuller points out that "African native music and early American jazz both originate in a total vision of life, in which music, unlike the 'art music' of Europe, is not a separate, autonomous social domain" (4). Such a totalizing impulse in African music expresses Nietzsche's Dionysian "urge to unity," what he described in *The Birth of Tragedy* as the "shattering of the individual and his fusion with primal being" (65). Schuller goes on to argue that the unique nature of jazz rhythm is based in part on "the consistent 'democratization' of rhythmic values" (6) and that the formal elements of African music that are most significant in relation to jazz are the "call and response pattern," "the repeated refrain concept," and "the chorus format" (27), something that Amiri Baraka has also noted. In his early book on African-American music (published under his former name, LeRoi Jones), Baraka writes that "the most salient characteristic of African, or at least West African, music is a type of song in which there is a leader and a chorus; the leading lines of the song sung by a single voice, the leader's, alternating with a refrain sung by the 'chorus'" (*Blues People* xi). These characterizations of totality of vision, democratization, chorus, and response that describe elements of jazz composition can best be summarized in the words of Fred Wei-han Ho: "The essence of African American music is a whole which is greater than the sum of its inseparable and mutually dependent parts—player and composer, notation and performance, composition and improvisation" (288).

Readers of Nietzsche will recognize many elements of his Dionysian principles in these descriptions of the elements of jazz. To associate democracy with Nietzsche may sound rather odd until we note such a word can be used to describe the multiple masks Nietzsche adopted in his various texts. In his insightful book *Nietzsche: Life as Literature,* Alexander Nehamas argues that because Nietzsche viewed life aesthetically, he fashioned himself as a work of art through his writings, and these writings were heterogeneous, varied, sometimes contradictory, and ever able to escape circumscription by a metaphysical metanarrative. Sarah Kofman, in one of her last works, *Explosion I: De "l'Ecce Homo" de Nietzsche,* examines Nietzsche along similar lines and concludes that Nietzsche's oeuvre, as well as his life, expresses the unstable subject. Thus, there are *Nietzsches,* not one Nietzsche, each akin to a performance in writing.

When we turn to the concept of the chorus, there are deeper connections. In the *Birth of Tragedy,* Nietzsche argues that tragedy arises from the chorus (BT 56) and that it serves as "the mirror image in which the Dionysian man contemplates himself" (BT 63). The chorus articulates the "terrible destructiveness of so-called world history as well as the cruelty of nature" (BT 59). For Nietzsche, the Dionysian insight into destructiveness informs the creative act as well. "Whoever must be a creator always annihilates," declares Zarathustra (59). This principle of reciprocity between creation and annihilation is a central component in African music. As Schuller indicates, an African master drummer begins with expositional material, and then the "seed pattern" is "varied, manipulated, augmented, diminished, fragmented, [and] regrouped in new variants" (58). In his description of John Coltrane, Amiri Baraka says much the same thing. Coltrane, according to Baraka, would destroy a song and reassemble it in his own way; he showed his followers "how to murder the popular song. To do away with weak Western forms" (*Black Music* 174). Thus, jazz composition enacts the destruction of the exposition through the call-and-response pattern of the melody and thereby recalls the role played by the chorus (as described by Nietzsche).

Jazz compositional style (fragmentation/reassembly, destruction/creation, call/response, etc.) can be observed in several components of Reed's novel, including its formal structure (which I will describe as a musical narrative employing both horizontal and vertical elements); in the temporal registers indexed in the narrative (what I see as Reed's attempt at establishing polyrhythms or cross rhythms in his text); and in the narrative focalization (an analogue to passing off solos to different instrumentalists). At the thematic level, for example, just as Jes Grew's fourteen textual parts came together in the ragtime of the 1890s, the Jazz Age of the 1920s, and the writing and music of the late 1960s and early 1970s, so will jazz compositional style come again, as Reed suggests. "Dionysus cut to pieces," writes Nietzsche, "is a *promise* of life; it will be eternally reborn and return again from destruction" (WP ¶ 1052). This promise and return is the hallmark of jazz composition. To my mind, this jazz idiom constitutes the poetic wisdom of *Mumbo Jumbo*, a truth expressed via a particular mode of narration. In the remainder of the chapter, I would like to turn my attention to three key aspects of jazz music and relate them specifically to Reed's novel. First, I want to focus on the musical concepts of melody and harmony as they specifically relate to jazz and show how Reed inscribes these elements in his novel. Second, I want to explore briefly the notion of rhythm and its place in jazz music and *Mumbo Jumbo*. Finally, I want to examine the notion of improvisation in jazz and how Reed constructs narrative analogues of this musical activity. Throughout the discussion of these three elements of the jazz idiom, I will be indicating how they relate to Nietzschean and Vichian philosophy.

Melody and Harmony in Jazz and the Narrative

Gunther Schuller contends that swing, one of the primary sources of jazz, "maintains the perfect equilibrium between the horizontal and vertical relationships of the musical sounds" (7) where melodies are "horizontal projections of harmonic substructure" and harmonies are "verticalizations of melodic segments" (39). In his magisterial *Thinking in Jazz: The Infinite Art of Improvisation*, Paul F. Berliner also describes how jazz soloists mix horizontal (melodic) and vertical (harmonic) elements in their musical conceptions (128–29, 197–98). I believe the textual components of Reed's novel can be interpreted using these jazz compositional principles such that certain intertextual interventions (photographs, playbills, charts, excerpts of histories, false bibliographies) can be read along these horizontal/vertical and melodic/harmonic axes to bring out the antipodal compositional approach and Reed's complex sense of timing.

In terms of its formal structure, one can characterize *Mumbo Jumbo* as consisting of a horizontal element of the detective fiction/film plot and a vertical element of historic and mythic dimensions. In other words, one main melody of *Mumbo Jumbo* is a standard, the detective fiction, complete with kidnappings, murders, a missing precious object, gangsters' molls, even the summary "explain it all to you" speech offered by the hero detective, PaPa LaBas. The harmonic elements or voices of the novel, however, express themselves first and foremost through the various narratives that appear and reappear throughout the novel—the straightforward narration of the activities of LaBas, the *Mu'tafikah*, Black Herman, Woodrow Wilson Jefferson, and others; the italicized portion of the text that records the machinations of the Wallflower Order and may, in fact, be the thoughts of Hinckle Von Vampton; and the intertextual citations of real and imagined books about American history, voodoo, jazz musicians, and so forth. The other harmonic aspect of the novel (which I will discuss in greater detail below) consists of the various insertions of other materials—handwritten letters, photographs, and drawings—that frequently crop up in the narrative. Take, for example, chapters 3, 4, and 5 (a total of three pages). We first encounter in chapter 3 a drawing (attributed to Jose Fuentes) depicting an angel handing a sword to a knight, followed by an italicized portion of text describing the activities of the Wallflower Order, which in turn shifts over to normal typeface that discusses the purpose of art museums in the West. In chapter 4, the typeface is normal, but the narrative voice is that of the professional (though somewhat irreverent) historian who describes America in 1920 and the events leading up to that decade. By the time we turn to chapter 5, we come across quotations attributed to a book entitled *The Harding Era;* we also read a description of a picture that will be found in the novel some twenty-four pages later. These voices contribute to the harmonics of the novel such that they announce certain phrases that will be embellished, elaborated, and developed in the subsequent pages of the novel.

At this point, we should digress and consider what has just been described in light of structuralist and formalist theories of language and literature. One could characterize the horizontal or melodic axis as being homologous to the Saussurian notion of synchrony, which in turn would mean that the vertical axis of harmony that expresses different historical moments would correspond to diachrony. Perhaps a stronger case can be made for using Jakobson's two polarities of language. In this case, the metonymic axis of contiguity corresponds to the horizontal melody of the detective plot, while the metaphoric axis of similarity corresponds to the vertical harmonics of historical introjection. In Jakobson's terms, the metaphoric, vertical insertion or substitution of the historico-mythic materials (photographs, history texts, playbills, drawings, etc.) would constitute the dominant. It is the substitutive principle that governs *Mumbo Jumbo;* and this should come as no surprise when we remind ourselves that Reed is himself a poet.

Yet another way of describing the melody and harmony of the text would be to adopt a structuralist narratological vocabulary. The horizontal melody would, in a certain sense, be the *histoire,* the story that we abstract from the narrative once we have read it in its entirety. The vertical harmony would, therefore, correspond to the *récit,* or the narration of the text (i.e., what we read). This descriptive approach, however, does not account for the richly complex nature of the novel as a whole.

Linguistic and narratological paradigms aside, one of the most unsettling effects that reading *Mumbo Jumbo* has on its readers is the odd sense of timing that we experience as we shift across the centuries from paragraph to paragraph and, on occasion, within single sentences. In addition to the descriptions of ancient Egypt, the Middle Ages in Europe, and 1920s America, there are numerous references to the 1970s cultural scene as well, and these various temporalities exist simultaneously, especially when PaPa LaBas narrates the history of Jes Grew. For example, pictures of Nixon's cabinet appear in a section of the narrative describing the administration of Warren G. Harding; when LaBas offers his summary in 1920, he refers to William Styron's *Confessions of Nat Turner.* Perhaps this accretion of various signifiers, a type of syncretism that has been used to describe Reed's aesthetic style, accords with the notion that "African rhythm is based on additive rather than divisive principles" (Schuller 11). But the notion of temporality and rhythm must be examined in greater detail because, in Reed's handling of these elements, we can find the key to the novel's jazz aesthetic.

Rhythm as a Category of Human Experience

Rhythm has long been considered a central component of African-American music in general and jazz in particular. As LeRoi Jones (Amiri Baraka) reminds us: "The most apparent survivals of African music in Afro-American music are its rhythms: not only the seeming emphasis in the African music on rhythmic, rather than melodic or harmonic, qualities, but also the use of polyphonic, or contrapuntal, rhythmic effects" (*Blues People* 25). It is precisely this rhythmicity that W. E. B. Du Bois pays homage to when he writes: "the Negro folksong—the rhythmic cry of the slave—stands to-day not simply as the sole American music, but as the most beautiful expression of human experience born this side the seas" (205). For both of these perspicacious observers of African-American experience, rhythm is the key; this point is not lost on Reed.

Having acknowledged the importance of rhythm in African-American music and experience, we must attempt a clearer definition of the term. Alf Gabrielsson defines three types of rhythm: (1) as experience, (2) as overt behavior, and (3) as psychophysiological response (140). Rhythm as experience refers to types of motion, the "grouping of accents" and "feelings of excitement, tension, calmness, release, etc." As overt behavior, rhythm would include hand clapping and foot tapping, whereas rhythm as psychophysiological response is connected to "changes in breathing, heart rate, muscle activity, activity of the brain, etc." (140). Gabrielsson even discusses certain rhythmic movement patterns that induce "kinaesthetic sensations" (135).

With respect to *Mumbo Jumbo*, one can easily identify each of Gabrielsson's definitions with Jes Grew itself. The antiplague induces physical movement, extreme overt behavior, and somatic changes. But beyond this connection, there is little these definitions can do to reveal the rhythmicities of Reed's novel. To do so, we must turn to other theories of rhythm.

In his seminal essay "Defining Rhythm: Aspects of an Anthropology of Rhythm," Haili You insists that rhythm is not a concept; rather, it is "a category of human experience" in the Aristotelian or Kantian sense (373–74). As he describes it, rhythm is "an all-purpose metaphor" that we can use to interpret the temporal experience of the body (374). Following Benveniste, You notes that the original meaning, *rhythmos*, referred to flow and not to the periodicity of waves. Our present-day notion of the connection between rhythm and meter stems from this confusion. For Aristotle, *rhythmos* is *schema* (or form), and other Greek writers—such as Herodotus,

Aeschylus, and Xenophon—use it in this way (365). Based on this etymological analysis, You concludes that, from the beginning, rhythm "means form, transform, proportion in the physical, relational and moral sense" (366), and he goes on to discuss how *rhythmos* was a key term in ancient atomist philosophy. As he characterizes it: "Improvisation and indeterminacy of the atomic dispositions are the first nature of *rhythmos*" (366).

You's definition of rhythm as form is particularly helpful when we examine the rhythms of Reed's novel; it allows us to move away from the accepted notion of rhythm as meter. Although it would be possible to examine the speech patterns reproduced in the novel with an eye toward their meter, it is far more fruitful, in my estimation, to develop the notion of rhythm as form to see how Reed's narrative establishes and changes its rhythms.

One of the more important dimensions of Reed's jazz aesthetic concerns improvisation through polyrhythmicality, what James Lincoln Collier considered "the essential . . . principle of African music" and characterized as "the setting of two or more time schemes against one another" (Ogren 13). The "polyrhythmic time relationships" that Schuller identifies in African drumming have their counterpart in the multitemporality of Reed's text. As Berliner points out: "Perhaps the most fundamental approach to improvisation emphasizes rhythm, commonly known in the jazz community as time or time-feel" (147). Improvisers, according to Berliner, "experiment with the vertical relationships of their ideas by applying vocabulary patterns within different parts of a piece's harmonic-rhythmic form where their blend assumes distinctive attributes. At the same time, improvisers pursue the linear relationships of their ideas by combining vocabulary patterns in different ways to create new phrases" (184). Combining vocabulary patterns is precisely what Reed does throughout his novel. In chapter 18, for example, we enter the headquarters of the Wallflower Order and are given a description of Hierophant 1, the leader. As part of the description, we learn of the U.S. invasion of Haiti (1915–34) and read quotations from Alain Locke's *New Negro*. Suddenly, the narrative shifts into the second-person singular, and we think the thoughts of Hierophant 1:

> You must capture its Celebration and then it will dissolve. It's a new age. 1920. Sword fighting only interests the kids who attend the matinees. Douglas Fairbanks can sell Liberty Bonds and act but he is no aid to you. The Teutonic Order is of no use. You must use something up-to-date to curb Jes Grew. To knock it dock it co-opt it swing it or bop it. If Jes Grew slips into the radiolas and Dictaphones all is lost. Luckily your scientists are working on microorganisms;

miniscule replicas of yourself capable of surviving the atmosphere of any planet. Your inventors are preparing a Spaceship that will transport these micro-
organisms to 3 planets you've had your eye on. You wish all of your subjects
were like them. Loyal, passive, "just doing our job." (64)

We can also assume that some white readers may experience an eerie feeling of *déjà vu* in that some of these thoughts may have crossed their minds
at some time or another. The fear of a vibrant and (to whites) incomprehensible black culture unsettles many whites; and the idea that there is
always the alternative of colonizing space is one that has great currency,
especially today. The time change effected here is one that takes the
thoughts of a character in the 1920s and interpolates them into the minds
of readers such that they echo a familiar tune, and the shift in pronoun
can be likened to a chord change.

Once the second-person narrative ends, we return to the third-person
line but soon are forced to read the Atonist creed, a poem denouncing
people who can dance:

> *Look at Them! Just look at Them!*
> *throwing their hips this way, that*
> *way while I, my muscles, stone,*
> *the marrow of my spine, plaster, my*
> *back supported by decorated paper,*
> *stand here as goofy as a Dumb Dora.*
> *Lord, if I can't dance, No one shall.* (65)

This is followed immediately by a photograph of a Black Panther march
(circa 1970). Such a dramatic temporal rhythm shift underscores the polyrhythmic principles that Reed adheres to in that we, as readers, must keep
up with the change from prose narrative to poem and then with the semiotic intrusion of the photograph—which itself raises questions of temporality (e.g., What is the connection between the Panthers and the events
described in the previous passage? Are the Panthers a variation on a theme
long known in America? Is the dance referred to throughout this novel a
metaphor for "dancin' in the street"?). These temporal rhythms inscribed
in both narrative and semiotic form—historical events in 1920s America,
mythico-historical accounts of the Knights Templar, events in 1970s
America, to name but a few—serve as Reed's vocabulary patterns; he varies these vertically along the horizontal axis of the detective melody, what
jazz musicians would call the theme, or head, of the novel.

Melodic variation occurs frequently in jazz composition, and it is important to understand how this takes place. Berliner elaborates further on the notion of the melody when he describes the head as follows: "Performers commonly refer to the melody or theme as the head, and to the progression as chord changes or simply changes. It has become the convention for musicians to perform the melody and its accompaniment at the opening and closing of a piece's performance. In between, they take turns improvising solos within the piece's cyclical rhythmic form" (63). When examining the themes of *Mumbo Jumbo*, we can find chord progressions as expressed through the changes of voices in the novel. As LeRoi Jones (Amiri Baraka) contends: "Melodic diversity in African music came not only in the actual arrangements of notes (in terms of Western transcription) but in the singer's vocal interpretation" (*Blues People* 26). Thus, we can identify each voice in the novel as a particular interpretation of a specific melody or theme. For example, one of the major themes consists of the diversity within the African-American community. *Mumbo Jumbo* expresses this melody and its changes through the articulation of different attitudes among Black Americans. Thus, we can identify PaPa LaBas as a proponent of HooDooism or, more generally, a return to certain West African traditions. Abdul Sufi Hamid, of course, articulates the views of Black Muslims, whereas W. W. Jefferson is a budding Marxist. Hank Rollings, "the Guianese art critic" and "authority on Vermeer" who momentarily comes to the defense of Hinckle Von Vampton when LaBas makes his arrest, represents the sycophantic element within the community; he is the type of person who wants to play the game according to white rules and show whites that African Americans can do just as well (160). In addition, there is the accomplished poet Nathan Brown, who may best convey Reed's own views on diversity within the African-American community. "Is it necessary for us to write the same way?" Brown asks. "I am not Wallace Thurman, Thurman is not Fauset and Fauset is not Claude McKay, McKay isn't Horne. We all have unique styles" (102). He summarizes his philosophy tersely: "I have been educated in both cultures and so I use the advantages of both" (117). These characters express the complex and rich array of some of the belief systems (there are many more) within the African-American community as part of a melody within Reed's novel. As many critics have observed, there is no single Black culture, and Reed develops this particular melody and its changes through the specific changes from one character's point of view to another's.

Berliner's notion of repeating the melody at the end of a performance also occurs in Reed's novel when the detective melody achieves its full elaboration as PaPa LaBas addresses the gathering at the Villa Lewaro. Yet even in this lengthy summation in chapter 52, which is a recapitulation of the grand history that has brought about Jes Grew, Reed cannot resist playing off the melody. In his speech, delivered to a crowd in 1920, LaBas reveals that Osiris received a "far-out" education. This verbal anachronism, not unlike a dissonant note in a Thelonious Monk solo, is overshadowed by an even greater textual discordance, the insertion of graphs indicating the bombing tonnage in three wars—World War II, Korea, and Vietnam. Once again, the vertical concept prevails, and Reed continues the tune of the story of Set's violence and militarism by shifting the rhythm, so to speak, and depicting twentieth-century American war efforts—which included, at that time, an ongoing war.

It is quite possible to imagine this entire sequence presented by a third-person, omniscient narrator without the previously described changes. In such a case, the novel would adhere to a strict melody and maintain a steady rhythm and inevitably be an irrelevant piece of fiction. It is precisely these harmonic-rhythmic shifts that make *Mumbo Jumbo* what it is. Without them, it would be a forgettable tune.

Having considered the aspects of polyrhythmicity found in the novel, we must also look at a related element of jazz composition crucial to our understanding of Reed's novel: what musicians call "crips" (short for crippled). "Veterans," writes Berliner, "refer to the discrete patterns in their repertory storehouses as vocabulary, ideas, licks, tricks, pet patterns, crips, clichés, and, in the most functional language, things you can do" (102). When a musician runs out of improvisatory moves and falls back on an old schtick, a crip is being used. One of the most obvious examples of this occurs when Woodrow Wilson Jefferson's father, the Rev. Jefferson, arrives and rescues his son from the control of Hinckle Von Vampton and "Safecracker" Gould. Reed parodies the language and style of an old country preacher when he has the Rev. Jefferson stretch his hands toward heaven and say: "Lawd we axes you to pray over this boy . . . mmmmmmmmmmmm An deliver this child away from these naked womens . . . mmmm And sweet back mens. And save his soul from torment . . . mm" (142). The obvious nature of the parody should not obscure the fact that this is a crip taken from a warehouse of vocabulary and language that is instantly familiar and recognizable but at the same time appreciated because of the timely fashion in which Reed inserts it into his fiction. This crip helps Reed to get on to the next phase of the composition; he can discard W. W. Jefferson and move on to the next theme and series of changes.

Improvisation: In the Music, in the Text

In *Thinking in Jazz*, Paul Berliner provides detailed analyses and discussions of what jazz musicians do during the performance of their music. Early on, he makes a distinction between noun and verbal forms of the word "improvisation." According to Berliner, "When players use *improvisation* as a noun referring to improvisations as artistic products, they typically focus on the products' precise relationship to the original models that inspired them" (221). When musicians use the word as a verb, writes Berliner, "they focus not only on the degree to which old models are transformed and new ideas created, but on the dynamic conditions and precise processes underlying their transformation and creation" (221). When examining *Mumbo Jumbo* as an improvisation in the first sense, we see that the original models Reed works with and against include: detective fiction, the African-American novel tradition, the genre of the novel as a whole, and historical discourse (traditional histories).

The detective genre is well known, and its famous practitioners—Dashiell Hammett, Raymond Chandler, and Ross Macdonald—produced the paradigmatic, ruthless, unfeeling, matter-of-fact detective who has long since become a cliché. Reed exploits this expectation in the opening pages of his novel as the antiplague Jes Grew begins to sweep the nation, and officials are stymied as to how to combat it. As the novel unfolds, we discover that, read as a detective fiction, PaPa LaBas becomes our Sam Spade, but he differs markedly from his generic forebear. LaBas is cool—he can unflinchingly deal with the remains of the murdered Abdul Sufi Hamid—but he is also spiritual, a high priest of HooDoo, in fact. This added component to his personality and approach gives him more than street smarts and toughness and constitutes Reed's transformation and deviation from the original model.

With respect to the novel as a genre, Reed's approach best exemplifies Bakhtin's notion of the novel as the genre that parodies all other genres. Much has been written on Reed's parodic style and approach, and I will only mention briefly a few aspects of it. Readers often remark on how the opening of the novel flows like the credits in a film. The opening scene in the office of the mayor of New Orleans eventually fades and the page/

screen of the text is filled with an epigraph by Louis Armstrong, then a definition of the word "mumbo jumbo," and finally the title itself (in a different typography and with different graphics). The cinematic qualities of Reed's text critique traditional realist techniques of novel writing (i.e., make us aware of what Barthes once called "l'effet du réel"), force us to consider how film structures our reality, and, as Bakhtin would have it, show how the novel appropriates yet another form of discourse (in this case, film).

The addition of discursive addenda—photographs, newspaper clippings, drawings, reproduced hand-written letters, graphs and statistics, and paintings—recalls techniques used earlier by novelists such as Döblin and Dos Passos, but Reed is not trying to present the reality of everyday life by reproducing the actual artifacts from that life. On the contrary, Reed's use of these added elements calls into question the veracity of these modes of discourse and their truth-producing potential. The addition of these elements fragments or breaks up the narrative and gives us pause to consider just "where truth lies," in every sense of that expression, for Reed's parodic interpolation of situation reports, newspaper articles, and historical accounts underscores the constructed nature of all truth.

By highlighting the relative truths produced by various discourses, Reed expresses strong affinities with Nietzsche, particularly the Nietzsche of *On the Genealogy of Morals*. When Reed parodies historical accounts through his use of pseudobibliographies and footnotes to books, both real and imagined, he transforms the model of historical discourse and opens up new ways of seeing the narrativization of the past. For Reed, as for Nietzsche, any account of the past masks a certain series of power relations that preceded the account in question, and any narrative that expresses the events as natural, inevitable, or immutable obscures the play of power that necessarily must always obtain in the formation of values.

We have determined that Reed's improvisational relationship with the form of the novel and historical discourse in particular is parodic, mocking, and critical. When it comes to his relationship to the African-American tradition of the novel, Reed's position is well known. In *The Signifying Monkey*, Henry Louis Gates Jr. argues quite persuasively that Reed parodies, or signifies, on writers such as Hurston, Wright, Ellison, and Baldwin. In Gates's estimation, *Mumbo Jumbo* signifies on the history of the African-American novel "by repeating received tropes and narrative strategies with a difference" (217). This accurately describes what Berliner says about improvisation in the jazz world: the relation between a model (in this case Hurston or Ellison) and the product created through the improvisation (*Mumbo Jumbo*). The concept of signifying relates to jazz itself as Gates reminds us of works such as Jelly Roll Morton's "Maple Leaf Rag (A Transformation)" and its relationship to Scott Joplin's "Maple Leaf Rag" and Oscar Peterson's "Signify" to Count Basie's "Signifyin'" (63).

Gates's notion of signifying can be extended when one considers Nathaniel Mackey's notion of "othering," which Mackey breaks down into two categories. "Artistic othering," he writes, "has to do with innovation, invention, and change, on which cultural health and diversity depend and thrive. Social othering has to do with power, exclusion and privilege, the centralizing of a norm against which otherness is measured, meted out, marginalized" (76). Mackey focuses on instances of the former produced by people who suffer from the latter; and, as he makes clear, jazz musicians comprise a large number of these people. I include Reed in this same camp in part because, unlike Gates, I am not primarily concerned with Reed's relationship to an aesthetic tradition; rather, I am most interested in Reed's axiological approach—one that parallels Nietzsche's approach in many ways, a topic I will return to later. Thus, Reed "others" the novel and its various forms, as well as history, because he wishes to overcome the relative powerlessness of his values by offering this creative and innovative form known as *Mumbo Jumbo*, just as John Coltrane othered "My Favorite Things," bringing attention to his musical values while at the same time critiquing the whiteness of the dominant culture that itself is mentioned repeatedly throughout the song (Monson 292–300).

"Improvisation" can also be used by musicians as a verb. In Berliner's words, the focus is on "the dynamic conditions and precise processes underlying their transformation and creation" (221), and this definition can best be explained by looking at a specific jazz musician. Miles Davis, one of the most celebrated and controversial figures in the history of jazz, offers us a good example of what transpires during acts of improvisation. In his essay "'Out of Notes,'" Robert Walser analyzes the famous 1964 recording of Davis performing "My Funny Valentine." Walser describes how Davis uses risky techniques such as half-valving, "which creates a split, unfocused airstream—to create a variety of timbres and effects" (175). As a result of Davis's using these techniques, many critics and listeners regard the performance unfavorably. As Walser summarizes it: "Davis's consistent and deliberate use of risky techniques and constant transgression of genre boundaries are antithetical to 'classicism' and cannot be explained by formalism; from such perspectives, unusual content looks like flawed form. That is why so many critics have responded to Davis's music with puzzlement, hostility, or an uneasy silence" (172). In describing his work with the Miles Davis Quintet, Herbie Hancock explains that he felt the group was trying to mix the various "influences that were happening to all of us at the time and amalgamate them, personalize them." In doing so, Hancock contends, the audience heard two things simultaneously: "they were hearing the avant-garde on one hand, and they were hearing the history of jazz that led up to it on the other hand—because Miles was that history. He was that link" (Berliner 341). The use of risky techniques, the amalgamation of influences, and the simultaneous presentation of the avant-garde and history produced an effect that Hancock characterized as an acrobatic act: "We were sort of walking a tightrope with the kind of experimenting we were doing in music, not total experimentation, but we used to call it 'controlled freedom'" (Berliner 341). Of course, the image of the tightrope walker recalls the pivotal scene in the prologue of *Zarathustra*. At an even more significant level, one can recognize Hancock's description of controlled freedom as being a perfect example of what Nietzsche meant when he spoke of "dancing in chains" (HTH 343). The Nietzschean free spirit must engage in a delicate balancing act; both tradition and innovation are combined to produce the playful activity of the child. The three metamorphoses Nietzsche speaks of in *Zarathustra*—the transformation from the camel to the lion and finally to the child—is in accord with what has been said about Davis and what will be said about Reed. The jazz musician and novelist master a tradition, rebel against it, and ultimately produce a free and playful performance that is life enhancing and affirming.

Much of what has been said to describe the improvisational technique of Davis can also be said for Reed's work in general. In the specific case of *Mumbo Jumbo*, we can detect risky narrative techniques, a combination of influences, and elements of stylistic innovation and history that characterize Reed's improvisational performance. The techniques Reed employs in chapters 16 and 17 offer us a good example of this.

The sixteenth chapter opens with a question in the form of a name: "Von Vampton?" (58). The lack of quotation marks raises doubts in the reader's mind as to who is speaking. We wonder if we are reading the thoughts of the narrator or simply a dialogue that just does away with the standard convention of quotation marks. The quick response to this initial uncertainty is that we are reading a dialogue between Von Vampton and his managing editor at the *New York Sun*. Von Vampton is being criticized for writing a story that detailed what U.S. occupation forces were really doing in Haiti. The managing editor extols the virtues of what he calls the "American style," which consists of "strong lively short verbs and present tenses" (58). When Von Vampton begins to rebut this argument, we sense some uncertainty again because much of what Von Vampton is saying concurs with what the narrator has been signaling to us all along: that the dominant white culture is hypocritical and vapid. Von Vampton vocalizes the central ideology of Reed's novel at this point by declaring that the newspaper panders to the salacious whims of the readers when it carries "ads for the cheapest Bijou, scandalous stories about Hollywood and photos which titillate" while at the same time running "highfalutin stories on the cover" (58). Von Vampton continues by rejecting the editor's notion of style because the "concept of briefness will lead to inaccuracy." In short, the newspaper's "style book is a racing form" (58). The focalization of the dominant narrative point of view through Von Vampton is a risky move because, in doing this, Reed disrupts the simple expectation that Von Vampton represents an anti–Jes Grew attitude and hence cannot possibly articulate a critique of culture that is in accord with Jes Grew principles.

As the chapter continues, we run across bold-print reproductions of the actual headlines to Von Vampton's article. This technique, reminiscent of stylistic maneuvers in Dos Passos, moves us beyond the boundaries of human consciousness and speech and into the material world, for the physical print of the headline receives emphasis through the use of bold typeface. A second use of typographic change occurs when the managing editor fires Von Vampton. His words are reproduced in capital letters, thus indicating the volume of his voice: "THAT DOES IT. YOU'RE CRAZY. GO PICK UP YOUR PAY AND GET OUTTA HERE BEFORE I CALL THE BULLS" (59). When Von Vampton leaves the office, we encounter yet another bold-print sentence that indicates what the newspaper boys are shouting. It is nearly identical to what we read in the earlier reproduction of the bold headline when Von Vampton was in the editor's office. However, when the boys shout, "**VooDoo Generals Surround Marines At The Poor Prince**," we recognize that they say "Poor Prince" instead of Port-au-Prince, thus underscoring the distinction between oral and written culture, one of the major themes of the novel.

When Von Vampton hears the newspaper boys, the narrator indicates that he smiles, and then we read: "That's America for you. Rumor stacked upon rumor like bricks in the Mason's Tower of Babel. 'Gamalielese,' as

Mencken described Harding's prose. A prose style so bad that it had charm" (59). Once again we are left in doubt as to who is really speaking. Are these the thoughts of Von Vampton or the narrator or both? The use of this form of free, indirect discourse is not unique to Reed, but it is yet another stylistic variation that he includes in rapid succession in this chapter. By quoting Mencken on Harding, Reed includes elements of the real world as Von Vampton, a fictional character, thinks the thoughts of an actual human being. Once again, such moves are quite common in novels, particularly historical novels. Yet the same can be said of jazz compositions. Jazz pieces are often compilations of elements of standards and phrases from other, often older, forms of music; the key to understanding, appreciation, and enjoyment, however, is not to be found in simply indentifying each element. The complete aesthetic experience obtains only when we recognize the parts through the whole. Or, better yet, the whole performance, its totality and completeness, draws attention to the changes that occur in the music and hence makes us aware of the technical and stylistic virtuosity of the performer. I see Reed doing much the same thing as he shifts typeface, focalization, and voice in these chapters.

Right on the heels of the commentary on Harding's prose comes a jarring shift. We encounter a situation report, or S.R., presented in typescript imitating telegraphic type, that describes rumors about a U.S. Marine becoming a victim of cannibalism, indicates how "Kongress" passes a resolution condemning Haiti, and includes a quotation attributed to James Weldon Johnson in which he argues that the Haitian custom of eating a human without cooking him at least serves a utilitarian purpose, whereas the U.S. custom of cooking a human without eating him is open to criticism. The Weldon quotation is footnoted at the bottom of the page, indicating that it appears in Johnson's autobiography *Along This Way* (59–60).

The S.R. contains a number of combinations of technique and style incorporating both history and hearsay. Once again, the S.R. appears in yet another typescript, thus offering us a different reading or visual experience. The reference to cannibalism raises serious questions about some of the deepest cultural stereotypes that haunt white America: that African peoples are uncivilized, that they are savages, or—in the words of Mr. Kurtz—"brutes." The simple use of the letter *K* when spelling "Kongress" signifies an institution that acts like King Kong and thus indicates who the real beast in the world is. In addition, the use of the Germanic *K* spelling, often invoked when critics speak of Amerika, also indicates a type of militaristic, perhaps quasifascist orientation to the institution as a whole. Finally, the humorous analysis of the situation supposedly offered by Johnson and attributed to a real book by the scholarly device of the footnote again focuses attention on the real and the imagined and the veracity of fiction. Aside from a simple play on the "raw and the cooked," Reed is ventriloquizing through Johnson and describing how the very economic and social structures of the United States harm certain of its citizens. The real scandal for "Johnson" consists simply in the fact that the United States cannot even invoke its fundamental philosophy of utilitarianism to justify such actions.

The S.R. gives way to the opening of chapter 17, which describes the recently fired Von Vampton wandering the streets and chuckling to himself in large print: "HEHEHEHEHEHEHEH . . ." (60). We then read an indented paragraph describing dance as a "universal art" and arguing: "Those who cannot dance are imprisoned in their own ego and cannot live well with other people in the world" (60). Once again, a footnote indicates that this quotation comes from a book, in this case a study authored by Joost A. M. Meerloo entitled *The Dance: From Ritual to Rock and Roll, Ballet to Ballroom*. To the best of my knowledge, no such book exists. (Is the name a pun—"Just a mere loo"?) But the argument presented here mirrors the argument of *Mumbo Jumbo*. Thus, we are reading the truth of a fiction in a fiction that masquerades as scholarly research.

Immediately after the quotation from Meerloo, we see the graphic symbols of two circles, one darkened in and the other white, that appear often in the novel and that Robert Elliot Fox describes as a *vé vé*, a design traced out on the ground that signifies a *loa*, or god of voodoo ("Blacking" 95). He goes on to associate these symbols with standard oppositions of black/white, left/right, yes/no, as well as textuality versus orality (95–96). Ultimately, Fox argues that these symbols, not unlike the symbol for the Tao, give us two sides of "the metaphysical coin" (97). So much is suggested by these two graphic signifiers (and so unsettling can be their effect) that it is even more shocking to move one's eyes just a few millimeters below the symbols and look at a photograph depicting a little girl and a woman looking off to the right of the page. Both are dressed in formal gowns. The little girl wears a tiara and holds aloft in her right hand a small American flag as she points off into the distance with her left hand. The woman is kneeling at the girl's right side. She wears an American flag in the form of a cape and places both hands above her eyes in the gesture of a lookout, as if she is scrutinizing the horizon in an attempt to see what the little girl is pointing out. Any effort to interpret this photograph is fraught with dangers. The prose below the photo describes a Knights Templar meeting that Von Vampton attends. Perhaps the photo signals the coming of the Knights Templar to the New World. Or perhaps it is a representation of looking or spying; for, in the prose that follows, we learn that Von Vampton's landlady has been watching him through the keyhole in the door. Whatever the case may be, this symbolization of America is yet another instance of mockery and, more important, a daring and risky move that makes up part of Reed's narrative technique.

On the two final pages of chapter 17, we read about Von Vampton's abduction by the Wallflower Order. We read excerpts from Jung's *Psychology and Religion,* in which he wonders if the inclusion of jazz in the unworldly Christian world would be viable. There is also a quotation attributed to David St. Clair, in what is apparently a fictitious book, that claims "'the African deities were fond of food, drink, battle, and sex'" (62). After this, we read the description of the synthetic world of the Wallflower Order (quoted above), which is written in a completely different voice—malevolent, cool, and direct. The chapter closes with a final quotation attributed to Jung that indicates how the "catastrophe of the first World War" was necessary to "arouse a doubt as to whether all was well with the white man's mind" (63).

As I have indicated, these two chapters—in the space of little more than five pages—contain a wide array of narrative techniques that include focalization and voicing, typographic alternation, symbolic graphics, extended quotations from real and imagined books, and photography. None of these techniques is unique to Reed, and none is new in the history of the novel. What is new, and what we must not lose sight of, is the performance, that is, the succession of these techniques, the particular mix of these styles, and the daring with which Reed, much like Miles Davis, puts into play a heterogeneous mix of narrative and writing techniques that can upset a traditionalist who is comfortable with novels following nineteenth- or even early twentieth-century forms of the novel.

How else, then, might we identify the act of improvisation in Reed's novel? One way is to consider how musicians see their improvisations as types of conversations they are having. Berliner identifies five main types of improvisation as "musical conversation." First, a "player converses with predecessors within the jazz tradition, creating new ideas in relation to established improvisation conventions and previous interpretations of the composition known to the player" (497). We have already referred to Gates's masterful description of Reed's signifying on the writers within the African-American tradition who preceded him (*Signifying* 217–38). No improvement can be made on Gates's observations, and they are so widely known that they need not be recapitulated here.

The next form of conversation consists of an "inner dialogue," what Berliner calls "a conversation that [band members] carry on with themselves" (497). One can relate this form of conversation to Reed's entire oeuvre. In his essay on Reed's experimental fiction, Neil Schmitz asserts that Reed attempts to avoid succumbing to the traditional approaches to the novel as well as to the fashionable forms of contemporary experimental fiction and metafiction. "To turn from the stiffening of the traditional novel James Baldwin shares with John Updike," writes Schmitz, "only to fall into the linguistic despair of William Burroughs or the elaborate glosses of metafiction is an artistic fate Reed has taken great pains to avoid" (126). Thus, Reed's body of work constitutes a continual transformation, an ongoing performance in flux, or a state of becoming that attempts to distance itself from literary antecedents—including those Reed has produced himself. Lizabeth Paravisini notes how Reed parodies a whodunit in *The Last Days of Louisiana Red*, the conventional western in *Yellow Back Radio Broke-Down*, and the fugitive slave narrative in *Flight to Canada* (113). Reed, in other words, is in dialogue with the tradition as well as himself, and, like Miles Davis, he attempts to avoid succumbing to a particular mode or style, tradition or subgenre.

Berliner describes the third form of conversation as one that is rooted in the idiosyncratic playing technique of an individual performer. He writes: "Artists' conversations also have a historical dimension on a personal level: in each performance, the player's unfolding ideas grow, moment by moment, out of a cumulative lifetime of performance and musical thinking" (497). Although the very fact that the novel is published may seem to preclude this type of conversation from occurring, there are in fact published *versions* of *Mumbo Jumbo*. The original hardback version, published in 1972, had a cover design that depicted Josephine Baker, a rose, and a medallion; this design does not appear on the cover of the 1988 Atheneum reprint. In addition, some of the photographs in the two versions are different. Thus, one could argue that these two publications are in fact separate performances of the novel—the two are not exactly alike, just as no two performances of a jazz piece are exactly alike.

The fourth form of conversation is described by Berliner as the "interaction between players and audience" (497–98). With respect to *Mumbo Jumbo*, the question of audience is a vexed one. Reed clearly communicates with members of both the African-American and European-American communities. Thus, he does not offer a monocultural perspective. Much of what he has to say is critical of certain elements within the African-American community as well as elements of the dominant white culture. As noted above, when Reed reproduces the thoughts of Hierophant 1 (64), white readers in particular may feel a bit uneasy because Reed expresses ideas that few whites have dared to voice publicly but that many may have thought privately. In this case, he presents his white audience with ideas they may have often denied espousing.

In chapter twelve, Reed addresses both audiences. When LaBas testifies in court, he refuses to swear on the Bible. The narrator tells us that LaBas "demands the right to his own idols and books." The narrative continues: "It reminds PaPa LaBas of the familiar epigram: 'Orthodoxy is my Doxy. Heterodoxy is the other fellow's Doxy'" (48). Here, one can discern a humorous address to certain segments of the African-American community that feel estranged from dominant and often intolerant Christian culture. One can imagine members of this audience nodding their heads in assent, saying, "Uh huh." Then the typescript becomes italicized, and we read that *"the late Teens and early 1920s are a bad time for civil liberties"* (48); what follows is a brief history of social and political struggle during this period, including incidents involving the Industrial Workers of the World, "Reds," and people who express anti-American sentiments. This history contains information that few (if any) contemporary U.S. history books would recount, and Reed is directly addressing members of the dominant white culture and asking them to consider what is often overlooked and obscured in conventional and popular accounts of the past. After this italicized account, Reed offers a two-sentence paragraph: "Fear stalks the land. (As usual; so what else is new?)" (48). The parenthetical comment is addressed to the nonwhite audience that has always known this. By placing this in close proximity to the italicized précis (which must be news to some white readers), it is clear that Reed is trying to signal how the two communities, based on their separate experiences, view events from radically different perspectives.

One of the most poignant examples of Reed specifically addressing the Black audience occurs at the very end of the novel, when PaPa LaBas is accosted by a "pitiful creature" who mouths the teachings of Freud and Marx and refers to Black studies as "'so much black eyed peas'" (216). The narrative continues to describe the divergent points of view these two men have:

LaBas felt everybody should have their own head or the head of God which the Atonist's mundane 'system' wouldn't admit. *Homo economicus.* The well-fed the will-less robot who yields his head to the Sun King. The sad old creature wanted the Jes Grew Carriers to have his head. Cut out this Jes Grew that keeps a working man up to all hours of the night with its carryings on. The Ballyhoo of its Whoopie. Its Cab Calloway hidihidiho.

He wanted them to have *his* head. An Atonist head. While LaBas wanted them to have their heads their people had left for them or create new ones of their own. A library of stacks a 1000 miles long. Therefore he and PaPa LaBas disagreed about what to do with the head, not the body. (216–17)

The struggle here is the key to understanding what Reed has been saying throughout the novel to his fellow African Americans. Rather than blindly espouse the cultural traditions of Europe, LaBas and Reed call for a return to non-European traditions *and* a transcultural mixture of traditions in the hopes of making something new. At the very end of his novel, Reed offers a warning to the Black community: either have the courage to leave the confines of the European tradition or perish.

The fifth, final, and highest level of conversation constitutes a "transcendental" experience "in which players feel, if only momentarily, 'in touch with the big picture'" (Berliner 498). Only at this level does the analogy with levels of conversation break down. Such a conversation is necessarily beyond our ken, not because *Mumbo Jumbo* is a novel, but because, as with jazz music itself, we as readers and listeners will never know if this dialogue is achieved; it is something only the performers and writers know themselves.

One should remember that all of these conversations are going on simultaneously. As Berliner describes it: "To use one of the metaphors favored by musicians, improvisation is a musical conversation that the improviser enters on many different levels simultaneously" (497). In addition to these complex, simultaneous expressions, there also occur in *Mumbo Jumbo* what we may describe as solo performances. There are moments in the novel when we encounter situation reports that sound like underground radio reports about what is actually happening in Haiti. I see these textual moments—as well as the letters of Abdul Sufi Hamid, the large portions of intertext, and even Reed's apparent parenthetical asides (initialed I.R.)—as brief textual solo performances in which individual instrumentals veer off from the narrative and reveal their own unique style through improvisatory moves.

Reed's jazz thinking, like Nietzsche's perspectival thinking, is essentially axiological, not metaphysical (Schrift 60). In *Mumbo Jumbo*, Reed poses questions of value and uses a jazz compositional style, one that I have associated with Dionysianism, to posit new, life-affirming values. It is my contention that, although Nietzsche's search proved unsuccessful, the musical manifestation of the Dionysian that he sought occurred in jazz, the origins of which can be traced to turn-of-the-century New Orleans. Some things, as Nietzsche would say, are born posthumously, and it is Reed's novel that demonstrates how jazz embodies the spirit of Nietzsche's Dionysian vision and articulates the cultural critique that Nietzsche tried to present in his own writings.

For me, this combination of jazz compositional style in pursuit of Nietzschean goals makes Reed a "satyric" writer, not a postmodern practitioner of historiographic metafiction. I borrow the term "satyrique" from Sarah Kofman, who, in her *Explosion I: De "l'Ecce Homo" de Nietzsche*, describes the tone of Nietzsche's text as being "toujours épicée de beaucoup de méchanceté et de bonne humeur où gravité et enjouement se donnent tendrement la main" (31; always spiced with a great deal of maliciousness and good humor where seriousness and cheerfulness delicately join forces). She perceives in Nietzsche's text an "alliance de deux tons 'contradictoires' qui piétine en dansant la morale et fait sauter toutes les oppositions métaphysiques" (31; alliance of two contradictory tones that trample on morals while dancing and shake up all metaphysical oppositions). Such a tone, she adds, "se moque de tous ceux qui ne savent pas rire du sérieux ou du 'tragique' de la vie en la traitant sur un mode parodique" (31; mocks all those who do not know how to laugh at the seriousness or the tragic element of life by treating it in a parodic mode). Kofman's description applies equally well to Reed's *Mumbo Jumbo*.

Reed would agree with Nietzsche: "the question of values is more *fundamental* than the question of certainty" (WP ¶ 588). This is why in *Mumbo Jumbo* Reed offers a new foundational myth: because he recognizes, as did Nietzsche, that "without myth every culture loses the healthy natural power of its creativity" (BT 143). And in *Mumbo Jumbo*, that myth is expressed in a jazz idiom that best exemplifies the cultural values that Reed associates with HooDooism, values that we might term transcultural.

The emphasis on myth returns us once again to the philosophy of Vico, which surprisingly enough has some affinities with jazz aesthetics. In an interview, Reed discussed his own works as "fictions":

When I say "own fictions," I mean that one can speak more accurately of the psychological history of a people if one knows the legends, the folklore, the old stories which have been handed down for generations, the oral tales, all of which tells you where you came from, which shows the national mind, the way a group of people looks at the world. I think you can ascertain that by going and reconstructing a past which I call Neo-Hoodoo in my work. I call it Neo-Hoodoo because you can have your own psychology rather than someone else's. In other words they are trying to make us Europeans in this country, and we don't think that way. (Nazareth 121–22)

Reed's emphasis on the legends and oral tales accords with the Vichian notion of the poetic wisdom of a culture. More than anything else, *The New Science* indicates that the only way we can understand a culture, past or present, is to examine what Reed calls "the old stories which have been handed down for generations." This is precisely what Vico does in book 3, "The Discovery of the True Homer." As Cecilia Miller puts it, in book three, Vico affirms that only "from oral history, and later codified versions of the same" could one "gain historical knowledge of the past" (76). Reed recognizes that the truths of a culture appear in their fictions, and his project, which is Vichian in design and spirit, is to purvey these fictions so as to promulgate cultural change.

The emphasis on stories and tales also has strong connections with jazz. LeRoi Jones (Amiri Baraka) relates that an "important aspect of African music was the use of folk tales in song lyrics, riddles, proverbs, etc., which even when not accompanied by music, were the African's chief method of education, the way the wisdom of the elders was passed down to the young" (*Blues People* 28). These influences appear in a modified form in jazz, often taking the form of musical riddles and puns. Berliner also emphasizes the connection between stories and jazz when he considers what musicians call "storytelling": "For early jazz players like Louis Armstrong and Sidney Bechet, and for swing players like Lester Young, storytelling commonly involved such designs for multiple choruses as devoting an initial chorus to interpreting a piece's melody, devoting the next to expressive liberties varying it, and then returning to the melody or proceeding on to the other events such as single-note riffing patterns" (201). Thus, the very origins of jazz music are rooted in legends and storytelling, and the performance of the music itself is also described as the telling of stories (through variations of chorus and melody interpretation).

A second Vichian connection appears when we consider the fact that jazz is a communal art form; it springs from the entire community. Just as Vico concentrated his efforts on delineating the wisdom of the people through their communal production of poetry and law, jazz critics, historians, and enthusiasts must take into account how the music springs from a communal effort and is not to be associated with single individuals. In her book *The Jazz Revolution*, Kathy Ogren repeatedly emphasizes that jazz is participatory in nature. The call and response and the very activities associated with jazz performance clearly indicate that communal activity is at the heart of jazz. Ingrid Monson is even more emphatic: "I view jazz improvisation as a mode of social action that musicians selectively employ in their process of communicating" (285).

In addition to the focus on legends and community, there is a third connection between Vico and jazz. In his most detailed analyses of what takes place during an act of improvisation, Berliner describes the effects in the minds of the musicians as follows: "The experience of negotiating through the ever-changing patterns around them from the perspective of their personal structural maps is a rich and dynamic one for improvisers. It potentially involves the imaginative play of sounds, physical gestures, colorful shapes, and abstract symbols, whose gestalt creates the impression of perpetual movement through the multidimensional musical realm" (92–93). Improvisers, claims Berliner, must engage mind and body with the surrounding environment. He describes how, during performances, musicians must "contend with different relationships between the singing mind and the body" (189). He continues: "The body plays an even more active role when, through its motor sensory apparatus, it interprets and responds to sounds as physical impressions, subtly informing or reshaping mental concepts" (190). Berliner then describes the very thoughts of the musician during an act of improvisation: "Like the improviser's store of musical knowledge, the ideas that occur during a solo assume different forms of representation: sounds, physical gestures, visual displays, and verbalizations. Each potentially involves distinctive thought processes and distinctive qualities of mediation with the body" (206).

Each of Berliner's descriptions has strong affinities with Vico's notion of *fantasia*. The imaginative acts that the musicians engage in are reminiscent of the body-centered, imagistic projections that Vico himself imagines when he tries to explain how humans first fashioned imaginative universals. It is through the combination of the sensual imaging—through sight, sound, smell, taste—and sensation that the first humans made their world. We know that the "intuitive and communal aspect of mental activity" was of central concern to Vico (Miller 51). And it seems that the same can be said for jazz musicians—they have an intuitive, body-oriented way of being in the world that grows from acts of the imagination. By extension, we can see that *Mumbo Jumbo* enacts the same processes; it constitutes a narrative representation of jazz thinking that makes manifest the multifarious ideas—linguistic, aural, semiotic, physical—that inform each jazz solo performance, and Reed presents all possible thinking modalities in his novel. Abstract shapes, images, various forms of texts and typescripts, all of these and other elements make the gestalt of Reed's jazz thoughts on history and culture. These radical combinations of textual materials that require our close attention to images, typescript, spacing, vocabulary, and tone of voice are, concomitantly, examples of the Vichian dimension of Reed's jazz aesthetic.

In its entirety, *Mumbo Jumbo* can be perceived as Reed's own solo improvisation on American history, African-American literary traditions, and the mythic foundations of Western culture. I would contend that Nietzsche's early description of Wagner can more aptly be applied to Reed. More so than Wagner, Reed is an "interpreter and transfigurer of the past" (UM 257). Reed's history of Western civilization, of 1920s and 1970s America, does what Nietzsche hoped all true histories would do: "tak[e] a familiar, perhaps commonplace theme, an everyday melody, and composing inspired variations on it, enhanc[e] it, elevat[e] it to a comprehensive symbol, and thus disclos[e] in the original theme a whole world of profundity, power and beauty" (UM 93). But this can only be achieved through creating by destroying. As Nietzsche points out: "The madly thoughtless shattering and dismantling of all foundations, their dissolution into continual evolving that flows ceaselessly away . . . all this may concern and dismay moralists, artists, the pious, even statesmen: *we* shall for once let it cheer us by looking at it in the glittering magic mirror of a *philosophical parodist* in whose head the age has come to an ironical awareness of itself" (UM 108). Reed has offered us that glittering magic mirror and called it *Mumbo Jumbo.*

What, then, is history for Reed, what would or could it mean? History as an act of improvisation raises the most fundamental questions about how one constructs historical narratives. By improvising history, Reed concurs with Amiri Baraka's succinct phrase "How *is* What" (*Black Music* 124). And as for history itself, Reed, like Duke Ellington, would simply respond, "It don't mean a thing . . ."

7

Narrating the Past:
Graham Swift's *Waterland*

The first communities were called *phratriai* by the Greeks, and the first lands were called *pagi* by the Latins, like the Dorian Greek for spring, *paga;* that is, water, the first of the two principal solemnities of marriage. For the Romans celebrated marriage *aqua et igni* because the first marriages were naturally contracted between men and women sharing the same water and fire, that is, of the same family; whence marriage must have begun between brothers and sisters.
—Vico, *The New Science*

Consider the cattle, grazing as they pass you by: they do not know what is meant by yesterday or today, they leap about, eat, rest, digest, leap about again, and so from morn till night and from day to day, fettered to the moment and its pleasure and displeasure, and thus neither melancholy nor bored.
—Nietzsche, *Untimely Meditations*

When we hear the term "history" used in everyday parlance, we must pause and consider whether the word refers to a written document about the past or the events themselves that transpired in the past. We must determine if we are speaking about the things in themselves or the description of those same things; usually, we must ask ourselves if the word refers to acts or writing. In *History and Memory*, Jacques Le Goff reminds us that in fact history has two or three different meanings. First, there is "the inquiry into 'the acts accomplished by men' (Herodotus) that has sought to establish itself as a science, the science of history; second, the object of that inquiry, what men have accomplished." "But," Le Goff continues, "history can also have a third meaning, which is precisely that of *narrative*" (102).

Le Goff's definition provides a useful starting point to consider many of the controversies surrounding the vexed term history. History aspiring to be a form of science, which Le Goff traces back to the writings of Herodotus, achieved its apogee in the nineteenth century, when historians such as Ranke, Marx, and Michelet attempted to uncover specific laws that governed historical development. Resting on the triumph of Enlightenment thinking (as embodied in the writings of Galileo, Bacon, Newton,

Descartes, Locke, and others), many nineteenth-century historians applied what has been termed "the heroic model of science" to their historical investigations. The hope was that, just as Newton and Kepler had uncovered the laws describing gravitational pull and planetary motion, the historian, armed with the scientific method, could determine laws governing human behavior. Marxism may provide the most famous example of this approach. In the words of Appleby, Hunt, and Jacob, Marxism "was a vision of history informed by heroic science that offered a concrete social and economic model of the meaning of progress . . . that sought the laws of change within the process of history itself . . . and that claimed a scientific status for the inexorable workings of social laws" (71). Marxism, as a form of history influenced by "heroic science," is not the exception but very much the rule, beginning with Hegel and Comte and continuing to the present day. The scientific approach still dominates historiography inasmuch as historians seek to verify their accounts based on evidence and, in some cases, statistical data. The key factor here is that the methods used to describe functions in nature were and are transposed to the realm of human activity. This approach, however, has revealed its limitations in the twentieth century, as historians have become increasingly frustrated with the possibility of ever uncovering actual laws that can explain the behavior of humanity. To cite just one example from the chorus of critical voices raised in opposition to the heroic science model used in the service of historical research, we can turn to G. M. Trevelyan, who argued that when historians adopted such a method, they went astray. As he observed: "The idea that the facts of history are of value as part of an exact science confined to specialists is due to a misapplication of the analogy of physical science" (230).

Le Goff's second definition is equally troubling. Acts committed in the past remain beyond our immediate observation. We will never see Caesar cross the Rubicon or Louis XIV at Versailles. Even events in the immediate past that, because of technology, can be witnessed on film or videotape are captured from a particular angle of vision, one that precludes other, multiple points of view. Thus, the ability to resurrect the past in all its manifestations, as it actually occurred, remains an ideal that no method or technology can guarantee.

Finally, there is Le Goff's third definition, one that has served as the focal point for much of the present book. The association of history and narrative creates a host of complications when we begin to consider how to distinguish truth claims in fictional narrative from truth claims in historical narrative. Thus, to utter "history" is to express a *con*fusion—one that is rich and troubling, indispensable and unresolvable.

Added to Le Goff's observations on the very definition of history, we should also consider what his eminent countryman, Fernand Braudel, has to say about the practice of history. "Nothing is more important, nothing comes closer to the crux of social reality than this living, intimate, infinitely repeated opposition between the instant of time and that time which flows only slowly," writes Braudel in his famous essay on *la longue durée* ("History" 26). It is precisely this notion of slow, durative time that undergirds Braudel's entire historical approach, especially as it appears in his magisterial work *The Mediterranean and the Mediterranean World in the Age of Philip II*. By focusing on *la longue durée,* Braudel emphasizes the crucial role geography plays in the development of history. Stating that his goal is to "divide historical time into geographical time, social time, and individual time" (*Mediterranean* 21), Braudel offers us a deeper understanding of the temporal dimensions that inform our comprehension of our own experience. Geographical time informs "a history whose passage is almost imperceptible"; it is a history that shows "man in his relationship to the environment, a history in which all change is slow, a history of constant repetition, ever-recurring cycles" (*Mediterranean* 20). Coupled with social time, which focuses on the history of "groups and groupings" (*Mediterranean* 20) and individual time, which presents a more "traditional history" of "individual men" (*Mediterranean* 21), geographical time opens up new and complex relations between the history made by humans and the natural environment in which this history is played out.

The observations of Le Goff and Braudel, therefore, leave us with some vexing problems. When speaking of history, we must consider the relationship between the written account of the past and the actual acts that people committed in the past. We must be careful to account for the similarities and differences between so-called fictional narratives and historical (i.e., truthful) ones. In addition, we must come to terms with a complex notion of layered temporalities while at the same time paying special attention to the role geography plays in contributing to the unfolding of historical events. These constitutive components of history are not the only ones, but they cannot be ignored when we try to gain a better understanding of what we mean when we speak of history.

Much of what has been presented up to this point in the examinations of works by Fuentes, Daitch, Rushdie, Tournier, and Reed has concerned the tensions among these definitions of history. In large part, each of these writers scrutinizes the various relations between the textual notion of history and the idea that history refers to the deeds accomplished by humans in days gone by. But none has made the focal point of his or her novel a meditation on history, its definitions and semantic contradictions, in so complete and direct way as has Graham Swift in *Waterland*. From the opening epigraph of the novel—which presents the following definition: "Historia, ae, f. 1. inquiry, investigation, learning. 2. a) a narrative of past events, history. b) any kind of narrative: account, tale, story"—through periodically described classroom lectures on the French Revolution, to the repeated references to the "wide world" that often becomes associated with such cataclysmic events as the First and Second World Wars, readers of *Waterland* recognize that the novel serves as the locus for a meditation on history—its meanings and metamorphoses.

Part detective fiction, part neosensationalist Victorian narrative (Marsh), part natural history, and part high school history lecture, *Waterland* presents us with the story of Tom Crick, an English secondary school history teacher who is about to be fired because his discipline is no longer considered essential for today's students and, perhaps more important, because Tom's wife has become involved in a scandal that has made him a public embarrassment. In order to cope with the trauma of his wife's mental breakdown (manifested in her kidnapping of a child from a supermarket and her claiming that God gave her the baby), as well as his own sense of professional insecurity as he is about to be fired, Tom changes his class lectures on the French Revolution. Rather than discuss such typical French Revolution topics as the storming of the Bastille, the Reign of Terror, and the emergence of Napoleon, Tom chooses to discuss the history of his family. He tells the story of the Cricks (his father's ancestors) and the Atkinsons (family members on his mother's side). In the course of his lectures, he also manages to describe the Fenlands—a region of East Anglia that is characterized by swampland and is ever subject to flooding and erosion—and the behavior of the European eel, a creature indigenous to the region. Viewed from the perspective of a typical novel, Tom's story reflects the struggles of an individual who is the product of a particular culture. The novel records his attempt to make sense of his own experience in the context of the two branches of his family. Viewed from the perspective of a meditation on history, however, *Waterland* is much more. Swift offers us a complex analysis of the relationship between history as acts in the past and history as a narrative about those past acts. He also presents a detailed examination of the multilayered temporal levels that inform history. In addition, he considers the connections between natural history and history proper, a line of inquiry that allows us to better understand the problem of history as a science.

Swift constructs his novel in such a way that he presents us with what Pamela Cooper describes as a "repertoire of interchanging binaries" (379). Beginning with the basic dichotomy of history as actions in the past versus history as an act of writing, Swift creates a series of oppositions—including the those of individual time versus geographical time and nature versus history—only to collapse these oppositions by showing how each is implicated in the other, how each depends on its other such that ultimately we are left with a state of indeterminacy or unresolvable ambiguity when it comes to disentangling the various threads of temporality, textuality, and space in and of history.

In the course of presenting an examination of these oppositions, Swift's novel also articulates key elements in the philosophies of Vico and Nietzsche that include the Vichian notion of *vera narratio*, or true narration, and the Nietzschean belief that life demands deception. In the pages that follow, I will trace the binaries that structure Swift's novel and show how they reveal the Vichian and Nietzschean dimensions of the text that express a philosophy of history that combines the perspectives of each philosopher.

History: Acts or Writing?

The very title of Swift's novel signifies the notion of opposition: water versus land. François Gallix correctly asserts that "c'est le titre dans toutes l'ambivalence et la force d'opposition de ses deux termes rapprochés et produisant une véritable déflagration au sens où l'entendait Eluard à propos de l'écriture surréaliste, qui servira de point de départ" (66; it is the title with all the ambivalence and the force of opposition of its two terms brought together and producing a veritable deflagration of meaning that Eluard understood to be appropriate to surrealist writing, which will serve as a point of departure). The title offers us a clue as to the philosophical meditation Swift inscribes in the pages of his novel. *Waterland* shows how the foundational conceptual oppositions (such as the simple distinction between water and land) exist in a form of metaphysical reciprocity such that a careful examination of any two binaries will yield a "déflagration au sens," an explosion of meaning.

The distinction we make between *history as a narrative* about actions

in the past and *history as a series of actions* that took place in the past constitutes one of the most important dichotomies that *Waterland* explores.
As Brewer and Tillyard noted in an early review of the novel, "Swift explores the tension between 'history' as something that really happened—
the events of the past—and 'history as construction and artifice,' a tale
which is told in much the same way as a novelist tells a story" (49–50).
Swift, however, chooses not to reinforce this dichotomy; rather, he sets
up the opposition of narrative and action and then, through Tom Crick's
meditative and rambling commentary, demonstrates how the meanings
of these terms are mutually dependent on one another. In short, Swift's
novel indicates that, just as history as narrative depends on an assumption of actions having taken place in the past, it is equally true that the
presumption of cognizing actions as having taken place depends on a
narrative function of some sort.

The opposition between action and narration receives its clearest expression in the comparison Tom makes between the two branches of his
family—the Atkinsons on his mother's side (the family gripped by ideas
and movement that, by brewing ale, make history) and the Cricks on his
father's side (the phlegmatic and fixed creatures of the Fens who drain the
land and simply tell stories). As Tom puts it tersely: "While the Atkinsons
made history, the Cricks spun yarns" (17). Tom expresses this stark contrast once again when he discusses the activities of Johannes Schmidt, a
Danish ichthyologist and oceanographer who set out to discover where
and how eels spawn, only to find his travels and research interrupted by
the First World War. In Tom's words: "There are those who fashion history and those who contemplate it; there are those who make things happen and those who ask why" (199). Later, this becomes elevated to the level
of what Tom must regard as a profound insight about his own profession,
something he characterizes as "the historian's besetting sin: how he pon-
ders contingencies, how he's no good at action" (291). But herein lies a
problem. Schmidt appears to be working in opposition to history, and his
activities are interrupted by the momentous historical event known, ap-
propriately enough, as the Great War. But in fact, his activities are themselves part of the history or accumulated narrative of the investigations
into the life cycle of the eel—something that has puzzled scientific observers since the time of Aristotle. In short, Schmidt makes things happen even
as he asks why. Can the same be said for someone who poses questions
about human behavior in the past?

In one of his numerous lessons on history, Tom asks his students to "liken the study of history to an inquest" (107). This analogy applies to Swift's novel in that the original pull of the narrative on the reader has its source in the detective subplot on the death of Freddie Parr. Tom tells his story about Freddie's death to show his students how the historian engages in the interpretive enterprise. "It's called reconstructing the crime. From last to first. It's an analogy of the historical method; an analogy of how you discover how you've become what you are. If you're lucky you might find out why," he tells his class (312). One of the key lessons Tom imparts by using this analogy is the danger of superimposing a preestablished narrative on new evidence. When the body of Freddie first appears, Tom notices a bruise on the head of the cadaver (a bruise that we learn was caused when Tom's brother, Dick, hit Freddie on the head with a bottle); this bruise is subsequently marred by a boat hook that Tom's father uses to try to fish the body out of the water. Tom, however, saw the original bruise as well as the new bruise caused by the boat hook. No one else, however, noticed this, and the final report listed the cause of death as death by drowning "because the examining pathologist, having been informed of the business of the boat-hook, did, indeed, have a casual eye and was concerned only to ascertain that Freddie's lungs were waterlogged" (35). So, when the pathologist examined the body, he concluded that the bruise to the head was solely caused by the hook itself because he took into account the narrative about the slip of the hook. The danger here, Tom implies, is that we can be swayed by covering stories that mask evidence that is right before our eyes.

Tom, however, is a better investigator, a better historian. Tom describes his own actions as a young boy, stating: "And we know what little Tom, whose initiative in this whole affair is so conspicuous by its absence, did. He watched; weighed evidence. Put facts together. Saw a new bruise on an old bruise. Fished a bottle—Ah yes, he's hooked by now, it's got serious, this historical method, this explanation-hunting. It's a way of getting at the truth" (263). True, Tom the boy sees things others miss; but, through this analogy, Tom the teacher offers an important lesson: despite his claims to the contrary, the rigid dichotomy between those who fashion and those who contemplate history simply does not hold. For it is precisely because of his contemplation of Freddie's body and his subsequent investigative activity that he pushes his brother to the brink of self-revelation. One could argue quite persuasively that Tom's contemplative behavior causes things to happen, that contemplation serves as the primary fashioning mechanism of a local historical event—the death of Dick

Crick. Had Tom not investigated the evidence he saw on Freddie's body, then Dick would not have been pushed to discover his own origins and, ultimately, take his own life. Far from his initiative being conspicuously absent, Tom actually takes purposive action through his investigative activities, the most extreme example of this being when he places the empty beer bottle in Dick's room.

One can make history or narrate it, claims Tom. But is this necessarily the case? The novel suggests otherwise. Can we not also make history by *narrating* it? Or narrate history by *making* it? Clearly one of the lessons Tom Crick tries to impart to his impatient students is that the revolution-aries of France were trying to narrate history by making it—their acts were perceived to be the unfolding of an earlier narrative, the narrative of the Roman Republic. In this regard, the Girondins, Montagnards, and Ja-cobins see in their actions the analogue of antecedent acts that come down to the historical players of 1789 in the form of a narrative. The deeds of the revolution had already been prescribed for the *citoyens;* by acting in accordance with a script from the past, they were able to narrate history. Conversely, one can also make history through an act of narration—this seems to be exactly what Tom is trying to do when he describes the saga of the Atkinsons and the Cricks; as he admits to his students, using their somewhat pejorative appellation for him: "old Cricky was trying to put himself into history; old Cricky was trying to show you that he himself was only a piece of the stuff he taught" (4). Yet the key to being a part of what he teaches hinges on Tom's ability to present his narrative.

The dichotomy becomes muddled even further if we pause to reexam-ine Tom's understanding of the Atkinsons as doers and the Cricks as nar-rators. Tom chooses the following figures of speech to characterize the contrast between the sedentary, yarn-spinning Cricks and the active, world-building Atkinsons: "The obstinacy of water. The tenacity of ideas" (69). Yet, these figures of obstinate water and tenacious ideas express notions opposed to those Tom hopes to convey. One can just as easily reverse the family oppositions because the Atkinsons succumb to the *story* of progress—ultimately, Ernest believes in the myth of the "Saviour of the World"—whereas the Cricks, although storytellers of sorts, continue their mundane activities on the Fens even as they recognize that the real world does not progress, that it is a flow of back and forth, an eternal cir-cularity, that human activity involves endless siltation and dredgery, and that the land exists in a constant state of being reclaimed. Thus, "tenac-ity of ideas," in addition to signaling the active principle that governs Atkinson behavior, also signifies the power of narrative, thereby suggesting that it is the Atkinsons who tell stories, perhaps *the* story of their time—the story of progress—and this story is actually more important than the physical activities they engage in. Similarly, the "obstinacy of water," rather than signaling a static environment that induces a pattern of endlessly repeated tales uttered to ward off boredom or keep at bay the recognition of life as a repeated pattern of never-changing, ultimately futile behavior, also signifies the constant *activity* that we as humans engage in. The obstinate waters require consistent human action and, during much of that time, preclude the possibility of storytelling. Comparing the two families and their respective activities can yield the equally valid conclusion that the Cricks are active all the time and there is not much of a story to tell when it comes to the mundane activity of drainage, whereas the Atkinsons are involved in articulating a grand Enlightenment narrative of progress and social advancement that far surpasses the specific activities associated with nineteenth-century ale brewing.

This reversal or inversion of the initially established dichotomy appears very early in the novel when Tom admits that his "father, as well as being a superstitious man, had a knack for telling stories" (2). Tom associates his father, a Crick, with the storytelling function, yet he quickly undercuts this affiliation two sentences later when he states the following: "It was a knack which ran in his family. But it was a knack which my mother had too—and perhaps he really acquired it from her. Because when I was very small it was my mother who first told me stories, which unlike my father, she got from books as well as out of her head, to make me sleep at night" (2). The novel's principal focus on the purpose, meaning, and function of history achieves its expression in the very beginning of the novel in the form of a simple and unresolvable question: who is the real storyteller in the family—Tom's father (Crick) or Tom's mother (Atkinson)? There is no clear and definitive answer to this question. When it comes to the larger pattern of opposition, as we have noted, Tom asserts that the Cricks "believed in fairy-tales. . . . they listened and repeated what they heard with wide-eyed awe, as if such things were not the stuff of fact but the fabric of a wondrous tale" (18). Yet, when it comes to his father, Henry, it is his future wife, Helen, an Atkinson, who heals Henry's psychic wounds from the Great War by telling him stories. Thus, we are unsure as to whether Henry tells stories because, being a Crick, he is prone to do so, or if in fact it is his encounter with the fabulating Helen that gives him the capacity to weave his own tales.

The ambiguity surrounding the source of tale-telling receives greater embellishment when Tom goes on to connect his mother's storytelling with his own fascination with history. "My earliest acquaintance with history was thus, in a form issuing from my mother's lips, inseparable from her other bedtime make-believe," he declares (62). Tom's early exposure to the stories his mother and father told him spurred him on to pursue history as a profession. His goal, it seems, was not to uncover particular truths or specific details about the past; rather, he wanted the big story. He admits quite openly: "And can I deny that what I wanted all along was not some golden nugget that history would at last yield up, but History itself, the Grand Narrative, the filler of vacuums, the dispeller of fears of the dark?" (62). In the course of his career, however, he experiences a transformation of sorts. As he reflects on his professional life, he notes: "So I began to demand of history an Explanation. . . . only to conclude forty years later . . . that history is a yarn" (62).

By focusing on Tom's changing attitudes about history and storytelling, Swift's novel makes possible a detailed examination of both the compelling drive to produce explanations in hopes of coming to an understanding of what we have experienced and the apparently inherent need to tell stories. These are not, Swift seems to be saying, mutually exclusive activities. In fact, the novel implies that the drive to narrate constitutes the primary means by which we explain our experience to ourselves as well as to others.

Speaking of humanity in the generic sense, Tom states: "Wherever he goes he wants to leave behind not a chaotic wake, not an empty space, but the comforting marker-buoys and trail-signs of stories" (63). The ultimate human desire, according to Tom, consists of leaving a legacy of language. Despite the manic activity of the Atkinsons, their forging of an empire of ale, it is the *story* of the building of the empire that is more important. The supremacy of narrative over action in the case of the Atkinsons achieves its apotheosis in the writings of Ernest Atkinson, which are contained in notebooks discussing his ideas about the "Saviour of the World." Although one could argue that it is the act of incest with his daughter that is most significant, one should not overlook the fact that the act itself is precipitated by Ernest's own idiosyncratic (some might say mad) narrative about the world. The story Ernest tells himself and his daughter Helen, the one he eventually produces in the form of a written narrative, leads to his unnatural act.

Waterland examines the centrality of narrative construction and the primacy of language in many ways throughout the entire length of the

novel. The very structure of Swift's narrative (which could be characterized as a looping back and forth and commingling of a present-tense classroom lecture on the French Revolution and short, philosophical diatribes
on the importance of history; a retrospective personal history of Tom
Crick's family; a meditation on the behavior of the eel; and intermittent
conversations between Tom and the headmaster Lewis, Tom and the student Price, and Tom and his wife Mary) purposely draws attention to the
form of the story Swift presents. What Tom says of history equally applies
to the very form of Swift's novel: "It goes in two directions at once. It goes
backwards as it goes forwards. It loops. It takes detours" (135). But aside
from the easy-to-identify and in some ways typical self-reflexive moves
of Swift's narrative, the novel also addresses what we might term an imagined origin of the narrative impulse. Midway through the novel, Tom
speculates on the early inhabitants of the Ouse River region, stating:
"What these first men and their waves of successors called the Ouse we
have no idea, having no inkling of their language. But how the Ouse regarded (for let us adopt the notion of these primitive peoples who very
probably thought of the Ouse as a God, a sentient Being) these two-legged
intruders who by daring to transmute things into sound were unconsciously forging the phenomenon known as History, we can say readily:
with indifference" (143). To begin with, I wish to focus on the notion of
transmutation of "things into sound" and its relation to history. Tom's
description of "these first men" corresponds exactly to Vico's account of
the first humans or "theological poets" who initially uttered imaginative
universals. According to Vico, the theological poets "attributed senses and
passions . . . to bodies, and to bodies as vast as sky, sea, and earth" (NS ¶
402). For Vico, "the first men, the children, as it were, of the human race,
not being able to form intelligible class concepts of things, had a natural
need to create poetic characters; that is, imaginative class concepts or
universals, to which, as to certain models or ideal portraits, to reduce all
particular species which resembled them" (NS ¶ 209). The most famous
of these poetic attributions was of course when "Jove was born naturally
in poetry as a divine character or imaginative universal" at the moment
he became thunder (NS ¶ 381). Tom, it appears, concurs with Vico; he
suggests that the initial acts of early humans were metaphoric and pro-
jective. Initially, humans quite literally sensed the world, projecting their
sensate bodies onto it in order to make sense of it (i.e., transmuting things
into sound and thereby forging history). It was only later that humans
developed an abstract vocabulary, one that made possible the distinction

between figurative and literal language. As Vico describes it, "all the tropes . . . were necessary modes of expression of all the first poetic nations, and had originally their full native propriety" (NS ¶ 409). In other words, the theological poets spoke the world; their utterances made the world; and thus their speech was true. "But," continues Vico, "these expressions of the first nations later became figurative when, with further development of the human mind, words were invented which signified abstract forms or genera comprising their species or relating their parts with their wholes" (NS ¶ 409).

To invoke Vico with respect to this brief comment made by the central character in Swift's novel constitutes more than idle fancy. The notion that the original stories of the "first men" were true receives confirmation in Tom's own pronouncement at the beginning of chapter 41, when he says: "But all the stories were once real" (297). According to Tom, "All the stories were once a feeling in the guts" (297). Tom confirms the visceral, body-centered origins of language and narrative utterance. We may view the historical accounts of ancient peoples with suspicion because the language of the ancients accords with their apperception of the world that they have made. Armed with an abstract, conceptual vocabulary that we often try to superimpose on ancient accounts, we find it nearly impossible to recapture the meaning-producing capacity of the language of a Homer or Hesiod because we live in a world of rational discourse. The barbarism of the senses has given way to the barbarism of reflection, in Vico's view, and the heroic world of Homer remains remote and can only be glimpsed from afar.

Viewed in the context of the novel, we can begin to recognize how the stories that Helen Atkinson told to the invalid Henry Crick and the infant Tom were true, how they helped to make a world that ultimately gave both men physical and psychological health. Like Vico's "children" of the human race, both Henry and Tom benefited from what we would call stories, fabrications, fictions, lies. As Tom notes, "in every myth there is a grain of truth" (215); narratives, even those we deem fabulous, contain within them particular meaning-producing capacities that Vico correctly associates with the use of metaphor. In the case of Tom's narrative about his family, we see how the dominant metaphors of "phlegmatic" Cricks and "active" Atkinsons provide Tom with the ability to make sense of the generational development of the two branches of his family.

Yet Swift's inclusion of Vichian insights does not end with the focus on the primacy of narrative construction and the invention of imagina-

tive universals. Vico's notion of ideal eternal history, in which each nation runs a course through "its rise, development, maturity, decline, and
fall" (NS ¶ 245), finds its analogue in the story of the "Rise of the Atkinsons," the industrious brewers who transform the Fenlands as they establish a mighty brewery along the Leem and build imposing structures at
Kessling and Gildsey throughout the nineteenth century, only to see their
fortunes decline and the last of their line engage in incestuous acts that
produce a potato-headed creature. When Dick plunges into the Ouse at
the end of the novel, he returns to his mythic origins; the Vichian cycle,
or *corso*, is complete. Having begun with the early accounts of land reclamation by the fabled Cornelius Vermuyden, the story of Tom's forebears
unfolds as the reason-centered, Enlightenment-inspired Atkinsons,
caught in the grip of an idea, pursue and promote progress and ultimately, as Vico would say, "grow dissolute, and finally go mad and waste their
substance" (NS ¶ 241). This trajectory, from mythic origins to enlightened,
industrious, rational activity to decline and a return to mythic origins,
appears vividly in Swift's novel. The Atkinsons emerge from the Fens,
espouse the story of progress and, in the end, succumb to the myth of the
"Saviour of the World." As Tom himself declares: "First it was a story—
what our parents told us at bedtime. Then it becomes real, then it becomes
here and now. Then it becomes a story again. Second childhood" (328).
Tom's observation accurately describes the Atkinson saga—as well as his
individual history. First he heard the stories his mother told, then he pursued the idea of history as a form of inquiry; but in the end, Tom comes
to see history as only a yarn. And the experience of Mary fits into this
paradigm as well. Spurred by a scientific curiosity to learn about sex, Mary
abandons the stories of childhood, pursues an experimental approach to
self-discovery, grows to adulthood, and ends up believing that God has
given her a baby. The cycle from story to investigative, reason-centered
activity to story occurs once again. As Tom puts it: "How it repeats itself,
how it goes back on itself, no matter how we try to straighten it out. How
it twists and turns. How it goes in circles and brings us back to the same
place" (142).

In addition to emphasizing both the primacy of speaking in metaphors
that create imaginative universals and the cycle of development and decline, Swift's novel expresses other Vichian philosophical principles as
well. When speaking of Louis XVI to his class, Tom states, "it is necessary
not only to reanimate in our imaginations his troubled life and times but
even to penetrate the generations before him" (107). And when speaking

of the French Revolution as a whole to his interlocutor and sometime antagonist, Price, he asks: "'Does it really lie in some impenetrable mesh of circumstances too complex for definition? It's a curious thing, Price, but the more you try to dissect events, the more you lose hold of them— the more they seem to have occurred largely in people's imagination'" (139–40). Once again, we see Vichian principles being articulated by Tom as he comes to understand just what his profession entails. The more Tom Crick contemplates what is necessary for the historian (particularly the historian who wishes to communicate to a nonprofessional audience) to make available to readers or auditors a vision of the past, the more he realizes that the historian must use his or her own imagination and invoke the imaginations of the audience. Tom expresses the idea that every historian must possess a powerful imaginative capacity; without it, every investigation would devolve into discrete particulars that would never amount to a coherent narrative. For Vico, imagination, or *fantasia*, constitutes the indispensable attribute every historian must have if he or she is to succeed in narrating the past. We recall that Cecilia Miller contends *fantasia* refers to three different things, one of which is the imaginative capacity of historians to "unlock the minds" of people who lived in the past so as to "reconstruct patterns of past cultures" (120). Without this imaginative capacity, we would be unable to picture how people from the past conceived of their world and, consequently, be unable to narrate the past.

As we have seen, *Waterland* establishes the dichotomy between history as a narrative and history as the object of that narrative only to collapse the dichotomy. The two meanings of history are interdependent; history as narrative and history as past action interpenetrate one another. The past does not exist outside of always already available narrativizing functions that make it possible for us as thinking, conceptualizing creatures to organize the multifarious phenomena that confront us. In Swift's world, the distinction between actors and observers of history simply does not hold. Members of both camps engage in both activities; to engage in one activity is necessarily to engage in the other. Swift's novel indicates that when it comes to making sense of the past, we always invoke a narrative-producing strategy—we are driven to create understanding through narration. We cannot do otherwise.

However, one of the early warnings Tom discloses about this drive to narrate should give us pause. When Tom reflects on just why his mother told so many stories, he declares: "she believes in stories. She believes that they're a way of bearing what won't go away, a way of making sense of madness" (225). It is precisely this notion of things that "won't go away," of recurring things, that informs us of an added dimension to the dialectic of history as actions in the past and history as narrative about the past; namely, the materiality, immutability, and irrefutability of the world—what many people ordinarily call the "real." Tom implies that his mother's storytelling was actually a coping strategy, one that made it possible to endure the madness of the unchanging world around her. Perhaps Tom refers here to the specific predicament Helen found herself in when it came to her father and his incestuous desires. But, perceived from the angle of interpreting the novel overall, Tom's observation raises serious questions about what role stories or narratives—even historical ones—play in our lives. Do we write history as "a way of making sense of madness"?

History, the Real, and Nothing

The opposition between history as narrative and the real achieves its most overt expression in Price's denunciation of history as a discipline. Price prefers to focus on the "here and now," the "real world," on "reality." In a confrontation with Tom in the classroom, Price declares unequivocally: "'What matters . . . is the here and now. Not the past. The here and now—and the future'" (6). For Price, reading history is a waste of time. The present moment—its crises and contingencies—are of all-consuming interest; the past is simply bunk. The headmaster, Lewis Scott, agrees with much of what Price says. In the conversation with Tom in which he informs the history teacher that "'we're cutting back History'" (21), Lewis makes the popular pedagogical argument that education should be centered on "equipping [students] for the real world" (23). Lewis even offers arguments from what he believes are the students' perspectives, claiming that they demand "'practical relevance to today's real world'" (22). But, in addition to this rather impoverished vision of the purpose of education, there is another dimension to the argument that Price offers, and it comes in the form of a blunt statement: "'The only important thing about history . . . is that it's got to the point where it's probably about to end'" (7). Price speaks neither of the Kojèvian interpretation of Hegel nor its popularized and simplistic version in the writings of Fukuyama; rather, Price alludes to the end of history in the form of nuclear disaster. The possibility of nuclear annihilation haunts the imagination of Price and some of his classmates, who together form the Holocaust Club. Thus, the "here and now" for Price and his followers consists of the ever-impending nuclear apocalypse, and they view with great suspicion anything that diverts attention away from this anxiety-producing fact.

But the phrase "here and now" leads to greater speculation on the part of Tom as he considers Price's challenge with a remarkable degree of seriousness. "But what is this much-adduced Here and Now?" he asks. "What is this indefinable zone between what is past and what is to come; this free and airy present tense in which we are always longing to take flight into the boundless future?" (60). Tom begins by posing the temporal question: how do we define the present—a dilemma that has plagued philosophers for millennia and perhaps achieved its clearest articulation in the writings of Augustine (*Confessions* XI). What we soon learn is that, for Tom, the here and now consists of singular (some might say catastrophic) and irreversible events. Examples of the here and now in Tom's narrative include: the injury to Sarah Atkinson that renders her catatonic: "Plenty of Here and Now" (77); the aborting of Mary's baby: "I'm here; it's now" (308); and the discovery of Freddie Parr's body. Each of these events involves a death of sorts, and none is reversible. Thus, Tom describes the here and now as "these surprise attacks of the Here and Now which, far from launching us into the present tense, which they do, it is true, for a brief and giddy interval, announce that time has taken us prisoner" (61). In each instance, the participants—Thomas and Sarah Atkinson, Tom Crick and Mary, Henry Crick and his two sons—are trapped in a temporal moment that will forever alter the course of their lives. Unlike the repeated, daily activities on the Fens—or in the brewery, for that matter—that take on a habitual quality that leads one to believe that each day is like the day before and will be repeated on the following day, the events of the here and now punctuate time with a sinister singularity that makes it impossible for the participants to escape through repetition and habitual behavior. This is what Tom means when he says: "history is a thin garment, easily punctured by a knife blade called Now" (36). The implication here seems to be that the narrative of history covers the raw body of data that itself can be exposed when one of these singular, and oftentimes violent, events punctures the surface of the covering story. Viewed in this manner, the narrative of history appears as a seamless text that follows a habitual pattern of development and (by implication, at least since the eighteenth century) progress.

What, then, is the relation between history and the here and now? For Tom, at the most personal level, the here and now pushed him into his study of history. When we reexamine the quotation presented earlier that describes the pivotal role his mother played in leading Tom to choose a profession, we have the following:

> My earliest acquaintance with history was thus, in a form issuing from my mother's lips, inseparable from her other bedtime make-believe. . . . And even as a schoolboy, when introduced to history as an object of study, when nursing indeed an unfledged lifetime's passion, it was still the fabulous aura of history that lured me, and I believed, perhaps like you, that history was a myth. Until a series of encounters with the Here and Now gave a sudden pointedness to my studies. Until the Here and Now, gripping me by the arm, slapping my face and telling me to take a good look at the mess I was in, informed me that history was no invention but indeed existed—and I had become a part of it. (62)

The mess to which Tom refers is the unwanted baby that he and Mary conceive and eventually abort. This encounter with potential life is what causes him to retreat into his studies. This may explain in part what Tom means when he states, "only animals live entirely in the Here and Now. Only nature knows neither memory nor history" (62). It is the natural world, that physical and, in many ways, cyclical world of birth, death, and regeneration, that constitutes the realm of the here and now, the realm that Tom contemplates further when he speaks of eels. But before we turn to the discussion of nature and natural history, we must first consider what Tom's other pronouncements about history and its relation to the here and now might mean. Given what we have noted as Tom's position on these issues, we might be puzzled by the following statement he makes: "How many times do we enter the Here and Now? How many times does the Here and Now pay us visits? It comes so rarely that it is never what we imagine, and it is the Here and Now that turns out to be the fairy-tale, not History, whose substance is at least for ever determined and unchangeable" (60–61). In response to Lewis and Price, who claim that history is a fairy tale (meaning that it is an untrue, fabricated tale designed to entertain, perhaps teach, and ultimately soothe the listener/reader), Tom claims that it is the notion of the here and now that is a fabrication. At one level, we can acknowledge that the notion of a present moment in contradistinction to the past and future, which themselves constitute part of the present (i.e., what Augustine terms "a present of things past, a present of things present, and a present of things future" [*Confessions* XI.20]), can only be perceived to be an abstract fabrication. In plain and simple terms, there is no here and now that is not itself inflected with the retrospective pull of the past and the anticipatory power of the future. However, when we consider what Tom also says about the here and now, we find that, just as in the case of the opposition between Cricks as storytellers and Atkinsons as doers, there is some semantic slippage when it comes to the opposition between the here and now and history.

Earlier, we noted that Tom associates the here and now with irreversible and significant events. How, then, do we reconcile this with the idea that history is unchangeable and determined and the here and now is a fairy tale? In order to answer this question, we must examine the concept here and now and its relation to reality and the notion of nothing.

At one point, Tom tries to soothe his students by telling them that "the reality of things—be thankful—only visits us for a brief while" (33). Like the phrase "here and now," the word "reality" poses problems for us readers when Tom employs it in his speech because he often uses the two terms in a similar fashion. When describing Mary jumping from a significant height in order to induce abortion, he states: "for the second time in two weeks, reality comes up" (293). The first time, of course, occurred when Freddie Parr's body surfaced near the lock. The word also appears when Tom speaks of the purpose of history in general. "What history teaches us," he declares, "is to avoid illusion and make-believe, to lay aside dreams, moonshine, cure-alls, wonder-workings, pie-in-the-sky—to be realistic" (108). Tom indicates that the historian's task consists of looking at events squarely in the eye, so to speak, of avoiding what we might term overarching metanarratives. The assumption made when someone argues for a realistic approach to history, however, is that one can be objective and avoid such metanarratives, that there exists a position from which one can render an unmediated, descriptive narrative of what took place in the past. Tom himself engages in such behavior when, in a moment of uncertainty, he tries to reassure himself that, although his wife is speaking about God giving her a child, he can come back to earth by simply identifying through nomination the objects around him: "this is Mary; this is a bench; this is a dog" (148).

Tom, however, does not entirely accept this notion of an unmediated interpretation. He begins to doubt it when he asks a pointed question about what it might mean for the so-called realistic historian to write about the French revolutionaries who were caught in the grip of ideas. "What every world-builder, what every revolutionary wants a monopoly in: Reality. Reality made plain. Reality with no nonsense. Reality cut down to size. Reality minus a few heads," declares Tom (206). Decapitation and death are real in the sense that they bring about the end of life. They are those moments of the here and now that forever alter a present situation. But what precipitated these acts of terror in 1793 were ideas—the Rights of Man, Liberty, Equality, Fraternity. Are these, too, real? And if so, in what sense? The notion that we are all born equal is precisely that, a notion. These ideas were forged in the imaginations of European intellectuals and made manifest in overt political acts that sought to transform the social and political landscape. The revolutionaries attempted to change not the natural world but the world created by humans. In this regard, they were substituting their constructs for others. In both cases, one could say that the social orders of post-1789 France, as well as those of the ancien régime, were not real in a metaphysical sense. Social reality consists of human-made institutions that we subject to modification, wholesale change, or complete destruction. The recognition of the constructed nature of the social order had, and in some cases still has, a dramatic effect on those who recognize that this signals the radical contingency of the human world. In other words, there is no human reality that remains immutable. This is precisely what Ernest Atkinson comes to recognize. As the last great scion of the Atkinson clan, and the inheritor of the progressive worldview that perceives a larger pattern of development, progress, and enlightenment in every act of economic and social development, Ernest comes to a different conclusion about the world. As Tom notes, on the final day of Ernest's life, "he was already confirmed in the belief that this world which we like to believe is sane and real is, in truth, absurd and fantastic" (233).

This may explain why, early in the novel, Tom announces to his class that "reality's not strange, not unexpected. Reality doesn't reside in the sudden hallucination of events. Reality is uneventfulness, vacancy, flatness. Reality is that nothing happens" (40). If we accept the notion that humans make their world through acts of imagination, ingenuity, and violence, then the real consists of that which humans do not make. And, as Vico pointed out, such a realm remains a mystery to us. "Whoever reflects on this cannot but marvel that the philosophers should have bent all their energies to the study of the world of nature, which, since God made it, He alone knows," writes Vico (NS ¶ 331). According to the Neapolitan philosopher, we simply cannot know what we do not make; it is far better for us to concentrate on studying the "world of nations, or civil world, which, since men have made it, men could come to know" (NS ¶ 331). Tom hopes to impart this same lesson to his students when he states:

"Children, there's this thing called civilisation. It's built of hopes and dreams. It's only an idea. It's not real. It's artificial. No one ever said it was natural. It's built by the learning process; by trial and error. It breaks easily. No one ever said it couldn't fall to bits. And no one ever said it would last for ever" (336).

When Tom describes the fragility of civilization, its artificiality, its ephemeral nature, he touches on one of the key themes in Nietzsche's writings: namely, the illusory nature of our understanding of the world. "One should not," writes Nietzsche, "understand this compulsion to construct concepts, species, forms, purposes, laws . . . as if they enabled us to fix the *real world;* but as a compulsion to arrange a world for ourselves in which our existence is made possible:—we thereby create a world which is calculable, simplified, comprehensible, etc., for us" (WP ¶ 521). Beginning with *The Birth of Tragedy* and the early philosophical notebooks—and, indeed, throughout his writing career—Nietzsche focused on the illusions we make through art, our language, and social constructs. According to Nietzsche, there is "a profound *illusion* that first saw the light of the world in the person of Socrates: the unshakeable faith that thought, using the thread of causality, can penetrate the deepest abysses of being, and that thought is capable not only of knowing but even of *correcting* it" (BT 95). For Nietzsche, we can never know what exists outside of our conceptual schemes of comprehension: what we ordinarily term the real world lies beyond our ken. The ominous conclusion Tom reaches (i.e., that "nothing happens") signals a Nietzschean recognition that, as humans, we are armed with our imaginative constructs (many of which are stories or narratives) with which we struggle against the void. Such a view achieves its most poignant expression when Tom reports that his father's reaction after his experience in the trenches of the First World War was as follows: "He thinks: there is only reality, there are no stories left. About his war experiences he says: 'I remember nothing'" (20). Like many a survivor of horrific wartime violence, Henry Crick expresses his adoption of a form of self-imposed amnesia. Yet, we can also take Henry's statement literally—he remembers "nothing" because that is what reality is—nothing, finitude, biological death, emptiness, and waste. Like Nietzsche, Henry caught a glimpse of the void; he peered behind the veil of illusion and emerged disarticulated and terrified. Unlike Nietzsche, however, Henry had someone to fill his ear with life-affirming stories that could shelter him from the knowledge that we are surrounded by a meaningless world of emptiness.

History and Nothing; or, History versus Nature

In his preface to *Human, All Too Human,* Nietzsche claims that no one "has ever before looked into the world with an equally profound degree of suspicion" (HTH 5). He goes on to speak of how he often "sought shelter in this or that—in some piece of admiration or enmity or scientificality or frivolity or stupidity" and how, when he "could not find what [he] *needed,* [he] had artificially to enforce, falsify and invent a suitable fiction for [him]self" (HTH 5). Nietzsche builds on this theme in the book and argues that we all *need* "suitable fictions" because, without them, we cannot face the ultimate truth that there is nothing beyond our illusions. One way of describing this is to say that Nietzsche's critique of metaphysics consists of arguing vehemently and consistently throughout his career that metaphysics is a garment that covers the nakedness of a body or the absence of a presence—much like the veil that covered the Holy of Holies in the Jewish temple.

In *Waterland,* Swift looks at the world with an amount of suspicion equal to that of Nietzsche's; and he, too, argues in favor of "suitable fictions" to combat the awesome terror of the void that surrounds us. Swift inscribes much of Nietzsche's philosophy in his novel by focusing his attention on the idea of "nothing." *Waterland* actually conducts a meditation on the concept of nothing, as Tom explores the meaning of the word and its relation to the Fens in which he grew up as a child. When reflecting on his waterlogged childhood home, he asks his students: "For what is water, which seeks to make all things level, which has no taste or color of its own, but a liquid form of Nothing? And what are the Fens, which so imitate in their levelness the natural disposition of water, but a landscape which of all landscapes, most approximates to Nothing?" (13). The level, water-filled land of the Fens provides Tom and Swift's readers with the best metaphor for the real. The Cricks, he claims, "know that what water makes, it also unmakes. Nothing moves far in this world. And whatever moves forwards will also move back. A law of the natural world: and a law, too, of the human heart" (73). The Fens teach us as well as Tom about the immutable nature of nature—its cyclicity, its endless rhythm, its patterned development to infinitude. It is this opposition, the one between history (*both* as narrative *and* events in the past) and nature, that constitutes a second oppositional dialectic that Swift's novel explores. This explains why Tom can reach the conclusion that history is just a yarn, just a story. As events recognized ex post facto, history must conform to some given narrative structure; and, as constituted in narrative, history is a story of some sort. Thus, the internal opposition contained in the term "history" becomes collapsed and is set up against nature, reality, nothing.

In addition to being associated with the Fens and Henry Crick's experiences in the Great War, the term "nothing" also becomes linked to other characters in the novel. After Sarah Atkinson's injury, she sits up in her room in a catatonic state looking out the window, which causes Tom to query, is she "keeping her watch over Nothing?" (91). Such a use of the term implies that she sees the Fenlands for what they are: nothing. In a similar fashion, the word becomes associated with Mary when Tom reflects on how she reacts to their barren marriage. "But she made do (so he thought) with nothing. Not believing either in looking back or looking forward, she learnt how to mark time. To withstand, behind all the stage-props of their marriage, the empty space of reality" (126). Like the empty land, the empty womb becomes associated with nothing. But of equal importance to these associations between places geographical and anatomical and the notion of nothing is the recognition that Henry, Mary, and perhaps even Sarah (in the deep recesses of her mind) glimpsed the truth that this human-made world is all illusion, that, like Tom, they would agree: "this thing called civilisation . . . is precious. An artifice— so easily knocked down—but precious" (239–40).

Praise for the artifice of civilization is not peculiar to Tom. Nietzsche said much the same thing: "if there is anything that is to be worshipped it is *appearance* that must be worshipped, that the lie—and *not* the truth— is divine!" (WP ¶ 1011). In order to survive in this world, we must, declares Nietzsche, create our world in opposition to the chaotic one given to us and simplistically identified as real. "Man must be a liar by nature, he must above all be an *artist*," writes Nietzsche (WP ¶ 853). The key to survival resides in the ability to "compel one's chaos to become form" (WP ¶ 842). Yet Nietzsche's call for a turn to artistic endeavor, his demand for ordering the chaos, is no simple task. Confronted with the inexplicable and vast array of natural phenomena and cognizant of the fact that all truths that we make are illusions, Nietzsche requires of us a tremendous degree of psychological and mental strength, perhaps too much, given what we know of Nietzsche's own mental breakdown. After Nietzsche, we find ourselves bereft of the soothing certainty that we can know things in themselves; yet, at the same time, we are impelled to create new illusions that we know to be illusions to quell the tide of nothingness that surrounds us. To be placed in such a position—to be "thrown" into it, as Heidegger might say—is exactly the position in which Swift places his character Tom and, subsequently, his readers.

Recognizing the illusory quality of civilization—as well as the fundamental opposition between human world-building activity and nature per se—creates a problem for Tom when he must consider just what history must be when placed next to the unfolding of the natural world, the vast nothing of the real. At one point, he asks rather provocatively: "How many of the events of history have occurred, ask yourselves, for this and for that reason, but for no other reason, fundamentally, than the desire to make things happen? I present to you History, the fabrication, the diversion, the reality-obscuring drama. History, and its near relative, Histrionics" (40). Conceived in this manner, history as acts that took place in the past is itself a behavior emitted by creatures beset by boredom. As Nietzsche once said, "when you look into an abyss, the abyss also looks into you" (BGE 89). Yet such a possibility is too much for us mortals to handle. We prefer, so Tom argues, to make things up. He continues: "And there's no saying what consequences we won't risk, what reactions to our actions, what repercussions, what brick towers built to be knocked down, what chasings of our own tails, what chaos we won't assent to in order to assure ourselves that, nonetheless, things are happening. And there's no saying what heady potions we won't concoct, what meanings, myths, manias we won't imbibe in order to convince ourselves that reality is not an empty vessel" (41). Once again, the notion that our world, the human one, is an illusion is simply too much to bear. Says Tom, "It's the old, old feeling, that everything might amount to nothing" (269) that terrifies us. As Nietzsche argued, "life is, after all, not a product of morality: it *wants* deception, it *lives* on deception" (HTH 6). We must, it seems, cling to our illusions, embellish them, recount them, make them true. As Tom points out early on: "How did the Cricks outwit reality? By telling stories" (17). "It's all a struggle," as Tom says, "to preserve an artifice" (241). But this struggle never reaches completion. The struggle continues ad infinitum, some might say ad nauseum, as each generation goes through much the same activity. The end result is the rather sinister conclusion that Tom arrives at when he asks rhetorically: "And why is it that every time the time before has taught us nothing?" (141). Once again, the word "nothing" functions in two ways. On the one hand, "taught us nothing" means we do not learn anything in the sense that we continue to make the same mistakes generation after generation. On the other hand, "taught us nothing" signifies that each generation learns that there is nothing, nothing at all, just the emptiness of reality—an inhuman landscape of endless regenerative process. This is what leads Tom to declare: "Are you beginning to feel that History is all made nonsense by that sensation in the pit of your stomach, that tingling in your finger-tips and that swimming feeling in your head and knees? It's called terror, children. The feeling that all is nothing. There is your subject, your lesson for today" (270).

But this nothing, this reality that lies beyond our grasp and drives us to acts of make-believe, has its manifestation in nature, in our physical being (at least metaphorically). "Women are equipped with a miniature model of reality: an empty but fillable vessel," says Tom (42). The womb as a figure of the real becomes one of the most significant insights Tom offers us. Ultimately, that is what reality is: nothing—an empty vessel, a womb of possibilities. The notion of the empty vessel appears again when Tom addresses his students as "heirs of the future, vessels of hope" (240). The image of emptiness appears here as the locus of possibility. Just as the empty womb can be filled with a developing fetus, so, too, can young children be perceived as potential future (and hopeful) life scenarios. Thus, the notion of nothing need not always be viewed with abject horror. On the contrary, the terror that nothing elicits from us can be positive, a type of productive anxiety that brings us to activity and thus makes us make history. Such a positive response accords with Nietzsche's notion of a joyful wisdom that stems from the recognition of the illegitimacy of positivist science and the concomitant understanding that we can affirm our lives and our world through asserting our values in opposition to the void, the nothing, the emptiness of the real.

In *Waterland*, the making and doing of nothing becomes figured in the form of silt, dredging, and drainage. This is why land reclamation becomes the metaphor of history proper—silt (the real) must be continuously reclaimed. Reclamation involves the making and unmaking of the world. "The Fens were formed by silt," declares Tom. "Silt: a word which when you utter it, letting the air slip thinly between your teeth, invokes a slow, sly, insinuating agency. Silt: which shapes and undermines contents; which demolishes as it builds; which is simultaneous accretion and erosion; neither progress nor decay" (8–9). Silt, as Tom is quick to point out, "obstructs as it builds; unmakes as it makes" (11). In Swift's novel, silt becomes the perfect metaphor for the real—for in fact it is nothing but an amorphous, ever-changing mass. Pushed to the extreme of a metaphor in the service of a meditation on history, Tom concludes: "So forget, indeed, your revolutions, your turning-points, your grand metamorphoses of history. Consider, instead, the slow and arduous process, the interminable and ambiguous process—the process of human siltation—of land reclamation" (10). History, as Tom discovers, becomes the struggle against the nothing of the real, a never-ending process of shifting the muck, an eternal recurrence of sorts of the repetitive behavior that makes illusions real for us, but that themselves are constructs of the human imagination.

For Tom, the Ouse River serves as the image of the "process of human siltation." In one of his lectures to his class, Tom demands of his students: "The great Ouse. Ouse. Say it. *Ouse*. Slowly. How else can you say it? A sound which exudes slowness. A sound which suggests the slow, sluggish, forever oozing thing it is" (142). Like the word "silt," the very name of the river contains its sense in its sound. The movement of the river contributes to the undoing of the human endeavors that signify history. When viewed in this manner, history, ostensibly a progressive activity, becomes a never-ending cycle of repeated endeavors as each generation resumes the behavior of the preceding one. This is what leads Tom to say that "the Ouse flows out to the sea, it flows, in reality, like all rivers, only back to itself, to its own source; and that impression that a river moves only one way is an illusion. . . . Because we are always stepping into the same river" (145–46). Thus, the idea of progress and change as it is associated with historical development really is illusory. The idea of progress—as imagined by the Atkinsons and realized in the labors of the Cricks—succumbs to the power of nature that itself opposes the world-building activities of human beings. As Tom so memorably characterizes it: "We have to keep scooping, scooping up from the depths this remorseless stuff that time leaves behind" (346). Consequently, for Tom, land reclamation is his "humble model for progress," an activity "which is repeatedly, never-endingly retrieving what is lost" (336).

At first glance, we should recognize that, by devoting a substantial part of his narrative to a discussion of the geography of the region and the seemingly never-changing aspects of the silt-filled Fens, Swift touches on yet another dichotomy, the opposition between what Braudel terms geographic and social (or individual) time. Throughout the novel, the Fens remain a constant in the background, an immutable force that forever stays "a landscape which, of all landscapes, most approximates to Nothing" (13). Opposed to this are the actions of the land reclaimers—men such as Cornelius Vermuyden and the generations of the Cricks. Geographical time, as figured in the Fens, is slow to change. Social and individual time, as embodied in the activities of the men who reclaim the land, is fast-paced (Vermuyden builds his sluices, drains, dikes, and ditches in a matter of years). However, viewed from another perspective, the Fens can express fast-paced changes, such as the time when "the Bedford River burst a sixty-foot gap in its banks" in the 1690s, when in "1713 the Denver Sluice gave way" (12), and—most significantly for Tom—when in 1947 "one of the most calamitous floods on record" occurred, resulting in the death of his father (340). Similarly, the Cricks and the Atkinsons, who exist in social and individual time, who through their respective efforts transform and maintain the landscape through tireless activity, also express aspects of the slow-to-change, durative time of geography. The Cricks are themselves phlegmatic and seemingly unchanging, forever spitting in the water, whereas the Atkinsons, who most clearly embody the Enlightenment's linear notion of time, eventually opt for a transcendental, mythic time when Ernest chooses to believe in the myth of the "Saviour of the World." Once again, the binary that Swift inscribes collapses: the Fens express both the slow, seemingly static nature of geographic time and volatile, rapidly changing physical transformations, just as the Atkinsons espouse both the notion of progress and linear, human time and the stasis of a mythic temporality.

Swift also opposes social to individual time. As Tom presents the history of his family, he repeatedly mentions what concurrently occurred in "the wide world." For example, he describes how "in 1813, while Napoleon, whose army once advanced so proudly in the opposite direction, retreats from Leipzig to the Rhine, Thomas Atkinson begins building the maltings at Kessling" (71). Tom continues to invoke this narrative technique, thereby implying that the "big picture" of world events and the activities of individuals somehow remain remote from one another, even opposed. The novel, however, undermines this opposition. The wide world intrudes on the lives of the Atkinsons and Cricks just as they themselves directly engage in activities associated with the wide world (most notably the First and Second World Wars).

As noted several times already, Swift's novel collapses, even as it establishes, oppositions. Individual and social time commingle. The time of nature and human time each possess aspects of the temporality of its other. Yet Swift's exploration of oppositions does not end here. When we reexamine the manner in which Swift develops Tom's narrative on the Fens, the silt, and the Ouse, we see that he wishes to look carefully at how history and nature relate.

Because of their association with land reclamation, the Cricks obtain greater insight into the nature of history and its relation to nature. As Tom points out, the Cricks "did not forget, in their muddy labours, their swampy origins; that, however much you resist them, the waters will return; that the land sinks; silt collects; that something in nature wants to go back" (17). The force of nature, so it seems, opposes the power of history as manifested in human ideas and actions. The Cricks recognize the power of nature, its constancy, its persistence, its immutability; their insight into nature's drive to return to origins offers readers another way of examining the problem of history, and Swift develops this new angle of vision in a complex and ingenious way.

When contemplating nature's principle of returning to origins, Tom asks his class: "What is this thing that takes us back, either via catastrophe and confusion or in our heart's desire, to where we were? Let's call it Natural History" (137). Herein lies one of the principal problems that confront us when we consider history as a mode of intellectual inquiry. As noted earlier, natural history grows out of the scientific method as applied to the phenomenal world. Tom makes explicit this problem when he states: "'*Historia*' or 'Inquiry' (as in Natural History: the inquiry into Nature). To uncover the mysteries of cause and effect" (107). The focus on identifying causal relationships, discovering laws, and determining principles that govern observed activity becomes a stumbling block to us once we leave the realm of the natural world of plants and animals and begin to investigate human behavior and activity. Le Goff speaks for many historians when he writes: "My feeling is that there are in history no *laws* comparable to those which have been discovered in the natural sciences" (124). Nietzsche is even more sweeping in his condemnation in that he challenges the notion of determining laws of nature at all. "When you speak so rapturously of a conformity to law in nature," he writes, "you must either assume that all natural things freely obey laws they themselves have imposed upon themselves—in which case you are admiring the morality of nature—or you are entranced by the idea of a creative mechanic who has made the most ingenious clock, with living creatures upon it as decorations.—Necessity in nature becomes more human and a last refuge of mythological dreaming through the expression 'conformity to law'" (HTH 216). Unlike Le Goff, Nietzsche does not even concede that nature has laws. Instead, he sees the laws of nature as a scientific wish fulfillment that constitutes a form of post-Enlightenment mythology. Similarly, as we have previously mentioned, Vico does not even think it possible for us to know nature, because we do not make it. Nevertheless, no matter how much we may or may not know about nature, our scientific approach toward it has left its mark on historiographic research. In its simplest form, the typical problem that faces any historian comes down to this: How can we determine the causes of the effects we call history? Consider any famous moment in history (e.g., World War One, the Holocaust, the Protestant Reformation). Can we possibly narrow down the causes and establish a linking of activities, behaviors, and circumstances that can explain these historical events as one would explicate photosynthesis? Like Vico and Nietzsche, Swift rejects the notion that the scientific approach can reveal the answers we seek in history. Instead, Swift relates nature and history in a different manner.

In the novel, Tom does not pursue a scientific line of analysis when it comes to his historical investigations into the origins of his family and larger historical events (no doubt because he recognizes the futility of such an endeavor). He does, however, make the following connection: "Natural history, human nature. Those weird and wonderful commodities, those unsolved mysteries of mysteries. Because just supposing—but don't let the cat out of the bag—this natural stuff is always getting the better of the artificial stuff. Just supposing—but don't whisper it too much abroad—this unfathomable stuff we're made from, this stuff that we're always coming back to—our love of life, children, our love of life—is more anarchic, more subversive than any Tennis-Court Oath ever was" (205). The problem for Tom is not so much trying to model historical investigation on scientific methodologies that have become the hallmark of natural science; rather, he wants us to acknowledge that nature drives our behavior and constitutes the true engine of history in spite of all our actions to the contrary. This, then, is the dialectic Swift's novel wishes to explore, and it becomes figured in the character of Dick, the child born through incest. Nevertheless, in *Waterland*, the opposition of nature and history, much like the earlier opposition we observed between history as narrative and history as action, does not hold.

Dick serves as the locus for the novel's examination of the nature-history dichotomy. Referred to derisively by his erudite brother as "potato head," Dick is also viewed as an atavistic amphibian who possesses characteristics that modern humans may have lost through evolution. In his everyday, simple existence, Dick, claims Tom, at first wants "to live an amphibious life. He hasn't begun to ask yet where the stories end and reality begins" (207–8). Yet it is Dick who will unleash all the forces that make Tom's personal history become a narrative, for Dick's murder of Freddie causes Mary to abort her baby, which in turn leads to Tom's retreat into the study of history, just as it leads to Dick's own suicide, and, eventually, to Mary's delusions about receiving a child from God. But herein lies the problem. Does Dick, as emblem of nature, act out of instinct, or are there other causes for his brutal behavior?

One could say that Dick serves as the reality principle of the novel. As we have noted, reality as presented by Swift in *Waterland* is "nothing," and Dick personifies that blank nothingness of the Fens as no one else does. If the typical Crick is phlegmatic, terse, and undemonstrative, Dick is a Crick to an extreme (although the curious biological fact remains that he is all Atkinson). The relationship between Dick and the principle of nothingness appears most boldly in the description of his underwater swim in the competition to see Mary's naked body. When Dick swims for Mary, the word "nothing" is repeated nine times in a single paragraph. Tom describes how Dick dives into the water and then states:

> Ripples. Bubbles. A glimmer of sallow limbs beneath the grey-brown surface. Then nothing. For a long time nothing. For fifteen, for thirty seconds, nothing. Then nothing again. Then when nothing must surely have gone on for the utmost period allowable to it, still nothing. And, after a further amazed stretching of credibility while Freddie, on all fours, expels onto the grass a stream of whiskey-scented vomit, still nothing. And still nothing. With the result that all (excepting Freddie) rise to their feet and Mary (neglecting the complete concealment of her nipples) lifts one hand to shield her eyes. Because, basing a spatial reckoning on the lapse of time, it is now a question of looking into the sun-glinting distance. (189)

The association between Dick and nothing is unmistakable. Despite the remarkable nature of his feat, he remains inarticulate, a mute expression of a basic instinctual drive—a return to the sea. Dick quite literally embodies the real as nothing, a key argument that *Waterland* posits in its pages. Just as Tom argues that "reality is that nothing happens," Dick lives in a constant state of the present. He knows "no Before, no After. Just another day. Another day on the dredger. Silt-shifting" (134). For Dick, everything is the same—everything is this blank nothing of the real. Like the cattle Nietzsche describes at the beginning of the second untimely meditation, Dick "do[es] not know what is meant by yesterday or today"; he is "fettered to the moment and its pleasure and displeasure, and thus neither melancholy nor bored" (UM 60).

Dick can be compared to Tom's dog, which loves to play fetch, an activity Tom describes as "watching instinct at work. Pursue; pick up; return; pursue again. Retriever. Golden retriever" (130). The novel reinforces

Dick's animal nature even further by drawing attention to the size of his penis (which is of "fabulous" proportions), and the sly double entendre of his name escapes no reader's notice. This being said, however, the best link between Dick and the instinctual animal world, of course, remains the relation between Dick and the eels.

In the chapters on eels and natural history, Tom tells the story of the endless search for the answers to the basic questions about the European eel's reproductive system and migratory habits. The eel, it seems, stumped Aristotle, Pliny, and Linnaeus, among others, when it came to determining if, in fact, eels had reproductive organs. It was not until the nineteenth century that both sets of reproductive organs were positively identified (197). Yet the most remarkable aspect of the eel saga, for Tom at least, involves the quest of Johannes Schmidt, the "votary of curiosity" (200), who sought out the breeding ground of the European eel. His long, complex, and often interrupted journey eventually took him to the Sargasso Sea, which is where he surmised that the European eel would breed after reaching adulthood and returning from freshwater regions like the Fens, thousands of miles away.

But Schmidt's thesis did not satisfy everyone. There still remains a series of unanswered questions that challenge Schmidt's findings: Does the European eel differ from the American eel? Does the European eel make the journey back to the Sargasso Sea? Is it not possible that some eels just journey to Europe and simply die there without reproducing at all? For Tom, questions such as these exemplify the overwhelming power of curiosity. "Curiosity will never be content," he declares. "Even today, when we know so much, curiosity has not unraveled the riddle of the birth and sex life of the eel. Perhaps these are things, like many others, destined never to be learnt before the world comes to its end. Or perhaps—but here I speculate, here my own curiosity leads me by the nose—the world is so arranged that when all things are learnt, when curiosity is exhausted (so, long live curiosity), that is when the world shall have come to its end" (203–4). Despite all of Schmidt's efforts, some questions remain unanswered, and many of his answers have been challenged. The eel embodies a mystery for us; and, in the realm of the novel, so does Dick. Like the eel, Dick is a creature of the water. Like the eel, he engages in instinctual behavior. The enormity of his erection at the sight of the seminude Mary seems to come not from pride in breaking social taboos or competition with the other boys so much as from a pure, instinctual reaction to her body. His display of swimming prowess also appears to be a natural reaction—he does not show up his rivals or parade in triumph before them. Instead, he gives his rivals a "blank glance" and sits by himself, "sulky-sullen" (191). He acts much as the eels act—instinctively—and, like the eels, his behavior remains largely inexplicable. From his strange interactions with his motorcycle to his final plunge into the Ouse, Dick's actions, like the actions of the eels, can never be satisfactorily explained.

The meditation on the eel also establishes another link between Dick and the aquatic creatures, for both are associated with the key concept of curiosity. Tom contends that the power of curiosity drove Schmidt to undertake his arduous investigative journey. This same curiosity drives the historian in general and Tom in particular when he tries to unravel the mystery of Freddie Parr's death and the origins of Dick. Curiosity is a driving force that fuels the investigative spirit of human beings. This accounts for why Tom can claim that when curiosity becomes exhausted, the world will come to an end. Tom asserts that curiosity functions in two ways: it can promulgate investigations that can lead to the writing of history, or it can precipitate action. "Curiosity," he declares, "which, with other things, distinguishes us from the animals, is an ingredient of love. Is a vital force. Curiosity, which bogs us down in arduous meditations and can lead to the writing of history books, will also, on occasion, as on the afternoon by the Hockwell Lode, reveal to us that which we seldom glimpse unscathed— for it appears more often (dead bodies, boat hooks) dressed in terror: the Here and Now" (51). The curiosity exhibited by the Hockwell Lode leads Mary and Tom to engage in sex, and one could argue that it is precisely this instinctual sexual drive that serves as the real culprit when it comes to determining what caused the chain of events that includes Freddie's death, Dick's suicide, and Mary's mental breakdown nearly forty years later. In this regard, curiosity becomes the driving force that ultimately leads to dissolution.

Perceived in this manner, curiosity, as presented in Swift's novel, expresses yet another element of Vico's philosophy. According to Mark Lilla, a central theme of The New Science is that "human curiosity is sinful and dangerous" because eventually it will "produce philosophical skepticism and, in the end, the rebarbarization of nations" (19). In other words, Lilla believes that just as Vico saw the decline of civilizations linked to their growing reliance on ratiocinative activity, he implied that curiosity, a key element in the scientific method that emerged from the scientific and philosophical writings of Galileo and Descartes, contributed substantially to the advancement of a reflective, philosophical speculation that undermined and eventually destroyed the traditions of Western culture. If Lilla is correct, we could argue that Swift's novel suggests the same thing. Curiosity, as exhibited by both Tom and Mary, pursuant to an experimental activity designed to reveal the truth about sex and death, only brings about the collapse of their world. In the same manner, curiosity, as displayed in the behavior of Ernest Atkinson, leads to acts of incest, a clear example of the "rebarbarization" of the Atkinson clan.

Tom insists that curiosity is a distinguishing characteristic that we possess but that other animals lack. As such, it joins the ranks of the other key characteristics that Tom speaks of when he discusses what makes us human. Tom offers the following definitions of Man in the generic sense: Man is the story-telling animal (62); Man is an animal that demands explanation (he always asks why) (106); and Man is the animal who craves meaning (140). Each of these definitions depends on the assumption that humans possess the impulse called curiosity. When it comes to the question of history, both the making and the writing of it, curiosity again holds sway. At a personal level, Tom's curiosity leads him to discover the truth of his family's past, the truth about the death of Freddie, and, in his professional life, the truths about the French Revolution. At a larger level, Tom raises the question about how curiosity fits within the vision of a progressive historical development. In rebuttal to Price's imagined contention that the discussion of mundane things such as human sexual behavior impedes the progress of revolutionary change, Tom declares:

> Supposing it's not like that, Price. Supposing it's the other way round. Supposing it's revolutions which divert and impede the course of our inborn curiosity. Supposing it's curiosity—which inspires our sexual explorations and feeds our desire to hear and tell stories—which is our natural and fundamental condition. Supposing it's our insatiable and feverish desire to know about things, to know about each other, always to be sniff-sniffing things out, which is the true and rightful subverter and defeats even our impulse for historical progression. Have you ever considered why so many historical movements, not only revolutionary ones, fail, fail at heart, is because they fail to take account of the complex and unpredictable forms of our curiosity? (194)

A stronger argument for the biological imperative would be difficult to find. As Tom would have it, curiosity is a drive in the Freudian sense of the term—a drive to rival both Eros and Thanatos. We might go so far as to say that, in accordance with Tom's view of things, curiosity is the motor that drives both Eros and Thanatos. Speaking of drives, Nietzsche wrote: "It is our needs that interpret the world; our drives and their For and Against. Every drive is a kind of lust to rule; each one has its perspective that it would compel all the other drives to accept as a norm" (WP ¶ 481). With Nietzsche's observation in mind, we should consider what need or needs curiosity addresses. We should be mindful that curiosity functions in two ways. As noted previously, curiosity in the service of contemplative activity "bogs us down," whereas curiosity in the service of physical activity inspires us to have sex and tell stories; and larger stories (such as the ideas of revolution and progress) prevent us from naturally fulfilling our function as sexual, storytelling animals. Such is Tom's thesis. But does *Waterland* support his thesis?

At a certain level one could read Swift's novel and come away with a rather mundane view of human activity. Observed from this angle, Swift would seem to be telling us that we are doomed to repeat the basic animal behaviors of eating, procreating, and dying and that, in large measure, we engage in destructive behavior even when we think we are improving our lot in life. Human existence consists of repetitive, meaningless behaviors that we cannot avoid. The best we can do is tell stories to ward off the fear that grips us when we realize that our lives are meaningless.

Perhaps such a thematic reading of the novel is warranted. Nevertheless, such a reading of *Waterland* fails to take into account the problematic of history that Swift examines. For when we consider the question of curiosity and its relation to nature as depicted in the novel, a different interpretation of the novel emerges.

Curiosity, which Tom contends fuels both meditative and active behaviors in humans, also has an effect on the figure of the nothingness of the real—Dick. One could argue that Dick, whom I have termed the reality principle of the novel, engages in a series of instinctive acts that precipitates the action of the novel. In other words, it is human instinct that is the real engine of history. Dick's desire to conceive a child with Mary leads to his feelings of jealousy and, ultimately, to his murderous act. The thin garment of Tom's family history is rent by the knife blade (or, in this case, bottle) of the here and now. In a general sense, Swift's novel would then be saying that impulsive human behavior, much of it irrational, propels history on an endless repetitive course of birth, death, and regeneration as expressed in various acts of pleasure and violence. But does Dick in fact act on impulse? Put another way, what motivates Dick, finally, to kill Freddie? Is it instinct or something else?

We can readily identify the instinctual aspects of Dick's personality. He is drawn to the water; he possesses an enormous penis that signifies his connection with the biological realm as opposed to the intellectual; he can neither read nor write; an adept at manual labor, he is characterized as "sort of a machine," a habitualized creature that engages in the same behavior repeatedly (38). But these factors do not compel him to murder Freddie. On the contrary, we can argue that it is education, not instinct, that makes Dick kill Freddie.

After she sees the size of Dick's penis, Mary, driven by her own curiosity, takes it upon herself to teach Dick about sex. They have a series of encounters that prove unsuccessful in the end because Dick is simply "too big." Yet, in the course of this instruction, Tom asks a crucial question: "So, is he learning?" (255). Taken in context, Tom is wondering if and when these lessons between his brother and his girlfriend will end. But taken at the level of the overall narrative of the novel, the question looms very large, for what we discover is that Dick wants to know where babies come from. When his father tells him that "'they're made with—Love'" (257), Dick succumbs to an idea that compels him to experience "lu-love" with Mary. "Curiosity," as Tom believes—and so it seems—"begets love" (206).

According to Tom, Dick is "not immune to love" (210). But where exactly did he obtain this notion of love? The novel indicates that "Love," the concept, with all its distorting power, comes to Dick in the form of a story, and it is the story of love that impels Dick to commit a series of acts that culminates in his own suicide. When pressed by Dick to explain what love is, his father responds with two short definitions. First, he declares: "'Love, Dick, is a feeling. A good feeling. It's like the feeling you felt for your poor Mum. Like the feeling she felt for you'" (257). He then adds: "'That's to say— it's a very important thing. It's a Wonderful Thing. It's the most Wonderful Thing there is—'" (257). Left with this typical unsatisfactory response to the perennial question on the nature of love, we can only conjecture what it might mean to the "potato-headed" auditor who is described as a "lost little boy" (257). The references to "Mum" and the equally enigmatic "Wonderful Thing," although grotesquely vague, have the power to conjure a very basic scenario, one that might include hugging, kissing, and feelings of warmth and comfort. It is also quite plausible to imagine that Dick's mother told him stories just as she told Tom stories and that these tales had an equally dramatic effect on Dick as they did on the future history teacher. More important, however, these few fatherly words move Dick to confront Mary with this question of love. This, in turn, leads to his shoulder-hugging, stomach-touching behavior, which he believes will ultimately result in the birth of a child. Love, it seems, also begets curiosity.

With this in mind, the following comment by Tom takes on new mean-ing: "Love. Lu-love. Lu-lu-love. Does it ward off evil? Will its magic word suspend indefinitely the link between cause and effect? Will it help those citizens of Hamburg and Berlin, clutching in anticipation their loved ones and whispering loving words in their feeble cellars and backyard bun-kers?" (300). Here, Tom refers to the terrifying encounter with Martha Clay. The love he and Mary felt for one another would never undo the causal relation between intercourse and conception. Similarly, the refer-ence to the victims of World War II firebombings reinforces this notion that love conquers nothing, that it is no match for the brute force of the causal chains that govern the material world. Yet the reference to larger historical events also raises in the reader's mind how the novel relates love and history. As noted earlier, the idea of love motivates Dick to try to conceive a child with Mary, and his jealousy over Freddie's purported paternity pushes him to murder. What, then, motivates this bit of family history? Can love, one of the great social fictions, be responsible for Dick's actions? The novel answers yes and reinforces this answer by having yet another narrative influence Dick's behavior.

When Dick demands to know the contents of his grandfather's chest, he learns about his origins. The source of this knowledge consists of a letter and some notebooks Ernest Atkinson has left for his son, the "Sav-iour of the World." Critical to an understanding of this scene is the rec-ognition that, in addition to the pivotal role played by Ernest Atkinson's narrative, there is an equally important role played by Tom as *interpreter* of Ernest's narrative. Dick cannot read the text—he must rely on his broth-er. But Tom cannot simply transmit the text directly to his brother; he must interpret, edit, embellish, and modify what he reads so as to make it comprehensible to his half-wit sibling. Once again, the precession of narrative and the equally important interpretation of narrative contrib-utes to the making of history. When it comes to the history-nature dichot-omy, we can also see the impossibility of determining which is primary. In Pamela Cooper's words, "*Waterland* emphasizes simultaneously the density of the organic and its constructedness: at once accentuating and denying the artificiality of the natural, the novel itself points to the cog-nitive inseparability of Tom's essentializing categories" (379). On the one hand, the instinctive drive of curiosity pushes Tom, Dick, and Mary to engage in acts that themselves lead to irreversible consequences. On the other hand, had certain narratives not been introduced into the lives of these youngsters, it is quite possible that Tom and Mary would have married as they had planned and would have led very different lives. Thus, *Waterland* underscores how the origins of history remain indeterminable: so-called events contribute to the crafting of narratives just as narratives make events possible. Similarly, an instinctive, natural impulse such as curiosity can precipitate action, but this curiosity itself can be fueled by a story or narrative. To borrow a worn metaphor, Swift offers us the Möbius strip of history; just as we are tracing the cause of a certain effect, we find ourselves twisting back to where we began. To use another well-worn analogy, one could argue that Swift offers us a meditation on the *différance* of history. The reader who believes that the cause of the activity narrated by Tom is to be found in instinct will also find the trace of narrative; the reader who stresses the narrative function will find embedded in it the trace of instinct.

To better understand this phenomenon, we should return to an earlier quotation, the one in which Tom offers us the genealogy of his interest in history:

> My earliest acquaintance with history was thus, in a form issuing from my mother's lips, inseparable from her other bedtime make-believe. . . . And even as a schoolboy, when introduced to history as an object of study, when nursing indeed an unfledged lifetime's passion, it was still the fabulous aura of history that lured me, and I believed, perhaps like you, that history was a myth. Until a series of encounters with the Here and Now gave a sudden urgency to my studies. Until the Here and Now, gripping me by the arm, slapping my face and telling me to take a good look at the mess I was in, informed me that history was no invention but indeed existed—and I had become a part of it. (62)

The key phrase here is: "in a form issuing from my mother's lips, inseparable from her other bedtime make-believe." Naturally, stories emerge from his mother's mouth, and bedtime make-believe refers to fairy tales. But "bed-time make believe" can also refer to her own sexual encounters with her father, the sexual encounters that were supposed to produce the "Saviour of the World." To put it bluntly, from his mother's lips emerged both stories and the body of his brother. Admittedly, I am referring to different lips, but the source is the same: the body of the mother.

This passage, perhaps more than any other, reveals the profound Nietzschean dimensions of Swift's novel. The idea that a truth issued from his mother's lips, from the body of a woman, echoes one of Nietzsche's most celebrated lines: "Supposing truth is a woman—what then?" (BGE 2). Nietzsche's opening query to *Beyond Good and Evil* sets up his entire investigation such that woman becomes the figure of truth. Woman, in Nietzsche's writing, emblematizes the need for artifice, the need for deception or veiling in order to mask an absence. I choose not to pause and consider the misogyny of much of what Nietzsche has to say about women. It is true: many of Nietzsche's pronouncements on women are misogynistic; several are simply stupid. Nor will I pursue a psychoanalytic line of analysis and discuss the notion of castration or the missing phallus that has already been written about by many people (e.g., Derrida, Irigaray, et al.). Rather, I choose to concentrate on the *figure* of woman as truth.

To suppose truth is a woman is to posit that truth consists of artifice and construction. Traditionally, woman serves as the cultural emblem for the natural, the corporeal, and the material; thus, it is opposed to the cultural, the mental, and the artificial. When Nietzsche invokes woman, he calls upon this traditional aspect of the word. At the same time, however, he invokes something else. Just as the woman masks her face with cosmetics and adorns her body with clothing that accentuates or distorts her physical form, she weaves an illusion that expresses the truth of her desire. In a similar fashion, Nietzsche suggests that we as humans must don masks (either cultural or conceptual) to construct a world of meaning. The veiled body of the woman also conceals the genitals that are themselves the portal to the womb—the empty vessel of potential life. Here Nietzsche implies that truth is a seduction, an invitation to the possibility of engendering something real. By embracing the illusions that we accept as being true, we create the so-called real world. Nietzsche sees the primary means by which we do this as manifesting itself in our language. As he views it: "The significance of language for the evolution of culture lies in this, that mankind set up in language a separate world beside the other world, a place it took to be so firmly set that, standing upon it, it could lift the rest of the world off its hinges and make itself master of it" (HTH 16). Our truths, it seems, lie (in every sense of the word) in language.

Jacques Derrida explains the "truth as a woman" metaphor in a slightly different manner. In *Spurs Nietzsche's Styles,* Derrida argues that the phrase "truth as a woman" expresses "three fundamental propositions" that "represent three positions of value which themselves derive from three different situations" (95). The first proposition consists of woman "as a figure or potentate of falsehood." She seduces man into believing something that knows itself to be false. In the second proposition, woman is the figure of truth (be it Christianity or philosophy); she believes in the truth of her seduction; but, like the first proposition, this belief is inimical to life. It is only in the third proposition that we see woman affirmed as a seductress. In Derrida's words: "woman is recognized and affirmed as an affirmative power, a dissimulatress, an artist, a dionysiac. And no longer is it man who affirms her. She affirms herself, in and of herself, in man" (97).

In her essay "Baubô: Theological Perversion and Fetishism," Sarah Kofman also examines the central Nietzschean trope of truth as a woman. Like Derrida, she identifies the trope of woman as sometimes being associated with the weak, who tempt us and charm us "by misrepresenting and disguising nihilistic values under gilded trim" (179). Here, woman figures thè values that are opposed to life; her body veils an abyss that leads to death. Philosophers, claims Nietzsche when he uses the figure of woman is this manner, are seduced into believing in the surface of things— in their ideas, which themselves are perversions of life-affirming values (hence, Christian morality that denies life, the body, and the world in pursuit of the afterlife, the soul, and heaven). Used in this way, the trope of woman signifies a negative and dangerous power that can be destructive. But, as Kofman asks, "is it really true that the art of seduction is thus scorned by Nietzsche? Is it not, rather, the special art of Dionysus?" (180). There is, according to Kofman, a second manner in which the trope of woman appears in Nietzsche's writings (this corresponds roughly to Derrida's third proposition).

Kofman argues that, in Nietzsche's philosophy, we can distinguish between perverse illusion, "a fictional metaphysical realm" whose goal is "to pass off the 'real' world as a world of 'appearances'" (180), and life-affirming illusion—the realms of dream, art, and play that express "positive accomplishments of desire and reflect the real world" (181). Put simply: if, as Nietzsche contends, we have set up a separate world in language, we always weave illusions. The real world exists—it is the world of drives and impulses, centered in the body and manifested in acts of will. Consequently, we must choose between weaving perverse illusions that posit values opposed to the life force (e.g., the metaphysics of Plato or the theology of Christianity) and life-supporting illusions that affirm the desires of the will-governed world of body-centered desire. In Kofman's words: "The true philosopher is a tragic philosopher, for he must will illusion as illusion, knowing that woman has a reason to hide her reasons. Mastery means . . . not to refuse appearance but to affirm it and to laugh, for if life is ferocious and cruel, she is also fecundity and eternal return: her name is *Baubô*" (196). Baubô, as Kofman explains, is the female figure who appears in the Eleusinian mysteries. She made the mourning Demeter laugh by "pulling up her skirts and showing her belly on which a figure had been drawn" (196). Baubô shows us what the lifting of the veil reveals. The veiled body of the naked woman hides not an abyss (or, in psychoanalytic terms, an absence, a missing phallus); rather, it signifies the very opposition of presence and absence, surface and depth, truth and illusion that serves as the originary oppositional structures that make meaning possible *for us*. Kofman explains: "The figure of Baubô indicates that a simple logic could never understand that life is neither depth nor surface, that behind the veil there is another veil, behind a layer of paint, another layer. It signifies also that appearance should cause us neither pessimism nor skepticism, but rather the affirming laugh of a living being who knows that despite death life can come back indefinitely and that 'the individual is nothing and the species all'" (197). Behind the veil is the absence that is the presence of the real, the womb of possibilities, the potential for further life. This, then, explains what Nietzsche meant when he wrote in the preface to *The Gay Science:* "Perhaps truth is a woman who has reasons for not letting us see her reasons?" And he continues to describe the Greeks as people who "knew how to live." "What is required for that," Nietzsche writes, "is to stop courageously at the surface, the fold, the skin, to adore appearance, to believe in forms, tones, words, in the whole Olympus of appearance. Those Greeks were superficial—*out of profundity*" (38).

With respect to *Waterland,* I am arguing that the image of history emerging from the lips of Tom's mother expresses the same truth of being superficial out of profundity. As Kofman has argued, Baubô veils the truth that is the fecundity of life. In a similar fashion, Helen Atkinson veils her truth in the form of her fairy tales, but she also articulates the fecundity of life in the form of her son Dick, the product of incestuous relations with her father. Swift's novel signals the mythic origins of culture through this incestuous gesture, but it also signifies the Nietzschean principle of being superficial out of profundity. Helen, as Tom reminds us, "had cause of her own to be no stranger to fairy-tales" (46). Like Baubô, Helen shows that, in Kofman's words, "behind the veil there is another veil." Helen told fairy tales to ward off the truth of her incestuous acts, acts that were themselves promulgated by a fairy tale. Thus, the oppositions collapse. Just as Kofman's Baubô shows us that "life is neither depth nor surface," Helen shows us that life is neither fairy tale nor the real.

Waterland articulates this basic Nietzschean insight: we make our truths, which themselves are illusions, in language. The fairy tales that Tom's mother told serve as the impetus for Tom's historical investigations;

and, in the end, he realizes that history is just a story—an important one, true, but just the same, a story. In this regard, Tom's intellectual development parallels Nietzsche's own, as it has been explained by Julian Young in *Nietzsche's Philosophy of Art*.

According to Young, Nietzsche's writings take a turn in *Human, All Too Human*, in which he espouses science, the notion of progress, and the belief in redeeming life in a future state of the world we inhabit. This optimistic view does not last, however; Young describes how Nietzsche began to doubt the capacities of science by the time he began *The Gay Science* (94–95). The entire trajectory of Nietzsche's career, according to Young, reveals a thinker who initially championed the redemptive power of art as illusion in *The Birth of Tragedy* and then turned briefly toward the power of science in *Human, All Too Human*. Young goes on to argue that, "during the period of *The Gay Science* and *Zarathustra*, Nietzsche's scientism evaporates, leading to a renewed sense of the importance of art, of viewing life aesthetically," something that Young characterizes as "an 'honest' confrontation with and acceptance of the reality of one's existence as an individual human being" (148). In the end, contends Young, Nietzsche returned to "the inauthenticity, the illusionism" of *The Birth of Tragedy* but with this major difference: both the Apollonian and Dionysian solutions are presented as illusions. For Young, Nietzsche's philosophy ultimately affirms the wisdom of Silenus: "Real life, the life of human individuality, is something it would be better we had never been born into" (148).

To my mind, the development of Tom's thinking resembles that of Nietzsche in some ways. Tom begins with the redemptive power of illusory fairy tales as a boy; as a young man, he espouses the scientific rationalism of historiography; eventually, as an adult, he returns to illusion by admitting that history is just a yarn. To push the parallel even further, I would say that Tom's solution is ultimately what Young would term a "late Apollonian solution"—one that expresses a profound superficiality but that, as Young reminds us, "is intended for 'we convalescents'" (101). Young here refers to the distinction Nietzsche makes between those who, like Zarathustra, herald the Overman but are not themselves the Overman and the genuine Overman himself. "We convalescents" have need of the illusory because we do not possess the strength and robust health that would be required if we were to face life in all its terror and power. Seen in this light, Tom is one of these convalescents; he has need of his mother's stories, for they ward off the terror of the real world, including the fiction that dominates his wife's thinking and drives her to steal a child. Note also that Tom's father (quite literally a convalescent) has need of Helen's stories as well. Both men espouse these illusions to ward off the terror of life. This can explain in part why Tom so insistently addresses his class as "children" and offers them dire warnings about the horror of the real and the here and now. For Tom, history becomes the official story—the Apollonian illusion that shields us from the horror of the emptiness of our collective lives.

But the late Apollonian solution described by Young is not the only one we find in Swift's novel. I contend that Swift, at the level of producing the text of *Waterland*, expresses what Young calls a "late Dionysian solution" as well—one that is an illusion but that constitutes a "nonsuperficial, truth-*embracing* approach to existence" (101). Although both solutions involve creating the self as an aesthetic phenomenon, the late Dionysian solution offers a complete "kind of coherent unity" (102), one that, "like the state, is the product of free creative activity" (103). Unlike the illusion Tom creates, Swift's illusion is coherent. Tom never really understands what has happened. He withdraws behind the belief in the power of tales, and he appears to be telling his students that this is all we have left. In response to the rallying cry of Price and his fellow students—"Fear is here"—Tom responds that we can draw comfort from stories. Swift, however, offers us an affirmation of the power of the illusion of narrative construction. Yes, *Waterland* is an illusion: there is no Tom Crick or Price or Martha Clay. There exists, however, the Dionysian sublimity that Young speaks of and in which we pretend "to belong to an order of being other than that of human individuality" because "life, real life, is unaffirmable" (139). As readers, we cannot affirm the death of Freddie Parr, the mental deterioration of Mary Crick, or the violation of Helen Atkinson. We can, however, affirm the power of the illusion of Swift's narrative—this, then, is the Nietzschean dimension of *Waterland*.

As Nietzsche said, we want deception. History, as Tom argues, is the story we tell to ward off the madness, the emptiness, the nothing of the real. Tom cannot explain the what and the why of it all. As we have seen, each of the oppositions that Tom establishes in the hopes of generating a foundation for making meaning—history/narrative, Atkinsons/Cricks, history/reality, instinct/learning, and so forth—collapses of its own accord within the boundaries of Swift's novel. In this manner, Swift demonstrates what Nietzsche called for in *Beyond Good and Evil;* he shows how something could originate out of its opposite. The closing remark of the novel, uttered by Stan Booth—"'Someone best explain'" (358)—can serve as the refrain for each of us. It comes at the end of Tom's attempt to explain precisely what happened, and yet the request still remains valid. Tom's narrative did not explain what happened. Indeed, no one will ever be able to satisfy the Booths of this world. The best explanation we have remains the novel Swift has constructed—one that presents truth as a woman. Swift's narrative is an illusion that knows itself to be an illusion; therefore, it is true. In this regard, I concur with Catherine Bernard. Swift succeeds in enlarging the definition of the referent such that it includes the creative act of narration itself. As Bernard notes, Swift shifts emphasis from, in Barthes's words, "l'énoncé à l'énonciation" (98). In the broader context, Swift instructs us that we can only offer our narrative of events we call history, but this creative act of narration constructs the referential world that we declare real. Swift's lesson also reminds us that we must organize the chaos of the past to meet our present needs, as Nietzsche would say, and this is exactly what *Waterland* does.

Swift's novel is true in the Vichian sense as well. In his novel, Swift constructs a true narrative, a *vera narratio*, one that through its very figuration expresses the truth of history, its cyclical nature, its unfolding in accordance with a paradigm of "rise, development, maturity, decline, and fall" (NS ¶ 245). The past of the Fens and the saga of Tom's family become the metaphor for each of us—our personal and collective histories. Expressed in Tom's own explanation of his fascination with history, Swift figures the conundrum he offers on history: story, action, instinct, story—an endless cycle with no beginning and no end. This accounts for the final word of the novel: "motor-cycle." Linked to Dick, and possibly his sexual surrogate, the motorcycle symbolizes both mystery and certainty. We are never sure just what function it serves for the atavistic Dick. Nevertheless, as a product of human labor, it signifies what we can make (and with its engine and speed it carries with it the sign of technological advancement and notions of Enlightenment progress). But its sign as cycle indicates that it continues endlessly in accordance with its own rhythms that will function independently, beyond our control.

As presented in *Waterland,* history follows a cyclical pattern; it is a mysterious machine of unfolding desire. As Tom describes it in chapter 47, "Goodnight": "First it was a story—what our parents told us at bedtime. Then it becomes real, then it becomes here and now. Then it becomes a story again. Second childhood" (328). A few lines later, we read: "First there is nothing; then there is happening. And after the happening, only the telling of it" (329). So, we might ask, which is it? *Waterland* suggests that it is both and neither.

"History," as Tom so eloquently describes it, "is that impossible thing: the attempt to give an account, with incomplete knowledge, of actions themselves undertaken with incomplete knowledge" (108). The lesson Swift's novel offers us corresponds to the lesson Tom offers his class when he says, "I taught you that by for ever attempting to explain we may come, not to an Explanation, but to a knowledge of the limits of our power to explain" (108). In Swift's vision of the world, we will forever come to this limit. As he explains to his students: "when the world is about to end there'll be no more reality, only stories. All that will be left to us will be stories. We'll sit down, in our shelter, and tell stories, like poor Scheherazade, hoping it will never . . ." (298).

8

Inventing the Past:
Mario Vargas Llosa's *El hablador*

The first gentile peoples, by a demonstrated necessity of nature, were poets who spoke in poetic characters. This discovery, which is the master key of this Science, has cost us the persistent research of almost all our literary life. . . .
—Vico, *The New Science*

The drive toward the formation of metaphors is the fundamental human drive, which one cannot for a single instant dispense with in thought, for one would thereby dispense with man himself.
—Nietzsche, "On Truth and Lies in a Nonmoral Sense"

In his now-famous essay "The Precession of Simulacra," Jean Baudrillard describes the day in 1971 when the Philippine government decided to "return to their primitive state the few dozen Tasaday discovered deep in the jungle, where they had lived for eight centuries undisturbed by the rest of mankind, out of reach of colonists, tourists, and ethnologists" (257). The moment is instructive because it signals how science always must destroy its object even as it discovers, identifies, measures, examines—in a word, *invents* it. By voicing support for the move that would place the Tasaday back in their natural, virgin environment, the anthropologists and ethnologists appeared to be making a sacrifice. After all, they renounced the opportunity to observe their objects of study. But, as Baudrillard cleverly observes, in this case science engaged in a "simulated sacrifice of its object in order to save its reality principle" (257). In other words, through their very acts of observation, ethnologists destroy the cultures they study; by renouncing the opportunity to observe these Tasaday in the virgin forest, the ethnologists preserved the idea of their object of study (i.e., the unobserved Tasaday). Or, in Baudrillard's terms, the Tasaday returned to the forest "becomes the simulation model for all conceivable Indians *before ethnology*" (257).

The paradox that Baudrillard describes is but one of many that have arisen since the Enlightenment concerning intercultural interaction. Even during the Enlightenment's inception, some of its thinkers expressed their own anxieties about the limits of reason and the relationship between

European, reason-centered societies and non-Western cultures; others championed the new way of thinking. For example, two years after Defoe published the ultimate Protestant myth of the self-made man, *Robinson Crusoe*, which unequivocally expresses the triumph of Western capitalist culture, Montesquieu published *Lettres persanes*, which presents a pointed critique of European society and calls into question universal values. In the post-Enlightenment era, the paradoxes have become more acute and, perhaps, more deadly. In an era of mullahs with modems who use free-speech laws to condemn authors and advocate their murder, we also witness international corporations justifying sweatshop labor as an improvement in the lives of workers in China, Korea, and Indonesia while indigenous revolutionary groups in Africa wear Chicago Bulls sports apparel and tote M-60 machine guns. The paradoxes abound, and we are just beginning to acknowledge that there really are no solutions to these problems, all comments from free-marketeers to the contrary.

One of the most effective literary works that addresses many of these issues—indigenous peoples and the rise of televisual, media-dominated culture, the role of government and interethnic conflict, economic development and cultural preservation, the artist and commodified culture, religion in a secular world, oral versus print culture, and so forth—happens to be Mario Vargas Llosa's *El hablador* (*The Storyteller*). In this novel, Vargas Llosa presents two narratives—one describes a Western-educated, successful writer from Peru who reflects on a college friend whom he thinks may have inserted himself into an Amazonian tribe as their bard or storyteller; the other records the actual tales told by this same storyteller. What ensues is a deep meditation on cultural interaction, language, and imagination that underscores many of the ideas expressed in the writings of Vico and Nietzsche.

Readers familiar with Vargas Llosa's work might well contend that *The War of the End of the World* (1981) actually addresses the issues of history and fiction in a much more thorough manner. According to Michael Valdez Moses, *The War of the End of the World* "involves a monumental narrative attempt, in the manner of Tolstoy's *War and Peace*, to define the nature of history in terms compatible with a set of liberal democratic reforms he [Vargas Llosa] advocates as the remedy for the immense social and political ills of Latin America in particular and the Third World in general" (151). While this may be the case, I would also add that Vargas Llosa's depiction of the actual rebellion that occurred in Canudos in 1897; his creation of the enigmatic presence of the Counselor, a symbol of the opacity of the Other, of Galileo Gall, the Scotsman who is both a revolutionary and a phrenologist and as such an exemplar of extremist Enlightenment ideologies, and of the unnamed journalist who represents the myopia of the modern press; and, finally, his reliance on Euclides de Cunha's *Os sertões* constitute a rich interpretive field that brings together issues of historical accuracy, the truth of fiction, the necessity of the imagination, and the generative power of intertextuality. Furthermore, I have addressed many of the issues explored in *The War of the End of the World* in my discussions of *Terra Nostra* and *Midnight's Children*. Consequently, I choose to focus on *The Storyteller* for two main reasons. First, it highlights the clash of cultures in the contemporary world, specifically as it applies to indigenous peoples and their interactions with Western societies. Second, in this finely distilled novel, Vargas Llosa concentrates his energies on examining the transformative potential of fiction in its literary form. In *The Storyteller*, we see firsthand how we construct our worlds through deliberate acts of the imagination. Implied in Vargas Llosa's novel is the notion that we now face a situation at the end of the twentieth century where we must abandon our exclusive reliance on the so-called scientific approach toward solving our global social problems and first invoke the various forms of the imagination to acknowledge cultural differences, project possible futures, and make new meanings based on alternative ways of organizing communities.

Vargas Llosa's tale in *The Storyteller* is in some ways a familiar one: a writer seeks solace in exile as he flees his native culture. As the writer-narrator puts it in the opening line of the novel: "I came to Firenze to forget Peru and the Peruvians for a while" (3). The novel, however, soon departs from the tradition of the writer who seeks a release from the burden of his past and his profession. As the novel unfolds, the writer-narrator's thoughts increasingly focus on the clash of cultures in what we might term a postmodern Peru and the role of the writer vis-à-vis this cultural confrontation. Much to his chagrin, the writer-narrator quickly learns that he cannot forget Peru because he finds in Florence a photo exhibit that records the activities of the Machiguenga tribe—a loosely connected group of peripatetic peoples who wander through the Amazon jungle. It is a tribe with which the narrator is familiar (we later learn that he visited Protestant missionaries who attended to the tribe when he worked for a television series called "The Tower of Babel" in 1981).

Viewing the photos sparks memories in the narrator, and he begins to recall his friendship with an eccentric college classmate named Saúl Zuratas, a Jewish student of history and anthropology who has a deep-red birthmark that covers half of his face. Because of this birthmark, Saúl earns the nickname Mascarita, but his attitude toward his disfigurement is rather sardonic. For Saúl, the birthmark gives him the perspective of an outsider, something that is reinforced by his Jewishness. As the writer-narrator contemplates the photographs of the Machiguenga, he pauses at a photo of a small group surrounding an *hablador,* a "speaker" or tribal storyteller, who looks like a white man with light red hair. It is this photo that ultimately leads the writer-narrator to imagine that his old friend, Mascarita, joined the Machiguenga and became their hablador.

As we read the novel, we move back and forth in alternating chapters from the reflections of the writer in Florence (chapters 1, 2, 4, 6, and 8) to the actual storyteller (chapters 3, 5, and 7), who recounts tales to the Machiguenga people. By contrasting the reflections of the writer and the articulations of the speaker, we have much more than a comparative examination of print versus oral culture. Rather, Vargas Llosa presents us with the reflections of a postmodern consciousness confronting a premodern actuality—a condition that currently obtains in present-day Peru. *The Storyteller* provides us with a rare opportunity to see how the philosophical writings of Vico and Nietzsche have much to teach us about what many term the postmodern, multicultural world of the late twentieth century. Specifically, *The Storyteller* depicts two cultures at opposite extremes: one exists at the earliest moment of Vico's *corso*—the age of the gods—while the other languishes in the third age of the barbarism of reflection. In addition to the concept of ideal eternal history, other Vichian ideas appear in the novel as well: imaginative universals, the centrality of the poet in culture, the relationship between memory and imagination, and recollective imagination. The Nietzschean dimension of the novel appears most clearly when we consider how the writer-narrator comes to adopt his personal interpretation of the photographs of the Machiguenga. Here we find a clear example of the expression of will to power in pursuit of art. Overall, *The Storyteller* presents us with a thought-provoking examination of the complexities of intercultural interaction at the end of the millennium, one that transcends the facile discussions of multiculturalism and magical realism. What follows, then, will be an examination of the Vichian and Nietzschean dimensions of the text.

I should express a word of caution here. I am not arguing that Vico or Nietzsche inform the text or that Mario Vargas Llosa has even read them. Unlike Fuentes, Vargas Llosa has not examined the ideas of either philosopher in detail in his critical writings or his public lectures; and, unlike Tournier, he is not trained as a philosopher. Whereas it is very likely that Rushdie read Nietzsche and perhaps even Vico while taking a degree in history, and it is certain that Daitch was exposed to Nietzsche (if only in a secondhand manner when she read Foucault while studying theory in art school), there is nothing to suggest that Vargas Llosa was exposed to the writings of either philosopher when he studied at Leoncio Prado Military Academy, the University of San Marcos, or the University of Madrid. What is clear is that Vargas Llosa studied the works of Karl Popper during his bid for the Peruvian presidency ("Fish" 56); and, in an article published in *PMLA*, he endorses Popper's view of history while rejecting Vico, whom he lumps together with Machiavelli, Spengler, and Toynbee. He characterizes those who follow these philosophers as being "idolatrous of history and, consciously or unconsciously, frightened of freedom, secretly afraid of assuming the responsibility that means conceiving of life as permanent creation" ("Updating" 1022). It should be very clear that the interpretation of Vico that I offer differs markedly from that glossed by Vargas Llosa. Judging from what he has said about Vico, I would suggest that perhaps the novelist has not studied Vico carefully. Whatever the case may be, I am not, as was the case with Fuentes, concerned with Vargas Llosa's conscious intentions or his understanding of either Vico or Nietzsche. I am concerned with what elements of Vichian and Nietzschean philosophy appear in Vargas Llosa's novel *malgré lui*. The key factor for me is that *The Storyteller*, as a work of literature, can better express, and in some ways extend, elements of both Vico and Nietzsche's philosophy. The task I set for myself, then, is to show how Vargas Llosa's novel succeeds in doing this.

Speaking the Real

Readers of *The Storyteller* are often struck by the two radically different narrative voices that appear in the novel. The first narrator—as critics such as Castro-Klarén, O'Bryan-Knight, Booker, and Kerr have noted—closely resembles Vargas Llosa himself. The second is that of the hablador, and it is this voice that most clearly expresses Vichian ideas in the course of telling tales. First and foremost, one should immediately recognize that the hablador is the Machiguenga poet. He is the voice of his people much as Homer was the voice of the Greeks. In book 3 of *The New Science*, Vico argues that Homer was the Greek people (NS ¶ 875);

Homer articulated the ethos of Greek culture through the description of the exploits of various characters and gods in the *Iliad* and the *Odyssey*. In a similar fashion, the hablador is the Machiguenga people because he recounts the activities of past and present members of the scattered community, whose male members are called Tasurinchi. Thus, when the storyteller encounters a new group of the Machiguenga, he describes the exploits or activities of Tasurinchi, and this designation makes possible the identification of each male listener with the activity being described. In doing so, the hablador binds together the Machiguenga people by underscoring the common experiences, attitudes, and behaviors that all members of the tribe share. The stories, therefore, constitute the collective consciousness of the tribe.

Much as Vico described the cultures of the first gentiles, Machiguenga culture locates its foundation in poetic acts, and it is from these imaginative projections that the Machiguenga world becomes real. As Mr. Schneil, the Protestant missionary to the Machiguenga, describes it to the writer-narrator, the term hablador is uttered with respect by the Machiguengas. Schneil conjectures that his function is to speak (92) and that he is perhaps a spiritual or religious leader (91). According to Schneil, the storyteller also "'speaks of the past. He is probably also the memory of the community, fulfilling a function similar to that of the jongleurs and troubadours of the Middle Ages'" (93). In short, the hablador is the soul of the culture; without him, there would be no continuity to the Machiguenga experience and no voice of their conceptualization of the world. This is what Vico had in mind when he contended that poets were the originators of culture, that "poets must therefore have been the first historians of the nations" (NS ¶ 820), and that "all the arts of the necessary, the useful, the convenient, and even in large part those of human pleasure, were invented in the poetic centuries before the philosophers came; for the arts are nothing but imitations of nature and in a certain way 'real' poems" (NS ¶ 217; see also NS ¶ 376).

We also find that the Vichian notion of the imaginative universal is related to the centrality of the poet in Machiguenga culture. In *The New Science*, Vico declares that poetic truth is metaphysical truth, and he notes an "important consideration on poetic theory: the true war chief, for example, is the Godfrey that Torquato Tasso imagines; and all the chiefs who do not conform throughout to Godfrey are not true chiefs of war" (NS ¶ 205). If a man were an exceptional fighter, he necessarily possessed the

attributes associated with Godfrey because that is what the name Godfrey meant; it did not signify a particular individual born at a specific time
in a single village. Rather, Godfrey was a universal, and the warrior was
identified with that universal. As Donald Verene explains it: "The individual is what it is because its being is the being of the type. Since the
figure of the fable or poetic character is not formed by abstraction from
individuals or particulars already commanding their own empirical reality, the poetic character is the reality" (*Vico's Science* 75).

We learn that among the Machiguenga the members of the group "did
not have personal names" (83). Each man was called Tasurinchi, and in
order to differentiate one from the other, the storyteller would designate
each Tasurinchi by some specific characteristic or location. For example,
the hablador refers to Tasurinchi the blind one (54), or Tasurinchi who
used to live by the Mitaya (48), or Tasurinchi who lived by the bend in the
river (45). This move toward individuation (i.e., designating the unique
characteristics of a Tasurinchi) runs counter to the universalization of the
members of the tribe and can be understood in terms of Vico's paradigm
of the three ages that all cultures must pass through.

By moving from the strict universal appellation of Tasurinchi to one
that contains qualifiers of differentiation, we can see how the Machiguenga tribe itself would be moving into the second of Vico's three ages—the
age of heroes. It is in the heroic age that the poet (like Homer) holds sway
and commemorates the deeds of the great members of the culture in the
past. The stories about the origins of Machiguenga culture, the repeated
emphasis on "before" and "after," indicate that the current Machiguenga
are removed from those events in time such that, much like Homer's auditors, they can listen to descriptions of the actions of gods and humans
in a polymorphic world. Perhaps the best indications of the Vichian dimensions of the text appear when the hablador relates the story of Pachakamue.

The storyteller begins by saying: "This is the story of Pachakamue,
whose words were born animals, trees, and rocks. / That was before" (132).
What follows is the description of a character who utters the real. Pachakamue has the uncanny ability to make manifest his utterances; when he
calls his sister's children monkeys, they become so, and when he pro-
nounces "sachavaca," his daughter turns into one. Eventually, he is tracked
down and killed, but his severed head still retains its tongue and speaks
from time to time from beneath the earth, wreaking havoc among the

members of the community. Although Pachakamue is accused of "upsetting the order of the world with the words he uttered" (133), he does represent the principle of making the world through language. His speech projects real presence. The still-extant though buried tongue serves as a reminder of the power of language to transform reality. As María Isabel Acosta Cruz points out, Pachakamue "creates unwittingly; the power belongs not to him but to the language he utters, to the words which are not bound to authorial intentionality" (137–38). The power of speech as exemplified by Pachakamue expresses two key Vichian principles. First, we see in his actions the parallel activities of Vico's first humans, who utter the world by making imaginative universals. Second, we also note that Pachakamue comes from another era. His time is "before"; in Vichian terms, he lives during the age of the gods, a time in which a "first nature" was "robust," "poetic or creative" (NS ¶ 916), a time also in which the theological poets attribute "senses and passions . . . to bodies, and to bodies as vast as sky, sea, and earth" (NS ¶ 402). As the storyteller himself explains: "Whoever knows all the stories has wisdom, no doubt. I learned the story of some of the animals from them. They had all been men, before. They were born speaking, or, to put it a better way, they were born from speaking. Words existed before they did. And then, after that, what the words said. Man spoke and what he said appeared. That was before. Now a man who speaks speaks, and that's all. Animals and things already exist. That was after" (131–32).

The world of "before" is the Vichian era of the gods, where language makes the world, and the actions of humans are indissociable from the words that describe those actions. In book 2 of *The New Science*, Vico discusses poetic wisdom and traces its origin to the "first founders of gentile humanity," giants who, when frightened by thunder, attributed their own nature to the effects observed in the phenomenal world. Thus, according to Vico, "they pictured the sky to themselves as a great animated body" (NS ¶ 377). Poetic thinking, characterized as a "felt and imagined" metaphysics (NS ¶ 375), led to the development of the "first divine fable" of Jove, "king and father of men and gods" (NS ¶ 379). The language of the theological poets "was not a language in accord with the nature of things it dealt with . . . but was a fantastic speech making use of physical substances endowed with life and most of them imagined to be divine" (NS ¶ 401). I contend that the story of Pachakamue exemplifies this type of fantastic speech. In many ways, it is reminiscent of Heidegger's observation that "language speaks" (191). "What is spoken purely," writes Heidegger, "is the poem" (194); and, in the case of *The Storyteller*, the hablador articulates the poetry of Machiguenga culture in the form of the stories he relates to the various members of the tribe. The story of Pachakamue can be considered in some sense the poem of poems in that it shows how language speaks the real and how this occurred in an earlier age, "before"—or, as Vico would say, in the time of the theological poets.

Vico's three ages also constitute the driving force that moves ideal eternal history. According to Vico, each culture goes through the cycle of development and decline in the same order. Thus, history can be said to follow a pattern; consequently, one can claim that, in general, history repeats itself. The cyclicity of the Vichian system has strong affinities with the cyclical nature of time as expressed in most premodern cultures. The Machiguenga prove to be no exception in that their culture exists in a constant state of repetition. According to the writer-narrator, the Machiguenga verb system "mixed up past and present" and contributed to "a form of speech in which before and now were barely differentiated" (93). Consequently, "for the Machiguengas, history marches neither forward nor backward: it goes around and around in circles, repeats itself" (241). The hablador plays a crucial role in maintaining this state of being in the present through the very stories he tells that, in effect, place all Tasurinchis in every situation at all times. As the auditors tell the storyteller: "'Thanks to the things you tell us, it's as though what happened before happens again, many times'" (61).

The Machiguenga engage in a form of mythical thought. According to Ernst Cassirer, the hallmark of mythical thinking can be summed up in the following manner: "Myth and language are inseparable and mutually condition each other"; in other words, "word and name do not designate and signify, they are and act" (40). The story of Pachakamue provides a perfect example of the power of mythical language to make manifest a state of being and action. In a community conditioned by mythical thinking, Cassirer contends that there exists no clear distinction between life and death, sleeping and waking; the two are related, he writes, "as two similar, homogeneous parts of the same being" (37). Once again, the Machiguenga conform to this principle in that they willingly commit suicide over issues that many Western readers would find trivial. When it comes to the very structure of the stories the hablador relates, we also see a clear manifestation of mythical thinking. For example, the hablador relates the story of how Kashiri got a stained face; and, in the process, he produces different versions of the story (113–16). Lévi-Strauss points out that a myth is not dependent on "its style, its original music, or its syntax, but in the *story* which it tells" (210), and it consists "of all its versions" (217). Unlike the overall novel, the segments of the hablador's tales or myths are not dependent on narrative framing devices and temporal shifts; they are, as Lévi-Strauss contends, communicable in all translations and can be felt as a myth by any reader. I have paused to consider the aspects of mythical thought expressed in *The Storyteller* not so much to say anything about the Machiguenga per se but to indicate how carefully Vargas Llosa conveys the profound difference that obtains between the two cultures depicted in his novel. It is precisely in this confrontation of cultures that we can discern certain elements of Vico's philosophy.

The Clash of Cultures: A Vichian Approach

As we have seen, in the speaker-narrator sections of Vargas Llosa's novel (chapters 3, 5, and 7), we can readily identify several aspects of Vico's philosophy. Nevertheless, the key Vichian element in *The Storyteller* appears at the thematic level of the novel in the forcefully expressed cultural debate that ensues between the writer-narrator and Saúl over how the modern world should interact with the Machiguenga. Profound problems confront us whether, like Saúl, we advocate leaving the Machiguenga alone in the jungle or, like the writer-narrator, we promote the assimilation of the tribe. In each case (and all cases in between), we must rely on interpretations based on incomplete information. Take, for example, the Summer Institute of Linguistics. What exactly was the role that this organization played in the Amazon? Some felt that it was an arm of U.S. imperialism in that it was gathering intelligence for the CIA. Catholic priests felt that it was a group of Protestant missionaries acting as linguists. Some anthropologists felt that the institute was corrupting and Westernizing the tribal peoples. Still others felt that the institute undermined the national sovereignty of Peru (71). Perhaps the institute played each of these roles; perhaps it did something altogether different. What is undeniable is that the institute did affect the Machiguengas. In this regard, the ambiguity surrounding the purpose and effects of the institute serves as a metaphor for the major theme of *The Storyteller*. Vargas Llosa asks difficult questions about what industrialized nations should do as economic development begins to envelop the entire globe, thereby changing nonindustrialized cultures irremediably.

In a series of lectures he delivered at Syracuse University in 1988 and later published under the title *A Writer's Reality*, Vargas Llosa speaks of the effects industrialization has on the Indian population of his native Peru. In Vargas Llosa's eyes, Peru consists of two cultures. However, these "two cultures, one Western and modern, the other aboriginal and archaic, hardly coexist, separated from one another because of the exploitation and discrimination that the former exercises over the latter" (*Writer's Reality* 34). The novelist describes what it is like for the Indians when they attempt to become assimilated into Western culture. "The price they must pay for integration is high—renunciation of their culture, their language, their beliefs, their traditions and customs, and the adoption of the culture of their ancient masters. After one generation they become *mestizos*. They are no longer Indians" (*Writer's Reality* 36). Vargas Llosa conjectures that "perhaps the ideal, that is, the preservation of the primitive cultures of America, is a utopia incomparable with this other and more urgent goal—the establishment of societies in which social and economic inequalities among citizens be reduced to human reasonable limits and where everybody can enjoy at least a decent and free life" (*Writer's Reality* 36). When it comes to whether or not Indians should be assimilated, Vargas Llosa, the living author, opts for assimilation. In his words: "If forced to choose between the preservation of Indian cultures and their complete assimilation, with great sadness I would choose modernization of the Indian population because there are priorities; and the first priority is, of course, to fight hunger and misery" (*Writer's Reality* 36). I have reproduced the reflections of Vargas Llosa on this issue not because I believe they express the central thesis in *The Storyteller*. On the contrary, I offer them precisely because I believe that Vargas Llosa's novel does not advocate *either* assimilation *or* utopian preservationism. *The Storyteller* presents the problematic of cultural interaction; and, by its very nature as a novel—a discursive form whose philosophical themes remain necessarily indeterminate—it explores the various possibilities that exist with respect to this global problem.

In the novel, the problem that confronts the world as a whole achieves its most poignant expression in the image of an Andean boy who appears in the background as the writer-narrator and Saúl debate the issue of assimilation. The writer-narrator describes him as follows:

> The Andean boy throwing bucketfuls of sawdust on the floor in the Palermo had on the sort of sandals—a sole and two cross-strips cut from an old rubber tire—made and sold by peddlers, and a pair of patched pants held up with a length of rope round his waist. He was a child with the face of an old

man, coarse hair, blackened nails, and a reddish scab on his nose. A zombie? A caricature? Would it have been better for him to have stayed in his Andean village, wearing a wool cap with earflaps, leather sandals, and a poncho, never learning Spanish? I don't know, and I still don't. But Mascarita knew. (27)

The Andean boy functions as an objective correlative for the problems with assimilationist policy. The benefits of global capitalism that have trickled down through the peddlers to the boy transform him into a servile, unskilled laborer who resembles an aging clown. The world that makes possible the leisure-filled life of the writer-narrator who travels to Florence to read Dante and Machiavelli for a while, the world that produces technology capable of transmitting images from one location to another in television shows such as "The Tower of Babel," is the same world that effects an incomplete metamorphosis of tribal and preindustrial societies and condemns them to a profound existence of alienation and self-alienation.

The image of the Andean boy serves as the backdrop for the major debate between the writer-narrator and Saúl. For the former, the major question revolves around global development. He asks himself:

> Should sixteen million Peruvians renounce the natural resources of three-quarters of their national territory so that seventy or eighty thousand Indians could quietly go on shooting at each other with bows and arrows, shrinking heads and worshipping boa constrictors? Should we forgo the agricultural, cattle-raising, and commercial potential of the region so that the world's ethnologists could enjoy studying at first hand kinship ties, potlatches, the rites of puberty, marriage, and death that these human oddities had been practicing, virtually unchanged, for hundreds of years? (21–22)

The rhetoric here is harsh and forceful, but the questions are genuine. The continued development of natural resources and the expansion of so-called free market capitalism in both its industrial and postindustrial modes constitute the material reality that confronts the inhabitants of this planet. The writer-narrator's utilitarian argument is a persuasive one if, in addition to accepting utilitarian principles, we pause to consider the alternative facing many developing nations throughout the world. As intellectuals from nations such as India and Brazil are quick to point out, it is hypocritical for ecologically minded, well-educated citizens from the United States to demand that developing nations cease industrial development or adopt prohibitively expensive pollution-controlling procedures; this is because to pursue either alternative would make it impossible for the developing nations to participate in the global economy in any way other than providing an obscenely cheap labor force for industries from countries such as the United States that outsource many of their production activities. In other words, if the option is free market capitalism that is dominated by the developed nations of the world, then a nation such as Brazil would condemn its population to perpetual servitude and abject poverty if it chose to turn the entire Amazon jungle into a global park. This is not to suggest that there are no responsible alternatives that would make it possible for both preservation and development to proceed in tandem. However, the pressures on developing nations are enormous; and, in the face of economic crises that confront many nations today, some leaders of developing nations would agree with the writer-narrator: the preservation of prehistoric cultures will harm more people than it will benefit.

The writer-narrator continues his critique of Saúl's position by contending that even if Mascarita's proposals were understandable, they were neither attainable nor desirable. First of all, he argues, social and cultural groups of every sort "were being contaminated by Western and mestizo influences" (73). "Was going on living the way they were," he asks, "the way purist anthropologists of Saúl's sort wanted them to do, to the tribes' advantage? Their primitive state made them, rather, victims of the worst exploitation and cruelty" (73–74). Here we find the typical argument that the power of industrialization is so great that its predominance is inevitable. But coupled with this argument is the far more troubling contention that even if the indigenous cultures were preserved, they would be exploited. To carve out a preserve for the Machiguenga so as to prevent interaction with other cultures is to create a living museum space that, much like the Tasaday mentioned in Baudrillard's essay, would make the Machiguenga a theoretical object. In addition, it would necessarily limit the movement of the people themselves. Sooner or later, the Machiguenga would come to the border that separated them from the others—and there would be no way of preventing this inevitability, short of reducing the Machiguenga preserve to a large petri dish. In such a preserve, they could become the object of study and tourism and, in a classic sense, exploited.

In the end, the writer-narrator compares Saúl's utopian vision to the socialist ideology he espoused as a young man. In the 1980s, he has rejected these socialist views and wonders why he ever embraced them. "Wasn't there already sufficient evidence," he asks, "that industrial development, whether capitalist or communist, inevitably meant the annihilation of those [indigenous] cultures? (78). He admits that "we were as unrealistic and romantic as Mascarita with his archaic, anti-historical utopia" (78). The sympathetic tone of the writer-narrator does nothing to undermine the clear rejection of what he perceives to be the foolhardy and romantic nature of Saúl's ideas.

Saúl, for his part, admits that some tribes, such as the Tahuantinsuyo, already have had too much contact with the industrialized world and should therefore be assimilated as quickly as possible (100). The Machiguengas, however, are different in that some of their people have not yet been affected by modern industrialized culture. "Their culture," he argues, "is adequate for their environment and for the conditions they live in" (100). Mascarita defends the Machiguenga even against charges that their cultural values include cruel menarche rituals, slavery, euthanasia, and a form of "perfectionism" in which infants born with defects are immediately killed (25). Counterbalancing these disturbing cultural practices are the more significant cultural values that, in the writer-narrator's words, Saúl describes as

> their understanding of the world in which they were immersed, the wisdom born of long practice which had allowed them through an elaborate system of rites, taboos, fears, and routines, perpetuated and passed on from father to son, to preserve that Nature, seemingly so superabundant, but actually so vulnerable, upon which they depended for subsistence. These tribes had survived because their habits and customs had docilely followed the rhythms and requirements of the natural world, without doing it violence or disturbing it deeply, just the minimum necessary so as not to be destroyed by it. The very opposite of what we civilized people were doing, wasting those elements without which we would end up withering like flowers without water. (27)

As many observers have noted about other tribal cultures around the world, the Machiguenga were in harmony with nature. Indigenists like Saúl prize tribal cultures precisely because they have struck a balance between themselves and nature, unlike developed nations that continue to damage the environment. Implied in Saúl's defense is the idea that we must preserve such tribal cultures because they may have something to teach us about how to achieve a balance between ensuring cultural viability and maintaining a natural environment. Perhaps even more deeply embedded in Saúl's defense is the admission that preserving such tribal cultures is in the best interest of the human species, for the developed world may in fact destroy itself, and only these tribal cultures will remain.

Irrespective of the deep, perhaps unconscious, motives of Saúl, which of course also may include his identification with the very marginality of the Machiguenga themselves, we can readily see that, as the writer-narrator admits, Mascarita idealizes the Amazonian tribe (23). This does not, however, invalidate his argument. As Saúl succinctly states: "'Though we don't understand their beliefs and some of their customs offend us, we have no right to kill them off" (26). Here, then, is the dilemma Vargas Llosa wishes to explore. On the one hand, there exists a global economy that voraciously ingests everything in its path in pursuit of profit. As Saúl argues: "'Our culture is too strong, too aggressive. It devours everything it touches. They [the Machiguenga] must be left alone'" (99). On the other hand, there exist pockets of cultures that have managed to remain outside the realm of global capitalism. The question posed in Vargas Llosa's book appears to be, to echo another book, What is to be done?

At this point, we should admit that there is nothing particularly remarkable about the presentation of the problems surrounding this issue as they appear in *The Storyteller*. The debate between the two Vargas Llosa characters is rather thin and reminiscent of discussions one can hear in the popular media or in political science, sociology, and anthropology classrooms on college campuses around the world. What is more significant, however, is the manner in which Vargas Llosa explores the problem of interaction between cultures. Rather than examine the method of hegemonic forms of influence wielded by dominant economic powers over tribal cultures, Vargas Llosa prefers to examine a potential method of cultural preservation as practiced by a member of that dominant culture. When he imagines a Western-educated man inserting himself into the Machiguenga tribe, Vargas Llosa raises serious questions about the possibility of ever preventing any culture from being influenced by a dominant culture. Thus, rather than ask "What is to be done?" Vargas Llosa asks: "What manner of thinking will we need to resolve intercultural disputes?" and "What role, if any, might imaginative literature play in helping us to understand cultural difference?"

Most readers are persuaded that we are supposed to believe that Mascarita infiltrated the Machiguenga tribe and became the most important member of their culture—the hablador. Ostensibly, Saúl comes from outside to preserve what is inside the culture. By reciting his stories, he maintains the traditions and customs of the Machiguenga people. Saúl's approach diametrically opposes the approach used by the Summer Institute of Linguistics, one that he characterizes as "'the worst of all.'" Referring to the members of the institute, Mascarita declares: "'They work their way into the tribes to destroy them from within, just like chiggers. Into their spirit, their beliefs, their subconscious, the roots of their way of being'" (95). Their goal, he declares, is "'to wipe out their [the Machiguenga] culture, their gods, their institutions off the map and corrupt even their dreams'" (97). He concludes by stating that "'what the Institute is doing is so damaging, taking away their gods and replacing them with their own, an abstract God'" (101).

Yet, as some readers and critics such as Acosta Cruz (136–43), Booker (131), and Kerr (*Reclaiming* 151–52) have noted, Mascarita does much the same thing when he interpolates Western narratives such as Kafka's "Metamorphosis" and stories from the Bible into the tales he tells the Machiguenga. When he speaks of Gregor-Tasurinchi or Jehovah-Tasurinchi or the son of Jehovah-Tasurinchi who was able to "change a few cassavas and a few catfish into a whole lot" (216), the storyteller is quite literally "taking away their gods and replacing them with [his] own." His purpose, it seems, is to alter the tribal values so that the Machiguengas respect the rights of women and abandon the practice of infanticide. In fact, as Acosta Cruz argues, "Saúl's obsession with Kafka is more powerful than the tribal wisdom and his 'conversion' into a Machiguenga is still problematic and unfinished" (141). Each time the storyteller attempts to make these suggestions through his stories, his auditors laugh. In the end, we are left with serious doubts as to whether or not Mascarita will (or even can) bring about change within the tribe and, perhaps even more important, if he should, given everything he said to his friend in 1958.

Yet another layer of complexity is added when we pause to consider just who the storyteller of *The Storyteller* may be. As M. Keith Booker has argued, the hablador is the construction of the writer-narrator. It is the Peruvian writer in Florence who is imagining the hablador in the Amazon, and it is he who decides that in fact the storyteller is his old friend Mascarita. By making this choice, the writer asserts his authority as a creator. As Lucille Kerr notes, in several of Vargas Llosa's novels, "the figure of the author is constructed as an unmistakably textualized figure at the same time that it is presented as a recognizably autobiographical entity" (*Reclaiming* 135). *The Storyteller* proves to be no exception; but of equal importance is the manner in which Vargas Llosa imagines what it might mean for a Western-educated individual to inhabit a premodern culture— even if that individual is a militant indigenist.

The speaker-narrator portions of the novel reveal that Mascarita cannot shed his cultural skin, that in fact no matter how much he identifies and empathizes with the Machiguenga, he cannot avoid expressing his own cultural values. Perhaps the most disturbing comment made by the hablador is the following: "Who is purer or happier because he's renounced his destiny, I ask you? Nobody. We'd best be what we are. The one who gives up fulfilling his own obligation so as to fulfill that of another will lose his soul" (220). If the storyteller is Mascarita, could one not argue that Saúl renounced an obligation to his father Don Salomón? By renouncing his father, perhaps even his father's culture (admittedly, it is his father and not his mother who is Jewish; therefore, Saúl would not be considered Jewish), to become an hablador, Saúl may very well have lost his soul. Paradoxically, even as he loses his soul, he cannot rid himself of the spiritual values of his past. The very manner in which he tells his tales reflects a literary culture—the biblical and Kafka stories are products of a print culture that has distanced itself from the oral traditions ordinarily associated with tribal groups such as the Machiguenga.

The question of cultural authenticity raised by Saúl serves as but one example of the overall theme of the novel. From my perspective, *The Storyteller* expresses Vargas Llosa's troubled view on cultural interaction in the postmodern world, one that can be best examined in light of Vico's philosophy. Vico, in many respects, is the first major philosopher of what we might term polyculturalism. Cecilia Miller conjectures that perhaps Vico became aware of the diversity of cultures when he conducted his study for the writing of a biography of Antonio Caraffa, a Neapolitan general who fought in the culturally diverse region of Hungary (35). Whatever the reason, once he recognized that cultures differed radically, Vico granted to each its own place and autonomy. Rather than designate one culture superior to all others or claim that all cultures eventually will reach a certain stage of organization, Vico identified three basic stages that all cultures can go through (should they survive long enough). His focus on the poetic origins of culture made it possible for him (unlike some Enlightenment thinkers) to regard so-called primitive cultures as anything but primitive. From Vico's perspective, tribal cultures based on oral traditions existed in an age that differed from the age of the Enlightenment. Such tribal cultures would be experiencing the "barbarism of the senses" just as eighteenth-century Europe was in the grip of the "barbarism of reflection." My contention here is that Vico's philosophy offers us something useful and important, especially when we encounter regions of the world such as Latin America, where prehistoric cultures and postmodern architecture can be within a few hundred miles of one another. The term often invoked when describing Latin America is the "magical real," a phrase usually associated with a particular style of writing in the twentieth century. To my mind, Vico can help us better understand what this term means, particularly in the context of Latin American culture.

Magical Realism Revisited

Tourists often remark on the fantastic nature of the culture of Latin America. For example, one can find in close proximity to one another a skyscraper, an ancient Mayan temple, and the remnants of sixteenth-century artifacts left by the conquistadores. In several countries, the geography varies such that, in a small space, a traveler can see towering mountains, dense tropical jungles, and arid deserts within the space of a few square miles. In terms of human populations, Indian, Spanish, Portuguese, and African cultures, as well as various mixtures of these groups, flourish. For an observer coming from a relatively homogeneous, monolingual culture, Latin America can look like a geographic, historical, and ethnic *carnaval*. The heterogeneity of Latin American reality can be so extreme that an outsider can find it incredible. Such feelings have gained greater currency in the last thirty years as a growing population of readers has picked up translations of literary works of the writers of the "Boom"—Cortázar, Fuentes, García Márquez, and Vargas Llosa—as well as works written by writers before and after the "Boom"—including Borges, Carpentier, Isabel Allende, Lispector, Puig, and Piñon.

To offer an example of the literary expression of the fantastic dimensions of Latin American culture, we need look no further than what may be the most widely read book produced by a Latin American author in the twentieth century: *One Hundred Years of Solitude*. García Márquez's 1967 novel remains a pivotal event in Latin American literature; and, for many readers outside Latin America, the most unforgettable scenes in that novel revolve around actions that defy logic, that cannot be explained rationally, that appear to be magical. Thus, when Remedios the Beauty ascends into the heavens; or the blood of José Arcadio Buendía runs from his ear and winds its way through the streets of Macondo only to arrive at the foot of his mother, Úrsula; or rain falls for four years, eleven months, and two days, we attribute these events to the fantastical nature of Latin

American reality that García Márquez describes in his novel. The term most widely used to describe the fantastic events depicted in novels such as *One Hundred Years of Solitude* is "magical realism," a phrase so popular that it has entered common parlance and is used to describe movies by Woody Allen and popular television shows. Of course, the term itself has a history that begins early in the twentieth-century and, as such, remains in a state of contestation as various definitions are championed and refuted. So significant is the term that, in 1995, Duke University Press published *Magical Realism: Theory, History, Community;* its nearly six hundred pages, edited by Wendy Faris and Lois Parkinson Zamora, attempt to map out the conceptual terrain for the term and its various uses in literature, cultural studies, film, and the arts. What follows is a brief review of the various definitions of the term and my positioning of Vichian philosophy within this context.

Most critics agree that the term "magic realism" was first coined by Franz Roh in his 1925 essay on postexpressionism. In this essay, Roh attempted to define a new movement that was opposed to both impressionism and expressionism. Roh believed that what this new art—as exemplified in the works of painters such as Georg Schrimpf, Otto Dix, and George Grosz—"principally evokes is a most prolific and detailed *tactile feeling,*" that when seeing these works one is "overcome by a much wider amalgam of colors, spatial forms, tactile representations, memories of smells and tastes, in short, a truly unending complex that we understand by the name of *thing*" (19). The new art evoked the senses and made the viewer much more aware of the sensual qualities of the thing depicted. The painted objects, therefore, took on an aura of strangeness as the viewer became more aware of their sensuous dimensions. Roh's term for this new phenomenon was "magic realism." In later years, the art community would settle for the term *Neue Sachlichkeit* rather than *Magischer Realismus,* but Roh's neologism would gain new life when a Spanish translation of his essay appeared in a 1927 *Revista de Occidente* article and reached a Latin American readership.

Roh's term, then, gained new currency in the New World. In their theoretical writings, three Latin American writers actually invoke the term magical realism or its near equivalent. In the preface to his 1949 novel *El reino de este mundo* (*The Kingdom of This World*), Alejo Carpentier discusses what he calls "the marvelous real" (*lo real maravilloso*). According to Carpentier, the New World, as exemplified by the culture of Haiti, experienced a different order of reality because its culture emerged from a different ontologic base. Unlike the exhausted and declining cultures of the West, the cultures of the New World were vibrant and alive because their spiritual foundations had not been enervated by rationalism. Carpentier sees in the New World the "virginidad del paisaje" (the virginity of the landscape), the "presencia fáustica del indio y del negro" (the Faustian presence of the Indian and the Negro), and the "fecundos mestizajes" (the fecund Mestizo population), thus making America, in its widest sense, a rich and heterogeneous amalgam of different mythologies, belief systems, and cultural practices that can produce a living, vibrant, exciting, oftentimes contradictory—but never stagnant—culture. Unlike Europe, America is far from using up its wealth of mythologies. "¿Pero," Carpentier asks at the conclusion of his preface to *El reino*, "qué es la historia de América toda sino una crónica de lo real-maravilloso?" (15–16; Yet, what is the history of the entirety of America if not a chronicle of the marvelous real?).

In an essay published nearly twenty years later, Carpentier continued his development of the definition of the marvelous real when he linked it to the concept of the baroque—something he claims is not limited to the literary and artistic movements of seventeenth-century Europe. According to Carpentier, the baroque exists as "a constant of the human spirit that is characterized by a horror of the vacuum" ("Baroque" 93). In other words, the baroque expresses an abundant proliferation of possibilities (both beautiful and ugly) that fill empty space—be it the space of a page, a bas-relief, a musical moment in time, or a canvas. The surface becomes filled with an ever-expanding array of possible expressions. "America, a continent of symbiosis, mutations, vibrations, *mestizaje*, has always been baroque" ("Baroque" 98), declares Carpentier. The key, then, to the marvelous real lies in this: the heterogeneity of American culture—its mutations and intermingling make of it a primary site of expressing new combinations and interactions of heretofore separate social, political, economic, religious, and philosophical worldviews.

In 1955, Angel Flores published an essay in which he argues that magical realism stems from a new phase in Latin American writing that began when Borges published *A Universal History of Infamy* in 1935 (113). Flores sees this as the moment in which two threads of Latin American writing—the realist writing of the nineteenth century and the magical writing that can be traced all the way back to Columbus—come together in the magical realist works of Borges and his followers. Luis Leal, in a 1967 article, rejects Flores's argument, claiming that magical realism does not constitute an aesthetic movement and therefore cannot be associated with fantastic or psychological literature. Instead, Leal argues that magical realism constitutes "an attitude toward reality that can be expressed in popular or cultured forms" (121). "In magical realism," writes Leal, "the writer confronts reality and tries to untangle it, to discover what is mysterious in things, in life, in human acts" (121). For Leal, magical realism shows us the undiscovered mysteries that bind humans to their environment.

The definitions of magical realism do not end here. Contemporary critics have added their voices to the chorus. For Wendy Faris, "magical realism combines realism and the fantastic in such a way that magical elements grow organically out of the reality portrayed" (163). Theo D'Haen, by way of contrast, associates magical realism with speaking from marginal cultures such that magical realist writers appropriate literary techniques from the dominant traditions "to create an alternative world *correcting* so-called existing reality, and thus to right the wrongs this 'reality' depends upon" (195). For Lois Parkinson Zamora, however, magical realism constitutes a critique of modernity and expresses "the nature and the limits of the knowable." In addition, she argues that magical realism opposes the ideology of individualism and instead universalizes the individual self ("Magical Romance" 498).

The many definitions of magical realism, beginning with Roh, offer us several interpretive routes to take when we wish to examine Latin American literature. From my perspective, critics such as Flores and Faris regard magical realism as an aesthetic phenomenon. Roh and Leal, on the other hand, see in magical realism a response to the world as we encounter it. Works that fall under the rubric of the magical real, claim the art critic and the literary critic, attempt to make us aware of the hidden in the apparent. For D'Haen and Zamora, magical realism is altogether different in that it constitutes a strategy adopted by certain writers so as to engage in cultural critique. For Carpentier, something else is at stake, and it is in Carpentier's writings on the marvelous real that I see strong affinities with Vichian philosophy.

Hoping to identify Latin America's unique cultural characteristics, Carpentier theorized first *lo real maravilloso americano* and then the broader definition of the baroque. These two moves were linked to his belief in a Spenglerian worldview that postulated the decline of Western culture. Inherent in Carpentier's definitions of the marvelous real is the assertion that these Latin American *criollo* cultures are superior to the deteriorating cultures of Western Europe. In a certain sense, the marvelous real becomes a philosopheme—a conceptual term that undergirds Carpentier's system of thinking. In his book on Carpentier, Roberto González Echevarría notes that the Cuban writer developed his theory of the marvelous real precisely because he was a Western-educated intellectual. From this perspective, Carpentier could theorize the ontologic difference that he claimed obtained between the declining cultures of the West and the still-vibrant cultures of the New World. But, as González Echevarría shrewdly points out: "To assume that the marvelous exists only in America is to adopt a spurious European perspective, since it is only from the other side that alterity and difference may be discovered—the same seen from within is homogeneous, smooth, without edges" (*Alejo Carpentier* 128). To my mind, Carpentier, because of who he was and how he was educated, could hardly be expected to adopt a non-European perspective. However, González Echevarría correctly criticizes Carpentier for assuming that the marvelous exists only in America. Clearly, the marvelous can exist outside of America (consider the heterogeneous cultures of Africa and Asia), but Carpentier's focus on ontologic difference opens the way for a deeper understanding of the magical real phenomenon.

Rather than accept *tout court* Carpentier's position—which posits a strict ontologic difference between the Americas and Europe and grants a superior status to the "marvellous" cultures of the Americas—I would begin with the notion of ontologic difference and add Vico's philosophy to this problematic. From my perspective, the magical real emerges from cultures that have within them elements of societies at different stages of development as theorized by Vico. In other words, what Carpentier recognized in the Haiti that he visited in the 1940s, and what appears in so many Latin American texts that we label with the contradiction "magical real," is the interanimation of cultures—some of which may be in the first age of gods, some of which may be in the second age of heroes, and some of which may be in the third age of humans. Magical realism, therefore, records this cultural interanimation and brings attention to an axiologic as well as an ontologic difference that obtains simultaneously in a particular society.

The hallmark of much of the fiction identified as possessing magical realist elements remains what we might call a deadpan narrative consciousness that describes in a matter-of-fact way an act of psychokinesis or a priest who levitates when he drinks chocolate. As Carpentier noted, "la sensación de lo maravilloso presupone una fe" (12; the sensation of the marvelous presupposes a faith). Authors who express magical realist elements in their works are bearing witness to the multiple belief systems that exist in their societies. To argue that magical realism corrects social injustice or critiques modernity may in fact be true in certain cases, but I believe that such a definition obscures the wider implications of the magical real in literature. The challenge that Vico lays before us is to use our imagination to piece together the past. In the context of magical realist fiction, the authors of this fiction struggle to imagine the world as perceived by societies, cultures, and communities that grow out of an ontological base and an axiological system that reflects a Vichian age that differs from the one in which the authors themselves live. García Márquez, Fuentes, Isabel Allende, Rushdie, Morrison, and of course Vargas Llosa are thinkers of the third age—they, like Vico, live in an era dominated by the "barbarism of reflection." But their art, like Vico's new science, attempts to recover the other ages that exist in conjunction with their own. The importance of seeing magical realism in the context of Vichian philosophy is that it moves the term away from aestheticism and even currently popular notions of multiculturalism that remain politically charged and places it in the context of a philosophical anthropology—one that generates a deeper understanding of human societies and history.

My turn to Vico in this context is not unprecedented. Two eminent contemporary writers—one a theorist, the other a novelist—have perceived in Vico's work a response to the growing recognition of the problems attendant on cultural interaction in a complex, interconnected global community. In *Beginnings,* his book on contemporary theory, Edward Said contends that "Vico is the prototypical modern thinker who . . . perceives beginning as an activity requiring the writer to maintain an unstraying obligation to practical reality and sympathetic imagination" (349). For Said, Vico's value lies in his focus on human institutions created over time in response to human experience. The key to understanding rests in imagination, not in abstract systems of thought or esoteric paradigm building.

Carlos Fuentes would agree with Said; but for this Mexican novelist, Vico holds even greater value for Latin American intellectuals because he provides an antidote to the abstract rationalism that remains the legacy of Enlightenment thinking (the progenitor of much of what Said finds irritating in some of the theorizing that permeates literary and cultural studies). In his 1990 collection of essays on the Hispanic-American novel, *Valiente mundo nuevo,* Fuentes amplifies many of the things Said said about Vico. To begin with, Fuentes prizes Vico because the Neapolitan saw that "el valor de la historia es su variedad concreta, no su uniformidad abstracta" (31; the value of history lies in its concrete variety, not its abstract uniformity). Fuentes goes on to assert that Vico hated the eighteenth-century Enlightenment because it suffered from a Eurocentric pretension: "su ficción de una universalidad comprensible sóla en términos europeos" (33; its fiction of a universality only achieves its realization in a European manner). From Fuentes's perspective, it would have been better had the Latin American peoples read Vico rather than Voltaire because, in their pursuit of the Eurocentric ideal, thinkers in the New World denied "lo que habíamos hecho—un mundo policultural y multiracial en desarrollo—y afirmanos le que no podíamos se—europeos modernos—sinasimilar lo que ya éramos—indoafroiberoamericanos" (35; what we had made—a polycultural and multiracial world in development—and affirmed what we were not able to be—modern Europeans—without taking into account what we already were—Indo-Afro-Ibero-Americans). Fuentes sees Vico as a hero of cultural tolerance; and, as such, he believes that Vico's new science could prove to be very useful to a multicultural society such as the one that exists in Latin America. If the legacy of the Enlightenment in Latin America has been a destructive rationalism and utopian idealism that resulted in the writings of Domingo F. Sarmiento and the *Sendero Luminoso,* then Vico might be the best philosopher to turn to, precisely because his thinking is a response to—and develops at the same time as—the philosophy of the Enlightenment. Thus, for both Said and Fuentes, Vico offers a potent alternative to a potentially destructive rationalism. Vico's turn toward the imagination, the key to his philosophical project, attracts both Said and Fuentes, and each man sees Vico's commitment to acknowledging the concrete reality that undergirds human experience as indispensable for a deeper understanding of the self and the other. I contend that Vargas Llosa expresses this same view through *The Storyteller.*

Memory as Imagination

In *The Storyteller,* Vargas Llosa presents us with the writer-narrator in Florence who must use his imagination to understand his past, his friend Saúl Zuratas, the Machiguengas, and his own role as a writer. To my mind, Vargas Llosa enacts what Said would call a beginning by focusing his attention on the most pressing issue of his native Peru (and, one could argue, of the world): what approach we must adopt to make sense of the heterogeneous, polyglot, postmodern world. Through the very construction of his novel, Vargas Llosa affirms that we must return to poetic beginnings if we ever hope to make sense of the complex world that surrounds us. The turn toward fables that appears in *The Storyteller* constitutes a Vichian strategy as Vargas Llosa demonstrates how acts of the imagination serve as the best means we have of understanding the Other.

The scene of writing for *The Storyteller* actually takes place in front of a photograph. Like the photographer in Cortázar's "Blow-Up," the writer-narrator imagines what he sees—in this case, Saúl Zuratas in the form of the hablador. By recording the writer-narrator's reflections on his past, his relationship with his old friend Mascarita, and, quite possibly, his own constructions of imagined storytelling events within the Machiguenga tribe itself, *The Storyteller* focuses attention on the power of the artistic imagination to order the world and make it whole.

For Vargas Llosa, imagination remains inextricably linked to memory. Like Vico, the Peruvian novelist recognizes how these two mental functions are coterminous. *The Storyteller* records the transformation of the writer-narrator's attitude about the relationship between memory and imagination. At first, the writer-narrator seems perplexed by the problem of reproducing past experience. He has difficulty distinguishing what really happened from what has become embellished over time. For example, after having provided a narrative description of a conversation he had with Saúl in 1953, he writes:

> Perhaps he went on being the same smiling, talkative Mascarita whom I knew in 1953, and my imagination has changed him so as to make him conform more closely to the other one, the one of future years whom I did not know, whom I must invent since I have given in to the cursed temptation of writing about him.
>
> I am certain, however, that memory does not fail me as far as his dress and his physical appearance are concerned. (35)

The writer-narrator admits that his memory cannot escape the influence of his present needs, that now, in retrospect, he must consider suspect every word he attributes to Mascarita because, through his present act of writing, he is inventing a Saúl he did not know. For the sake of continuity, the writer-narrator fears he has altered the past. When relating another conversation he had with Saúl in 1958, he asks: "Is that what he said? Could one at least infer something of the sort from what he was saying?

I'm not sure. Perhaps this is pure invention on my part after the event"
(99). Earlier, he emphatically states: "But my memory cannot have entirely
invented Mascarita's fierce diatribe against the Summer Institute of Linguistics" (95). For the writer-narrator, there at first exists a profound tension between memory and imagination. He begins being committed to
distinguishing what really happened in the past from what he must necessarily invent to place an event or statement he is certain he witnessed
or heard in a plausible context.

The tension between memory and imagination does not end with the
writer-narrator's recollections of Saúl. When he describes his work on
"The Tower of Babel" television series and discusses how technical
difficulties plagued him and his three coworkers, he asks himself: "Am I
exaggerating things so that they stand out more clearly? Perhaps. But I
don't think I'm stretching things much. I could tell dozens of stories like
this one. And many others to illustrate what is perhaps the very symbol
of underdevelopment: the divorce between theory and practice, decisions
and facts" (151). Much like Proust's narrator of the *Recherche,* the writer-
narrator lifts one incident from the past and reconstructs it through an
act of imagination to exemplify a recurrent phenomenon from a past life
experience over a given length of time. In addition, the writer-narrator
also invokes this imaginative act to communicate an idea or concept—
what he terms the symbol of underdevelopment. Thus, the writer-narrator considers the mixture of imagination and memory as inevitable, perhaps even necessary, for the re-presentation of the truth of his past and
his cultural experience. Nor is he alone in this activity. When he describes
how, after he lost contact with Mascarita, he attempted to conduct research on the Machiguengas and how he learned the most important information through a series of conversations with Fray Elicerio Maluenda, who described Machiguenga mythology, he wonders: "But how much
of this—and the many other details that Fray Maluenda had given me—
was true? Hadn't the admirable missionary added to or adapted much of
the material he had collected?" (106).

It seems that one cannot avoid invoking imaginative embellishment
when recounting or writing anything. Profoundly disturbed by the dawning recognition that memory and imagination cannot be easily distinguished from one another, the writer-narrator experiences a minor crisis
when he admits that he "thought for a moment that habladores didn't
exist: that [he]'d invented them and then housed them in false memories

so as to make them real" (173). The crisis of memory and its relationship to the past constitutes the central concern of his entire narrative enterprise. "Memory is a snare, pure and simple: it alters, it subtly rearranges the past to fit the present," states the writer-narrator. He continues: "I have tried so many times to reconstruct that conversation in August 1958 with my friend Saúl Zuratas in the seedy café on the Avenida España, with its broken-down chairs and rickety tables, that by now I'm no longer sure of anything" (95). This revealing admission on the part of the creative consciousness of the novel accords with Vico's declaration that "memory is the same as imagination" (NS ¶ 819).

As the novel progresses, the writer-narrator comes to understand that to re-present the past as he experienced it, he must invoke the powers of imagination. When, toward the end of the novel, he declares, "after turning the pieces of the puzzle around and around many times and shuffling them this way and that I see they fit" (241), he expresses a key Vichian concept, one that calls for the "clean[ing], piec[ing] together, and restor[ing]" of "great fragments" (NS ¶ 357). This process itself is governed by the principle that a "physical truth which is not in conformity with [a metaphysical truth] should be considered false" (NS ¶ 205). The writer-narrator, then, learns the major lesson of *The New Science:* the imagination serves as the foundation for the entire process of making things fit in that it brings together phenomena in a meaningful way. In the end, the writer-narrator also recognizes that imagination is in fact the key to memory.

In essence, the writer-narrator agrees with Vico's idea that memory has three aspects: "memory when it remembers things, imagination when it alters or imitates them, and invention when it gives them a new turn or puts them into proper arrangement and relationship" (NS ¶ 819). The narrative of chapters 1, 2, 4, 6, and 8 of *The Storyteller* constitutes the writer-narrator's remembering of his past. The writer-narrator alters and rearranges the images from the past and in the end constructs his own truth when, after contemplating the photograph on several occasions, he declares: "I have decided that it is he who is the storyteller in Malfatti's photograph. A personal decision, since objectively I have no way of knowing" (240). For the writer-narrator, "the hump on the left shoulder of the storyteller in the photograph is a parrot" (241); in other words, the writer-narrator wills his truth by making the storyteller Mascarita.

We should pause here and note that this move to make things fit even if they fly in the face of so-called reality repeats itself when the writer-narrator first admits that, on seeing the Machiguenga in 1981, "quite evidently, they no longer fitted the images of them that my imagination had invented. They were no longer that handful of tragic, indomitable beings, that society broken up into tiny families, fleeing, always fleeing, from the whites" (163). At this point, the reality of the tribe failed to measure up to his imagination. However, by the end of the novel, he announces that "even though the damage to the community has been considerable because of all this, it is likely that many of them, faced with the upheavals of the last few years, will have opted for the traditional response ensuring their survival: diaspora. Start walking. Once again. As in the most persistent of their myths" (240). The writer-narrator asserts his prerogative to imagine the Machiguengas as returning to their beginnings; it is an act of willful imagination on his part.

The assertion of individual will in conjunction with the reconstructive or recollective imagination signals the point at which Vargas Llosa's novel moves from a Vichian outlook toward a more Nietzschean one. If the novel indicates that acts of memory must involve the process of imaginative reconstruction (as Vico rightly contends), then it also signals that these reconstructive acts are themselves related to particular needs in the present. For Vico, recollective imagination makes possible our gaining access to the past. It is through imagination that we can understand and in some sense experience what happened in the past. In this regard, Vico offers imagination as the alternative to scientific information gathering. In other words, we would do better to use our imagination in conjunction with a reading of a past culture's poetry and art than talk about crop production yields and demographics. In the context of *The Storyteller,* Vargas Llosa concurs with Vico's main thesis on memory and imagination because the writer-narrator of the novel slowly recognizes how indispensable his imagination becomes when he attempts to reconstruct the past. However, the writer-narrator does not simply want to represent the past— he has other pressing needs; primary among them is understanding the role of the storyteller not only in Machiguenga culture but particularly in his own.

Few readers fail to notice how the writer-narrator becomes obsessed with the notion of the hablador, and O'Bryan-Knight, Standish, and Perricone, among others, have argued that *The Storyteller* serves as Vargas Llosa's reading of the relationship between a given culture and its writers or storytellers. Early in the novel, when the writer-narrator first learns of the function of the hablador in a conversation with Mascarita, he admits that he wanted to say to Saúl that, when it came to the concept of *habladores*: "'They're a tangible proof that storytelling can be something more than mere entertainment. . . . Something primordial, something that the very existence of a people may depend on'" (94). Many years later, when the writer-narrator interviews the Schneils for "The Tower of Babel" television broadcast, Edwin Schneil argues that, for the Machiguengas, the storytellers "'are their entertainment.'" According to the missionary, the habladores constitute "'their books, their circuses, all the diversions we civilized peoples have. They have only one diversion in the world. The storytellers are nothing more than that.'" To this comment, the writer-narrator offers a one-sentence paragraph rebuttal: "'Nothing less than that,' I corrected him gently" (178).

The writer-narrator regards the storyteller as the cornerstone of Machiguenga society. Later in the novel, he admits that he "had forged that curious emotional link between the Machiguengas and my own vocation (not to say, quite simply, my own life)" (157). As the novel proceeds, we become aware of the stronger parallelisms that exist between the writer-narrator and Saúl as storyteller; we begin to recognize that it is the writer-narrator and not Saúl who is the true outsider with respect to his own culture. By forging a link between himself and the hablador, the writer-narrator opens up a line of analysis that makes us consider just what purpose a writer serves in contemporary industrial and postindustrial societies. As a modern-day storyteller in a late twentieth-century culture, the writer-narrator does not wield nearly as much influence as does the hablador in his culture. The Peru of the 1980s and 1990s does not look to writers of novels, poetry, and plays for the answers to its problems (consider, for example, the decision Peruvians made at the polls in 1990 when they selected Alberto Fujimori, an economist, over Mario Vargas Llosa, a novelist, for president). As Acosta Cruz points out, "the Western narrator in *El hablador* is frustrated because he does not have as vital a social role as he believes the hablador has in the tribe. He dwells on what he perceives as the difference in literary 'production' in an urban and capitalistic society as opposed to the communal and 'natural' transactions of the hablador with his primitive society" (135).

This shift away from what we might term poetry toward other discursive forms, the move from "natural transactions" to "literary production," corresponds to the shift Vico describes as the move from the "barbarism of the senses" to the "barbarism of reflection." The Vichian paradigm indicates that, in the early stages of a culture's development, the language of the poets, which is steeped in a body-centered consciousness, expresses the ethos of that culture in a rich and imaginative language—Homer serves as the prime example of a poet who expresses the spirit of a culture. In the later stages of development, other forms of discourse—scientific, rational, abstract, conceptual—dominate a culture, and we see in our own post-Enlightenment societies the role of poetry radically diminished and the discourses of science, computer technology, economics, and sociology reigning supreme. Stated simply, in a crisis situation, members of an industrialized society are far more likely to turn to a scientist than a poet. The writer-narrator of *The Storyteller* senses this profound difference, this displacement of the poet in culture, and this engenders in him a profound sense of nostalgia. His identification with the hablador expresses a form of wish-fulfillment, something M. Keith Booker believes to be the writer-narrator's own predilection for the "metanarrative of the Romantic artist" (132). This is evinced when he establishes a link between himself and the hablador, thus signaling his desire to be just as important to Peruvian culture as the storyteller is to the Machiguengas.

The writer-narrator describes the essence of the storyteller as "being able to feel and live in the very heart of that culture" (244). And he admits that "the tradition of that invisible line of wandering storytellers, is something that memory now and again brings back to me . . . it opens my heart more forcefully than fear or love has ever done" (244–45). The writer-narrator, caught in the grip of a profound nostalgia, desperately wants to believe that the storyteller still retains his position of importance, that the hablador he sees in the photograph is his old friend Mascarita, and that the reason so little information was forthcoming about habladores in general is that the Machiguengas were trying to protect Saúl specifically. When the writer-narrator asserts that the Machiguenga "were not protecting the institution or the idea of the storyteller in the abstract. They were protecting him" (185), he makes a rather remarkable leap in that he attributes to the Machiguenga an acknowledgement of individualized existence, something that runs counter to everything we have learned about their culture up to this point. This move on the writer-narrator's part betrays his own desires in that he would like to see his own culture respect the writer; and, much like the hablador as he imagines him in Machiguenga culture, the writer-narrator would like to see creative writers hold key positions in society that are so significant that members of that society would do everything to protect them. We should recall how the writer-narrator opposes this view of the centrality of the storyteller to the role television plays in industrialized society. The experiences the writer-narrator has on "The Tower of Babel" television series reveal how the storyteller function has been submerged in a series of technological structures that alter irremediably the nature by which the story becomes told. The very restrictions of the television format, the frames of reference, the limitations of the technology, and ultimately its connection with a commodified culture have eviscerated the transformative potential and the spiritual power of the storyteller function in culture. Now it has become little more than entertainment.

The move on the writer-narrator's part to associate himself with the hablador—as well as his desire to imagine that the Machiguenga tribe perceived Mascarita as an individual—does not, in my eyes, constitute a failure on the writer-narrator's part, an escape into nostalgia or, as Booker would have it, a return to Romanticism. On the contrary, I contend that Vargas Llosa intentionally has his writer-narrator make this move because the novel as a whole expresses the need of present-day Peruvian (and, I would argue, world) culture to look to imaginative literature as opposed to specialized scientific discourses as the primary locus of intellectual inquiry. I concur with Marie-Madeleine Gladieu when she writes that the storyteller haunts the writer-narrator because "romancier et 'hablador' sont à la fois une manifestation et les garants de la liberté pour une société donnée" (247; novelist and storyteller are both a manifestation and the guarantors of liberty for a given society). Vargas Llosa himself has said much the same thing in his own nonfiction prose.

In *A Writer's Reality*, Vargas Llosa relates that when he was writing *Historia de Mayta*, he "discovered that in fact fiction is indispensable for mankind" (149). His discovery led to a deeper understanding of what the term "fiction" means. Vargas Llosa discerns two bases of fiction: one he associates with literature, the other with ideology. Fictions as expressed in literature "have not only enriched mankind psychologically but also ethically; and they have encouraged progress in many ways," writes Vargas Llosa. He continues: "At the same time fiction has been a major instrument of suffering in history because it was behind all the dogmatic doctrines that have justified repression, censorship, massacres, and genocides" (150). For Vargas Llosa, literature can best serve us as a means to understand the structures of our reality. As a goal, Vargas Llosa "would like the novel to make this paradox evident, that when fiction is perceived as fiction and accepted as such, it becomes part of reality and is transformed into something that is objective and factual reality" (154). Unlike

290 History Made, History Imagined

ideology, as Vargas Llosa terms it, fiction in the form of literature points to itself as being a fiction. Literature does not declare itself to be true. In this regard, Vargas Llosa echoes Nietzsche's observation that "art treats *illusion as illusion;* therefore it does not wish to deceive; it is *true*" (PT 96). Vargas Llosa explains:

> The fiction that is accepted as fiction, accepted as an illusion, can very easily be incorporated into our real experiences and give us a better understanding of ourselves and of what society is. On the other hand, fiction considered as objective science, as in the case of this ideology that compels Mayta and his comrades to act as they do, is something that precipitates in reality a very destructive process because it misguides people about what reality is and sometimes establishes a gap between the mind, ideas, and the possibility to make effective changes. (154)

Marxism, the ideology that sways Mayta, leads to damaging consequences. And a deformed Marxism—as expressed in the actions of the Shining Path, examined by Vargas Llosa in his 1993 novel *Lituma en los Andes* (*Death in the Andes*)—has produced even more disastrous results. The novel and other forms of literary fiction, as opposed to ideologies that appeal to science, can offer us new opportunities to truly experiment with imagined possibilities for our collective futures. This, then, is how I perceive the Vichian and Nietzschean threads in Vargas Llosa's work. In *The Storyteller*, we witness an act of will *and* imagination as expressed in the form of literature that draws attention to the need for acts of imagination and will in the contemporary world, particularly when we consider how we structure the past to build our future.

With respect to expressions of Nietzschean will, we can acknowledge how the writer-narrator asserts his will when he identifies with the hablador, contends that the Machiguengas are protecting a specific storyteller, and, most important of all, declares that Mascarita *is* the storyteller. The writer-narrator's interpretation grows out of acts of imagination—he *sees* Mascarita in the photograph, he *reconstructs* the past—his own and Saúl's; and, through his interpretation, he *asserts* his will. *The Storyteller* culminates in an expression of a will to power, one that signals to us readers that the key to the future according to Vargas Llosa lies in eschewing the rational discourses ordinarily associated with positivist science and ideology and embracing more imaginative—some might say, more literary— forms of writing.

Perhaps the very notion of the hablador provides us with the most stunning example of the use of imagination as a form of will to power. Although several critics have attested to the fact that Vargas Llosa carefully studied and accurately portrayed many of the elements of Machiguenga life and that several people and works mentioned in the novel are in fact real, Jean O'Bryan-Knight has determined that there is no available evidence to suggest that habladores—or community storytellers, bards, or traveling poets—exist among the Machiguenga people (100). Such a revelation may disappoint if not outrage readers who demand accuracy, verisimilitude, or truth when it comes to narrative, even in the form of a novel. Nevertheless, the creation of the hablador constitutes an act of creative will on Vargas Llosa's part. By imagining the hablador as a member of the indigenous culture, he engages in an interanimative intervention that affirms the central role that imagination in general and literary imagination in particular should play in the future as we consider the options available to us in a world becoming more and more homogeneous.

Just as Vico argued that we must use imagination to reconstruct the past, Vargas Llosa indicates that we must do the same if we are to understand the Other, our own past, and the possibilities for the future. Through the act of creating the hablador, Vargas Llosa furthers life—the life of the Machiguenga, in that he preserves an unforgettable image of their culture, and the life of global, polycultural society, in that he makes us pause to consider what values we will choose to promote and preserve. The poetic imagination, Vargas Llosa appears to be saying, will be necessary for us if we are to resolve our problems, including the question of assimilation.

As I mentioned earlier, we should not confuse Vargas Llosa's opinions on assimilation as they appear in *A Writer's Reality* with the ideas expressed in the novel. *The Storyteller* remains indeterminate on this issue. I argue that through his novel, Vargas Llosa hopes to reopen this and other issues by demonstrating how necessary art, in the form of literary texts, will become for us as we struggle with these problems. The main idea expressed in *The Storyteller* is not so much that indigenous cultures can or cannot be preserved as it is that we must first use our poetic imagination to better understand indigenous cultures and, what may be more important, consider new possibilities of intercultural interaction.

First, we should acknowledge just how central a role imagination plays in the novel. We have already mentioned the manner in which the writer-narrator invokes his own imagination as he regards the photographs of Malfatti and attempts to reconstruct conversations he had years earlier with Saúl. In addition, I agree with critics who argue that it is the writer-narrator who constructs the hablador's tales, that the Peruvian writer is *imagining* what the storyteller says to the various Machiguengas. To regard the writer-narrator as the author of the hablador's stories not only underscores how *The Storyteller* places primary importance on imagination as the key to intercultural understanding and problem solving but also highlights Vargas Llosa's own powerful expression of imagination as he presents a portrait of Machiguenga culture based on careful research. As Jean O'Bryan-Knight contends, the representation of "indigenous characters in their natural rural environment" constitutes a "significant narrative achievement for the author" (98).

In addition to emphasizing the primacy of imagination, *The Storyteller* also unfolds the cultural problematic and situates the reader such that each one of us must decide what is to be done. Rather than construct a dogmatic text, Vargas Llosa presents a novel that leaves open the question of what path the global community must take. Consider the recurrent expressions the hablador uses when he tells his tales. When the storyteller employs the words "perhaps" and "that is what I have learned," he leaves open the possibility that what he relates may not be everything there is to know on the topic. In short, the principle of uncertainty governs his discourse. Catherine Poupeney Hart considers this a type of positioning that the hablador adopts with respect to his narration. She claims: "Cette posture contraste avec l'imposition d'un version des faits, d'une vérité, dérivée d'une origine certaine et identifiable, traits propres au discours dominant mis en question par ce roman de Mario Vargas Llosa" (535; This position contrasts with the imposition of a version of facts, of a truth, derived from a certain and identifiable origin, facts characteristic of the dominant discourse placed into question by the novel of Mario Vargas Llosa). I agree; the uncertainty expressed in the storyteller's very act of narration undermines the notion of positivist approaches to intercultural problem solving.

The expressions of uncertainty go even deeper. Jeanne Raimond claims that both narrators—the writer-narrator and the hablador—seek a world in flux that is circumscribed by fixed laws that generate fear of intellectual repression and fear of cultural invasion. Does each of these narrators, Raimond asks, "s'enfoncer dans un monde préexistant, pour y faire retraite ou y renaître?" (118; sink himself in a preexisting world, to retreat there or to be reborn there?). Indeed, is the move executed in *The Storyteller* as a whole a retreat or a rebirth?

The level of uncertainty increases further when we pause to consider how much *The Storyteller* is an ironic novel about masks and metamorphoses. The irony of masking that pervades the novel brings to mind Vico's observation that irony itself "certainly could not have begun until the period of reflection because it is fashioned of falsehood by dint of a reflection which wears the mask of truth" (NS ¶ 408). Vico contrasts this "mask of truth" with the first fables that "could not feign anything false" and were therefore "true narrations" (NS ¶ 408). Vargas Llosa, a writer living in the period of reflection, cannot but use irony to create his fictional world that includes the stories told by the hablador, a speaker of true narrations. Much like Vico himself, who had to struggle for decades to overcome the systematic thinking of the Enlightenment era so as to imagine how the first humans thought about their world, Vargas Llosa must write in the "mythos of winter," to borrow Northrop Frye's schema, a season of irony that characterizes the modern era. From Descartes' motto "I advance masked" to the metatheater of Pirandello, masks have pervaded the discourse of modernity, and *The Storyteller* proves to be no exception.

In addition to the obvious reference to Saúl as Mascarita, there is also the masking of the writer-narrator. Sara Castro-Klarén identifies four "Vargas Llosas": (1) The famous writer in Florence; (2) the Vargas Llosa in Lima working on a television show; (3) the Vargas Llosa visiting the jungle; and (4) Vargas Llosa, creator of the hablador's world (210–11). As readers, we become stymied, trying to wend our way through the various levels of narration as the living Vargas Llosa creates his simulacra in the forms of the Vargas Llosas that Castro-Klarén identifies while at the same time ventriloquizing Saúl. Page after page, we find ourselves asking the now-famous question: Who is speaking? This shifting back and forth creates an uncertainty in our minds as readers. Indeed, one can only state with certainty that, as is so often the case in the works of Flaubert (one of Vargas Llosa's literary heroes), *The Storyteller* remains irreducibly ambiguous.

The intentional ambiguity and irony in the novel have perplexed some readers. Acosta Cruz observes: "By making the hablador, the supposed representative of pure native culture, an example of cultural intervention the novel makes clear that there are no easy solutions, perhaps no solutions at all to the problems of cultural intervention in the case of the Machiguengas" (139). But I would argue that novels, by their very nature, are not supposed to provide solutions. Novels pose questions; they engage in a form of intellectual inquiry that puts into play various discursive forms. Nevertheless, the novel does leave us with a very clear message: just as the writer-narrator chooses to make Mascarita the hablador, in the end, we must choose. More important, the novel indicates that we must will our future choice through an act of the imagination. Whether we choose to preserve indigenous cultures, as does Saúl, or advocate assimilation, as does the writer-narrator, we must exercise our imaginative capacities. Mascarita and the writer-narrator use their respective imaginations—Mascarita in the form of crafting stories for the Machiguenga, the writer-narrator in his construction of the narrative of his past experiences as well as of the imagined scenarios of the hablador.

By underscoring the necessity for using the imagination, Vargas Llosa does several things. First, he attempts to preserve an image of a vanishing culture. Mary Davis identifies the lines of affiliation that associate the theme of metamorphosis in *The Storyteller* with other instances of metamorphoses in literature when she notes that both Kafka and Ovid witnessed and, through their writing, tried to "save vanishing worlds for the delight and education of future readers" (136). Vargas Llosa also attempts to save a vanishing world, that of the Machiguenga. Second, by invoking the power of the imagination, Vargas Llosa affirms Nietzsche's philosophy of the will to power as the will to art. If, as Nietzsche contends, we make ourselves and our worlds through acts of will, that "what is needed is that something must be held to be true—not that something is true" (WP ¶ 507), and these acts are themselves aesthetic, then Vargas Llosa shows us how as individuals and collectively as a culture we must learn to fashion our future through the imagination.

In an entry contained in *The Will to Power* and written in 1877, Nietzsche states: "One should not understand this compulsion to construct concepts, species, forms, purposes, laws ('a world of identical cases') as if they enabled us to fix the *real world;* but as a compulsion to arrange a world for ourselves in which our existence is made possible:—we thereby create a world which is calculable, simplified, comprehensible, etc., for us" (WP ¶ 521). Although specifically referring to the scientific method, paragraph 521 expresses Nietzsche's conviction that we make sense of the world through an ordering process, one that makes it possible for us to live. This same ordering principle governs poetic construction as well, in that aesthetic phenomena grow out of particular arrangements—be they temporal or spatial—and juxtapositions—material, typographic, chromatic, sonic, and so forth. When the writer-narrator interprets the photographs in such a way that he declares the hablador to be Mascarita, he creates a world in which it is possible for him to live. He enacts what Nietzsche calls for in that he has "produced a conception in order to be able to live in a world, in order to perceive just enough to endure it" (WP ¶ 568).

Above all else, *The Storyteller* portrays the severe shortcomings of world-building based on scientific, rationalistic approaches. The efforts on the part of governments and religions to change indigenous peoples result in disaster. The end results can be either the incompletely assimilated Andean boy or the tortured and oppressed Jum, a headman who attempted to participate in the global economy by circumventing the middleman (74–76). As we see in the accounts of "The Tower of Babel" television show, the technologies of the postmodern world fail. Given the insurmountable obstacles that confront us at the end of the millennium, Vargas Llosa signals that we must will the future through creative acts.

In tandem with the observation that willed creative acts provide the best means of building a future, Vargas Llosa's emphasis on the vital role played by the imagination also expresses a key Vichian notion contained in paragraph 405 of *The New Science*. It states: "as rational metaphysics teaches that man becomes all things by understanding them (*homo intelligendo fit omnia*), this imaginative metaphysics shows that man becomes all things by *not* understanding them (*homo non intelligendo fit omnia*); and perhaps the latter proposition is truer than the former, for when man understands he extends his mind and takes in the things, but when he does not understand he makes the things out of himself and becomes them by transforming himself into them" (NS ¶ 405). Unlike traditional metaphysics, imaginative metaphysics—as practiced by the theological poets in their creation of imaginative universals—necessitates the extension and transformation of the self. Rather than resort to the mapping of abstract paradigms onto the complexities of the polycultural world of today, we must, Vargas Llosa suggests, transform ourselves through imaginative projections that will make our world. Just as the writer-narrator imagines his past as well as the future through a creative impulse to make the pieces fit, so too must we create our future using our poetic capacities.

In a polemical essay written in 1980, Julio Ortega describes "the contemporary trivialization of the work of art into a mere commodity." "These mechanisms of production and consumption," he writes, "have led to the writer's conversion—from independent critic to spokesman: a qualified specialist in 'public opinion'—which is the social pact controlled by the bourgeoisie. . . . Moreover, this conversion of the writer from critic to spokesman leads to a more serious consequence: the loss of connection between writing and craft; the loss of a genuine relationship to language" (294–95). Vargas Llosa's position on the spectrum Ortega describes is a dual one. At times he has been a spokesman—most notably in the Peruvian presidential election campaign. But in *The Storyteller*, Vargas Llosa returns to the role of the critic. He challenges us to imagine the future so as to create it. Fiction serves as the means by which we can create this future; but for Vargas Llosa, we must turn to the fiction of literature, not the fiction of ideology. *That* is what he has learned; his hope is that we learn it, too.

Postscript:
Annihilating the Past

As rational metaphysics teaches that man becomes all things by understanding them (*homo intelligendo fit omnia*), this imaginative metaphysics shows that man becomes all things by *not* understanding them (*homo non intelligendo fit omnia*); and perhaps the latter proposition is truer than the former, for when man understands he extends his mind and takes in the things, but when he does not understand he makes the things out of himself and becomes them by transforming himself into them.
—Vico, *The New Science*

Change of values—that is a change of creators. Whoever must be a creator always annihilates.
—Nietzsche, *Thus Spoke Zarathustra*

The late, great Austrian novelist and playwright Thomas Bernhard records that his maternal grandfather once said to him: "In der Theorie vernichte ich jeden Tag alles" (23) This comment served as a constant reminder to the young Bernhard of what lies at the heart of the writer's craft. The daily (theoretical) annihilation of everything may be the one fundamental activity shared by the novelists presented in this study, if not by all novelists in general. Indeed, I would argue that a true theory of the novel would develop this line of analysis and show how the novel constitutes an act of annihilation—formal, verbal, social, political, philosophical. But such a study lies beyond the scope of this project and will have to wait. As a prolegomenon to such a theory, let me offer the following.

The novelists presented in this study sought to destroy accepted notions of the past in general and history in particular. Appearing to have learned Zarathustra's dictum—"Whoever must be a creator always annihilates" (Z 59)—they set about in their own ways to take the discourses of history, the various extant historiographies related to particular periods (be they sixteenth-century Europe or twentieth-century India), interpolate them with other discourses, and modify, mythologize, transform, and crush them under the weight of an opposing discourse of the novel that at the same time articulates distinct values opposed to the values in the dominant historical discourses. Because of this, I reject the claim that the authors I studied here are postmodern novelists.

According to Linda Hutcheon, postmodern novelists engage in a "compromised politics" that enacts a "complicitous critique" of the cultures they represent in their works of fiction (*Politics* 2). It is not so much that postmodernism can *do* something, claims Hutcheon, as it is that "it may at least show what needs undoing first" (*Politics* 23). By theorizing the genre of "historiographic metafiction" and then claiming that such work "is written today in the context of a serious contemporary interrogating of the nature of representation in historiography" (*Politics* 50), one that "foregrounds the postmodern epistemological questioning of the nature of historical knowledge" (*Politics* 71), Hutcheon is forced to conclude that postmodern novels engage in a form of parody that "is a value-problematizing, de-naturalizing form of acknowledging the history (and through irony, the politics) of representations" (*Politics* 94).

If Hutcheon is right about postmodern novels, then the novelists I have examined are not postmodernists, for they seek to create through destroying—theirs is an axiological endeavor, not an act of indeterminacy that focuses exclusively on questions of epistemology. The seven novels I have studied do more than problematize values; they actively promote them. Fuentes quite openly calls for the reintegration of Islamic and Jewish elements into Spanish history and culture, just as Rushdie repudiates a monumentalist approach and calls for a radical form of critical history for India, and Reed denounces the Judeo-Christian culture and champions Neo-HooDooism. To suggest that postmodern novelists interrogate systems of representation is to overlook the fact that novelists since Cervantes have always drawn attention to the various systems of representation that constitute the real. To those who would object and claim with Hutcheon that the postmodern novel takes this one step further by calling into question the systems of representation within historiography, I would respond by saying that once we have problematized the epistemological foundations of historiography, we are still left with the question of what we should do next. The novelists I have studied do pose difficult epistemological questions, but they also go one step further than the type of novelist Hutcheon theorizes—they *do* something. They promote new values.

With this in mind, I am far more comfortable with Fredric Jameson's notion of postmodernism as a "cultural dominant" rather than a style (*Postmodernism* 4). For Jameson, postmodernism is an expression of and a response to multinational capitalism, something that few postmodern theorists, Hutcheon included, pay much attention to. Despite her claims that "although postmodern art does indeed acknowledge the commodification of art in capitalist culture, it does so in order to enable a critique of it through its very exploitation of its power" and that the "postmodernist practice is also, however, a challenging and an exploiting of the commodification of art by our consumer culture" (*Poetics* 207), Hutcheon never really explains how this is accomplished. From my perspective, the commodification of all forms of cultural production appears to be so pervasive that, as Jameson points out, the works of an artist such as Warhol, which "*ought* to be powerful and critical political statements" on the very nature of commodification (*Postmodernism* 9), fail to communicate that critical statement. Jameson's turn toward a totalizing strategy that allows him to place postmodernism within a broader Marxist framework that involves cognitive mapping is something with which I have great sympathy. I would only add that totalizing strategies need not be limited to theoretical discourse and that, despite Jameson's claim that "the novel is the weakest of the newer cultural areas and is considerably excelled by its narrative counterparts in film and video" (*Postmodernism* 298), the novels I have examined here succeed in providing totalizing strategies that do offer critical political statements.

In response to Hutcheon's facile notions that postmodern art is "politically 'unmarked'" (*Poetics* 205) and that "what postmodern theory and practice has taught is less that 'truth' is illusory than that it is institutional" (*Poetics* 178), I would offer the words of Terry Eagleton:

> those who have developed the nervous tic of placing such vulgar terms as 'truth' and 'fact' in fastidiously distancing scare quotes should be careful to avoid a certain collusion between their own high-toned theoretical gestures and the most banal, routine political strategies of the capitalist power-structure. The beginning of the good life is to try as far as possible to see the situation as it really is. It is unwise to assume that ambiguity, indeterminacy, undecidability are always subversive strikes against an arrogantly monological certitude; on the contrary, they are the stock-in-trade of many a juridical enquiry and official investigation. (379–80)

Suffice it to say that, like Appleby, Hunt, and Jacob, I, too, emphasize "the human need for self-understanding through a coherent narrative of the past" (229). I differ with them in that, whereas they see "the need for admittedly partial, objective explanations of how the past worked" (229), I prefer totalizing explanations in the form of the novel, not because I see such explanations as complete or inescapable, but because I see the drive to totalize as necessary if we are to comprehend fully the ramifications of our conceptualizations of the past. Once again, I find Jameson helpful in this regard. In *Postmodernism; or, The Cultural Logic of Late Capitalism*, Jameson distinguishes totalization from totality by defining the latter as an attempt to obtain a privileged position of observation so as to see the whole of something and the former as the rejection of the possibility of securing such a privileged position. Borrowing heavily from Sartre, Jameson sees totalization as the process whereby we move from moments of contemplation to action. In Sartre, acts of negation or nihilation (what he termed *néantisation*) made action possible because the perceived world was negated and transformed into a realm of possible action. As Jameson phrases it: "Totalizing, in Sartre, is, strictly speaking, that process whereby, actively impelled by the project, an agent negates the specific object or item and reincorporates it into the larger project-in-course" (333). Jameson goes on to associate totalization with praxis and concludes that the hostility postmodern theorists express toward the concepts of totalization "would thus seem to be most plausibly decoded as a systematic repudiation of notions and ideals of praxis as such, or of the collective project" (333). I agree with Jameson's assessment; but for me, it is the novel, as exemplified in the works that I have studied in the previous chapters, that best brings about totalization. The novel, as I conceive of it here, engages in acts of annihilation in that it actively destroys the object (in this case, history) as part of a larger project of action. Put differently, the acts of contemplation and perception required of the reader of such novels will bring about the rejection of history—both as actions in the past and as a narrative of the past—and will replace it with notions of a "project-in-course," a continuing unfolding of narrative alternatives that make action for the future possible (be it a reconceptualization of a heterogeneous Hispanic culture, a deeper understanding of fascism, a critical reappraisal of revolutions, etc.).

I also join with Appleby, Hunt, and Jacob in their renunciation of "an ironic stance" (229). By this I do not mean that irony does not exist in the novels I have examined. On the contrary, as I have shown, these novels abound with irony. But they do not express irony in the sense that Hutcheon would have it; once again, the poietic novelists champion particular values, they do not retreat into the realm of moral indeterminacy. Finally, I concur with Appleby, Hunt, and Jacob's observation that "postmodernism cannot provide models for the future when it claims to refuse the entire idea of offering models for the future. In the final analysis, then, there can be no postmodern history" (237). If I have made nothing else clear in my analyses of these novels, one thing that should escape no reader's notice is that the seven novelists are very much concerned with the future. Theirs is a future-oriented discourse as much as it is a form of writing about the past. Thus, given what has been said and theorized about postmodernism in general and postmodernist novels in particular, I stand by my claim—the novels I have examined here are *not* postmodern novels.

I will conclude this short excursus on my complaints against postmodern theory by pointing out that fictional constructions in the form of the novel may be what Christopher Norris is looking for when he attempts to obtain a position from which to conduct a critique of the aporias of postmodernism. In his book *What's Wrong with Postmodernism*, Norris argues that deconstruction, as practiced by Jacques Derrida, carries on the Kantian tradition of Enlightenment critique. Norris believes that only through the rigorous practice of deconstructive analysis can we hope to produce a rational critique of the postmodern condition that he defines as "a generalised crisis in the order of signs and representation that works to efface all sense of the difference between truth and falsehood, reality and illusion, serious and non-serious discourse" (42). I would argue, however, that if, as Norris himself concludes, "the aesthetic has been installed within Western philosophy since Kant as the problematic ground where various faculties or truth-claims have established a provisional court of appeal whereby to adjudicate their often conflicting interests" (26), and if, as he remarks, "there is, undeniably, a sense in which history—or the history of the Western 'free-world' democracies—has entered a phase of absurd self-parody which can only be captured by some such wildly exorbitant means of representation" (36), then perhaps the novel is the most fruitful ground on which to cultivate a rational critique. Norris defends Derrida against Jürgen Habermas by claiming that one text "might possess both literary value (on account of its fictive, metaphorical or stylistic attributes) and philosophic cogency (by virtue of its power to criticise normative truth-claims)" (65).

The same argument can be used for works written by writers other than Derrida. There is nothing to preclude a novel from performing the same critique that Derrida offers in his later works, works that Norris and others characterize as being literary. In fact, one could argue that Derrida has often written novels. My contention would be, however, that novels such as *Midnight's Children*, *The Ogre*, and *Mumbo Jumbo* are more effective than

Glas or *La Carte postale* in that they allow us to participate in the imagined reconstruction of the past. We can experience vicariously the events that surround Saleem, Abel, and PaPa LaBas because they are depicted in a world with which we are familiar. At the same time, these narratives pose serious questions about those depicted worlds and cause us to reconsider the actions taken by those characters. With all due respect to Derrida, whose work I admire, I must admit that few are the numbers of readers who can participate in the imagined reconstruction of the philosophical investigations he embarks on. It is precisely the representation of the historical world and its everyday features that allows us to enter into a novel. This does not mean, however, that the novel avoids serious critical engagement with that which it represents. As the eminent historian Simon Schama has pointed out, "the asking of questions and the relating of narratives need not . . . be mutually exclusive forms of historical representation" (325). The novel form, as Schama's own work indicates, may be the best means through which we understand our past and our selves.

Our World

I embarked on this particular project because I believe that, despite what Lyotard may say, rumors of the death of the grand narrative have been greatly exaggerated. His contention that "the grand narrative has lost its credibility, regardless of what mode of unification it uses, regardless of whether it is a speculative narrative or a narrative of emancipation" (37), strikes me as being totally false when we consider world politics, particularly events that have occurred in Eastern Europe, South Africa, and the Islamic nations over the last fifteen years. Even in the United States during the decade of the 1980s, and especially during the 1990s, the overwhelming power of narrative in politics can hardly be denied. The popular political slogans such as "traditional American values," "pulling yourself up by the bootstraps," "the rule of law," not to mention the construction of specious historical parallelisms that sanctioned overt military action in defense of "freedom and democracy" and in opposition to "the dictator," appealed directly to narratives already inscribed in the popular consciousness of the American people, who for the most part uncritically accepted these narratives as expressing some sort of fundamental truth. These assumed-to-be-true narratives were used to justify some of the most despicable governmental practices in the history of the United States, and no amount of celebrating the obsolescence of the *grands récits* will undo the damage already done.

Consider the 1991 Persian Gulf War. The war was prosecuted only after the U.S. administration figured out which narrative would make sense to the American people. The early first drafts that talked about natural resources and jobs gave way to the more popular notion of recreating the Second World War scenario, which cast Saddam Hussein as Hitler and depicted the United States acting as the last bastion of freedom coming to the defense of the Kuwaiti democracy that had been lovingly preserved by the Al-Sabah family. Over 158,000 Arabs were killed with ruthless technological efficiency, and this triumph of the will was capped off with joyous American parades and celebrations that included the commander of Allied Forces gamboling with Mickey Mouse at Disney World.

Some may object that I have distorted the notion of the grand narrative. I can only say that *that* is precisely my point. It may be apparent to well-paid intellectuals that we can blithely pronounce the death of certain ideas; but, in the world of practical politics, ideas derived from narratives are very much alive. As Kumkum Sangari reminds us: "The West expands into the world; late capitalism muffles the globe and homogenizes (or threatens to) all cultural production—this, for some reason, is one 'master narrative' that is seldom dismantled as it needs to be if the differential economic, class, and cultural formation of 'Third World' countries is to be taken into account" (183). With the collapse of the Communist Bloc, the totalizing power of the narrative that describes and explains free-market capitalism will remain uncontested, and no amount of subtle theorizing, coming from the Université de Paris or elsewhere, will have any measurable effect.

Their World

I have focused attention on the novel because novels in themselves present whole narratives that concretize particular concepts and require the reader to think those concepts through to their conclusions. In constructing their poietic histories, Fuentes, Daitch, Rushdie, Tournier, Reed, Swift, and Vargas Llosa present counternarratives that challenge, debunk, or modify the accepted narratives of history that we today use to justify our political practices. As we have seen, in *Terra Nostra,* Fuentes restructures the past to suggest possibilities for the future of a Hispanic culture that would reintegrate a Judeo-Islamic past that has been forgotten. The overlooked and often forgotten aspects of modern revolutions serve as the central focus of Daitch's novel. *L.C.* critiques the notion of any revolutionary politics that repeatedly reinstitutes gender inequality. By employing a genealogical method that maintains a tension between perspectival free play and philological rigor, her novel demonstrates how all historiographies are dependent on linguistic structures and interpretations. Rushdie engages in a form of political praxis in *Midnight's Children* by overturning the already congealing narrative of the history of India. By presenting his counterhistory as an act of narrating, he challenges the political power of the state, which very often constructs its own histories by means of representation, and he reminds his readers that they configure their own realities and can imagine other possibilities for their collective future.

Tournier, by way of contrast, reminds us how powerful narrative constructions can be, and he disabuses us of the notion that the turn to fascism was the inevitable outcome of the combination of Western philosophical thought, which itself constructs totalizing narratives, and myth. On the contrary, Tournier demonstrates that all narratives grow out of mythic structures of some sort. Some of these narratives are malign whereas others are benign, and it remains for us to choose among narratives— we cannot abandon them altogether. With *The Ogre*, Tournier shows us that only through a totalized narrative can we truly think through and understand the fascist phenomenon.

In a similar fashion, Reed investigates the mythic underpinnings of all historical narratives, and he asks his readers to consider the consequences of choosing one mythic foundation over another. Through an examination of the past, he forces us to imagine how a future based on Judeo-Christian cultural paradigms would differ from one based on African and African-American cultural models. Swift delves even further into the myth-history dynamic. *Waterland* demonstrates how these competing and seemingly opposed narrative forms fold in on one another. Metaphoric structuration and projection from the body constitute the meaning-producing activities of us humans as we continue to tell stories in perpetuity.

Finally, Vargas Llosa examines the interaction of myth-based and history-based cultures. Through his novel, he makes clear that the powers of the imagination, as manifested in the construction of novels, will prove to be indispensable to us, because only through such imaginative engagement can we ever hope to comprehend the manner in which the Other conceives of the world. Without such an imaginative engagement, Vargas Llosa seems to be saying, we will never understand those cultures that remain outside the orbit of late-capitalist paradigms, and we will therefore condemn ourselves to a continued policy of cultural eradication and destruction.

I chose to analyze the previously mentioned seven novels using a theoretical, interpretive lens that grows out of philosophical discourse. My philosophical schema of historiography that combines Nietzschean and Vichian philosophy at first appears to be much more symmetrical than the narratives to which I have applied it. Readers should have noticed, however, that by moving from Fuentes to Daitch, through Rushdie and Tournier, on to Reed and Swift, and eventually to Vargas Llosa, the direct influence of Nietzsche and Vico on each author diminishes considerably. Whereas Fuentes openly acknowledges his debt to Vico and quotes Nietzsche in his novel, Swift makes no mention of either philosopher. I do not consider this to be a significant problem. My purpose was not to create a ready-made template that can be superimposed on any novel, nor was I hoping to trace influences. Rather, I sought to show how seven very different novelists construct counternarratives that articulate historical truths. In this regard, the combination of Nietzschean and Vichian philosophy offers a potent vocabulary and conceptual base from which to conduct detailed analyses of particular novels. The philosophies of Vico and Nietzsche can be combined in various ways to provide an effective means for examining the inner workings of a novel so as to determine its meaning-producing capacities. Through metaphoric structuration and emplotment, these novelists construct a truth about the past; and, in doing so, they underscore the notion that we as humans make our own truths.

Of equal importance is the fact that these novelists espouse particular values. These authors of poietic histories offer a praxis in the form of novels that do more than problematize the boundary between history and fiction. It is not sufficient to say, "History is a text; now let us see what fun we can have." To my mind, an author worthy of our consideration must think the problem of history by writing novels that depict the forgotten possibilities of the past, construct a counternarrative of cultural critique, or present history as myth. Another way of saying this would be that to the Nietzschean injunction to "organize the chaos" must be added the Vichian insight of the power of metaphoric structuration to produce the real.

I believe that the novel still remains the best means of reconceiving our reality, because it is based on structuring narratives. As this study has shown—and critics such as Hayden White and Louis O. Mink have argued—we understand our experiences through the stories that we tell. The so-called facts of the past actually emerge through contextualizing narratives; they do not exist prior to their being configured in a story structure of some sort. In other words, we make our world through acts of the imagination; in this regard, the past is made and not found. *Poiesis*, the act of making in language, remains the one meaning-producing activity that we as humans possess. Rather than being trapped by a scientific method that seeks to establish demonstrable truths serving to validate epistemological claims, the novelists I have studied here show us how the novel form can be used to construct narrative contexts that make the truths of the past. History, imagined in this way, becomes a living narrative, one that responds to the recontextualizations to which we submit it in response to our present needs and future goals.

The authors I have examined demonstrate the novel's immense power and appeal. With respect to our commodified, postmodern culture, Salman Rushdie says it best when he writes: "But the truth is that of all forms, literature can still be the most free. The more money a piece of work costs, the easier it is to control it. Film, the most expensive of art forms, is also the least subversive. . . . I continue to believe in the greater possibilities of the novel. Its singularity is its best protection" ("Is Nothing Sacred?" 12). By showing us how to write poietic histories of our own, the seven authors whose works I have studied indicate how the novel provides us with the most effective means to combat the narratives we are forced to live through.

The Next World

Given what I have already said about the seven novels I have analyzed, I would like to mention briefly what I see as the potential future of the novel in this context. Two writers strike me as having taken poietic history to a new level. The first is Cormac McCarthy. In his early fiction—which culminates in his 1985 masterpiece *Blood Meridian*—McCarthy develops literary language in such a way that he creates a new, potent style of writing that carries with it an awesome power that approximates the protean capacities of mythic language.

Consider for example the closing two paragraphs of the first full chapter of *Outer Dark*, McCarthy's second novel, published in 1968. The scene depicts a man abandoning his newborn child (the offspring of an incestuous relationship) in the woods. The man, Holme, is struggling to run away:

> When he crashed into the glade among the cotton-woods he fell headlong and lay there with his cheek to the earth. And as he lay there a far crack of lightning went bluely down the sky and bequeathed him in an embryonic bird's first fissured vision of the world and transpiring instant and outrageous from dark to dark a final view of the grotto and the shapeless white plasm struggling upon the rich and incunabular moss like a lank swamp hare. He would have taken it for some boneless cognate of his heart's dread had the child not cried.
>
> It howled execration upon the dim camarine world of its nativity wail on wail while he lay there gibbering with palsied jawhasps, his hands putting back the night like some witless paraclete beleaguered with all limbo's clamor. (17–18)

The obvious first question that leaps to mind is: Who *writes* like this? McCarthy has often been compared to Melville, Faulkner, even Homer; others make comparisons between the language of the Bible and McCarthy's prose. Clearly, no other American writer crafts language in this way. Many of the hallmarks of McCarthy's style are here—the gripping use of adjectives ("*shapeless white* plasm," "*incunabular* moss," "*boneless* cognate," "*dim camarine* world"), unusual adverbial forms ("bluely," "instant"), the startling similes ("lank swamp hare," "witless paraclete"), the unique nouns ("jawhasps")—but what is most important for me in this particular example is how this mythic prose coincides with a description of a dawning world. The primitive characters depicted in McCarthy's early novels possess a violence both physical and linguistic that offers up a terrible beauty. Here is a world culled from the chaos, pronounced in all its elemental fury. The type of language Vico described as being characteristic of the theological poets and the type of language implied in Nietzsche's calls for us to create a world of new values is very much in evidence in the writing of Cormac McCarthy. The language that appears in McCarthy's early novels in many instances supports the constitution of mythic worlds that are themselves part of history—turn-of-the-century Tennessee, the far West in the 1850s, and so forth.

In the passage quoted above, we have several mythic components—primordial landscape, birth through incest, cosmic portents—and these elements come to us through the inimitable style McCarthy has developed over his writing career. This drive toward describing originary moments, be they the origins of a culture or a person, reaches its apogee in *Blood Meridian, the* novel of the American West. In this 1985 novel, McCarthy

sets about forging the true myth, the *vera narratio* of the West. We witness the activities of a renegade army of scalp hunters, led by a man named
Glanton, who kill indiscriminately and make possible the so-called west-
ward expansion because their acts of extreme violence destroy all other
human beings in the area. These activities are described in a McCarthy
prose that has reached its most developed stage. Readers are struck by the
Homeric overtones in unforgettable scenes that include: a depiction of a
band of Comanches sweeping over a group of soldiers, a description of a
village in which all the members have been massacred and scalped, por-
trayals of individual gun and knife battles between drunk and disgruntled
men around campfires and in barrooms, and mystical descriptions of the
varied landscapes of the West.

The novel follows the movements of a character referred to simply as
"the kid" as he escapes from Tennessee and eventually joins up with Glanton and his gang, a group that includes an ex-priest, a black named Jack-
son, former soldiers, and several members of the Delaware tribe. The most
important character in the group—indeed, in the entire novel—is "the
judge," who serves as a Nietzschean figure par excellence. A towering man
of bald pate, keen wit, and unsurpassed ruthlessness, the judge forges new
values based on acts of will.

The Nietzschean dimensions of the novel are unmistakable. The judge
is a philosopher and scientist who conducts geological experiments, gathers herbal specimens, records his observations in a notebook, and offers
up philosophical sermons from time to time to the other members of
Glanton's gang. He often speaks of fate and history in tones reminiscent
of Nietzsche and possesses an air of immortality, as if he truly is superior
to all those around him. At one point, he makes a general observation
about the men he works with, saying: "It is not necessary . . . that the
principals here be in possession of the facts concerning their case, for their
acts will ultimately accommodate history with or without their understanding" (85). The judge sees the world in a completely different light.
For him, the words of God are the rocks that litter the desert (116). There
is no higher power except that which man forges through his own will.
As the judge puts it: "The way of the world is to bloom and to flower and
die but in the affairs of men there is no waning and the noon of his expression signals the onset of night. His spirit is exhausted at the peak of
its achievement. His meridian is at once his darkening and the evening
of his day. He loves games? Let him play for stakes. This you see here, these
ruins wondered at by tribes of savages, do you not think that this will be

again? Aye. And again. With other people, with other sons" (146–47). In this sermon, we hear echoes of Nietzsche's pronouncements on the will to power, Zarathustra at noon, the seriousness of a child at play, and the notion of the eternal recurrence. At another point, the judge tells his interlocutor that "whatever in creation exists without my knowledge exists without my consent" (198). Placing his hands on the earth, he declares: "This is my claim. . . . And yet everywhere upon it are pockets of autonomous life. Autonomous. In order for it to be mine nothing must be permitted to occur upon it save by my dispensation" (199). This is an extreme version of the will to power stripped of its aesthetic overtones and laid bare in all its terrible splendor. The judge states Nietzschean philosophy quite plainly: "that man who sets himself the task of singling the thread of order from the tapestry will by decision alone have taken charge of the world and it is only by such taking charge that he will effect a way to dictate the terms of his own fate" (199). Once again, we hear the unmistakable articulation of the will to power, *amor fati*, and the call to create a cosmos out of chaos.

The Nietzschean dimension of *Blood Meridian* achieves its most overt expression in the final chapter; its last subtitle reads: "Sie müssen schlafen aber Ich muss tanzen" (316; You must sleep but I must dance). Early on in the novel, the judge is described as a dancer (123); and, in the final scene, he approaches the kid, telling him: "You're here for the dance" and "it's a great thing, the dance" (327). The final tableau shows us the naked judge dancing nimbly in an entourage of crazed drunks and motley whores, and the novel closes with the following words: "He never sleeps, the judge. He is dancing, dancing. He says that he will never die" (335). I do not believe it necessary for me to belabor the point—the spirit of Nietzsche inhabits this novel.

By identifying the Nietzschean element in the novel and what I have characterized as its Vichian element (i.e., prose that resembles the expressions of Vico's theological poets), I find that Cormac McCarthy continues on the path of poietic histories as I have described them. If, in fact, America can be best understood through the myth of the West, then I contend that the best articulation of that myth is *Blood Meridian*, because in this novel we experience through the power of mythic language the essence of an American culture that was forged through horrific levels of violence in pursuit of a will to power.

The second writer of what I consider to be the next phase of poietic history is Roberto Calasso. In two of his works, he has created such a synthesis of history, literature, myth, anthropology, philosophy, and poetry that he has baffled readers who crave neat categorizations; at the same time, he has reminded us just how powerful and creative the novel can be.

In *The Ruin of Kasch,* first published in Italian in 1983, Calasso explores the very idea of history as he interweaves a pseudobiography of Talleyrand with meditations on French literature, nineteenth-century European politics, and the theories of Marx, Freud, and, in particular, Max Stirner. The ghosts of Sainte-Beuve and Proust haunt the entire narrative, and at its heart lies the myth of the "Ruin of Kasch," a story recorded in the writings of anthropologist Leo Frobenius that chronicles the downfall of a culture based on ceremonial sacrifice.

For Calasso, Talleyrand is the ideal subject—not because he was the prototypical modern politician who aligned himself with the prevailing side in a political argument (or, in contemporary parlance, listened to the polls), but because he was the first to perceive that "sacredness had to become fiction" (19). For Talleyrand:

> the challenge was to make it a powerful fiction: to invent, along with Napoleon, a dynasty; to claim, along with the Congress of Vienna, that it was still possible to rely on a "principle"—specifically on that "legitimacy" only recently buried; to ensure, along with Louis-Philippe, that society would find even an uprising acceptable. Talleyrand believed less than anyone in the fictions he proposed. "Legitimacy" had become something akin to what the "ego" would be in the age of Mach: an unsteady but useful guidepost. . . . But the transmission of power (as well as the transmission of thought) would still be—could not fail to be—a chain of those slippery, precarious fictions, which would manage briefly to capture the essence of power one more time, or at least momentarily remove the stopper from its bottle. (19–20)

The road to this recognition of the powerful fictions that constitute legitimacy and power was a long one; but, at its source, Calasso finds the legend of Kasch, a fable about an ancient city whose kings were selected by a class of priests who read the astrological signs and determined when the reigning king should be put to death and replaced by a new king. As Calasso tells it, Kasch was changed forever when a storyteller, Far-li-mas, told such captivating tales to the king, his court, the people, and ultimately the priests that the city lost touch with the sacred script of heavenly signs that sanctioned sacrifice and ultimately gave their culture meaning.

"With Far-li-mas," writes Calasso, "another sort of power is introduced: the reign of the word, which follows that of blood. It is a reign that does not kill according to ritual, but causes death through a disorder that arrives rapidly, invincibly. The words of Far-li-mas replace the sacrifice; like sacrifice, they have the power to command obedience, but they do not have the power to determine the length of the cycle" (132–33). The earlier society, based on sacrifice, disappears and gives way to the "reign of the word." This, for Calasso, is important because "the idea of *what is historical* has come into being here. This creation represents in a certain way the process through which decisive parts of the field of civilization have dissociated themselves from the rest and have entered the profane" (128). The effects of this transition are enormous; in the years following this transformation, technology and experimentation replace sacrifice such that we now live in an age where the innocent do not know that they are victims and the priests have no names. As Calasso describes it, "once sacrifice is dissolved, the whole world reverts, unawares, to a great sacrificial workshop" (138). Thus, following the French Revolution, we have huge conscripted armies crossing Europe back and forth, wreaking havoc through total war. By the time we reach the twentieth century, we witness campaigns of genocide and atomic warfare. What made this possible, Calasso appears to be saying, was the abandonment of the sacred—specifically, acts of ritualized sacrifice—in favor of the profane—or, more to the point, *the historical.*

I see *The Ruin of Kasch* as an ingenious narrative that reveals the central thesis of Vico's *New Science:* cultures move from a period dominated by the barbarism of the senses to a final period dominated by the barbarism of reflection. In Calasso's narrative, the priests of Kasch are like Vico's theological poets; they interpret the heavens. Seen from this perspective, Talleyrand becomes the consummate player in the age of the barbarism of reflection. He, more than anyone else, understands that there are quite literally "only interpretations," and he is content to entertain as many as possible in pursuit of power.

Calasso deepens our understanding of the course that nations run by showing us how the transitions occur and the place occupied by recorded history or history as narrative in this process. Of equal importance is the manner in which Calasso constructs his narrative. The complex interweaving of textual materials makes *The Ruin of Kasch* a veritable polygraphy, a poetic expression of collective human consciousness over time.

It is precisely this stylistic technique that Calasso polishes to perfection in his 1988 book, translated as *The Marriage of Cadmus and Harmony* (1993). In this work, Calasso renarrates the great Greek myths, beginning with Zeus and Europa, and in the process reproduces a history of antiquity. Bringing together fragments and passages from Homer, Plutarch, Euripides, Virgil, Ovid, Sophocles, Aeschylus, Pindar, Herodotus, Horace, and Lucian, to name but a few, Calasso quite literally pieces together "the great fragments of antiquity" (NS ¶ 357) and produces a truly poietic history of the ancient world, giving new voice to the words of the ancients themselves.

Circling back on the repeated question, "But how did it all begin?" Calasso's narrative wends its way through a rhizomatic network of interconnected tales, each of which illuminates the barbaric acts of violence that lie at the heart of ancient culture. As with *The Ruin of Kasch*, we witness a transition from a culture based on the immanence of the gods to one that reverts to the alphabet, the word. "With the alphabet," writes Calasso, "the Greeks would teach themselves to experience the gods in the silence of the mind, and no longer in the full and normal presence" (390). It is on this sad note that *The Marriage of Cadmus and Harmony* ends. At that moment, we as readers recognize that we have witnessed a culture move from the age of the gods to the age of heroes (i.e., the time of Cadmus) to the age of humans (the age that begins with the appearance of the poems, plays, and histories commemorating the earlier ages and continues on to include the time in which Calasso writes his own beautiful history). Once again, the Vichian dimensions of the text are unmistakable, and Nietzsche's notion of the robust nature of the ancients and their acknowledgment of good versus bad (i.e., strong versus weak) rather than good versus evil appears in all its terrifying majesty.

Any description of Calasso's work is utterly inadequate; it would be comparable to trying to describe a lyric by Rilke. I can only say that one must read Calasso's texts. I would argue that both of Calasso's works that I have discussed are, in fact, novels. Observing from a broad Bakhtinian perspective, one can clearly see how he incorporates other genres and texts into his own writings; but, to my mind, his goal is not parody per se. Rather, I see Calasso engaged in a two-part enterprise. In *The Ruin of Kasch*, he shows us the waning of the Vichian third age—a culture quite clearly going mad and losing its substance. Only a character such as Talleyrand—who, in his own words, "speak[s], as always, to deceive" (1)—can bring about some semblance of order in a world without foundations. With *The Marriage of Cadmus and Harmony*, Calasso returns to the mythic origins of Western culture to found new cultural myths. Once again, we read about the collapse of a civilization; yet, in his own way, Calasso attempts to inaugurate a new age through his very use of language. In other words, through powerful poetic language, he returns to the past to build a way toward the imaginative projections of the future.

Taken together, the works of McCarthy and Calasso constitute a new phase in the novel as poietic history. Both authors deliberately annihilate notions of the past and found new understandings of specific cultures through their novels. In this regard, they indicate the essence of what I have called poietic histories, novels comprised of acts of memory and imagination that transform the fictions of the world that concerns us.

Works Cited

Acosta Cruz, María Isabel. "Writer-Speaker? Speaker-Writer? Narrative and Cultural Intervention in Mario Vargas Llosa's *El hablador.*" *INTI* 29–30 (1989): 133–45.

Alazraki, Jaime. "*Terra Nostra:* Coming to Grips with History." *World Literature Today* 57.4 (1983): 551–58.

Ali, Tariq. *An Indian Dynasty: The Story of the Nehru-Gandhi Family.* New York: Putnam's, 1985.

Allen, Esther. "Sentimental Educations." *Review of Contemporary Fiction* 13.2 (1993): 117–20.

Amanuddin, Syed. "The Novels of Salman Rushdie: Mediated Reality as Fantasy." *World Literature Today* 63.1 (1989): 42–45.

Améry, Jean. "Ästhetizismus der Barberei: Über Michel Tourniers Roman *Der Erlkönig.*" *Merkur* 26 (1973): 73–79.

Appignanesi, Lisa, and Sara Maitland, eds. *The Rushdie File.* Syracuse, N.Y.: Syracuse University Press, 1990.

Appleby, Joyce, Lynn Hunt, and Margaret Jacob. *Telling the Truth about History.* New York: Norton, 1994.

Aristotle. *Aristotle's Theory of Poetry and Fine Art.* Trans. S. H. Butcher. New York: Dover, 1951.

Augustine. *The City of God.* Trans. Marcus Dods. New York: Modern Library, 1950.

———. *The Confessions.* In *Basic Writings of Saint Augustine.* Vol. 1. Ed. Whitney J. Oates. New York: Random House, 1948. 3–256.

Baraka, Amiri. *Black Music.* New York: William Morrow, 1967.

Barthes, Roland. "The Discourse of History." In *The Rustle of Language.* Trans. Richard Howard. New York: Hill and Wang, 1986. 127–40.

———. "From Work to Text." In *Image/Music/Text.* Trans. Stephen Heath. New York: Hill and Wang, 1977. 155–64.

Bataille, Georges. *Visions of Excess: Selected Writings 1927–1939.* Trans. Allan Stoekl et al. Minneapolis: University of Minnesota Press, 1985.

Batia, Krishnan. *Indira: A Biography of Prime Minister Gandhi.* New York: Praeger, 1974.

Baudrillard, Jean. "The Precession of Simulacra." In *Art after Modernism: Rethinking Representation.* Ed. Brian Wallis. Boston: David R. Godine, 1984. 253–81.

Belaval, Yvon. "Vico and Anti-Cartesianism." In *Giambattista Vico: An Interna-tional Symposium.* Ed. Giorgio Tagliacozzo and Hayden V. White. Baltimore: Johns Hopkins University Press, 1969. 77–91.

Benjamin, Walter. *Illuminations.* Trans. Harry Zohn. New York: Schocken, 1969.

Berlin, Isaiah. "Comment on Professor Verene's Paper." In *Vico and Contempo-rary Thought.* Ed. Giorgio Tagliacozzo, Michael Mooney, and Donald P. Verene. Atlantic Highlands, N.J.: Humanities Press, 1979. 36–39.

———. *Vico and Herder: Two Studies in the History of Ideas.* London: Hogarth Press, 1976.

Berliner, Paul F. *Thinking in Jazz: The Infinite Art of Improvisation.* Chicago: Uni-versity of Chicago Press, 1994.

Bernard, Catherine. *Graham Swift: La Parole chronique.* Paris: Presses Universi-taires de Nancy, 1991.

Bernhard, Thomas. *Ein Kind.* Munich: Deutschen Taschenbuch Verlag, 1985.

Booker, M. Keith. *Vargas Llosa among the Postmodernists.* Gainesville: University Press of Florida, 1994.

Borges, Jorge Luis. *Borges: A Reader.* Ed. Emir Rodriguez Monegal and Alistair Reid. New York: E. P. Dutton, 1981.

———. *Labyrinths: Selected Stories and Other Writings.* Ed. Donald A. Yates and James E. Irby. New York: New Directions, 1962.

Bougnoux, Daniel. "Des Métaphores à la phorie." *Critique* 28 (1972): 527–43.

Bouloumié, Arlette. *Michel Tournier: Le Roman Mythologique.* Paris: Librarie José Corti, 1988.

———. "Tournier face aux lycéens." *Magazine Littéraire* 226 (January 1986): 20–25.

Braudel, Fernand. "History and the Social Sciences: The *Longue Durée.*" In *On History.* Trans. Sarah Matthews. Chicago: University of Chicago Press, 1980. 24–54.

———. *The Mediterranean and the Mediterranean World in the Age of Philip II.* Trans. Siân Reynolds. New York: Harper Colophon, 1976.

Brewer, John, and Stella Tillyard. "History and Telling Stories: Graham Swift's *Waterland.*" *History Today* 35.1 (1985): 49–51.

Brochier, J. J. "Dix-huit questions à Michel Tournier." *Magazine Littéraire* 138 (June 1978): 11–13.

Brooks, David. "Salman Rushdie: An Interview." *Helix* 19 (1984): 55–69.

Calasso, Roberto. *The Marriage of Cadmus and Harmony.* Trans. Tim Parks. New York: Vintage, 1994.

———. *The Ruin of Kasch.* Trans. William Weaver and Stephen Sartarelli. Cam-bridge, Mass.: Harvard University Press, 1994.

Caponigri, A. Robert. *Time and Idea: The Theory of History in Giambattista Vico.* London: Routledge and Kegan Paul, 1953.

Carpentier, Alejo. "The Baroque and the Marvelous Real." In *Magical Realism: Theory, History, Community*. Ed. Lois Parkinson Zamora and Wendy B. Faris. Durham, N.C.: Duke University Press, 1995. 89–108.

———. "Prólogo." In *El reino de este mundo*. Santiago: Editorial Universitaria, 1967. 9–16.

Cassirer, Ernst. *The Philosophy of Symbolic Forms*. Vol. 2: *Mythical Thought*. Trans. Ralph Manheim. New Haven, Conn.: Yale University Press, 1955.

Castillo, Debra. "Travails with Time: An Interview with Carlos Fuentes." *Review of Contemporary Fiction* 8.2 (1988): 153–165.

Castro, Américo. *The Structure of Spanish History*. Trans. Edmund L. King. Princeton, N.J.: Princeton University Press, 1954.

Castro-Klarén, Sara. *Understanding Mario Vargas Llosa*. Columbia: University of South Carolina Press, 1990.

Chaudhuri, Una. "Imaginative Maps: Excerpts from a Conversation with Salman Rushdie." *Turnstile* 2.1 (1990): 36–47.

———. "Writing the Raj Away." *Turnstile* 2.1 (1990): 26–35.

Chowdhury, Subrata Roy. *The Genesis of Bangladesh*. New York: Asia Publishing House, 1972.

Collingwood, R. G. *The Idea of History*. Oxford: Oxford University Press, 1956.

Cooper, Pamela. "Imperial Topographies: The Spaces of History in *Waterland*." *Modern Fiction Studies* 42.2 (1996): 371–96.

Cowart, David. *History and the Contemporary Novel*. Carbondale: Southern Illinois University Press, 1989.

Cronin, Richard. "The Indian English Novel: *Kim* and *Midnight's Children*." *Modern Fiction Studies* 33.2 (1987): 201–13.

Daitch, Susan. *L.C.* New York: Harcourt, 1986.

Daly, Maura A. "An Interview with Michel Tournier." *Partisan Review* 52.4 (1985): 407–13.

Daniel, Stephen H. *Myth and Modern Philosophy*. Philadelphia: Temple University Press, 1990.

Davis, Colin. *Michel Tournier: Philosophy and Fiction*. Oxford: Clarendon Press, 1988.

Davis, Mary E. "Mario Vargas Llosa and Reality's Revolution: *El hablador*." In *Literature and Revolution*. Ed. David Bevan. Amsterdam: Rodopi, 1989. 135–44.

Davis, Natalie Zemon. *The Return of Martin Guerre*. Cambridge, Mass.: Harvard University Press, 1983.

De Certeau, Michel. *The Writing of History*. Trans. Tom Conley. New York: Columbia University Press, 1988.

Deleuze, Gilles. *Nietzsche and Philosophy*. Trans. Hugh Tomlinson. New York: Columbia University Press, 1983.

De Man, Paul. *Blindness and Insight: Essays in the Rhetoric of Contemporary Criti-cism.* 2d ed. Minneapolis: University of Minnesota Press, 1983.

De Rambures, Jean-Louis. *Comment travaillent les écrivains.* Paris: Flammarion, 1978.

Derrida, Jacques. *Spurs: Nietzsche's Styles.* Trans. Barbara Harlow. Chicago: University of Chicago Press, 1979.

D'Haen, Theo L. "Magical Realism and Postmodernism: Decentering Privileged Centers." In *Magical Realism: Theory, History, Community.* Ed. Lois Parkinson Zamora and Wendy B. Faris. Durham, N.C.: Duke University Press, 1995. 191–208.

Dilthey, Wilhelm. *Meaning in History: W. Dilthey's Thoughts on History and Society.* Ed. and Trans. H. P. Hickman. London: Allen and Unwin, 1961.

Dray, William. *Laws and Explanation in History.* Oxford: Oxford University Press, 1957.

Du Bois, W. E. B. *The Souls of Black Folk.* New York: Penguin, 1989.

Eagleton, Terry. *The Ideology of the Aesthetic.* Cambridge: Basil Blackwell, 1990.

Faris, Wendy B. "Scheherazade's Children: Magical Realism and Postmodern Fiction." In *Magical Realism: Theory, History, Community.* Ed. Lois Parkinson Zamora and Wendy B. Faris. Durham, N.C.: Duke University Press, 1995. 163–90.

Fisch, Max H. Review of *Time and Idea: The Theory of History in Giambattista Vico,* by A. Robert Caponigri. *Journal of Philosophy* 54.21 (1957): 648–52.

Fischer, Manfred S. *Probleme Internationaler Literaturrezeption: Michel Tourniers "Le Roi des Aulnes" im deutsche-franzosischen Kontext.* Bonn: Bouvier Verlag Herbert Grundmann, 1977.

Flores, Angel. "Magical Realism in Spanish American Fiction." In *Magical Realism: Theory, History, Community.* Ed. Lois Parkinson Zamora and Wendy B. Faris. Durham, N.C.: Duke University Press, 1995. 109–17.

Fontenot, Chester J. "Ishmael Reed and the Politics of Aesthetics; or, Shake Hands and Come Out Conjuring." *Black American Literature Forum* 12 (1978): 20–23.

Foucault, Michel. *Language, Counter-Memory, Practice: Selected Essays and Interviews.* Ed. Donald F. Bouchard. Trans. Donald F. Bouchard and Sherry Simon. Ithaca, N.Y.: Cornell University Press, 1977.

———. *The Order of Things: An Archaeology of the Human Sciences.* New York: Vintage, 1973.

———, ed. *I, Pierre Rivière, having slaughtered my mother, my sister, and my brother . . . : A Case of Parricide in the 19th Century.* Trans. Frank Jellinek. New York: Pantheon Books, 1975.

Fox, Robert Elliot. "Blacking the Zero: Toward a Semiotics of Neo-HooDoo." *Black American Literature Forum* 18.3 (1984): 95–99.

———. *Conscientious Sorcerers: The Black Postmodernist Fiction of Leroi Jones/Amiri Baraka, Ishmael Reed, and Samuel R. Delany.* Westport, Conn.: Greenwood Press, 1987.

Franchini, Raffaello. "Vico, Historical Methodology, and the Future of Philosophy." In *Giambattista Vico: An International Symposium.* Ed. Giorgio Tagliacozzo and Hayden V. White. Baltimore: Johns Hopkins University Press, 1969. 543–52.

Friedlander, Saul. *Reflections on Nazism: An Essay on Kitsch and Death.* New York: Harper and Row, 1984.

Fuentes, Carlos. "The Art of Fiction LXVIII: Carlos Fuentes." *Paris Review* 23 (1981): 141–75.

———. *The Buried Mirror.* Boston: Houghton Mifflin, 1992.

———. "Central and Eccentric Writing." *American Review* 21 (October 1974): 84–104.

———. *Christopher Unborn.* Trans. Alfred MacAdam and Carlos Fuentes. New York: Vintage, 1989.

———. *The Death of Artemio Cruz.* Trans. Alfred MacAdam. New York: Noonday Press, 1991.

———. *Don Quixote; or, The Critique of Reading.* Austin: Institute of Latin American Studies, University of Texas at Austin, 1976.

———. *El mundo de José Luis Cuevas.* Trans. Consuelo de Arenlund. New York: Tudor, 1969.

———. *Terra Nostra.* Trans. Margaret Sayers Peden. New York: Farrar, 1976.

———. *Valiente mundo nuevo: Épica, utopía y mito en la novela hispanoamericana.* Madrid: Narrativa Mondaori, 1990.

Gabrielsson, Alf. "Rhythm in Music." In *Rhythm in Psychological, Linguistic, and Musical Processes.* Ed. James R. Evans and Manfred Clynes. Springfield, Ill.: Charles Thomas, 1986. 131–67.

Gallie, W. B. *Philosophy and the Historical Understanding.* London: Chatto and Windus, 1964.

Gallix, François. "Au nom de l'anguille: *Waterland* de Graham Swift." *Études Anglaises* 45.1 (1992): 66–80.

Gandhi, Sonia, ed. *Freedom's Daughter: Letters between Indira Gandhi and Jawaharlal Nehru, 1922–1939.* London: Hodder and Stroughton, 1989.

Gantrel, Martine. "Les Romans de Michel Tournier: Une 'folie raisonneuse et systematique'?" *French Review* 63.2 (1989): 280–89.

Gates, Henry Louis, Jr. "The 'Blackness of Blackness': A Critique of the Sign and the Signifying Monkey." *Critical Inquiry* 9.4 (1983): 685–723.

———. *The Signifying Monkey: A Theory of African-American Literary Criticism.* Oxford: Oxford University Press, 1988.

Gemrich, Anna J. "La identidad latinoamerican en *Terra Nostra.*" *Dactylus* 10 (1990): 36–41.

Gerbi, Antonello. *Nature in the New World: From Christopher Columbus to Gonzalo Fernández de Oviedo.* Trans. Jeremy Moyle. Pittsburgh: University of Pittsburgh Press, 1985.

Gertel, Zunilda. "Sémiotica, historia y ficción en *Terra Nostra.*" *Revista Iberoamericana* 47.116–17 (1981): 63–72.

Gillespie, Michael Allen. "Nietzsche's Musical Politics." In *Nietzsche's New Seas.* Ed. Michael Allen Gillespie and Tracy B. Strong. Chicago: University of Chicago Press, 1988. 117–49.

Ginzburg, Carlo. *The Cheese and the Worms: The Cosmos of a Sixteenth-Century Miller.* Trans. John Tedeschi and Anne Tedeschi. London: Routledge, 1980.

Gladieu, Marie-Madeleine. "*El hablador* de Mario Vargas Llosa." In *De la Peninsule Iberique à l'Amérique Latine: Mélanges en l'honneur de Jean Subirats.* Ed. Marie Roig Miranda. Nancy: Presses Universitaire de Nancy, 1992. 237–48.

González, Eduardo. "Fuentes' *Terra Nostra.*" *Salmagundi* 41 (1978): 148–52.

González Echevarría, Roberto. *Alejo Carpentier: The Pilgrim at Home.* Ithaca, N.Y.: Cornell University Press, 1977.

———. "*Terra Nostra:* Theory and Practice." In *The Voice of the Masters: Writing and Authority in Modern Latin American Literature.* Austin: University of Texas Press, 1985. 87–97.

Gossman, Lionel. *Between History and Literature.* Cambridge, Mass.: Harvard University Press, 1990.

Goytisolo, Juan. "Our Old New World." *Review* 19 (1976): 5–24.

Gutiérrez, Carl. "Provisional Historicity: Reading through *Terra Nostra.*" *Review of Contemporary Fiction* 8.2 (1988): 257–65.

Gyurko, Lanin A. "Novel into Essay: Fuentes' *Terra Nostra* as Generator of *Cervantes o la crítica.*" *Mester* 11.2 (1983): 16–35.

Haar, Michel. "Nietzsche and Metaphysical Language." In *The New Nietzsche.* Ed. David B. Allison. Cambridge, Mass.: MIT Press, 1985. 5–36.

Haffenden, John. *Novelists in Interview.* London: Methuen, 1985.

Harrison, James. "Reconstructing *Midnight's Children* and *Shame.*" *University of Toronto Quarterly* 59.2 (1989/90): 399–412.

Hazard, Paul. *The European Mind (1680–1715).* Trans. J. Lewis May. London: Hollis and Carter, 1953.

Hegel, G. W. F. *Phenomenology of Spirit.* Trans. A. V. Miller. Oxford: Oxford University Press, 1977.

———. *Reason in History.* Trans. Robert S. Hartmen. Indianapolis: Bobbs-Merrill, 1953.

Heidegger, Martin. "Language." In *Poetry, Language, Thought.* Trans. Albert Hofstadter. New York: Harper and Row, 1971. 189–210.

———. *Nietzsche.* Trans. David Ferrell Krell. 4 vols. San Francisco: Harper Collins, 1991.

Hesse, Mary B. "Vico's Heroic Metaphor." In *Metaphysics and Philosophy of Science in the Seventeenth and Eighteenth Centuries: Essays in Honour of Gerd Burchdahl.* Ed. R. S. Woolhouse. Dordrecht: Kluwer, 1988. 185–212.

Heuston, Penny. "An Interview with Michel Tournier." *Meanjin* 38.3 (1979): 401–5.

Hinnells, John R., and Eric J. Sharpe, eds. *Hinduism.* Newcastle, U.K.: Oriel Press, 1972.

Holt, Candace K. "*Terra Nostra:* Indagación de una identidad." *Revista de Estudios Hispanicos* 17.3 (1983): 395–406.

Holt, Hamilton, ed. *The Life Stories of (Undistinguished) Americans as Told by Themselves.* 1906. Rpt., New York: Routledge, 1990.

Houlgate, Stephen. *Hegel, Nietzsche, and the Criticism of Metaphysics.* Cambridge: Cambridge University Press, 1986.

Howells, Carol Ann. "Rudy Wiebe's *The Temptations of Big Bear* and Salman Rushdie's *Midnight's Children.*" *Literary Criterion* 20.1 (1985): 191–203.

Hume, Kathryn. "Ishmael Reed and the Problematics of Control." *PMLA* 108.3 (1993): 506–18.

Husserl, Edmund. *The Crisis of European Sciences and Transcendental Phenomenology.* Trans. David Carr. Evanston, Ill.: Northwestern University Press, 1970.

Hutcheon, Linda. *A Poetics of Postmodernism: History, Theory, Fiction.* New York: Routledge, 1988.

———. *The Politics of Postmodernism.* London: Routledge, 1989.

Jameson, Fredric. "Postmodernism; or, The Cultural Logic of Late Capitalism." *New Left Review* 146 (1984): 53–92.

———. *Postmodernism; or, The Cultural Logic of Late Capitalism.* Durham, N.C.: Duke University Press, 1990.

Jones, LeRoi. *Blues People: Negro Music in White America.* 1963. Rpt., Westport, Conn.: Greenwood Press, 1980.

Kant, Immanuel. *On History.* Trans. Lewis W. Beck, Robert E. Anchor, and Emil L. Fackenheim. Ed. Lewis W. Beck. Indianapolis: Bobbs-Merrill, 1963.

Kaufmann, Walter. *Nietzsche: Philosopher, Psychologist, Anti-Christ.* Princeton, N.J.: Princeton University Press, 1968.

Kerr, Lucille. *Reclaiming the Author: Figures and Fictions from Spanish America.* Durham, N.C.: Duke University Press, 1992.

Klossowski, Pierre. "Nietzsche's Experience of the Eternal Return." In *The New Nietzsche.* Ed. David B. Allison. Cambridge, Mass.: MIT Press, 1985. 107–20.

Kofman, Sarah. "Baubô: Theological Perversion and Fetishism." In *Nietzsche's New Seas: Explorations in Philosophy, Aesthetics, and Politics.* Ed. Michael Allen Gillespie and Tracy B. Strong. Chicago: University of Chicago Press, 1988. 175–202.

———. *Explosion I: De "l'Ecce Homo" de Nietzsche.* Paris: Éditions Galilée, 1992.

————. *Nietzsche et la métaphor.* Paris: Éditions Galilée, 1983.

The Koran. Trans. N. J. Dawood. New York: Penguin, 1990.

Koster, Serge. *Michel Tournier.* Paris: Éditions Henri Veyrier, 1986.

LaCapra, Dominick. "Rethinking Intellectual History and Reading Texts." In *Rethinking Intellectual History: Texts and Contexts.* Ithaca, N.Y.: Cornell University Press, 1983. 23–71.

Lacoue-Labarthe, Philippe. *Heidegger, Art, and Politics.* Trans. Chris Turner. Oxford: Basil Blackwell, 1990.

Lampert, Laurence. *Nietzsche's Teaching: An Interpretation of "Thus Spoke Zarathustra."* New Haven, Conn.: Yale University Press, 1986.

Leach, Edmund. "Vico and Lévi-Strauss on the Origins of Humanity." In *Giambattista Vico: An International Symposium.* Ed. Giorgio Tagliacozzo and Hayden V. White. Baltimore: Johns Hopkins University Press, 1969. 309–18.

Leal, Luis. "Magical Realism in Spanish American Literature." In *Magical Realism: Theory, History, Community.* Ed. Lois Parkinson Zamora and Wendy B. Faris. Durham, N.C.: Duke University Press, 1995. 119–24.

Le Goff, Jacques. *History and Memory.* Trans. Steven Randall and Elizabeth Claman. New York: Columbia University Press, 1992.

Le Roy Ladurie, Emmanuel. *Montaillou: The Promised Land of Error.* Trans. Barbara Bray. New York: George Braziller, 1978.

Lévi-Strauss, Claude. "The Structural Study of Myth." In *Structural Anthropology.* Trans. Claire Jacobson and Brooke Grundfest Schoepf. New York: Basic Books, 1963. 206–31.

Lilla, Mark. *G. B. Vico: The Making of an Anti-Modern.* Cambridge, Mass.: Harvard University Press, 1993.

Lukács, Georg. *The Historical Novel.* Trans. Hannah Mitchell and Stanley Mitchell. Atlantic Highlands, N.J.: Humanities Press, 1978.

————. *The Theory of the Novel.* Trans. Anna Bostock. Cambridge, Mass.: MIT Press, 1971.

Lyotard, Jean-François. *The Postmodern Condition: A Report on Knowledge.* Trans. Geoff Bennington and Brian Massumi. Minneapolis: University of Minnesota Press, 1984.

MacAdam, Alfred J. "Carlos Fuentes: The Burden of History." *World Literature Today* 57.4 (1983): 558–63.

Mackey, Nathaniel. "Other: From Noun to Verb." In *Jazz among the Discourses.* Ed. Krin Gabbard. Durham, N.C.: Duke University Press, 1995. 76–99.

MacShane, Frank. "A Talk with Carlos Fuentes." *New York Times Book Review,* 7 November 1976, 3+.

Malhotra, Inder. *Indira Gandhi: A Personal and Political Biography.* London: Hodder and Stoughton, 1989.

Mali, Joseph. *The Rehabilitation of Myth: Vico's "New Science."* Cambridge: Cambridge University Press, 1992.

Márquez Rodríguez, Alexis. "Aproximación preliminar a *Terra Nostra:* La ficción como reinterpretación de la historia." In *La Obra de Carlos Fuentes: Una Vision Multiple.* Ed. Ana María Hernandez Lopez. Madrid: Editorial Pliegos, 1988. 183–92.

Marsh, Kelly A. "The Neo-Sensationalist Novel: A Contemporary Genre in the Victorian Tradition." *Philological Quarterly* 74.1 (1995): 99–123.

Martin, Reginald. *Ishmael Reed and the New Black Aesthetic Critics.* New York: St. Martin's Press, 1988.

Masani, Zareer. *Indira Gandhi: A Biography.* New York: Thomas Y. Crowell, 1976.

Mathieu, Vittorio. "Truth as the Mother of History." In *Giambattista Vico's Science of Humanity.* Ed. Giorgio Tagliacozzo and Donald P. Verene. Baltimore: Johns Hopkins University Press, 1976. 113–24.

May, Georges. "L'Histoire: A-t-elle engendré le roman?" *Revue d'Histoire Littéraire de la France* 55 (1955): 155–76.

McCaffery, Larry. "An Interview with Susan Daitch." *Review of Contemporary Fiction* 13.2 (1993): 68–82.

McCarthy, Cormac. *Blood Meridian.* New York: Vintage, 1985.

———. *Outer Dark.* New York: Vintage, 1968.

McKeon, Michael. *Origins of the English Novel, 1660–1740.* Baltimore: Johns Hopkins University Press, 1987.

Megill, Allan. "Vico and Marx after Nietzsche." In *Vico and Marx: Affinities and Contrasts.* Ed. Giorgio Tagliacozzo. Atlantic Highlands, N.J.: Humanities Press, 1983. 388–400.

Miller, Cecilia. *Giambattista Vico: Imagination and Historical Knowledge.* New York: St. Martin's Press, 1993.

Mink, Louis O. "History and Fiction as Modes of Comprehension." *New Literary History* 1.3 (1970): 541–58.

———. "Narrative Form as Cognitive Instrument." In *Historical Understanding.* Ed. Brian Fay, Eugene O. Golob, and Richard T. Vann. Ithaca, N.Y.: Cornell University Press, 1987. 182–203.

Monson, Ingrid. "Doubleness and Jazz Improvisation: Irony, Parody, and Ethnomusicology." *Critical Inquiry* 20.2 (1994): 283–313.

Moraes, Dom. *Indira Gandhi.* Boston: Little, Brown and Co., 1980.

Moses, Michael Valdez. *The Novel and the Globalization of Culture.* Oxford: Oxford University Press, 1995.

Nazareth, Peter. "An Interview with Ishmael Reed." *Iowa Review* 13.2 (1982): 117–31.

Nehamas, Alexander. *Nietzsche: Life as Literature.* Cambridge, Mass.: Harvard University Press, 1985.

Nehru, Jawaharlal. *Glimpses of World History: Being Further Letters to His Daughter Written in Prison, and Containing a Rambling Account of History for Young People.* New York: John Day, 1942.

Nericcio, William Anthony. "Rend[er]ing L.C.: Susan Daitch Meets Borges & Borges, Delacroix, Marx, Derrida, Daumier, and Other Textualized Bodies." *Review of Contemporary Fiction* 13.2 (1993): 101–16.

Nietzsche, Friedrich. *The Anti-Christ*. In *Twilight of the Idols and The Anti-Christ*. Trans. R. J. Hollingdale. New York: Penguin, 1968.

———. *Beyond Good and Evil*. Trans. Walter Kaufmann. New York: Vintage, 1966.

———. *The Birth of Tragedy*. In *The Birth of Tragedy and The Case of Wagner*. Trans. Walter Kaufmann. New York: Vintage, 1967.

———. *The Case of Wagner*. In *The Birth of Tragedy and The Case of Wagner*. Trans. Walter Kaufmann. New York: Vintage, 1967.

———. *Daybreak*. Trans. R. J. Hollingdale. Cambridge: Cambridge University Press, 1982.

———. *Ecce Homo*. Trans. Walter Kaufmann. New York: Vintage, 1969.

———. *The Gay Science*. Trans. Walter Kaufmann. New York: Vintage, 1974.

———. *Human, All Too Human: A Book for Free Spirits*. Trans. R. J. Hollingdale. Cambridge: Cambridge University Press, 1986.

———. *Nietzsche contra Wagner*. In *The Portable Nietzsche*. Ed. and trans. Walter Kaufmann. New York: Penguin, 1968.

———. *On the Genealogy of Morals*. Trans. Walter Kaufmann. New York: Vintage, 1969.

———. *Philosophy and Truth: Selections from Nietzsche's Notebooks of the Early 1870's*. Ed. and trans. Daniel Breazeale. Atlantic Highlands, N.J.: Humanities Press, 1990.

———. *Philosophy in the Tragic Age of the Greeks*. Trans. Marianne Cowan. Chicago: Gateway Editions, 1962.

———. *Thus Spoke Zarathustra*. Trans. Walter Kaufmann. New York: Penguin, 1954.

———. *Twilight of the Idols*. In *Twilight of the Idols and The Anti-Christ*. Trans. R. J. Hollingdale. New York: Penguin, 1968.

———. *Untimely Meditations*. Trans. R. J. Hollingdale. Cambridge: Cambridge University Press, 1983.

———. *The Will to Power*. Trans. Walter Kaufmann and R. J. Hollingdale. Ed. Walter Kaufmann. New York: Vintage, 1968.

Norris, Christopher. *Uncritical Theory: Postmodernism, Intellectuals, and the Gulf War*. Amherst: University of Massachusetts Press, 1992.

———. *What's Wrong with Postmodernism: Critical Theory and the Ends of Philosophy*. Baltimore: Johns Hopkins University Press, 1990.

Nouhaud, Dorita. "De l'amour de toutes à l'amour de soi ou Don Juan démasqué." *Langues Neo-Latines* 80.2 (1986): 5–33.

Obeyesekere, Gananath. *The Apotheosis of Captain Cook: European Mythmaking in the Pacific*. Princeton, N.J.: Princeton University Press, 1992.

O'Bryan-Knight, Jean. *The Story of the Storyteller: "La tia Julia y el escribidor," "Historia de Mayta," and "El hablador" by Mario Vargas Llosa.* Amsterdam: Rodopi, 1994.

O'Gorman. Eduardo. *The Invention of America.* Bloomington: Indiana University Press, 1961.

Ogren, Kathy J. *The Jazz Revolution: Twenties America and the Meaning of Jazz.* New York: Oxford University Press, 1989.

Ortega, Julio. "Latin American Literature Facing the Eighties." *New Orleans Review* 7.3 (1980): 294–96.

Oviedo, José Miguel, Richard Reeve, John Skirius, and Raymond Paredes. "Carlos Fuentes at UCLA: An Interview [1980]." *Mester* 11.1 (1982): 3–15.

Parameswaran, Uma. "Handcuffed to History: Salman Rushdie's Art." *Ariel* 14.4 (1983): 34–45.

Paravisini, Lizabeth. "*Mumbo Jumbo* and the Uses of Parody." *Obsidian II: Black Literature in Review* 1.1–2 (1986): 113–27.

Parry, David M. "The Aesthetics in Vico and Nietzsche." *New Vico Studies* 9 (1991): 29–42.

———. "Vico and Nietzsche." *New Vico Studies* 7 (1989): 59–75.

Parsons, Robert A. "Mirror Symbolism in Carlos Fuentes' *Terra Nostra.*" *College Language Association* 31.1 (1987): 77–86.

Peden, Margaret Sayers. "A Reader's Guide to *Terra Nostra.*" *Review* 31 (1982): 42–48.

Perricone, Catherine R. "Mario Vargas Llosa's *El hablador:* Variations on a Theme." *South Eastern Latin Americanist* 35.1 (1991): 1–11.

Petit, Susan. "Fugal Structure, Nestorianism, and St. Christopher in Michel Tournier's *Le Roi des Aulnes.*" *Novel* 19.3 (1986): 232–45.

Pompa, Leon. "Vico and the Presuppositions of Historical Knowledge." In *Giambattista Vico's Science of Humanity.* Ed. Giorgio Tagliacozzo and Donald P. Verene. Baltimore: Johns Hopkins University Press, 1976. 125–40.

Pound, Ezra. *Guide to Kulchur.* New York: New Directions, 1970.

Poupeney Hart, Catherine. "Le Rejet de la chronique ou la construction de l'utopie archaïque dans *L'Homme qui parle* de Mario Vargas Llosa." In *Parole exclusive, parole exclue, parole transgressive: Marginalisation et marginalité dans les pratiques discursives.* Ed. Antonio Gómez-Moriana and Catherine Poupeney Hart. Paris: Collection l'Univers des Discours les Éditions du Préambule, 1990. 517–42.

Raimond, Jeanne. "Notes sur *El hablador* de Mario Vargas Llosa." *Sociocriticism* 6.11–12 (1990): 113–22.

Reed, Ishmael. "Neo-HooDoo Manifesto." In *Conjure: Selected Poems, 1963–1970.* Amherst: University of Massachusetts Press, 1972. 20–25.

———. *Mumbo Jumbo.* New York: Atheneum, 1972.

Reed, Walter L. *An Exemplary History of the Novel: The Quixotic versus the Picaresque.* Chicago: University of Chicago Press, 1981.

Reimenschneider, Dieter. "History and the Individual in Anita Desai's *Clear Light of Day* and Salman Rushdie's *Midnight's Children.*" *World Literature Written in English* 23.1 (1984): 196–207.

Ricoeur, Paul. *Hermeneutics and the Human Sciences.* Trans. and ed. John B. Thompson. Cambridge: Cambridge University Press, 1981.

———. *Interpretation Theory: Discourse and the Surplus of Meaning.* Fort Worth: Texas Christian University Press, 1976.

———. *The Rule of Metaphor: Multidisciplinary Studies of the Creation of Meaning in Language.* Trans. Robert Czerny. Toronto: University of Toronto Press, 1977.

———. *Time and Narrative.* Trans. Kathleen McLaughlin and David Pellauer. 3 vols. Chicago: University of Chicago Press, 1984–88.

Roh, Franz. "Magical Realism: Post-Expressionism." In *Magical Realism: Theory, History, Community.* Ed. Lois Parkinson Zamora and Wendy B. Faris. Durham, N.C.: Duke University Press, 1995. 15–31.

Rorty, Richard. *Contingency, Irony, and Solidarity.* Cambridge: Cambridge University Press, 1989.

Rushdie, Salman. *Imaginary Homelands: Essays and Criticism 1981–1991.* London: Granta Books, 1991.

———. "Introduction." In *An Indian Dynasty: The Story of the Nehru-Gandhi Family*, by Tariq Ali. New York: Putnam's, 1985. xi–xv.

———. "Is Nothing Sacred?" The Herbert Read Memorial Lecture: 6 February 1990. London: Granta, 1990.

———. *Midnight's Children.* New York: Penguin, 1980.

———. "*Midnight's Children* and *Shame.*" *Kunapipi* 7.1 (1985): 1–19.

———. *The Moor's Last Sigh.* New York: Pantheon, 1995.

Ryan, Judith. "Out of the Mouths of Monsters: Perspectives on Nazism in Grass and Tournier." *Simon Wiesenthal Center Annual* 5 (1988): 97–108.

Sahlins, Marshall. *How "Natives" Think: About Captain Cook, for Example.* Chicago: University of Chicago Press, 1995.

Said, Edward. *Beginnings.* New York: Columbia University Press, 1975.

Sangari, Kumkum. "The Politics of the Possible." *Cultural Critique* 7 (1987): 157–86.

Scarry, Elaine. *The Body in Pain: The Making and Unmaking of the World.* New York: Oxford University Press, 1985.

Schama, Simon. *Dead Certainties (Unwarranted Speculations).* New York: Knopf, 1991.

Schmitz, Neil. "Neo-HooDoo: The Experimental Fiction of Ishmael Reed." *Twentieth Century Literature* 20.2 (1974): 126–40.

Schrift, Alan D. "Between Perspectivism and Philology: Genealogy as Hermeneutic." *Nietzsche-Studien* 16 (1986): 91–111.

———. *Nietzsche and the Question of Interpretation: Between Hermeneutics and Deconstruction.* New York: Routledge, 1990.

Schuller, Gunther. *Early Jazz: Its Roots and Musical Development.* New York: Oxford University Press, 1968.

Scott, Joan W. "The Evidence of Experience." *Critical Inquiry* 19 (1991): 773–91.

Seamon, Roger G. "Narrative Practice and the Theoretical Distinction between History and Fiction." *Genre* 16.3 (1983): 197–218.

Shepherd, Ron. "Growing Up: A Central Metaphor in Some Recent Novels." In *The Writer's Sense of the Contemporary: Papers in Southeast Asian and Australian Literature.* Ed. Bruce Bennett, Ee Tiang Hong, and Ron Shepherd. Perth: Vanguard Press, 1982. 51–54.

Showalter, English, Jr. *The Evolution of the French Novel, 1641–1782.* Princeton, N.J.: Princeton University Press, 1972.

Sollors, Werner. "Introduction." In *The Life Stories of (Undistinguished) Americans as Told by Themselves.* Ed. Hamilton Holt. Rpt., New York: Routledge, 1990. xi–xxviii.

Spence, Jonathan. *The Question of Hu.* New York: Vintage, 1989.

Srivastava, Aruna. "'The Empire Writes Back': Language and History in *Shame* and *Midnight's Children.*" *Ariel* 20.4 (1989): 62–78.

Stambaugh, Joan. *Nietzsche's Thought of Eternal Return.* Washington, D.C.: Center for Advanced Research in Phenomenology and University Press of America, 1988.

Standish, Peter. "Vargas Llosa's Parrot." *Hispanic Review* 59.2 (1991): 143–51.

Steiner, Wendy. *The Scandal of Pleasure: Art in an Age of Fundamentalism.* Chicago: University of Chicago Press, 1995.

Swann, Joseph. "'East Is East and West Is West'? Salman Rushdie's *Midnight's Children* as an Indian Novel." *World Literature Written in English* 26.2 (1986): 353–62.

Swift, Graham. *Waterland.* New York: Vintage, 1992.

Tittler, Jonathan. "Interview: Carlos Fuentes." *Diacritics* 10.3 (1980): 46–56.

Tolstoy, Leo. *War and Peace.* Trans. Aylmer and Louise Maude. Ed. George Gibian. New York: Norton, 1966.

Tournier, Michel. "Comment j'ai construit *Le Roi des Aulnes.*" *Cahiers de l'Oriente* 9 (1971): 76–89.

———. *Friday.* Trans. Norman Denny. New York: Pantheon, 1969.

———. *Gaspard, Melchior, et Balthazar.* Paris: Gallimard Folio, 1980.

———. *Le Médianoche amoureux.* Paris: Gallimard, 1989.

———. *Les Météores.* Paris: Gallimard Folio, 1975.

———. *The Ogre.* Trans. Barbara Bray. Baltimore: Johns Hopkins University Press, 1997.

———. *Le Roi des Aulnes.* Paris: Gallimard Folio, 1970.

———. "Treize clés pour un ogre." *Le Figaro littéraire* 30 (November 1970): 20–22.

————. *Le Vagabonde immobile*. Paris: Gallimard, 1984.

————. *Le Vent Paraclet*. Paris: Gallimard Folio, 1977.

————. *Le Vol du vampire: Notes de lecture*. Paris: Gallimard, 1981.

Trevelyan, G. M. "Clio, a Muse." In *The Varieties of History: From Voltaire to the Present*. Ed. Fritz Stern. New York: Vintage, 1973. 227–45.

Turner, Joseph W. "The Kinds of Historical Fiction: An Essay in Definition and Methodology." *Genre* 12.3 (1979): 333–55.

Ullán, José-Miguel. "Carlos Fuentes: Salto Mortal Hacia Mañana." *Insula* 22.245 (1967): 1+.

Vargas Llosa, Mario. "A Fish Out of Water." *Granta* 36 (1991): 15–75.

————. *The Storyteller*. Trans. Helen R. Lane. New York: Penguin, 1990.

————. "Updating Karl Popper." *PMLA* 105 (1990): 1018–25.

————. *The War of the End of the World*. Trans. Helen R. Lane. New York: Avon Books, 1984.

————. *A Writer's Reality*. Ed. Myron I. Lichtblau. Syracuse, N.Y.: Syracuse University Press, 1991.

Verene, Donald P. "Vico's Philosophy of Imagination." In *Vico and Contemporary Thought*. Ed. Giorgio Tagliacozzo, Michael Mooney, and Donald P. Verene. Atlantic Highlands, N.J.: Humanities Press, 1979. 20–36.

————. *Vico's Science of Imagination*. Ithaca, N.Y.: Cornell University Press, 1981.

————. "Vico's Science of Imaginative Universals and the Philosophy of Symbolic Forms." In *Giambattista Vico's Science of Humanity*. Ed. Giorgio Tagliacozzo and Donald P. Verene. Baltimore: Johns Hopkins University Press, 1976. 295–317.

Vico, Giambattista. *The Autobiography of Giambattista Vico*. Trans. Max Harold Fisch and Thomas Goddard Bergin. Ithaca, N.Y.: Cornell University Press, 1944.

————. *The New Science of Giambattista Vico*. Trans. Thomas Goddard Bergin and Max Harold Fisch. Ithaca, N.Y.: Cornell University Press, 1988.

————. *On the Most Ancient Wisdom of the Italians*. Trans. L. M. Palmer. Ithaca, N.Y.: Cornell University Press, 1988.

————. *On the Study Methods of Our Time*. Trans. Elio Gianturco. Ithaca, N.Y.: Cornell University Press, 1990.

Walser, Robert. "'Out of Notes': Signification, Interpretation, and the Problem of Miles Davis." In *Jazz among the Discourses*. Ed. Krin Gabbard. Durham, N.C.: Duke University Press, 1995. 165–88.

Wei-han Ho, Fred. "What Makes 'Jazz' the Revolutionary Music of the 20th Century, and Will It Be Revolutionary for the 21st Century?" *African American Review* 29.2 (1995): 283–90.

Wesseling, Elisabeth. *Writing History as a Prophet: Postmodernist Innovations of the Historical Novel*. Amsterdam: Johns Benjamins, 1991.

White, Hayden. *The Content of the Form: Narrative Discourse and Historical Representation.* Baltimore: Johns Hopkins University Press, 1987.

————. *Metahistory: The Historical Imagination in Nineteenth-Century Europe.* Baltimore: Johns Hopkins University Press, 1973.

————. *Tropics of Discourse: Essays in Cultural Criticism.* Baltimore: Johns Hopkins University Press, 1978.

Wilson, Keith. *"Midnight's Children* and Reader Responsibility." *Critical Quarterly* 26.3 (1984): 23–37.

Wisman, Josette A. "Idéologie chrétien et idéologie nazi: Une Lecture herméneutique du *Roi des Aulnes* de Michel Tournier." *Romanic Review* 80.4 (1989): 591–606.

Wolpert, Stanley. *A New History of India.* 3d ed. Oxford: Oxford University Press, 1989.

Woodhull, Winifred. "Fascist Bonding and Euphoria in Michel Tournier's *The Ogre.*" *New German Critique* 42 (1987): 79–112.

You, Haili. "Defining Rhythm: Aspects of an Anthropology of Rhythm." *Culture, Medicine, and Psychiatry* 18 (1994): 361–84.

Young, James E. *Writing and Rewriting the Holocaust: Narrative and the Consequences of Interpretation.* Bloomington: Indiana University Press, 1988.

Young, Julian. *Nietzsche's Philosophy of Art.* Cambridge: Cambridge University Press, 1992.

Zamora, Lois Parkinson. "Magical Romance/Magical Realism: Ghosts in U.S. and Latin American Fiction." *Magical Realism: Theory, History, Community.* Ed. Lois Parkinson Zamora and Wendy B. Faris. Durham, N.C.: Duke University Press, 1995. 497–550.

————. *Writing the Apocalypse: Historical Vision in Contemporary U.S. and Latin American Fiction.* Cambridge: Cambridge University Press, 1989.

Index

Aeschylus, 197, 312
À la Recherche du temps perdu (Proust), 10, 284
Allende, Isabel, 276, 281
Améry, Jean, 154
The Anti-Christ (Nietzsche), 184
Appleby, Joyce, 182, 217, 299–300
Aristotle, 26, 245; Poetics, 26, 30
Armstrong, Louis, 202, 213
Augustine, 30, 231–32; City of God, 30; Confessions, 231, 232
axiology (systems of values), 2, 3, 4, 5, 8, 12, 54, 55, 78, 108, 203, 212, 296–97, 298

Bacon, Francis, 216
Bakhtin, Mikhail, 101, 201, 312
Baldwin, James, 202
Balzac, Honoré de, 95
Bangladeshi War (1971), 141, 147–48, 149
Baraka, Amiri, 181, 190, 191–92, 192–93, 196, 199, 213, 215
Barthes, Roland, 101, 111, 114, 120
Basie, Count, 203
Bataille, Georges, 168
Baubô, 253, 254
Baudrillard, Jean, 259, 271
Bechet, Sidney, 213
Benjamin, Walter, 1, 8, 29, 77, 113
Bergman, Ingmar, 53
Berlin, Isaiah, 37, 63, 64
Berliner, Paul F., 193–94, 197, 199, 200, 201, 203, 204, 208, 209, 211, 213, 214
Bernhard, Thomas, 297
Beyond Good and Evil (Nietzsche), 13, 38, 47, 92, 117, 160, 164, 251, 256
The Birth of Tragedy (Nietzsche), 56, 57, 93, 158, 159, 160, 190, 191, 192, 212, 235, 255
Blood Meridian (McCarthy), 306–9
Bloy, Léon, 157
Bonaparte, Napoleon, 95, 112, 219
Borges, Jorge Luis, 48, 51, 73, 78, 278

Borowski, Tadeusz, 29
Bouloumié, Arlette, 158
Braudel, Fernand, 218
Brecht, Bertolt, 80
Buddenbrooks (Mann), 10
The Buried Mirror (Fuentes), 75
Burke, Edmund, 86
El burlador de Sevilla (de Molina), 48, 73
Burns, Ken, 81, 82

Cabrera Infante, Guillermo, 48
Calasso, Roberto, 309–13; The Marriage of Cadmus and Harmony, 311–12; The Ruin of Kasch, 310–12
Caponigri, Roberto, 63
Carpentier, Alejo, 48, 276–80
The Case of Wagner (Nietzsche), 191
Cassirer, Ernst, 267
Castro, Américo, 48, 68, 70, 71
La celestina, 48
Cervantes, 298
Chandler, Raymond, 201
Christopher Unborn (Fuentes), 61
City of God (Augustine), 30
Coetzee, J. M., 10
Cohn, Norman, 68
Collingwood, R. G., 19–20
Coltrane, John, 192, 203
communeros, 3, 56, 64, 68
Comte, Auguste, 217
Confessions (Augustine), 231, 232
The Content of the Form (White), 24
Cook, Captain James, 86–87
Coras, Jean de, 88
Cortázar, Julio, 48, 276
countermemory, 3, 8, 17, 42, 44
counternarrative, 3, 113, 114, 116, 123, 135, 139, 303, 305
Cowart, David, 14
cultural identity, 50, 60–61, 70, 71, 122–23, 187, 189–90, 199, 210, 268–76

Daitch, Susan, 4, 15, 17, 44–47, 79, 88–120
passim, 152, 181, 218, 263, 303–5; *L.C.*, 15,
45, 79, 88–120 passim, 181, 304
Daniel, Stephen, 106, 107, 117
Dante, 270
Daumier, Honoré de, 95
Davis, Colin, 155, 156
Davis, Miles, 203–4, 208, 209
Davis, Natalie Zemon, 81, 88
Daybreak (Nietzsche), 39, 114
Death in the Andes (Vargas Llosa), 290
The Death of Artemio Cruz (Fuentes), 75
de Certeau, Michel, 42, 47, 103, 111, 118–19
de Cunha, Euclides, 261; *Os sertões*, 261
Defoe, Daniel, 260; *Robinson Crusoe*, 260
Delacroix, Eugène, 91, 106, 108–9, 115
Deleuze, Gilles, 59
de Man, Paul, 90, 94
Derrida, Jacques, 252, 253, 301, 302; *La
Carte postale*, 302; *Glas*, 302; *Spurs Nietz-
sche's Styles*, 252–53
Descartes, René, 38, 176–77, 217, 246, 293
Des Pres, Terrence, 29
de Staël, Germaine Necker, 112
Devi. *See* Kali
différance, 174, 251
Dilthey, Wilhelm, 31–32
Dix, Otto, 277
Döblin, Alfred, 202
Donoso, José, 48
Don Quixote (Cervantes), 48, 70, 73–74
Don Quixote; or, The Critique of Reading
(Fuentes), 56, 57, 68
Dos Passos, John, 202, 205
Dray, William, 32
Du Bois, W. E. B., 190, 196
Durga. *See* Kali

Eagleton, Terry, 299
Ecce Homo (Nietzsche), 59, 161
Eco, Umberto, 28
Ellington, Duke, 215
Ellison, Ralph, 182, 202, 203
Enlightenment, 61, 224, 228, 241, 242, 257,
259, 262, 275, 281, 282, 288, 293
epic tradition, 19, 20
epistemology (theories of knowledge) 2, 3,
4, 5, 12, 20, 27, 38, 39, 54, 78, 107, 108,
298, 306
Eternal Recurrence (Return), 58–59, 161,

162, 164, 173. *See also* Nietzsche,
Friedrich
Euripides, 312
experience, 26, 40, 79–90 passim, 115, 120,
124, 169
expulsion: of Jews and Moors from Spain,
3, 55, 56, 71, 140

fable/récit (or *fabula/sjuzet*), 68, 118
fabula, 179. See also *fable/récit*
fascism/fascist thought, 167–71, 174, 175
Faulkner, William, 307
figuration/figurative language, 3, 4, 5, 13,
17, 94, 97, 104, 106, 144, 227
Finnegans Wake (Joyce), 61
Flaubert, Gustave, 102, 166, 293; *Madame
Bovary*, 21, 166; *Salammbô*, 21; *Sentimen-
tal Education*, 101, 166
Flight to Canada (I. Reed), 209
Flinker, Moshe, 169
Foucault, Michel, 12, 27, 51, 96, 101, 118,
137–38, 263; *I, Pierre Rivière*, 89–90; *The
Order of Things*, 51
Frank, Anne, 84, 169
French Revolution, 20, 23, 86, 219, 223,
226, 229, 247, 311
Freud, Sigmund, 103, 210, 247, 310
Friday (Tournier). See *Vendredi* (Tournier)
Frobenius, Leo, 310
Fuentes, Carlos, 3, 4, 15, 16, 17, 44–78
passim, 123, 140, 152, 171, 181, 218, 262,
263, 276, 281, 303, 305; *The Buried Mirror*,
75; *Christopher Unborn*, 61; *The Death of
Artemio Cruz*, 75; *Don Quixote; or, The Cri-
tique of Reading*, 56, 57, 68; *El mundo de
José Luis Cuevas*, 59; *Terra Nostra*, 3, 15, 16,
45, 48–78 passim, 123, 140, 154, 181, 261,
303; *Valiente mundo nuevo*, 60, 61, 281–82
Fujimori, Alberto, 287
Fukuyama, Francis, 15, 230

Gadamer, Hans-Georg, 24
Galileo, 216, 246
Gallie, W. B., 21, 22
Gandhi, Indira, 129, 131, 132, 133, 134
Gandhi, Mahatma, 132, 137, 140
García Márquez, Gabriel, 48, 276, 281; *One
Hundred Years of Solitude*, 276, 277
Gaspard, Melchior, et Balthazar (Tournier),
153, 163

Gates, Henry Louis, Jr., 188, 202, 208, 209
The Gay Science (Nietzsche), 39, 58, 160,
    162, 185, 186, 254, 255
genealogical method, 7, 51, 88, 92, 94, 114,
    137, 138, 304. *See also* Nietzsche,
    Friedrich
Ginzburg, Carlo, 80–81
global economy/global capitalism, 10, 15,
    270–73, 295, 299, 303, 305
Goering, Hermann, 153, 158, 164
Goethe, J. W. F. von, 174
Goldman, Emma, 102
González Echevarría, Roberto, 48, 280
Gossman, Lionel, 20–21
La Goutte d'Or (Tournier), 153
grand récit (grand narrative), 92, 96, 111,
    115, 118, 224, 302, 303
Grosz, George, 277
Grundrisse (Marx), 136, 138
Guizot, François, 95

Habermas, Jürgen, 12, 301
El hablador (Vargas Llosa), 15, 45, 259, 261–
    96 passim
Hadith, 122, 138
Hammett, Dashiell, 201
Hancock, Herbie, 204
Harding, Warren G., 195, 206
Hart, Catherine Poupeney, 292
Hazard, Paul, 20, 27
Hegel, G. W. F., 12, 31, 152–55, 168, 171, 230;
    The Phenomenology of Spirit, 155–56
Heidegger, Martin, 12, 34, 93, 170, 237,
    266–67; on art in Nietzsche's philoso-
    phy, 34, 93
Hempel, C. G., 32
Herder, J. G. von, 63
Hermeneutics and the Human Sciences
    (Ricoeur), 24, 27, 28, 32, 37, 45, 76
Herodotus, 1, 19, 20, 196, 216, 312
Hesiod, 19, 106
histoire: and *récit*, 195
Historia de Mayta (Vargas Llosa), 270, 289
The Historical Novel (Lukács), 9
historical novels, 5–6, 8–10, 21
Historical Pyrrhonism, 27
Historikerstreit, 1, 84
historiographic metafiction, 10, 298. *See
    also* Hutcheon, Linda
history: as action in the past, 98, 118, 221,

223, 229, 236; antiquarian, 33, 34, 43, 115,
    124–28 passim, 139; and art, 57; counter-
    memory of, 17, 42; critical, 33, 34, 43, 52,
    70, 115, 124, 125, 126, 135, 138, 139, 150,
    288; and dreams, 56–57; events as part
    of, 22, 37, 42, 46; explanation vs. under-
    standing, 2, 32, 38, 42, 44, 154, 258; facts
    in relation to, 2, 23–24, 27, 117, 292; for-
    gotten possibilities of, 16–17, 42; modal-
    ities of, 16–18, 23–24, 42; monumental,
    33, 34, 43, 52, 53, 54, 124, 125, 126, 129,
    130, 132, 134, 138, 139, 298; as myth, 17–
    18, 42, 305; mythic dimensions of, 4, 16,
    17–18, 44, 88, 106, 108, 109, 153, 155, 163,
    171, 172, 175, 177, 178–79, 304; as narra-
    tive, 2, 70, 98, 105, 106, 110, 118, 219, 220,
    221, 223, 229, 236, 310; and nature, 241–
    45; philosophy of, 4, 19–20, 30–37, 43,
    46, 50, 69; *Poietic*, 2–3, 4, 5, 7, 8, 12, 42–
    43, 44, 46, 47, 52, 77, 78, 123, 300, 303,
    305, 306, 309, 312, 313; relation with
    fiction, 14, 20–25, 28, 43, 46, 55, 289
Holocaust, 16, 29, 84, 85, 169. *See also*
    Shoah
Holt, Hamilton, 79
Homer, 19, 20, 39, 40, 65, 213, 227, 263, 264,
    265, 288, 307, 308, 312
Horace, 312
Houlgate, Stephen, 159
Huizinga, Johan, 28
Human, All Too Human (Nietzsche), 204,
    236, 237, 242, 252, 255
Hunt, Lynn, 182, 217, 299–300
Hurston, Zora Neale, 182, 202, 203
Husserl, Edmund, 153, 177
Hutcheon, Linda, 10, 11, 90, 298, 299; *The
    Poetics of Postmodernism*, 10, 11, 299; *The
    Politics of Postmodernism*, 298

Imaginary Homelands (Rushdie), 135, 150
imagination, 3, 4, 11, 13, 15, 17, 39, 51, 52, 69,
    70, 72, 119, 139, 141, 146, 149, 151, 177,
    187–88, 214–15, 229, 262, 282–86 passim,
    290–96 passim, 313
India: Emergency in (1975–74), 129
interpretation, 2, 14, 27–28, 34, 38, 39, 50,
    69, 70, 77, 81, 82, 86–95, 96, 100, 102,
    104, 106, 109, 111, 115, 116, 117, 137, 142,
    181, 248
Interpretation Theory (Ricoeur), 27, 74

I, Pierre Rivière (Foucault), 89–90
I Promessi Sposi (Manzoni), 21
Irigaray, Luce, 253

Jacob, Margaret, 182, 217, 299–300
Jakobson, Roman, 195
Jameson, Fredric, 11, 135, 298, 299, 300;
    "Postmodernism; or, The Cultural Log-
    ic of Late Capitalism, 135; *Postmodern-
    ism; or, The Cultural Logic of Late Capital-
    ism*, 11, 298, 299
jazz: call and response pattern in, 191–92;
    crips, 200; idiom, 213; harmony (hori-
    zontal projections), 193–94, 199, 200;
    improvisation, 201, 202–3, 204, 208,
    214, 215; melody (verticalizations), 193–
    94; musical conversations in, 208–10,
    211; rhythm, 195–97
Jones, Le Roi. *See* Baraka, Amiri
Joplin, Scott, 203
Joyce, James, 10, 61, 123; *Finnegans Wake*,
    61; "Two Gallants," 10
Jung, Carl, 208

Kafka, Franz, 73, 274, 275, 294
Kali, 130, 131, 134, 138
Kant, Immanuel, 31, 168, 171, 301
Kepler, Johannes, 217
Kerr, Lucille, 274
Kierkegaard, Søren, 105
Klein, Melanie, 168
Kofman, Sarah, 116, 192, 212, 253, 254
Kojève, Alexandre, 230
Kristeva, Julia, 101

LaCapra, Dominick, 12, 22–23
Lacoue-Labarthe, Philippe, 170
language, limits of, 83–88, 118
The Last Days of Louisiana Red (I. Reed),
    209
L.C. (Daitch), 15, 45, 79, 88–120 passim,
    181, 304
Le Goff, Jacques, 216, 217, 218, 242
Leibniz, G. W. F. von, 153, 168, 171
Le Roy Ladurie, Emmanuel, 81
Le Sueur, Guillaume, 88
Lévi-Strauss, Claude, 172, 267–68
Lilla, Mark, 246, 247
Linnaeus, 245
Lispector, Clarice, 276

Lituma en los Andes (Vargas Llosa), 290
Locke, Alain, 197
Locke, John, 217
Louis-Philippe (king of France), 95, 310
Lucian, 31
Lukács, Georg, 9, 10, 19; *The Historical Nov-
    el*, 9; *The Theory of the Novel*, 19
Luxemburg, Rosa, 102
Lyotard, Jean-François, 12, 84, 302

Mably, Abbé de, 23
MacDonald, Ross, 201
Machiavelli, 263, 270
Madame Bovary (Flaubert), 21, 166
magical realism, 276–82
Mali, Joseph, 187, 188
Mann, Heinrich, 9
Mann, Thomas, 35; *Buddenbrooks*, 10
Manzoni, Alessandro, 9; *I Promessi Sposi*, 21
The Marriage of Cadmus and Harmony (Ca-
    lasso), 311–12
Marx, Karl, 6, 7, 8, 52, 102, 136, 181, 199, 210,
    216, 217, 299, 310; *Grundrisse*, 136, 138
Masani, Zareer, 129
McCarthy, Cormac, 306–9, 313; *Blood Me-
    ridian*, 306–9; *Outer Dark*, 306–7
McKeon, Michael, 21
Le médianoche amoureux (Tournier), 164
Melville, Herman, 123, 307
memory, 13, 29, 36, 41, 52, 65–69 passim,
    75, 100–101, 110, 113, 117, 145, 187, 262,
    283, 284, 285, 286, 313
Mencken, H. L., 206
Metahistory (White), 6, 23
metaphor, 6, 7, 13, 15, 25, 28, 36–37, 39, 40,
    42, 44, 66, 68, 74, 76, 78, 97–98, 118, 139,
    142–43, 144, 150, 163, 168, 169, 170, 174,
    179, 182
Les Météores (Tournier), 153, 162, 163
Michelet, Jules, 86, 216
Midnight's Children (Rushdie), 15, 45, 121–51
    passim, 261, 301, 304
Miller, Cecilia, 188, 189, 213, 215, 229, 275
mimesis, 24, 25, 26, 30, 45, 76, 114, 170
Mink, Louis O., 21–22, 27, 42, 46, 306
Monk, Thelonious, 200
Montaigne, Michel de, 88
Montesquieu, 260
Moore, Charles, 10
The Moor's Last Sigh (Rushdie), 121, 122, 134

Morrison, Toni, 281
Morton, Jelly Roll, 203
Moses, 35, 141
Moses, Michael Valdez, 15, 260
Muhammad, 141
Mumbo Jumbo (I. Reed), 15, 16, 45, 180–215
    passim, 301
El mundo de José Luis Cuevas (Fuentes), 59
Musa, 141
muthos (emplotment), 26, 44, 68, 155, 166,
    170, 305
mythical thinking, 267–68

narration, 8, 22, 24–25, 52, 53, 57, 59, 60, 70,
    84, 101–2, 107, 142, 143, 144, 163, 164,
    189, 190, 223, 225–26, 227, 229, 257
Nehamas, Alexander, 93, 192
Nehru, Jawaharlal, 129, 131, 132, 133
"Neo-Hoodoo Manifesto" (I. Reed), 185
Newton, Sir Isaac, 216, 217
Nietzsche Friedrich, 4, 6, 7, 8, 11–18
    passim, 32, 37, 40, 42, 43, 45, 47, 50–60
    passim, 64, 65, 70, 77, 85, 88–98 passim,
    102, 103, 108, 113–37 passim, 144, 150,
    154, 155, 156, 159–64 passim, 168, 171,
    182–86 passim, 190, 191, 192, 193, 202,
    204, 212, 215, 220, 235, 236, 237, 238, 247,
    248, 251, 254, 255, 256, 262, 263, 286, 290,
    294, 295, 305, 307, 308, 312; *amor fati*,
    161–62, 309; antiquarian history, 33, 34,
    43, 115, 124–28 passim, 139; Apollo and
    the Apollonian, 56, 57, 58, 158, 159, 160,
    170, 255, 256; on art, 41, 57, 93, 94, 130,
    235, 237, 255–57, 290; on body-centered
    reason, 41, 185–86; critical history, 33,
    34, 43, 52, 70, 115, 124, 125, 126, 135, 138,
    139, 150, 288; Dionysus and the Diony-
    sian, 41, 56, 57, 58, 157, 158, 159, 160, 163,
    170, 182, 183, 185, 192, 193, 212, 255, 256;
    Eternal Recurrence (Return), 58–59, 161,
    162, 164, 173; on furthering life, 4, 32–33,
    34, 92, 93, 124, 126; genealogical meth-
    od, 7, 51, 88, 92, 94, 114, 137, 138, 304; on
    metaphor, 13; monumental, 33, 34, 43,
    52, 53, 54, 124, 125, 126, 129, 130, 132, 134,
    138, 139, 298; *ressentiment*, 55, 184; on
    science, 38, 39; on the transvaluation of
    values, 182; on truth, 6–7, 39; on truth as
    a woman, 251–54; on the unhistorical,
    32, 113–14; views on antipositivism, 38

—works by: *The Anti-Christ*, 184; *Beyond
    Good and Evil*, 13, 38, 47, 92, 117, 160,
    164, 251, 256; *The Birth of Tragedy*, 56,
    57, 93, 158, 159, 160, 190, 191, 192, 212,
    235, 255; *The Case of Wagner*, 191; *Day-
    break*, 39, 114; *Ecce Homo*, 59, 161; *The
    Gay Science*, 39, 58, 160, 162, 185, 186,
    254, 255; *Human, All Too Human*, 204,
    236, 237, 242, 252, 255; *On the Genealogy
    of Morals*, 39–40, 40–41, 54, 157, 183,
    184, 202; "On the Uses and Disadvan-
    tages of History for Life," 32, 33, 34,
    41, 42, 43, 47, 53, 54, 72, 92, 113, 120,
    124–38 passim; *Philosophy and Truth*
    (early notebooks), 7, 13, 39, 94, 95, 97–
    98, 290; *Philosophy in the Tragic Age of
    the Greeks*, 41; *Thus Spoke Zarathustra*,
    34, 39, 40, 41, 157, 162–63, 185–86, 192,
    204, 255, 297, 309; *Twilight of the Idols*,
    45–46, 183, 185, 191; *Untimely Medita-
    tions*, 191, 215; *The Will to Power*, 13, 34,
    38, 39, 41, 45, 85, 93, 98, 108, 191, 193,
    235, 237, 247–48, 294, 295
Nixon, Richard, 132, 195
Norris, Christopher, 301

Obeyesekere, Gananath, 86, 87
The Ogre (Tournier). See *Le Roi des Aulnes*
    (Tournier)
Ogren, Kathy, 214
One Hundred Years of Solitude (García
    Márquez), 276, 277
On the Genealogy of Morals (Nietzsche), 39–
    40, 40–41, 54, 157, 183, 184, 202
"On the Uses and Disadvantages of Histo-
    ry for Life" (*Second Untimely Mediation*;
    Nietzsche), 32, 33, 34, 41, 42, 43, 47, 53,
    54, 72, 92, 113, 120, 124–38 passim
Ontology, 2, 12, 72, 73, 108, 278, 280
The Order of Things (Foucault), 51
Os sertões (de Cunha), 261
Outer Dark (McCarthy), 306–7
Ovid, 294, 312

Parvati, 131. *See also* Kali
Persian Gulf War, 303
perspectival philosophy, 52, 53, 88, 92, 137,
    212
Peterson, Oscar, 203
The Phenomenology of Spirit (Hegel), 155–56

Philosophy and Truth (early notebooks; Nietzsche), 7, 13, 39, 94, 95, 97–98, 290
Philosophy in the Tragic Age of the Greeks (Nietzsche), 41
Pindar, 312
Piñon, Nelida, 276
Pirandello, Luigi, 293
Plato, 26, 40, 163, 165, 171, 185, 253; *Symposium*, 163
Pliny, 245
Plutarch, 1, 312
Poetics (Aristotle), 26, 30
The Poetics of Postmodernism (Hutcheon), 10, 11, 299
poetic thinking, 40, 188, 266
poetry vs. philosophy, 19
poiesis, 8, 45, 76, 306
poietic history, novels of, 2–3, 4, 5, 7, 8, 12, 42–43, 44, 46, 47, 52, 77, 78, 123, 300, 303, 305, 306, 309, 313; modalities of, 16–18, 42
The Politics of Postmodernism (Hutcheon), 298
Polybius, 20
Popper, Karl, 32, 263
postmodernism, 10, 11, 12, 14, 15, 49, 90, 182, 283, 298
Postmodernism; or, The Cultural Logic of Late Capitalism (Jameson), 11, 135, 298, 299
Pound, Ezra, 12, 163
La Princèsse de Clèves (Lafayette), 20
Proudhon, Pierre Joseph, 102
Proust, Marcel, 135, 284, 310; *À la Recherche du temps perdu*, 10, 284
Puig, Manuel, 276
Purana, 122, 138
Pynchon, Thomas, 123, 185

Quetzalcoatl, 57, 64, 74
Qur'an, 122, 138, 141

Rabelais, François, 123
Ramayana 146
récit, 195. See also *fable/récit; grand récit*
Reed, Ishmael, 15, 16, 17, 44, 45, 46, 47, 180–215 passim, 218, 298, 303, 304, 305; *Flight to Canada*, 209; *The Last Days of Louisiana Red*, 209, *Mumbo Jumbo*, 15, 16, 45, 180–215 passim, 301; "Neo-Hoodoo Manifesto," 185; *Yellow Back Radio Broke-Down*, 209

Reed, Walter L., 21
Ricoeur, Paul, 8, 24, 29, 30, 44, 45, 65, 66, 67, 68, 70, 74, 76, 150, 164, 166, 167, 170; on disclosure, 27; on distanciation, 27, 28; mimesis$_1$ (prefiguration), 26, 43, 67, 68, 146, 164, 165; mimesis$_2$ (configuration), 8, 26, 43, 51, 68, 146, 165; mimesis$_3$ (refiguration), 26, 43, 73, 146, 167; on second-order referential field, 29, 45, 46; threefold mimesis, 25, 26, 43, 66, 146, 155, 164
—works by: *Hermeneutics and the Human Sciences*, 24, 27, 28, 32, 37, 45, 76; *Interpretation Theory*, 27, 74; *The Rule of Metaphor*, 25, 45, 168, 169, 170; *Time and Narrative*, 24, 25, 26, 29, 45, 67, 68, 69, 70, 73, 150, 151, 166, 167
Rilke, Rainer Maria, 312
Robinson Crusoe (Defoe), 260
Le Roi des Aulnes (Tournier), 15, 17, 45, 123, 148, 152–79 passim, 301, 304
Rorty, Richard, 29, 30, 46
The Ruin of Kasch (Calasso), 310–12
The Rule of Metaphor (Ricoeur), 25, 45, 168, 169, 170
Rushdie, Salman, 4, 15, 16, 17, 44, 45, 46, 47, 121–51 passim, 218, 263, 281, 298, 303, 304, 305, 306; *Imaginary Homelands*, 135, 150; *Midnight's Children*, 15, 45, 121–51 passim, 261, 301, 304; *The Moor's Last Sigh*, 121, 122, 134; *The Satanic Verses*, 121, 122; *Shame*, 122

Sahlins, Marshall, 86, 87
Said, Edward, 37, 77, 175, 281, 282
Sainte-Beuve, Charles Augustin, 310
Saint-Simon, Claude Henri, 102
Salammbô (Flaubert), 21
Santayana, George, 1
Sarmiento, Domingo F., 282
Sartre, Jean-Paul, 300
The Satanic Verses (Rushdie), 121, 122
Saussure, Ferdinand de, 195
Scarry, Elaine, 82, 83
Schama, Simon, 302
Schrift, Alan D., 51, 59, 88, 90, 92–93, 94, 212
Schrimpf, Georg, 277
Schuller, Gunther, 191, 192, 193, 195, 197
Scott, Joan W., 85, 87, 90, 93–97 passim, 116, 119, 169, 181

Scott, Sir Walter, 8, 9; *Waverly*, 9, 21
Sendero luminoso (Shining Path), 282, 290
Sentimental Education (Flaubert), 101, 166
Shame (Rushdie), 122
Shaw, G. B., 133
Shoah, 29, 55, 154, 166, 174, 243. *See also* Holocaust
Showalter, English, Jr., 20
sjuzet. See *fable/récit*
Socrates, 185, 235
Sollors, Werner, 79
Sophocles, 312
speculation/speculative narrative, 3, 4, 11, 14, 24, 42, 43, 46, 51, 76, 78
Spence, Jonathan, 80, 81
Spengler, Oswald, 263
Spinoza, Baruch, 171
Stambaugh, Joan, 58
Steiner, Wendy, 90
Stendhal, 47, 75
Stirner, Max, 310
The Storyteller (Vargas Llosa). See *El hablador* (Vargas Llosa)
Styron, William, 195
Swift, Graham, 15, 16, 17, 18, 44, 45, 46, 47, 143, 152, 216, 219–58 passim, 303, 304, 305; *Waterland*, 143, 216, 219–58 passim, 304
Symposium (Plato), 163

Tales from a Thousand and One Nights, 122
Talleyrand-Périgord, Charles Maurice de, 310, 312
temporal dimensions: of human experience and narrative constructions, 24, 67, 73, 106, 111, 166, 193, 218, 241
Terra Nostra (Fuentes), 3, 15, 16, 45, 48–78 passim, 123, 140, 154, 181, 261, 303
The Theory of the Novel (Lukács), 19
Thucydides, 20
Thus Spoke Zarathustra (Nietzsche), 34, 39, 40, 41, 157, 162–63, 185–86, 192, 204, 255, 297, 309
Time and Narrative (Ricoeur), 24, 25, 26, 29, 45, 67, 68, 69, 70, 73, 150, 151, 166, 167
Tolstoy, Leo, 5, 6, 7, 8, 170, 260; *War and Peace*, 5, 6, 8, 21, 170, 260
Tournier, Michel, 4, 15, 17, 18, 44, 45, 46, 47, 123, 148, 152–79 passim, 218, 263, 303, 304, 305; *Gaspard, Melchior, et Balthazar*,

153, 163; *La Goutte d'Or*, 153; *Le médianoche amoureux*, 164; *Les Météores*, 153, 162, 163; *Le Roi des Aulnes*, 15, 17, 45, 123, 148, 152–79 passim, 301, 304; *Vendredi*, 153; *Le vent paraclet*, 152, 153, 157, 158, 160, 161, 164, 168, 175, 176, 179; *Le vol du vampire*, 163
Toynbee, Arnold, 263
tragedy, 39, 52, 54, 55, 58, 64, 65, 78, 163
Tristram Shandy (Sterne), 122
Tropics of Discourse (White), 23, 24, 27, 37, 44
tropology, 4, 23, 78, 88
Twilight of the Idols (Nietzsche), 45–46, 183, 185, 191
"Two Gallants" (Joyce), 10

Uma. *See* Kali
Untimely Meditations (Nietzsche), 191, 215

Valiente mundo nuevo (Fuentes), 60, 61, 281–82
values, conflicting: play of, 2, 3, 4, 5, 9, 12, 42, 46, 52, 54, 55, 56, 108, 182, 184, 202, 296–97
Van der Rohe, Mies, 10
Vargas Llosa, Mario, 4, 15, 16, 17, 44, 46, 47, 48, 152, 187, 259, 260–96 passim; on Indians, 269
—works by: *El hablador*, 15, 45, 259, 261–96 passim; *Historia de Mayta*, 270, 289; *Lituma en los Andes*, 290; *The War of the End of the World*, 260, 261; *A Writer's Reality*, 269, 289, 291
Vendredi (Tournier), 153
Le vent paraclet (Tournier), 152, 153, 157, 158, 160, 161, 164, 168, 175, 176, 179
Verene, Donald P., 36–37, 38, 40, 63, 64, 265
Vico, Giambattista, 7, 8, 11, 12, 13, 16, 18, 32, 35, 36, 37, 40–44 passim, 47, 50, 51, 52, 60–69 passim, 72, 76, 77, 85, 88, 106, 107, 117, 118, 119, 122, 123, 124, 125, 139, 143, 144, 145, 146, 149, 155, 171–80 passim, 187, 188, 189, 190, 212, 213, 214, 215, 220, 226, 227, 228, 229, 234, 242, 246, 257, 262–68 passim, 275, 276, 279–87 passim, 290, 291, 293, 295, 305, 307, 311, 312; on the barbarism of reflection, 38, 40, 176, 177, 178, 187, 227, 262, 281, 287, 311; *bestioni*, 189; *corso e ricorso*, 35, 41, 62, 173, 188, 262; *fantasia*, 36, 42, 43, 63, 64, 65,

68, 69, 72, 74, 78, 146, 149, 189, 190, 214;
on the fragments of antiquity, 35, 180,
285; on Ideal Eternal History, 36, 62, 63,
64, 106, 179, 228, 267; on Imaginative
Universals, 36, 40; *ingegno*, 36, 42, 43, 65,
72, 73, 78, 88, 117, 120, 146; on the Jove
experience, 36, 40, 85, 226; *memoria*, 36,
42, 43, 65, 67, 68, 78, 146; on Providence,
106, 174, 175; on the refutation of Descartes, 38; on science, 39; *sensus communis*, 37, 38, 173, 174; on Three Ages
(Gods, Heroes, and Men), 61, 265, 312;
threefold memory, 13, 36, 42, 43, 51, 52,
75, 145, 285, 286; *vera narratio*, 36, 37, 76,
107, 155, 174, 179, 189, 190, 220, 257, 293,
308; *verum-factum* principle, 35, 39, 66,
144
—works by: *New Science*, 7, 13, 35, 36, 40,
41, 43, 61–66 passim, 76, 85, 106, 107,
144, 145, 146, 149, 171–80 passim, 187,
188, 213, 226, 227, 228, 234, 246, 257, 263,
264, 266, 285, 293, 295, 311, 312; *On the
Most Ancient Wisdom of the Italians*, 35,
38, 39, 144–45, 176; *On the Study Methods
of our Time*, 176, 178; "Polemiche," 117
Virgil, 312
Le vol du vampire (Tournier), 163
Voltaire, 23, 152, 153, 282
Von Ranke, Leopold, 24, 216
Von Schirach, Baldur, 165
Voragine, Jacques, 165

Wagner, Richard, 190, 191, 215
War and Peace (Tolstoy), 5, 6, 8, 21, 170, 260

The War of the End of the World (Vargas
Llosa), 260, 261
Waterland (Swift), 143, 216, 219–58 passim,
304
Waverly (W. Scott), 9, 21
Weber, Max, 185
Wesseling, Elizabeth, 14
White, Hayden, 6, 12, 23, 24, 27, 42, 44, 46,
77, 88, 175, 306; *The Content of the Form*,
24; *Metahistory*, 6, 23; *Tropics of Dis-
course*, 23, 24, 27, 37, 44
The Will to Power (Nietzsche), 13, 34, 38, 39,
41, 45, 85, 93, 98, 108, 191, 193, 235, 237,
247–48, 294, 295
Wittgenstein, Ludwig, 124
Wittig, Monique, 118
World War I, 221, 224, 235, 237, 241, 243
World War II, 241, 250
Wright, Richard, 182, 202
A Writer's Reality (Vargas Llosa), 269, 289,
291

Xenophon, 197

Yates, Frances, 68
Yeats, W. B., 63
Yellow Back Radio Broke-Down (I. Reed),
209
Young, James B., 84, 169
Young, Julian, 255, 256
Young, Lester, 213

Zamora, Lois Parkinson, 62, 64, 277
Zola, Émile, 152, 153

DAVID W. PRICE is an assistant professor of English and comparative literature at Keene State College. He has published articles on Hegel and Diderot, Michel Tournier, Salman Rushdie, and Pina Bausch in *Clio, Studies in Twentieth Century Literature, ARIEL,* and *Theatre Journal.* He is working on a book-length study on the concept of annihilation.

Typeset in 10.5/13 Cycles
with Cycles display
Designed by Dennis Roberts
Composed by Celia Shapland
for the University of Illinois Press
Manufactured by Quinn-Woodbine, Inc.

University of Illinois Press
1325 South Oak Street
Champaign, IL 61820-6903
www.press.uillinois.edu